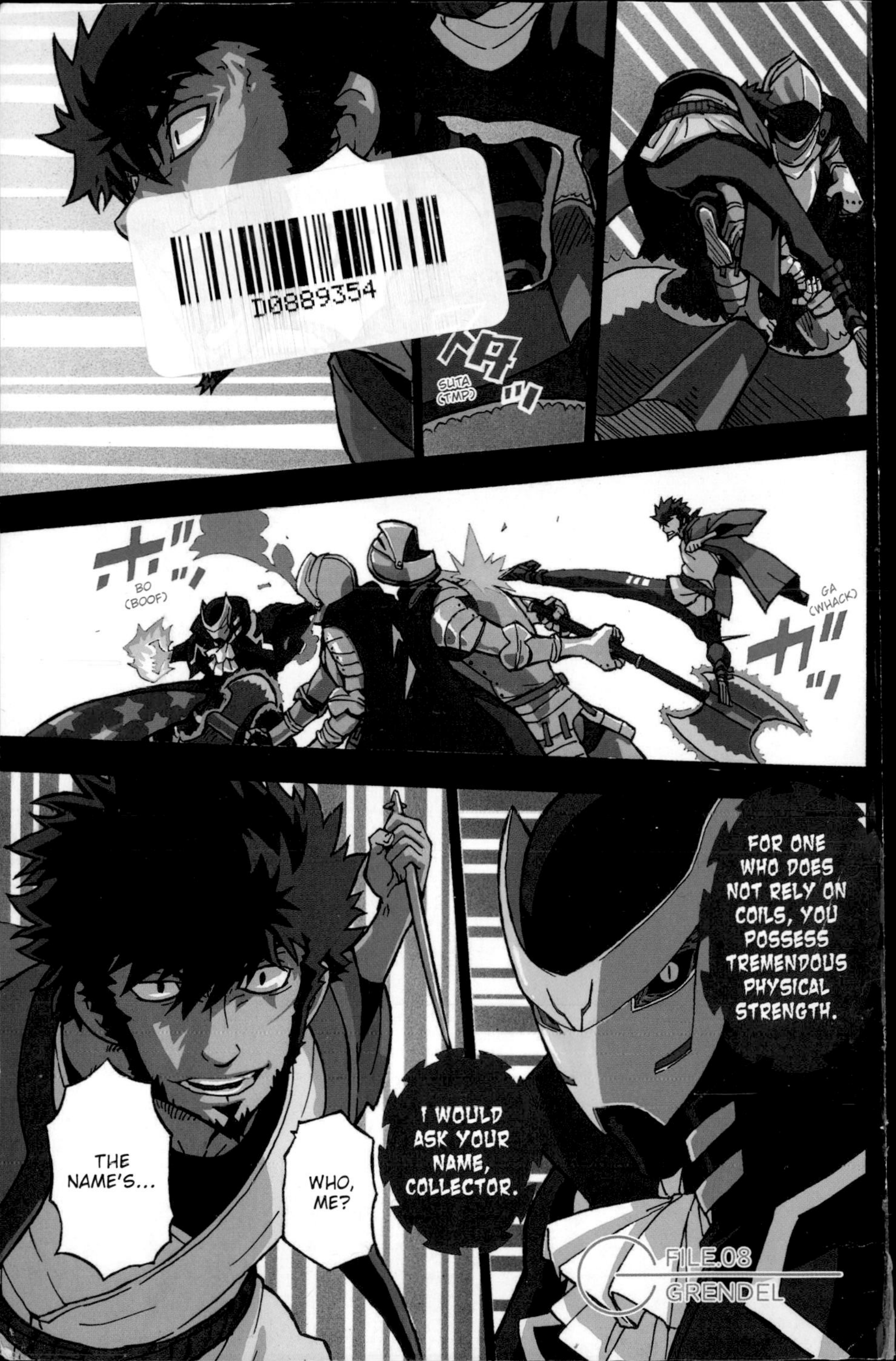
SUTA (TMP)
GA (WHACK)
BO (BOOF)
FOR ONE WHO DOES NOT RELY ON COILS, YOU POSSESS TREMENDOUS PHYSICAL STRENGTH.
I WOULD ASK YOUR NAME, COLLECTOR.
FILE.08 GRENDEL
WHO, ME?
THE NAME'S...

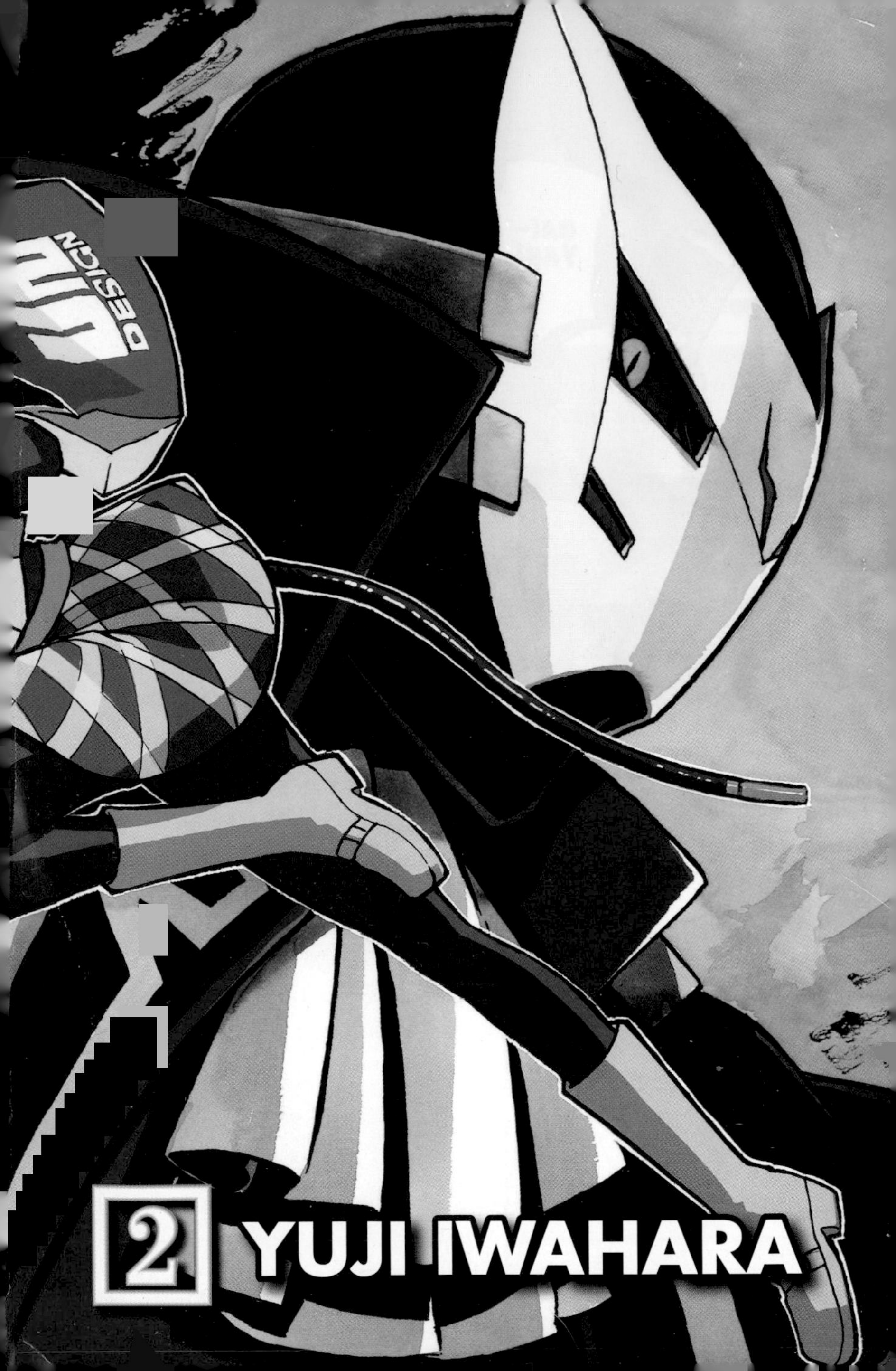
DESIGN
2
YUJI IWAHARA

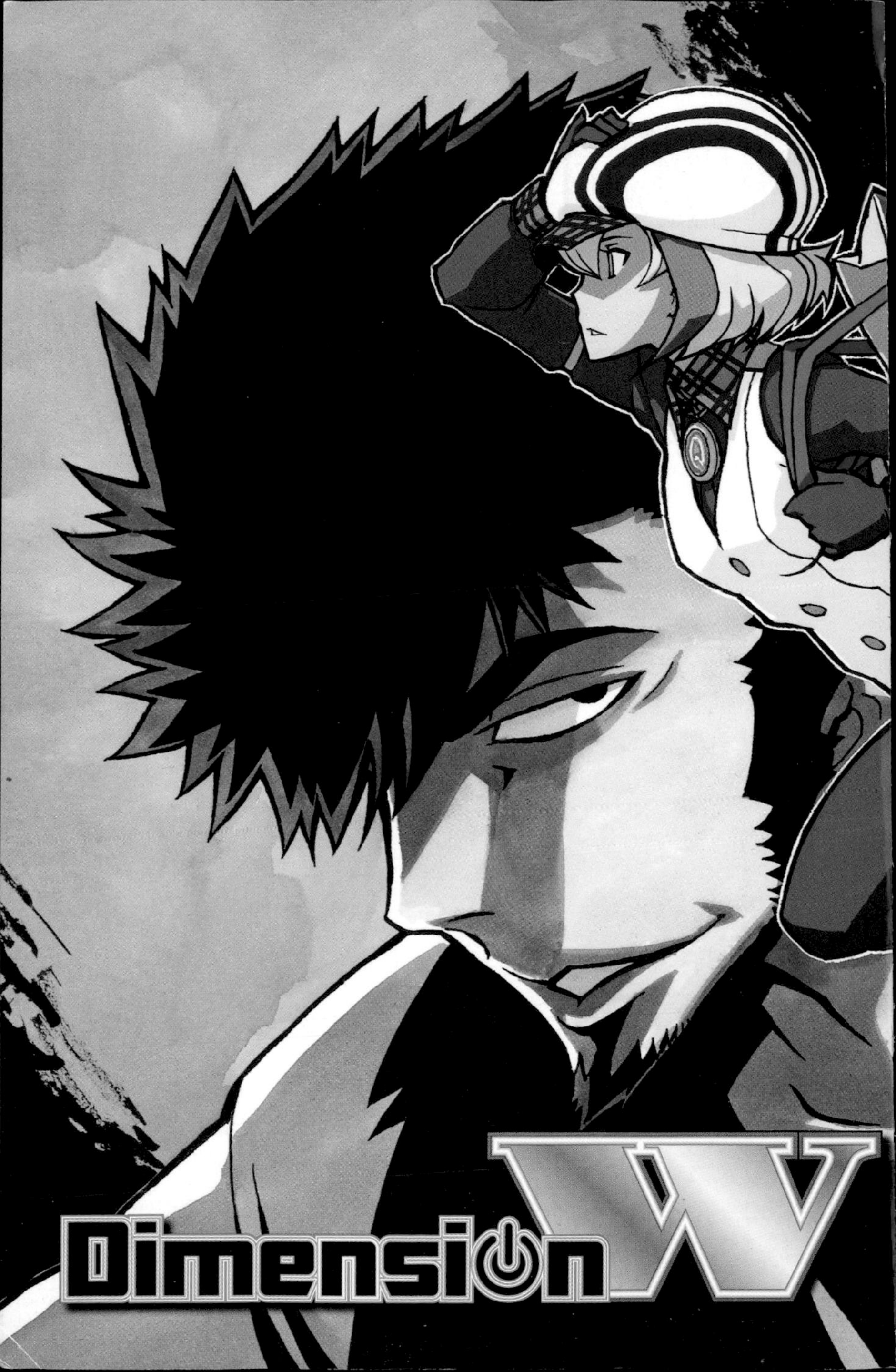
Dimension W

CONTENTS

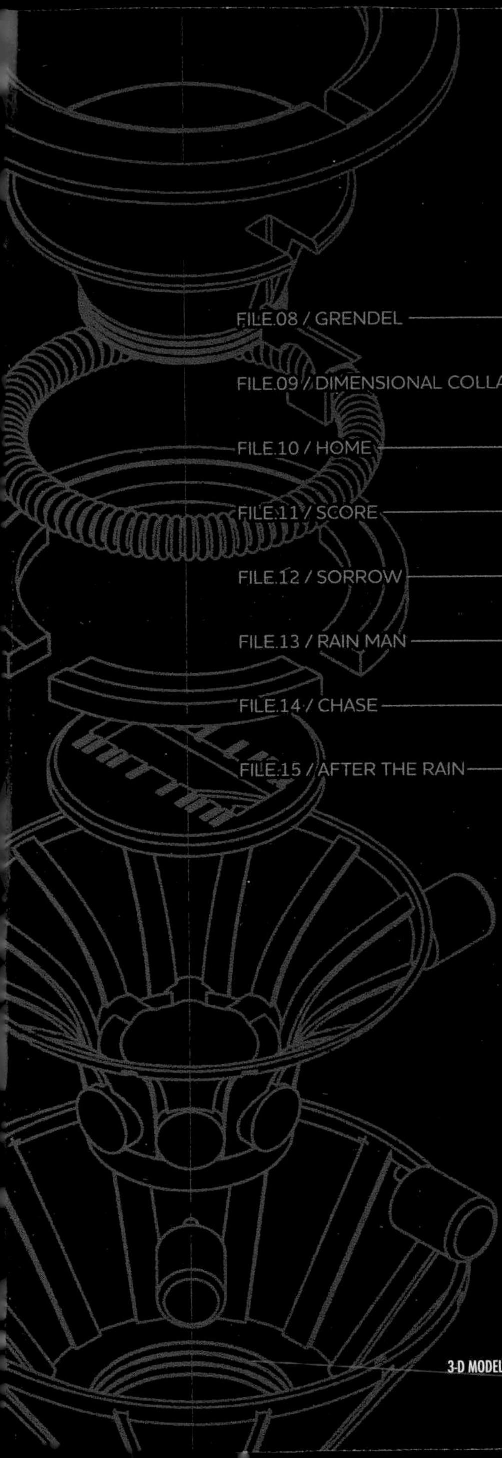

3-D MODEL DESIGN: TOSHIKAZU SENBA

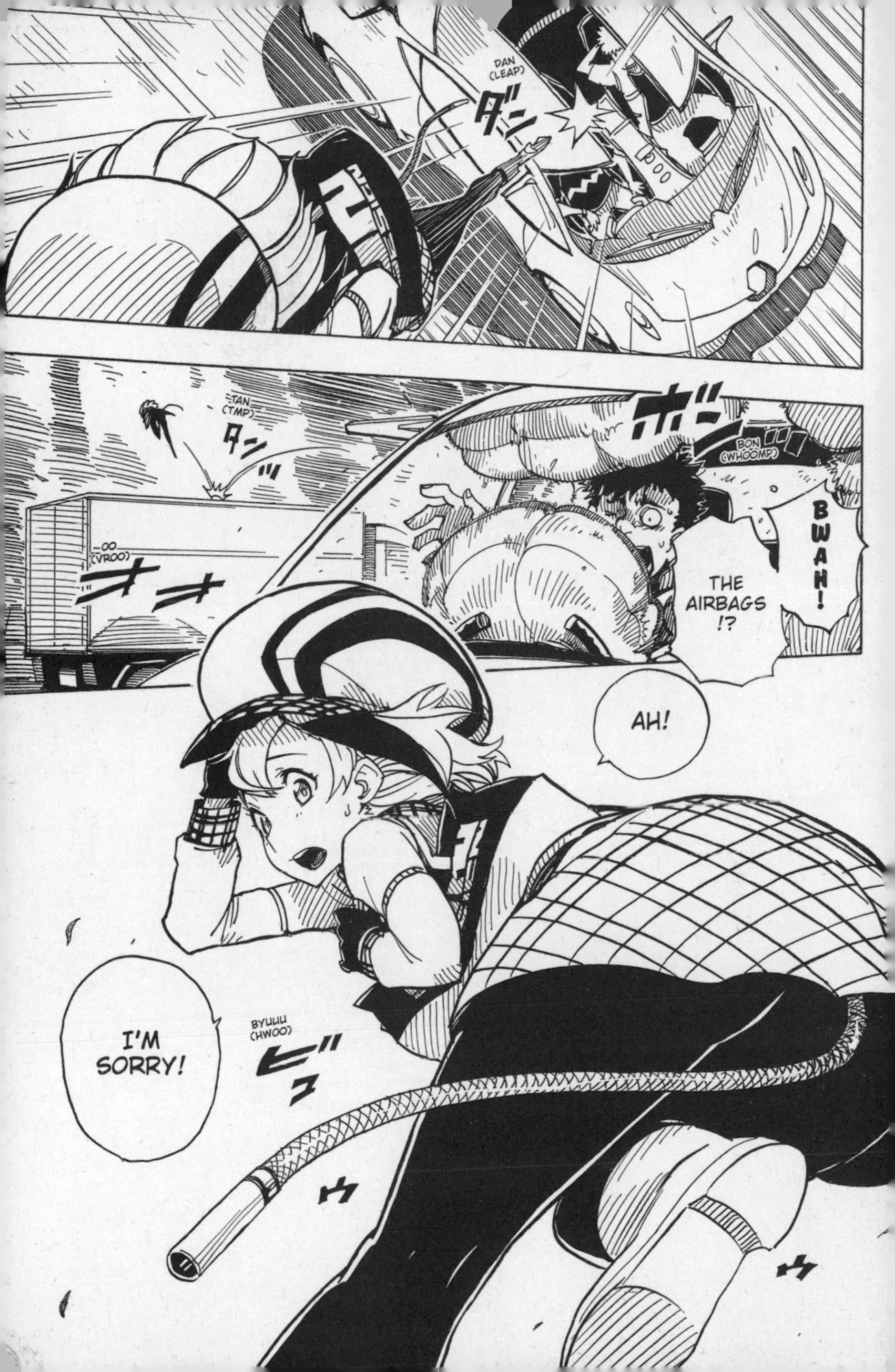
DAN (LEAP)
BON (WHOOMP)
BWAH!
THE AIRBAGS !?
TAN (TMP)
-OO (VROO)
AH!
BYUUU (HWOO)
I'M SORRY!

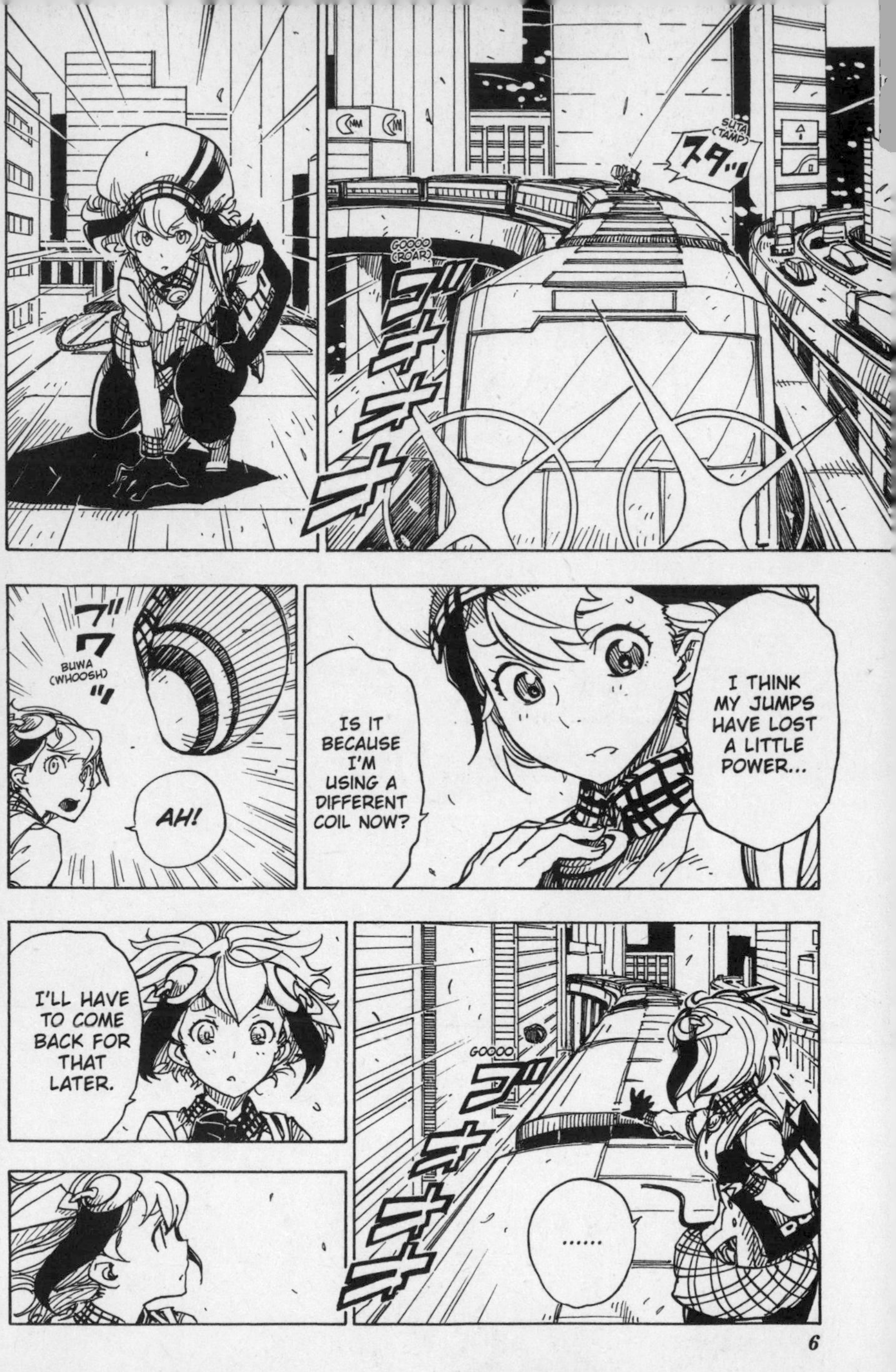
SUTA (TAMP)
スタッ
GOOOO (ROAR)
ゴオオオオ
I THINK MY JUMPS HAVE LOST A LITTLE POWER...
IS IT BECAUSE I'M USING A DIFFERENT COIL NOW?
ブワッ
BUWA (WHOOSH)
AH!
GOOOO
ゴオオオ
......
I'LL HAVE TO COME BACK FOR THAT LATER.

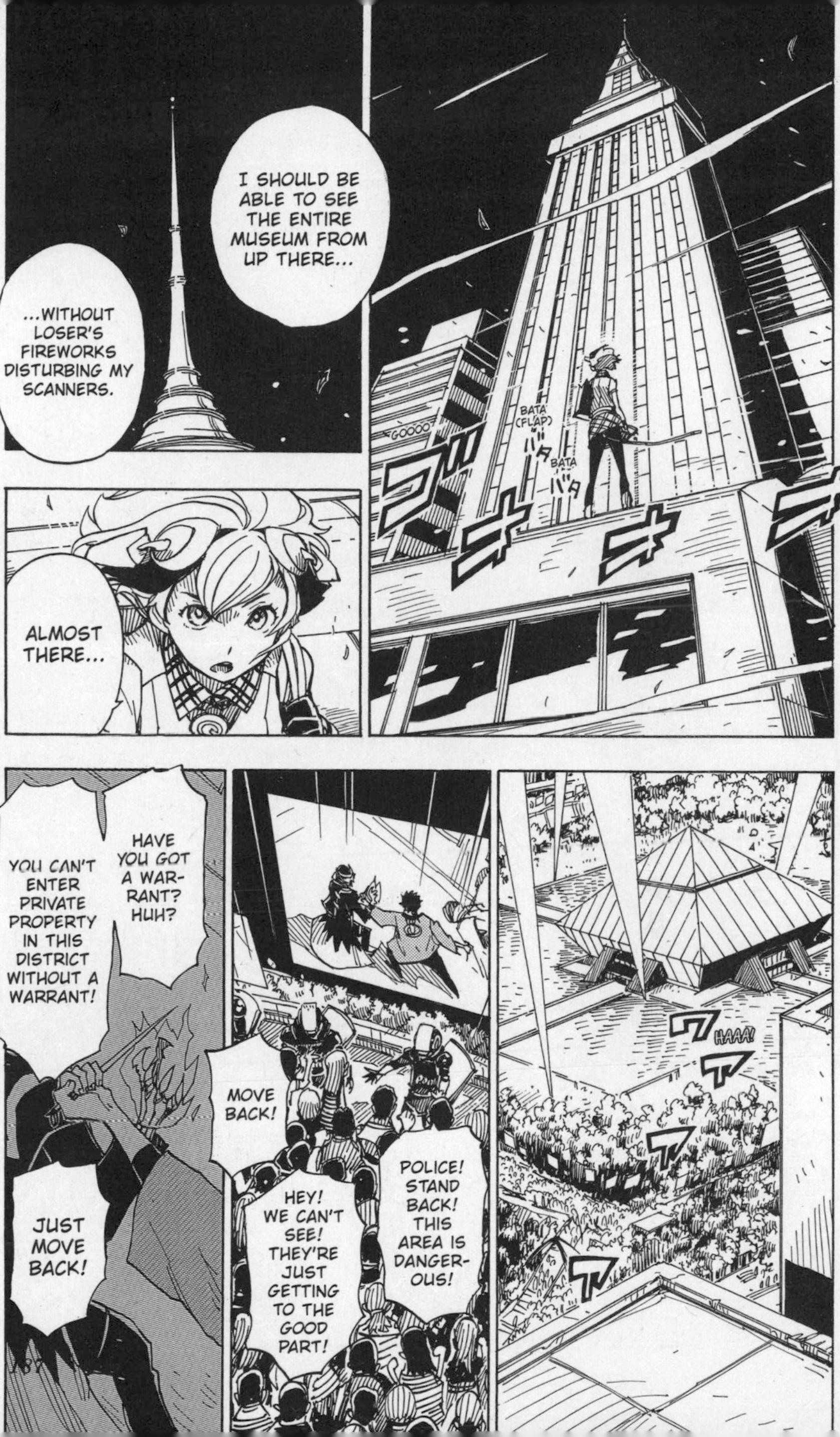
GOOOO
BATA (FLAP)
BATA
I SHOULD BE ABLE TO SEE THE ENTIRE MUSEUM FROM UP THERE...
...WITHOUT LOSER'S FIREWORKS DISTURBING MY SCANNERS.
ALMOST THERE...
HAAA!
MOVE BACK!
POLICE! STAND BACK! THIS AREA IS DANGER-OUS!
HEY! WE CAN'T SEE! THEY'RE JUST GETTING TO THE GOOD PART!
HAVE YOU GOT A WAR-RANT? HUH?
YOU CAN'T ENTER PRIVATE PROPERTY IN THIS DISTRICT WITHOUT A WARRANT!
JUST MOVE BACK!

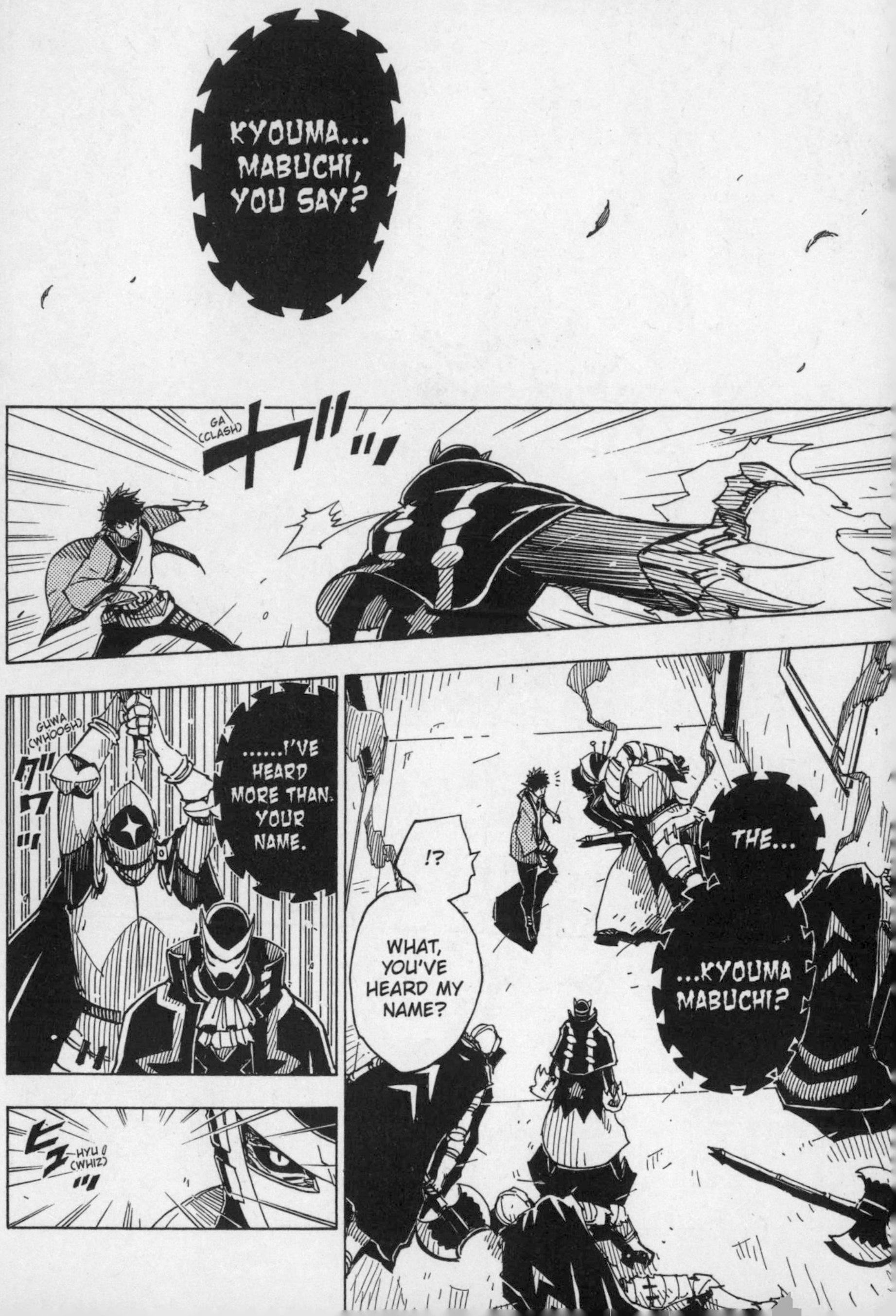
KYOUMA... MABUCHI, YOU SAY?
GA (CLASH)
THE...
...KYOUMA MABUCHI?
!?
WHAT, YOU'VE HEARD MY NAME?
GUWA (WHOOSH)
......I'VE HEARD MORE THAN YOUR NAME.
HYU (WHIZ)

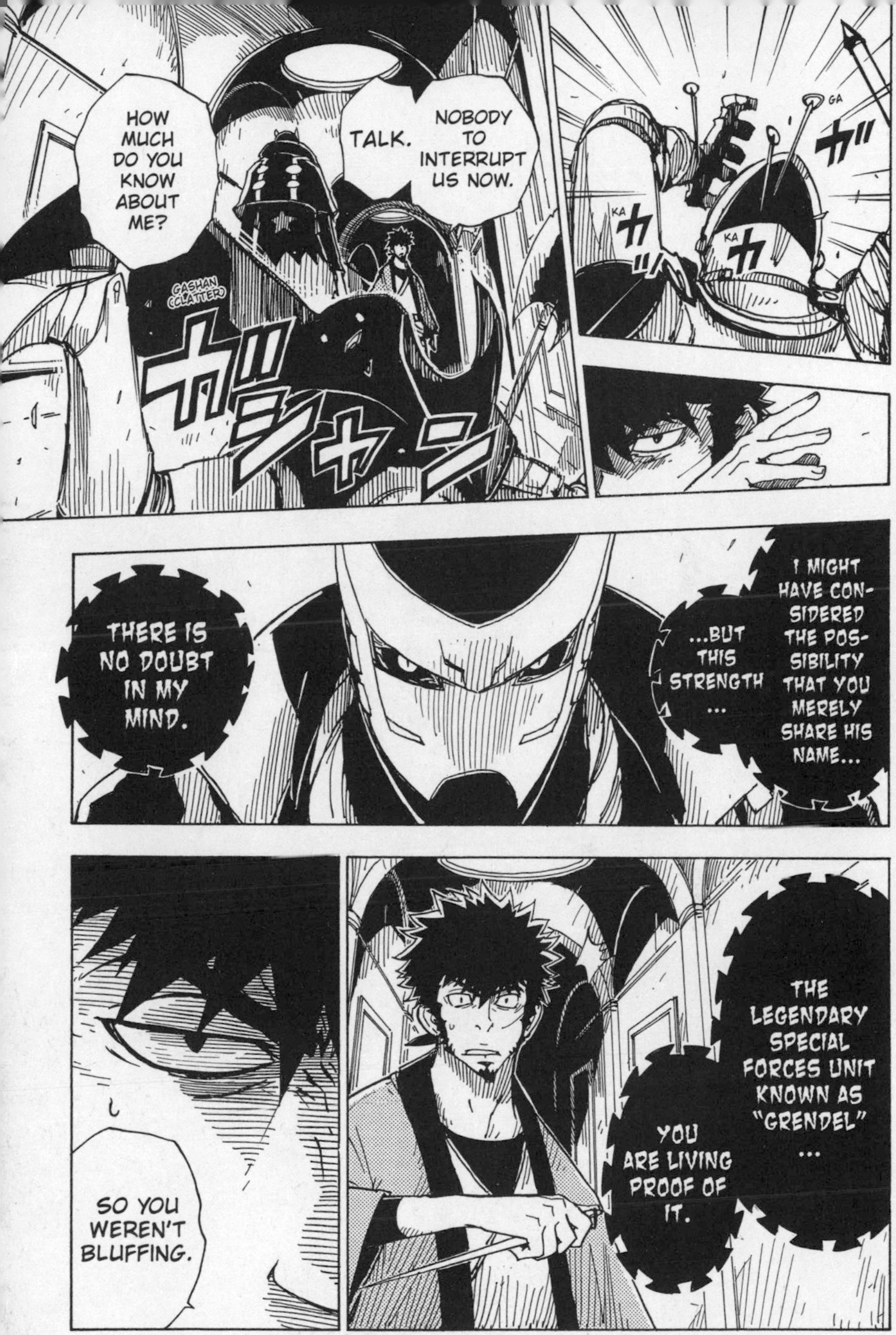
GA
ガ
KA
カ
KA
カ
NOBODY TO INTERRUPT US NOW.
TALK.
HOW MUCH DO YOU KNOW ABOUT ME?
GASHAN (CLATTER)
ガシャン
I MIGHT HAVE CONSIDERED THE POSSIBILITY THAT YOU MERELY SHARE HIS NAME...
...BUT THIS STRENGTH...
THERE IS NO DOUBT IN MY MIND.
THE LEGENDARY SPECIAL FORCES UNIT KNOWN AS "GRENDEL"...
YOU ARE LIVING PROOF OF IT.
SO YOU WEREN'T BLUFFING.

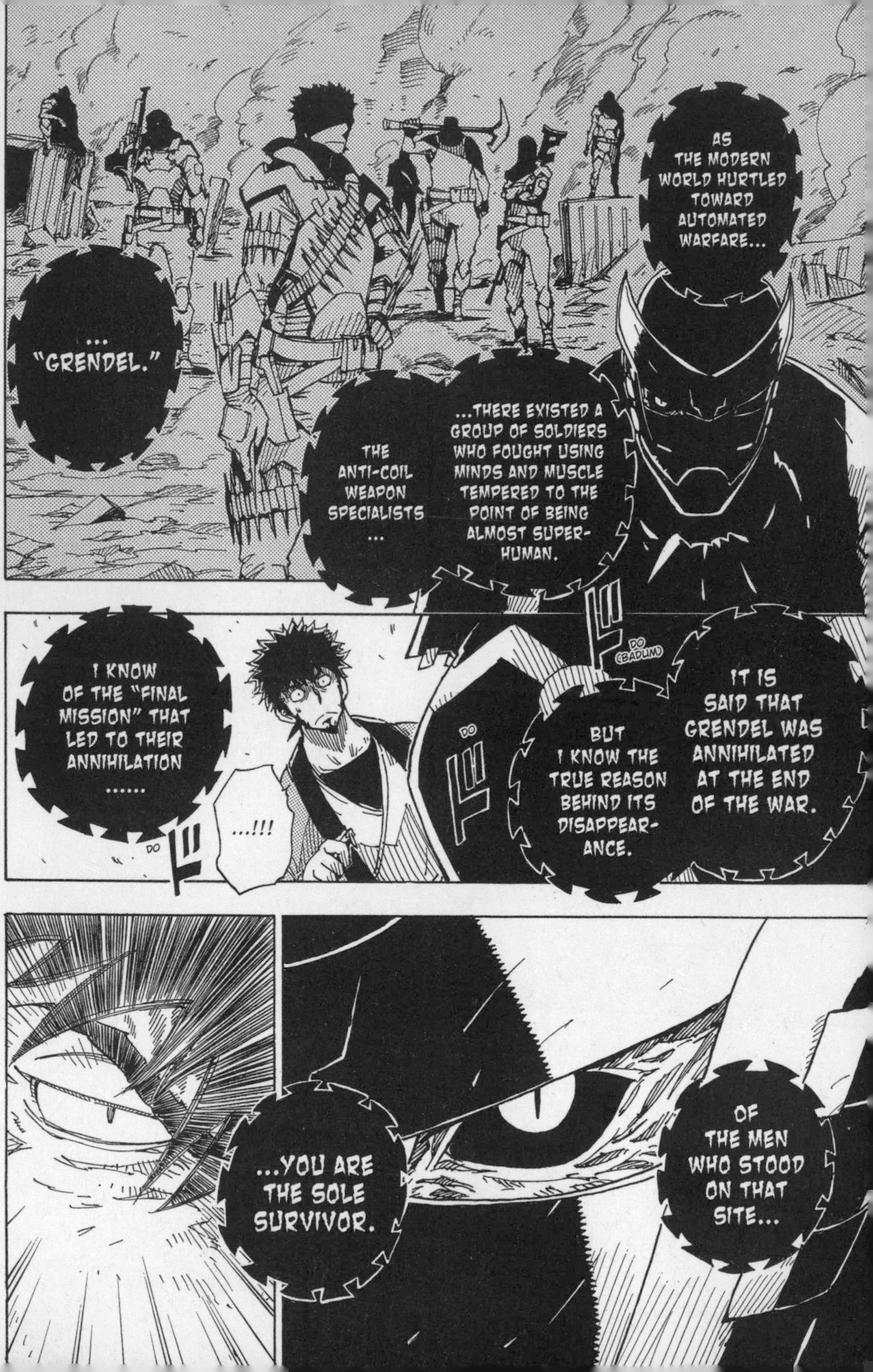
AS THE MODERN WORLD HURTLED TOWARD AUTOMATED WARFARE...
...THERE EXISTED A GROUP OF SOLDIERS WHO FOUGHT USING MINDS AND MUSCLE TEMPERED TO THE POINT OF BEING ALMOST SUPER-HUMAN.
THE ANTI-COIL WEAPON SPECIALISTS ...
... "GRENDEL."
IT IS SAID THAT GRENDEL WAS ANNIHILATED AT THE END OF THE WAR.
DO (BADUM)
BUT I KNOW THE TRUE REASON BEHIND ITS DISAPPEAR-ANCE.
DO
I KNOW OF THE "FINAL MISSION" THAT LED TO THEIR ANNIHILATION ......
...!!!
DO
OF THE MEN WHO STOOD ON THAT SITE...
...YOU ARE THE SOLE SURVIVOR.

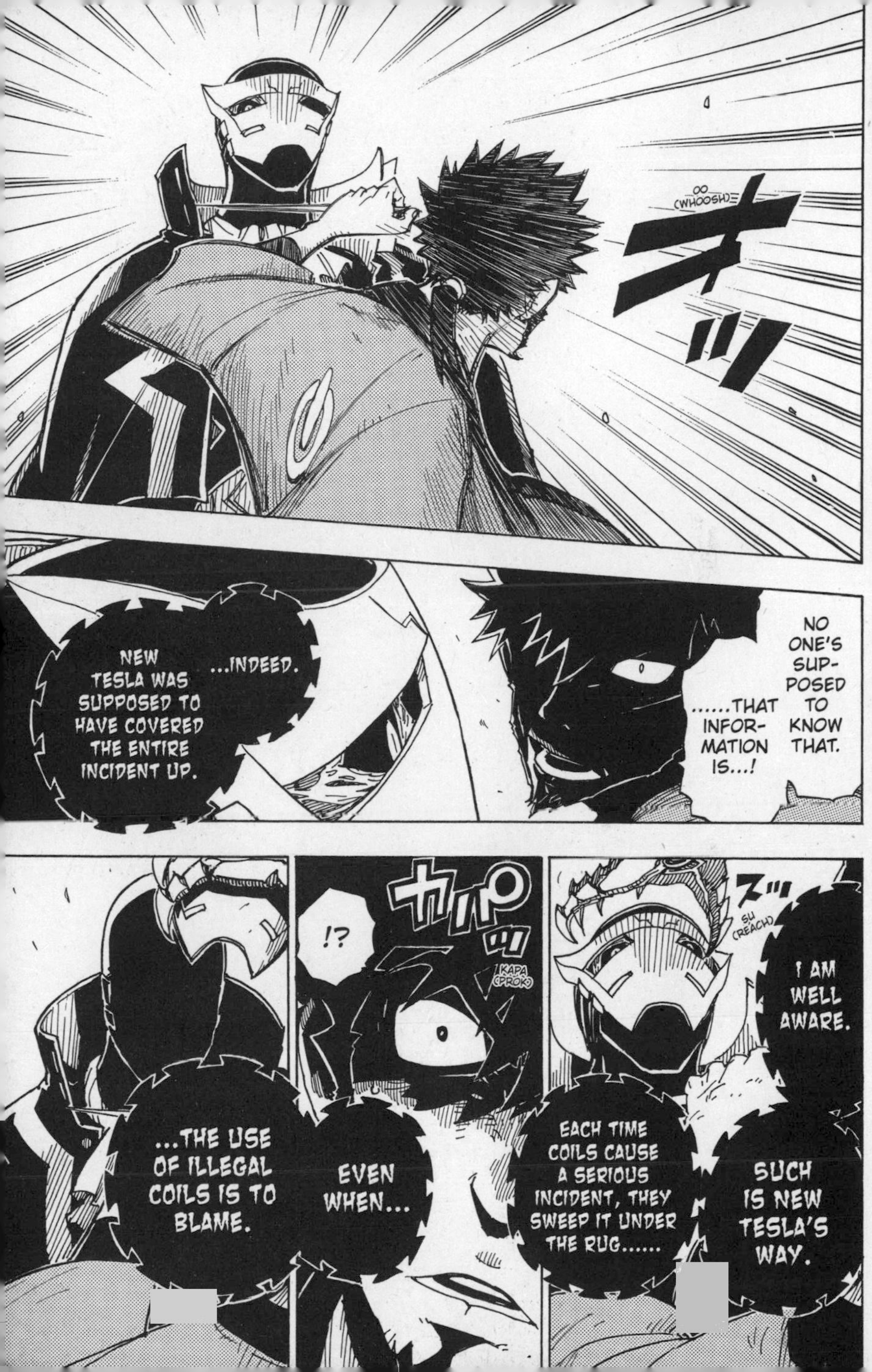

オッ
OO (WHOOSH)
NO ONE'S SUPPOSED TO KNOW THAT.
......THAT INFORMATION IS...!
...INDEED.
NEW TESLA WAS SUPPOSED TO HAVE COVERED THE ENTIRE INCIDENT UP.
スッ
SU (REACH)
I AM WELL AWARE.
SUCH IS NEW TESLA'S WAY.
EACH TIME COILS CAUSE A SERIOUS INCIDENT, THEY SWEEP IT UNDER THE RUG......
カパッ
KAPA (PROK)
!?
EVEN WHEN...
...THE USE OF ILLEGAL COILS IS TO BLAME.

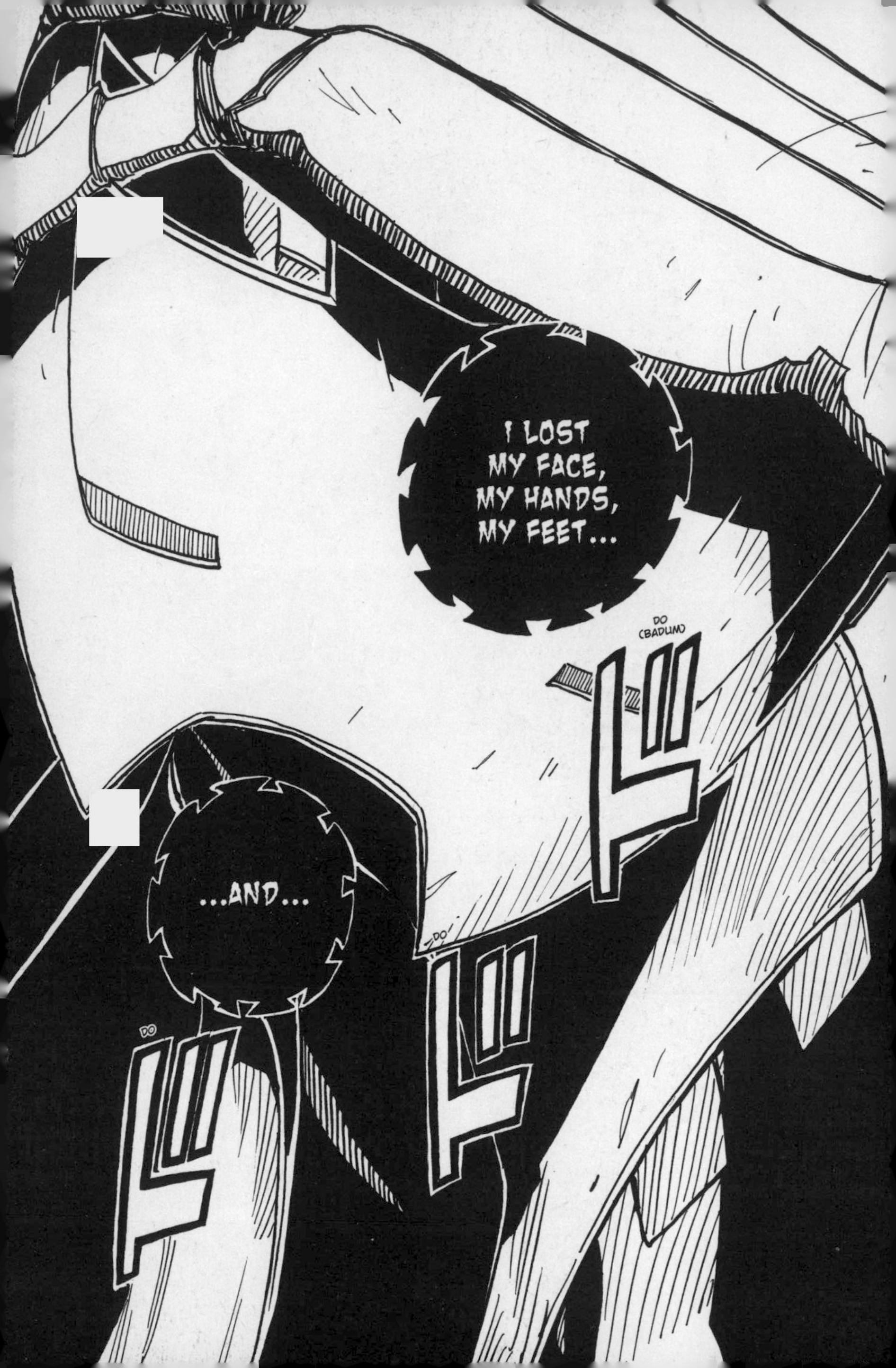
I LOST MY FACE, MY HANDS, MY FEET...
DO (BADUM)
...AND...
DO
DO

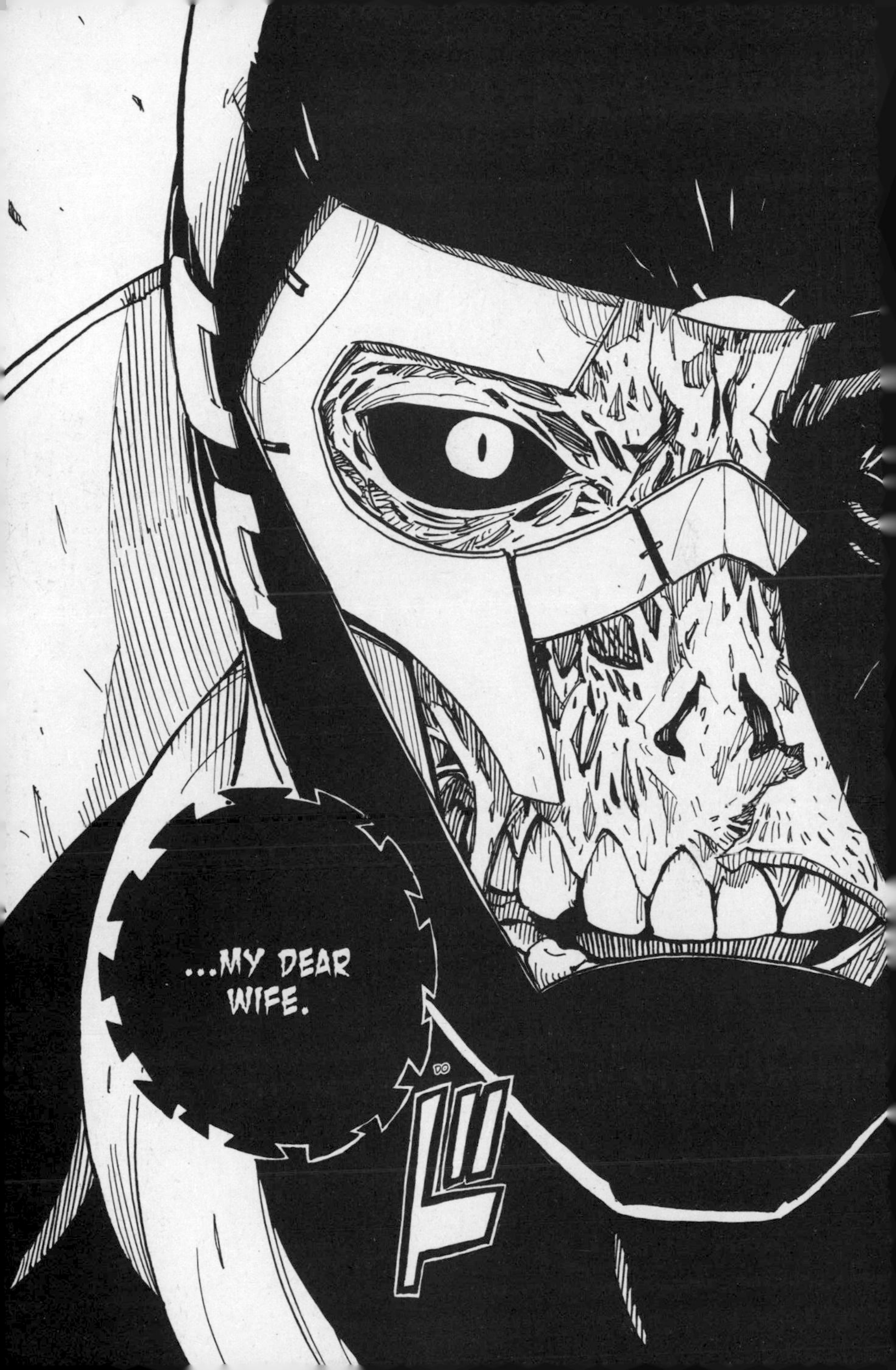
...MY DEAR WIFE.
DO

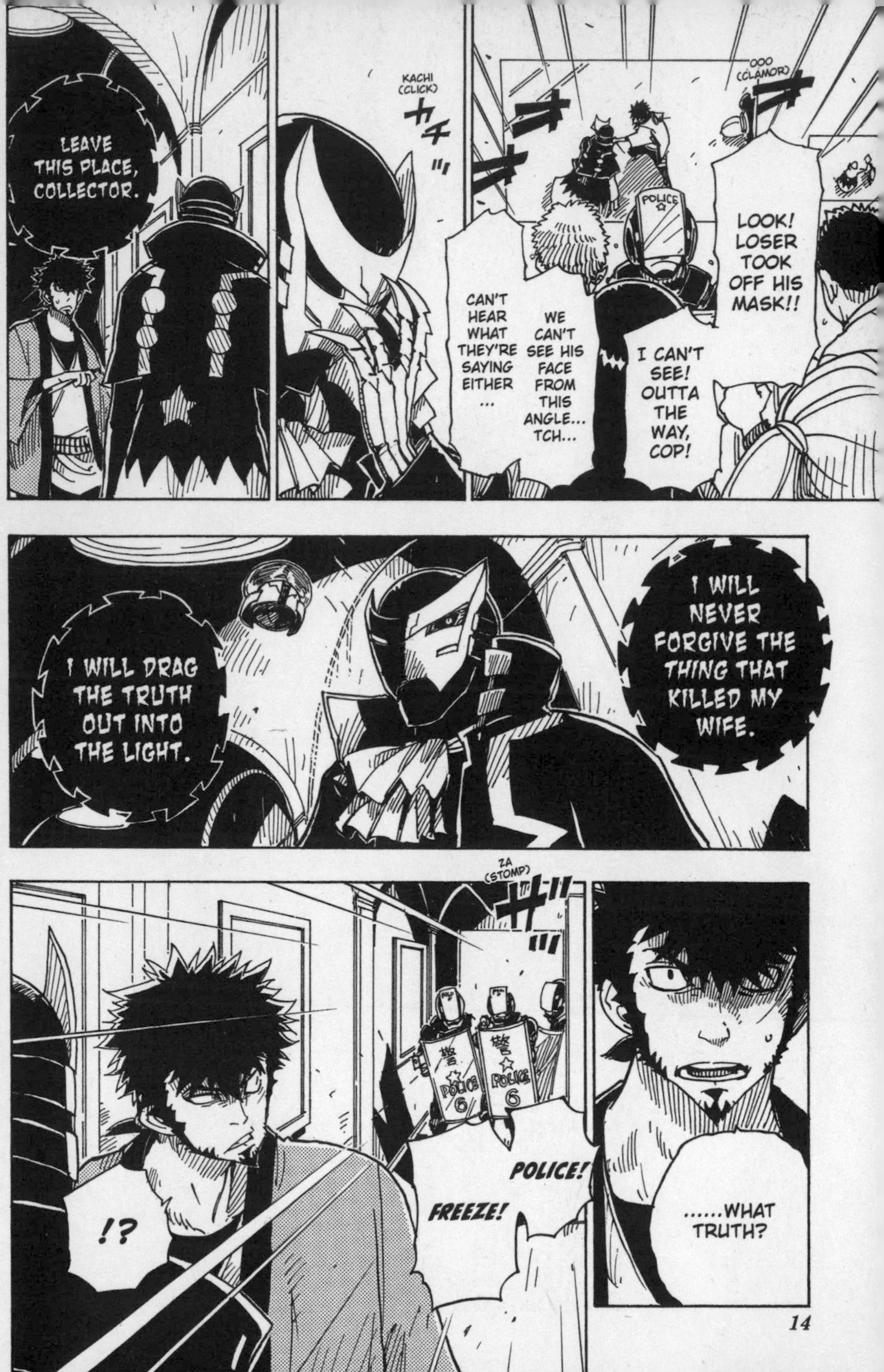
OOO (CLAMOR)
LOOK! LOSER TOOK OFF HIS MASK!!
I CAN'T SEE! OUTTA THE WAY, COP!
WE CAN'T SEE HIS FACE FROM THIS ANGLE... TCH...
CAN'T HEAR WHAT THEY'RE SAYING EITHER ...
KACHI (CLICK)
LEAVE THIS PLACE, COLLECTOR.
I WILL NEVER FORGIVE THE THING THAT KILLED MY WIFE.
I WILL DRAG THE TRUTH OUT INTO THE LIGHT.
......WHAT TRUTH?
ZA (STOMP)
POLICE!
FREEZE!
!?

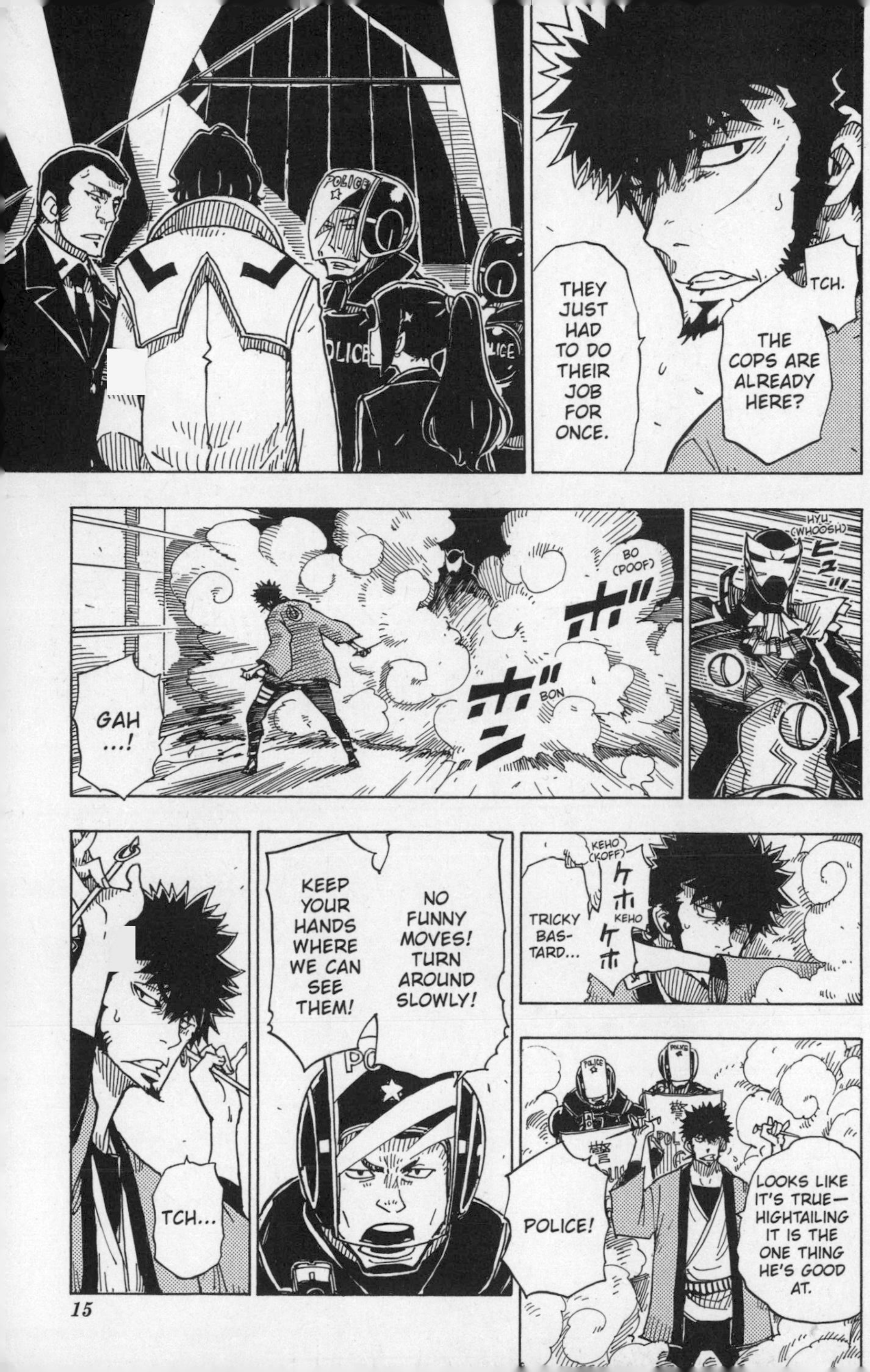
TCH.
THE COPS ARE ALREADY HERE?
THEY JUST HAD TO DO THEIR JOB FOR ONCE.
HYU (WHOOSH)
ヒュ
BO (POOF)
ボ
BON
ボン
GAH ...!
KEHO (KOFF)
ケホ
KEHO
ケホ
TRICKY BAS- TARD...
LOOKS LIKE IT'S TRUE— HIGHTAILING IT IS THE ONE THING HE'S GOOD AT.
POLICE!
NO FUNNY MOVES! TURN AROUND SLOWLY!
KEEP YOUR HANDS WHERE WE CAN SEE THEM!
TCH...

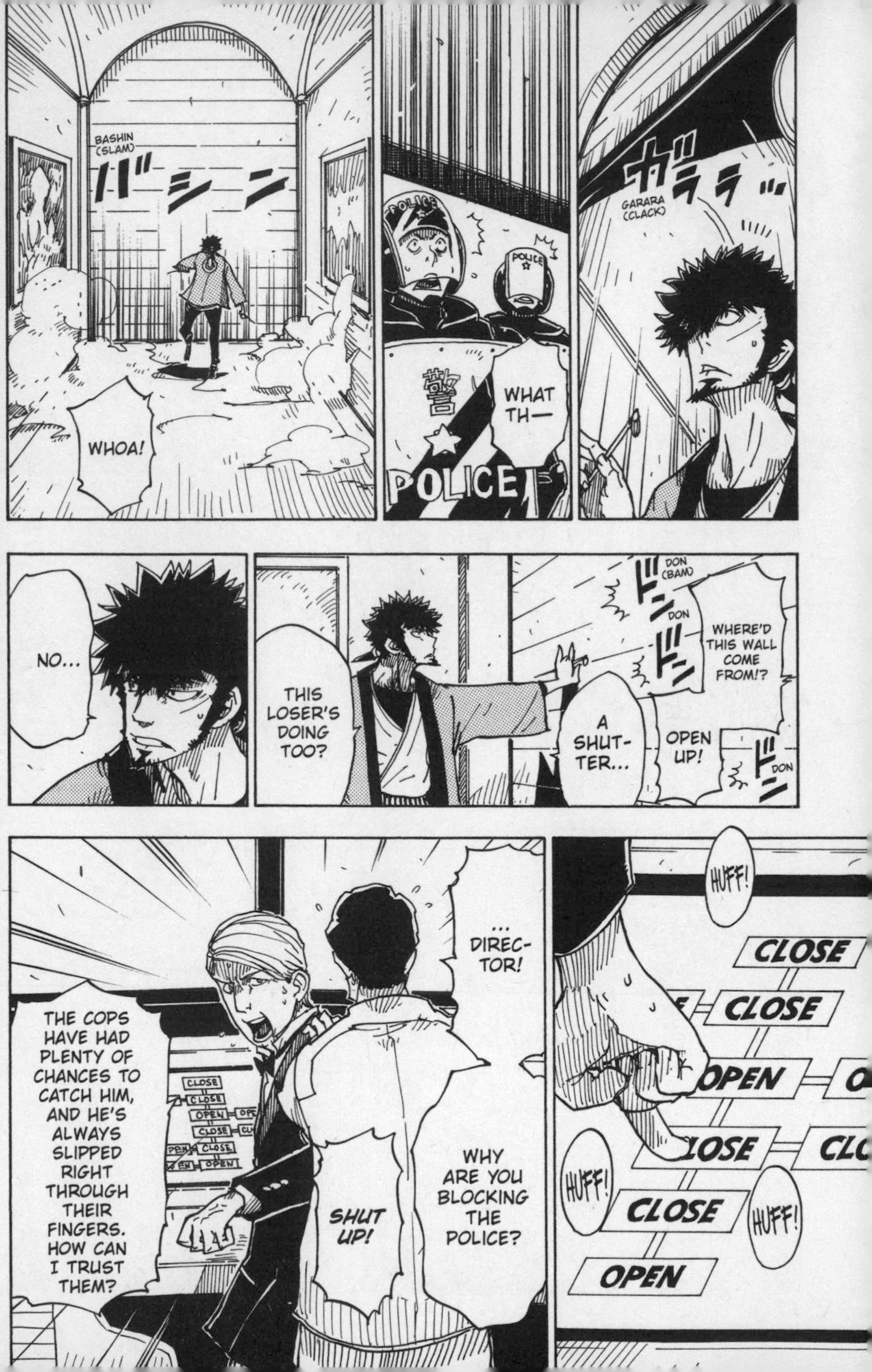
GARARA (CLACK)
WHAT TH—
POLICE
BASHIN (SLAM)
WHOA!
DON (BAM)
WHERE'D THIS WALL COME FROM!?
DON
OPEN UP!
A SHUT-TER...
THIS LOSER'S DOING TOO?
DON
NO...
HUFF!
CLOSE
CLOSE
HUFF!
CLOSE
HUFF!
OPEN
...DIREC-TOR!
WHY ARE YOU BLOCKING THE POLICE?
SHUT UP!
THE COPS HAVE HAD PLENTY OF CHANCES TO CATCH HIM, AND HE'S ALWAYS SLIPPED RIGHT THROUGH THEIR FINGERS. HOW CAN I TRUST THEM?

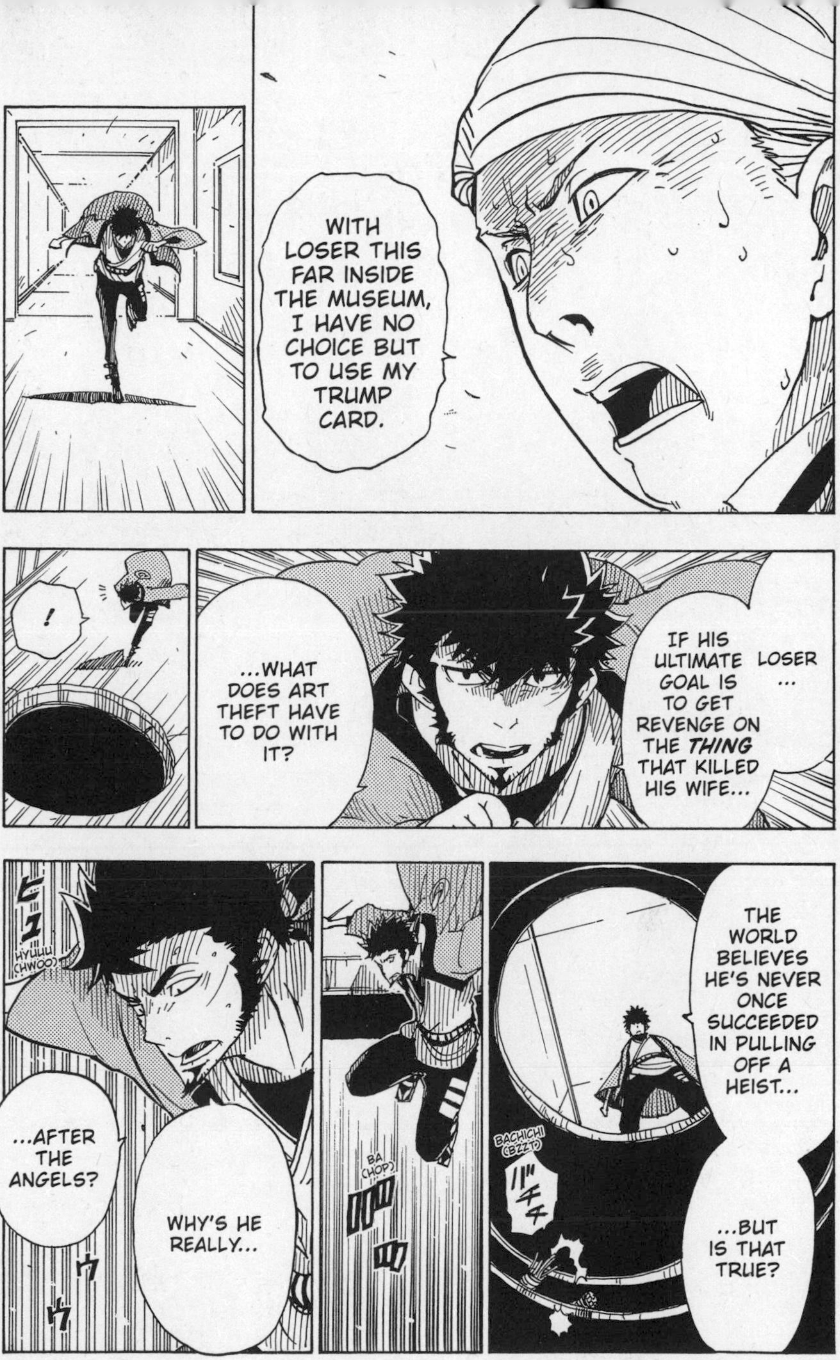
WITH LOSER THIS FAR INSIDE THE MUSEUM, I HAVE NO CHOICE BUT TO USE MY TRUMP CARD.
IF HIS ULTIMATE GOAL IS TO GET REVENGE ON THE THING THAT KILLED HIS WIFE...
LOSER ...
...WHAT DOES ART THEFT HAVE TO DO WITH IT?
!
THE WORLD BELIEVES HE'S NEVER ONCE SUCCEEDED IN PULLING OFF A HEIST...
BACHICHI (BZZT)
...BUT IS THAT TRUE?
BA (CHOP)
HYUUU (CHWOO)
WHY'S HE REALLY...
...AFTER THE ANGELS?

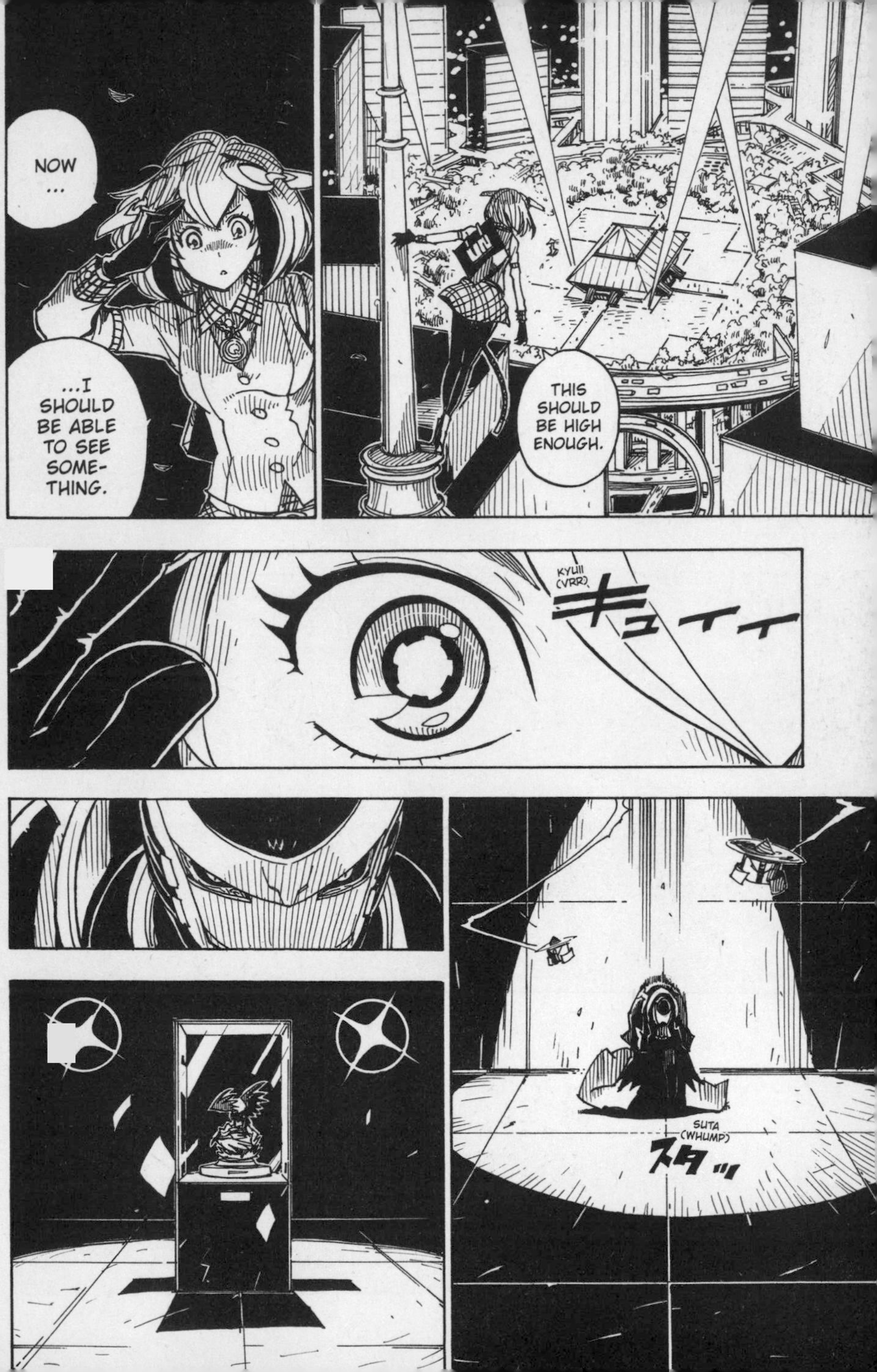
THIS SHOULD BE HIGH ENOUGH.
NOW ...
...I SHOULD BE ABLE TO SEE SOME-THING.
KYUII (VRR)
キュイイ
SUTA (WHUMP)
スタッ

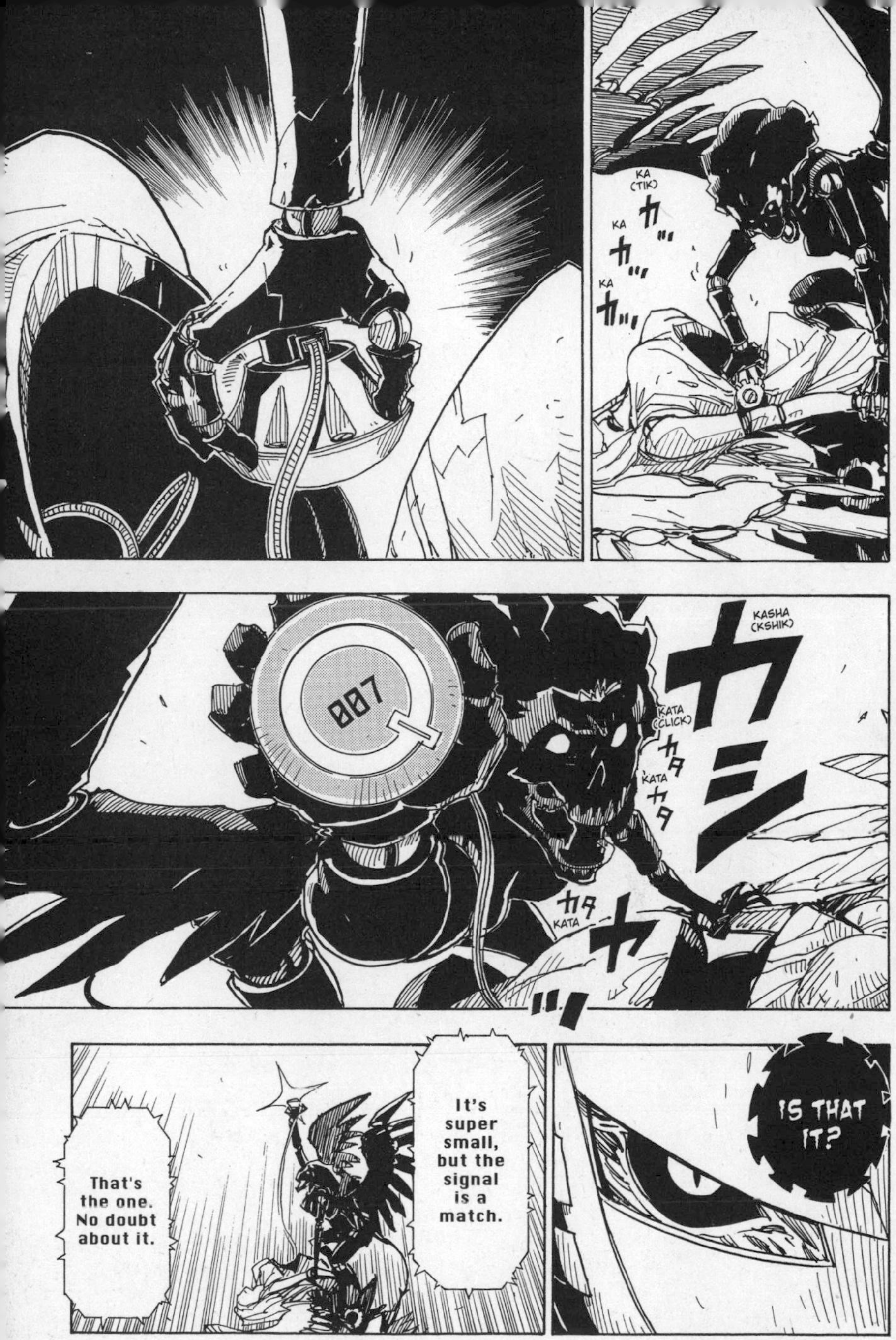
KA (TIK)
KA
KA
KASHA (KSHIK)
KATA (CLICK)
KATA
KATA
IS THAT IT?
It's super small, but the signal is a match.
That's the one. No doubt about it.

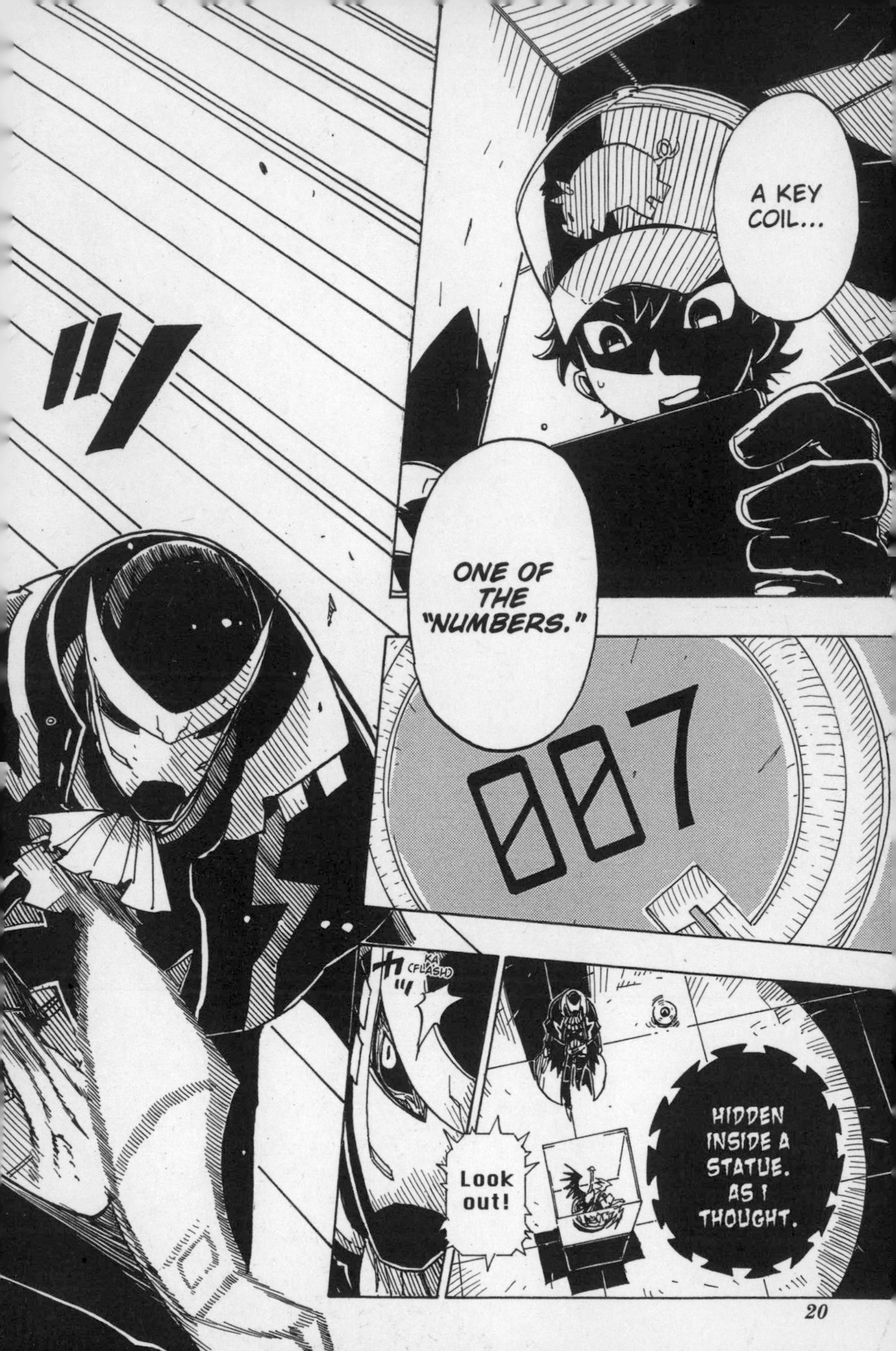
A KEY COIL...
ONE OF THE "NUMBERS."
007
HIDDEN INSIDE A STATUE. AS I THOUGHT.
KA (FLASH)
Look out!

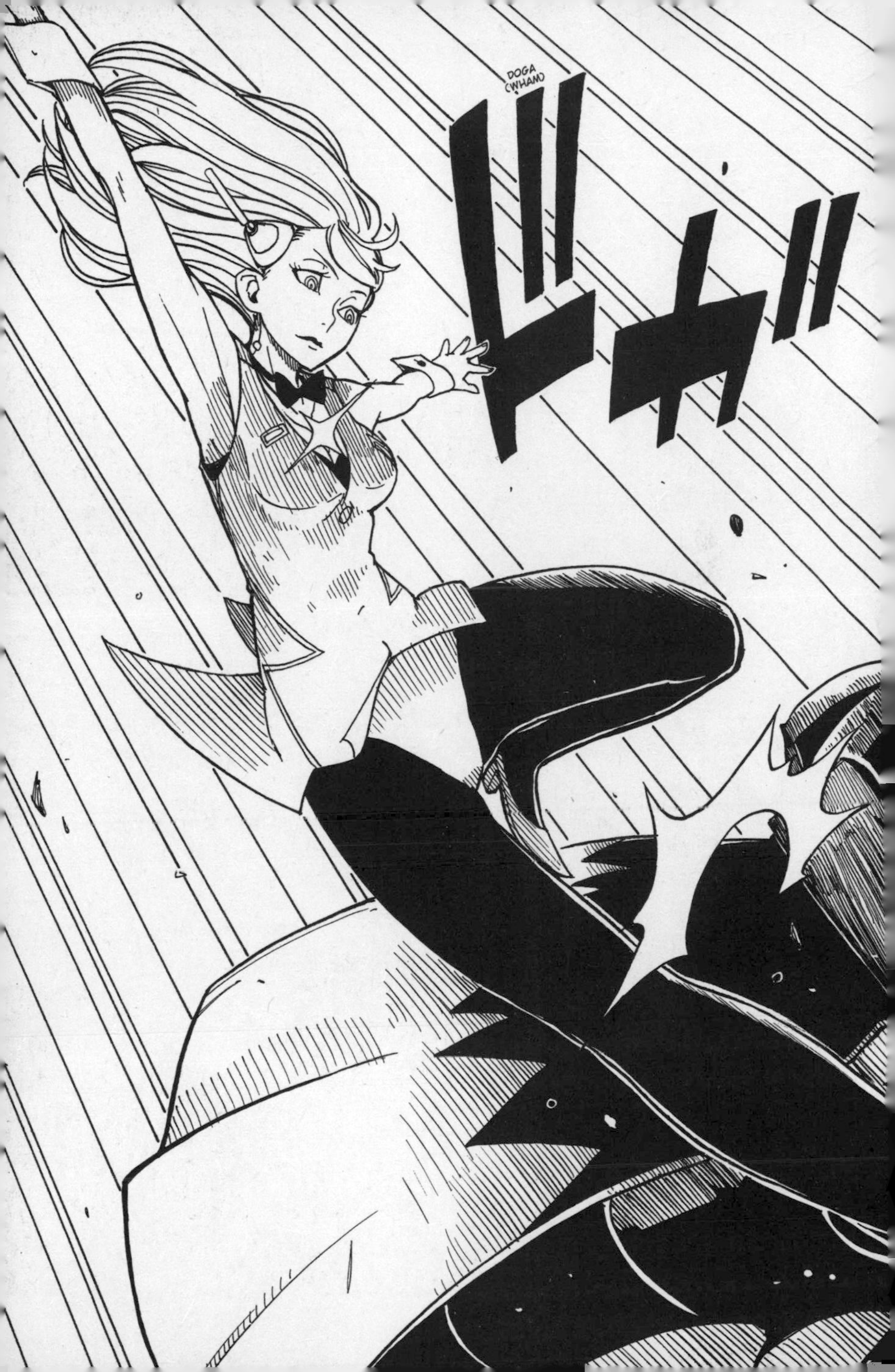
DOGA
(WHAM)
ドガ

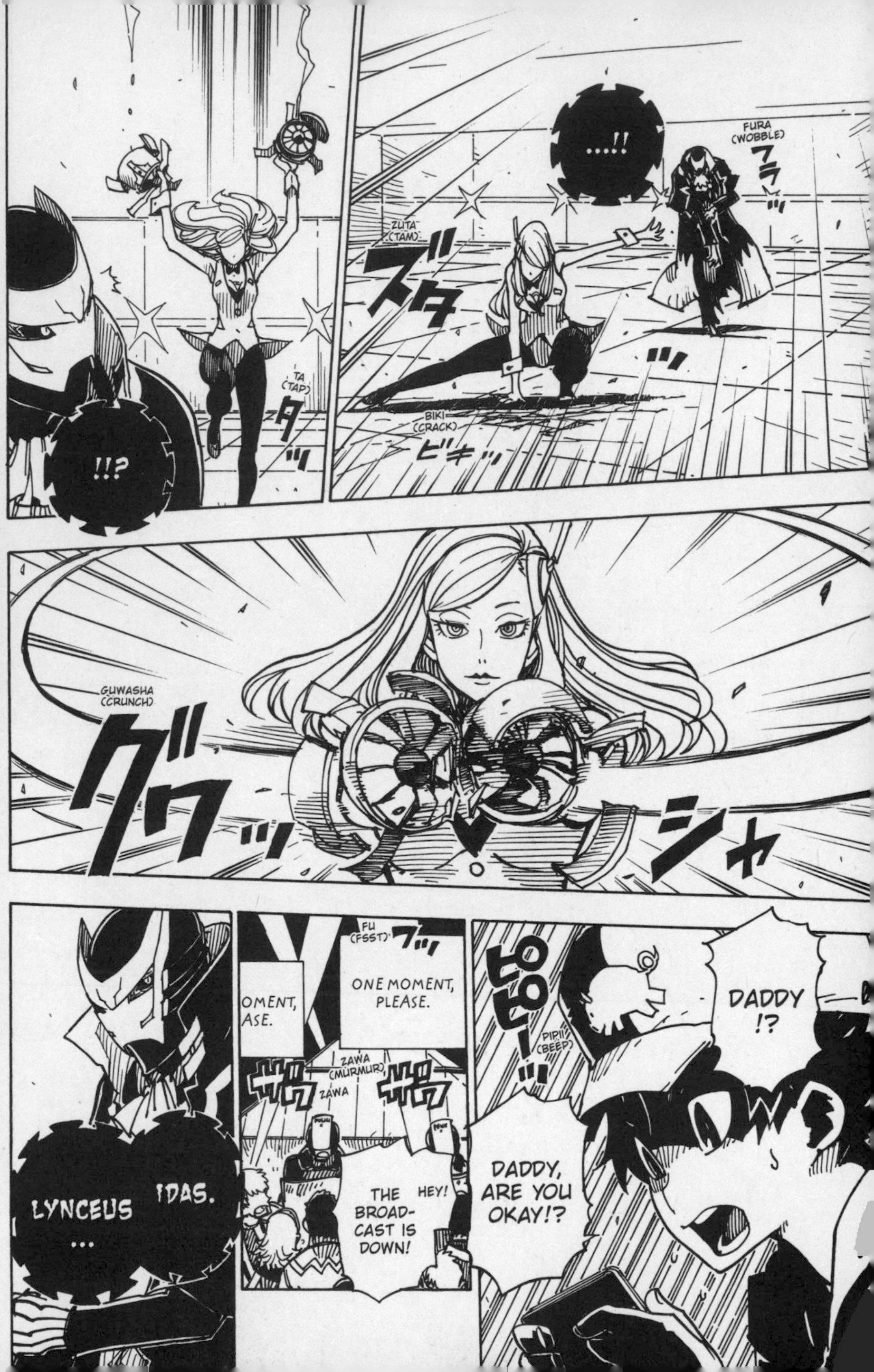
FURA (WOBBLE)
フラッ
....!!
ZUTA (TAM)
ズダッ
BIKI (CRACK)
ビキッ
TA (TAP)
タッ
!!?
GUWASHA (CRUNCH)
グワッシャ
DADDY !?
PIPI (BEEP)
ピピー!!
DADDY, ARE YOU OKAY!?
FU (FSST)
フッ
ONE MOMENT, PLEASE.
MOMENT, ASE.
ZAWA (MURMUR)
ザワ ZAWA ザワ
HEY!
THE BROADCAST IS DOWN!
IDAS.
LYNCEUS ...

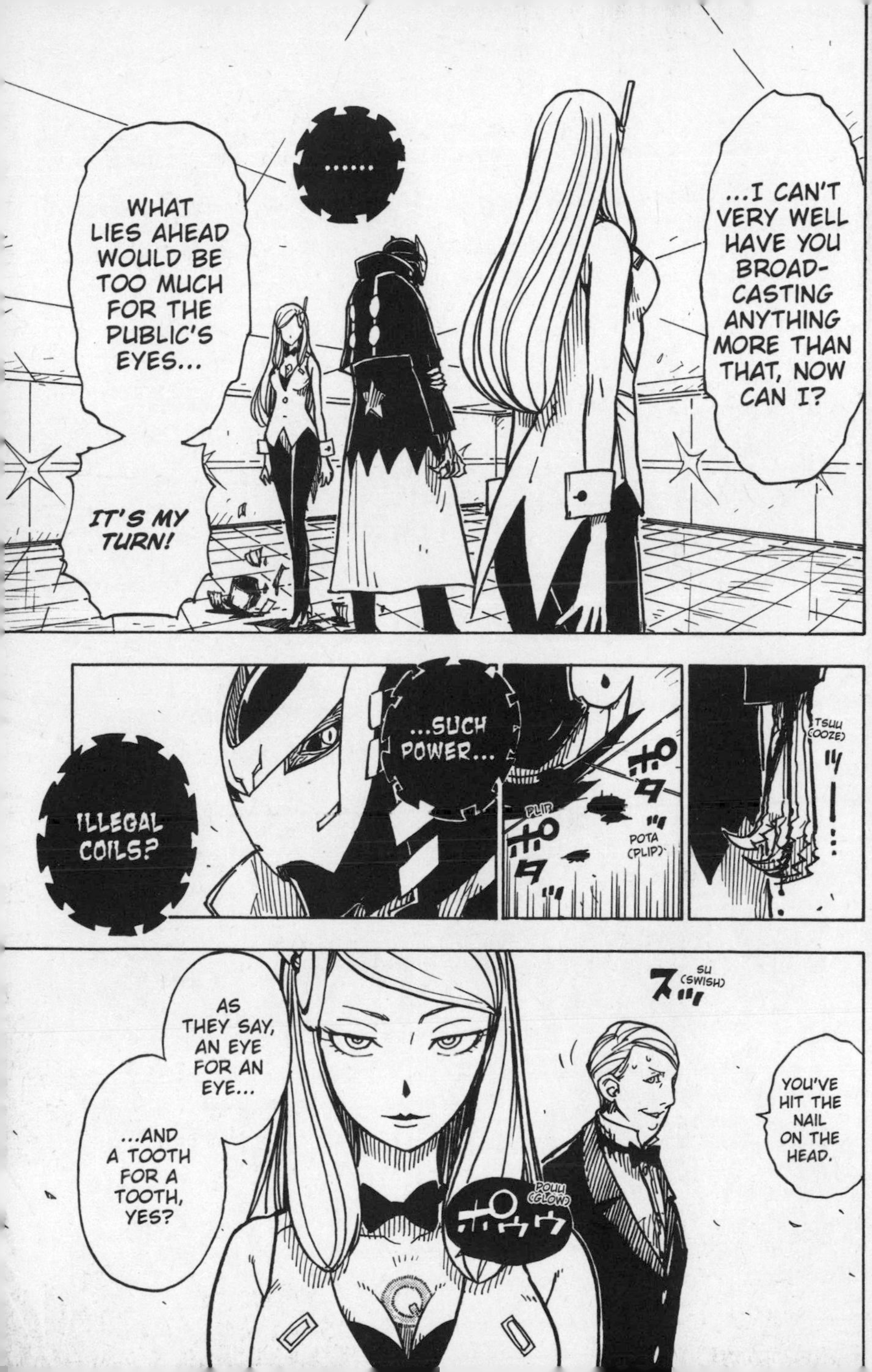
...I CAN'T VERY WELL HAVE YOU BROAD-CASTING ANYTHING MORE THAN THAT, NOW CAN I?
......
WHAT LIES AHEAD WOULD BE TOO MUCH FOR THE PUBLIC'S EYES...
IT'S MY TURN!
TSUU (OOZE)
ツー…
ポタッ
POTA (PLIP)
PLIP
ポタッ
...SUCH POWER...
ILLEGAL COILS?
SU (SWISH)
スッ
YOU'VE HIT THE NAIL ON THE HEAD.
AS THEY SAY, AN EYE FOR AN EYE...
...AND A TOOTH FOR A TOOTH, YES?
POUU (GLOW)
ポウウ

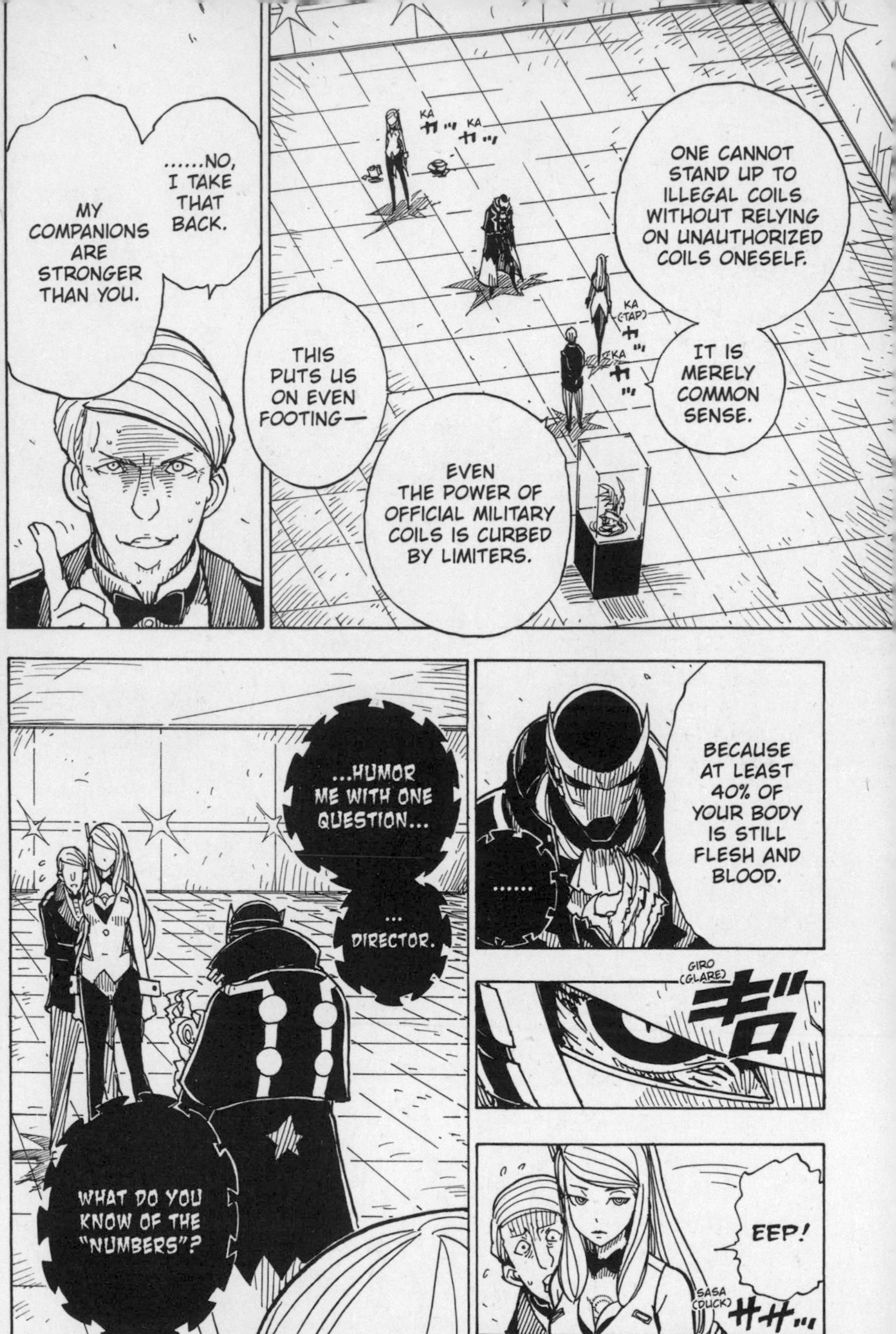

KA KA
ONE CANNOT STAND UP TO ILLEGAL COILS WITHOUT RELYING ON UNAUTHORIZED COILS ONESELF.
KA (TAP)
IT IS MERELY COMMON SENSE.
KA
EVEN THE POWER OF OFFICIAL MILITARY COILS IS CURBED BY LIMITERS.
THIS PUTS US ON EVEN FOOTING—
......NO, I TAKE THAT BACK.
MY COMPANIONS ARE STRONGER THAN YOU.
BECAUSE AT LEAST 40% OF YOUR BODY IS STILL FLESH AND BLOOD.
......
GIRO (GLARE)
EEP!
SASA (DUCK)
...HUMOR ME WITH ONE QUESTION...
... DIRECTOR.
WHAT DO YOU KNOW OF THE "NUMBERS"?

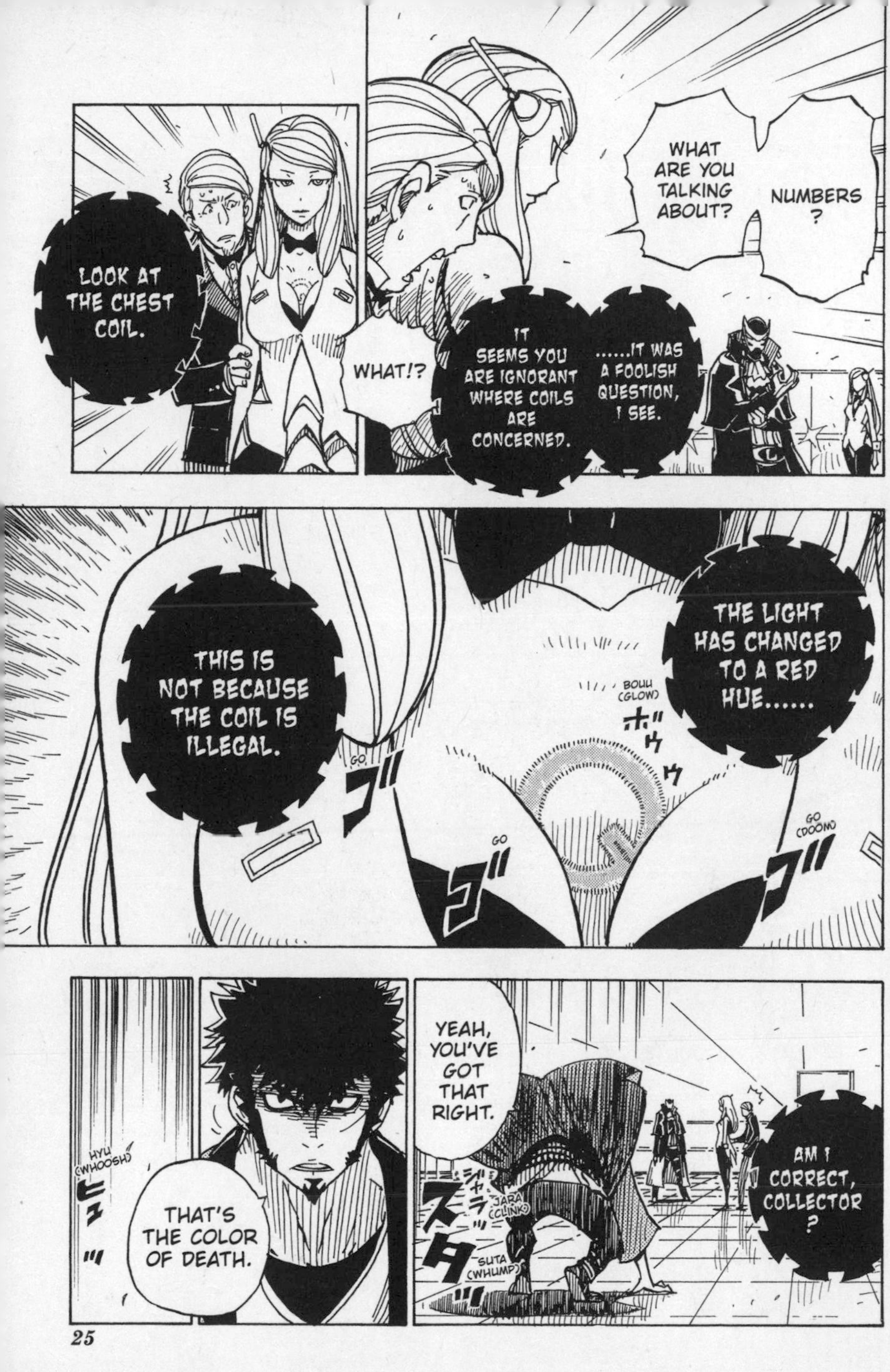
NUMBERS?
WHAT ARE YOU TALKING ABOUT?
......IT WAS A FOOLISH QUESTION, I SEE.
IT SEEMS YOU ARE IGNORANT WHERE COILS ARE CONCERNED.
WHAT!?
LOOK AT THE CHEST COIL.
THE LIGHT HAS CHANGED TO A RED HUE......
BOUU (GLOW)
GO (DOOM)
GO
GO
THIS IS NOT BECAUSE THE COIL IS ILLEGAL.
AM I CORRECT, COLLECTOR?
YEAH, YOU'VE GOT THAT RIGHT.
JARA (CLINK)
SUTA (WHUMP)
THAT'S THE COLOR OF DEATH.
HYU (WHOOSH)

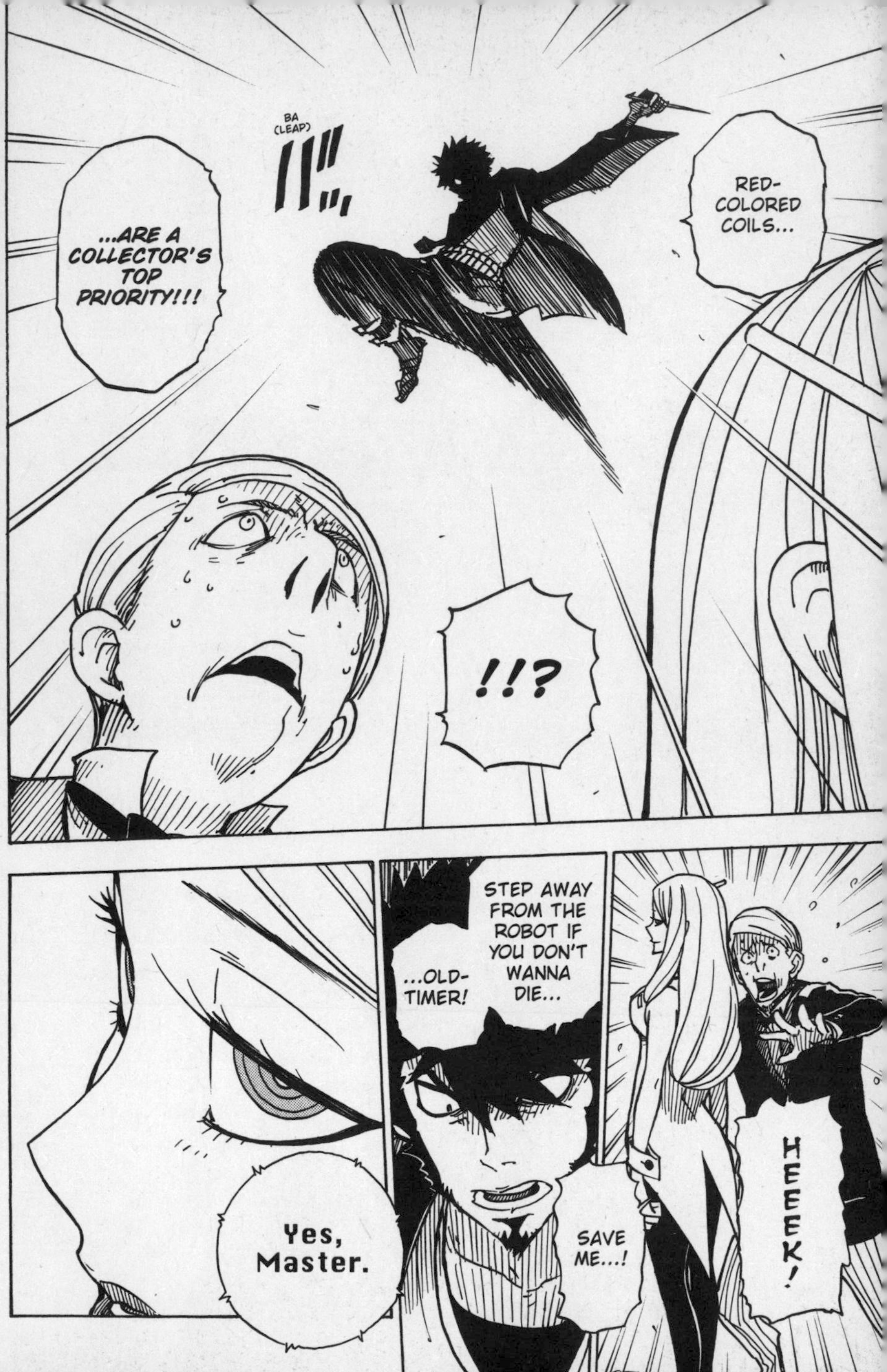
RED-COLORED COILS...
BA (LEAP)
...ARE A COLLECTOR'S TOP PRIORITY!!!
!!?
HEEEK!
SAVE ME...!
STEP AWAY FROM THE ROBOT IF YOU DON'T WANNA DIE...
...OLD-TIMER!
Yes, Master.

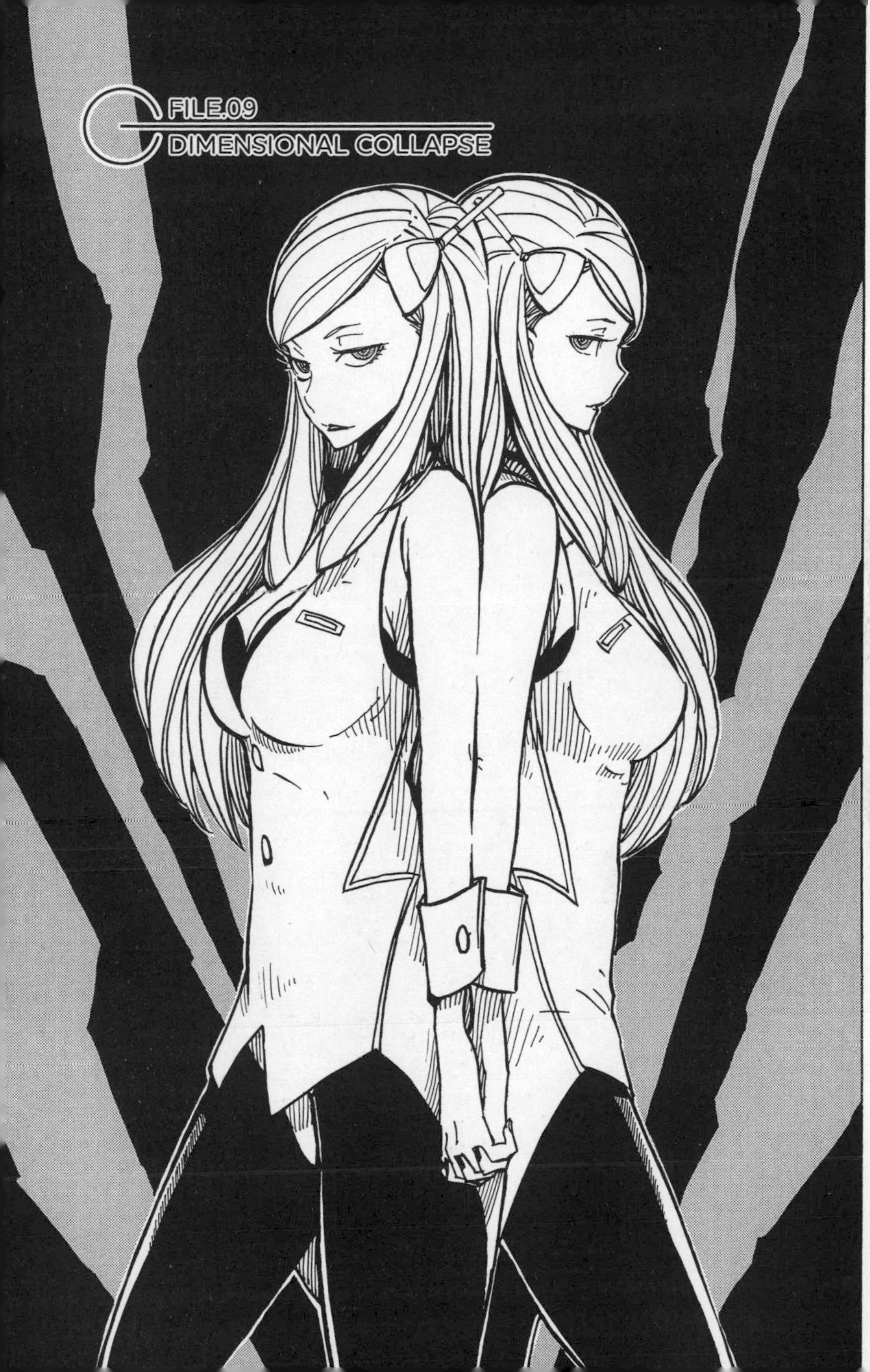
FILE.09
DIMENSIONAL COLLAPSE

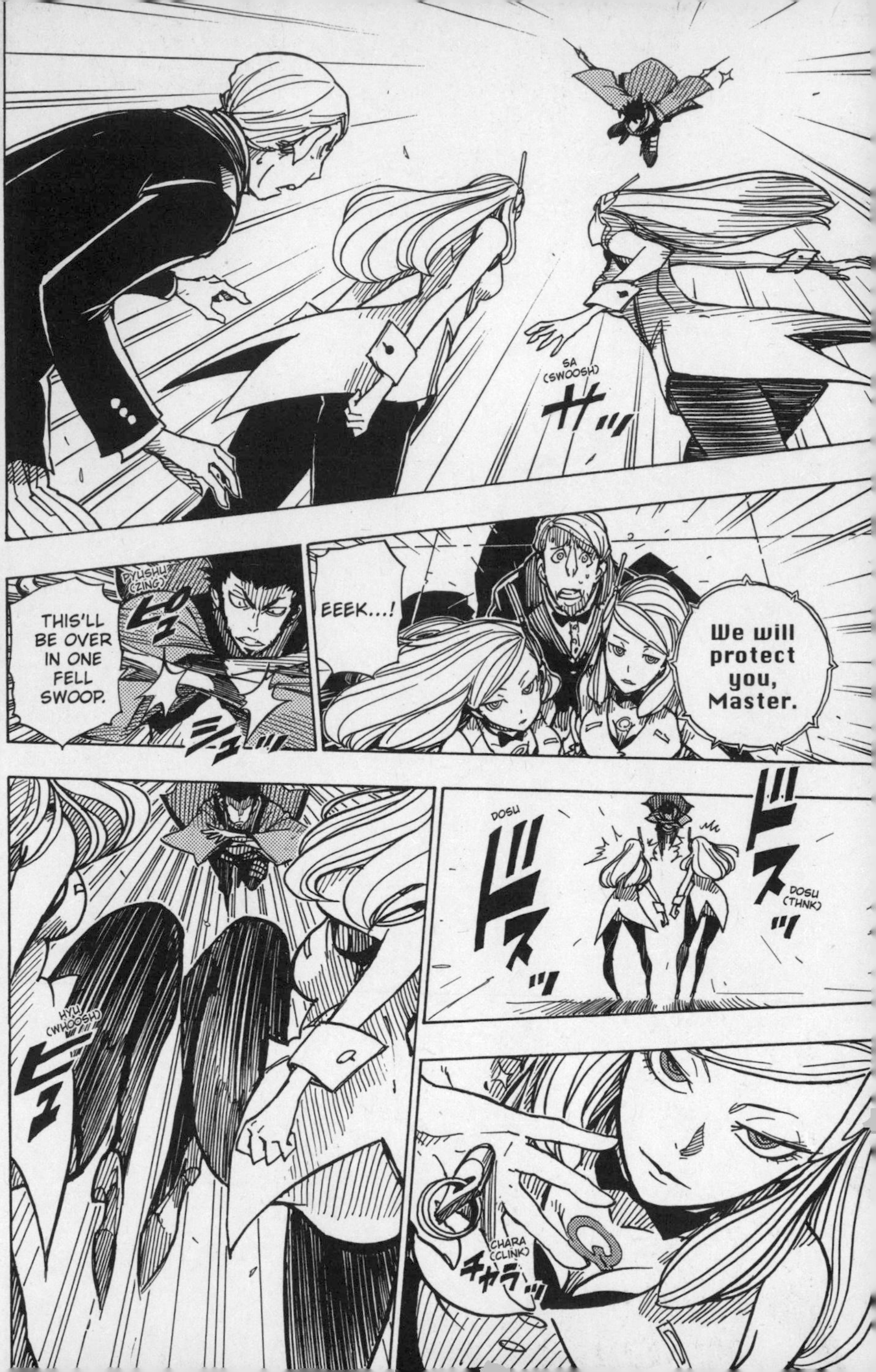
SA (SWOOSH)
ザッ
We will protect you, Master.
EEEK...!
PYUSHU (ZING)
ピュ
THIS'LL BE OVER IN ONE FELL SWOOP.
シュッ
DOSU (THNK)
ドスッ
DOSU
ドスッ
CHARA (CLINK)
チャラッ
HYU (WHOOSH)
ヒュ

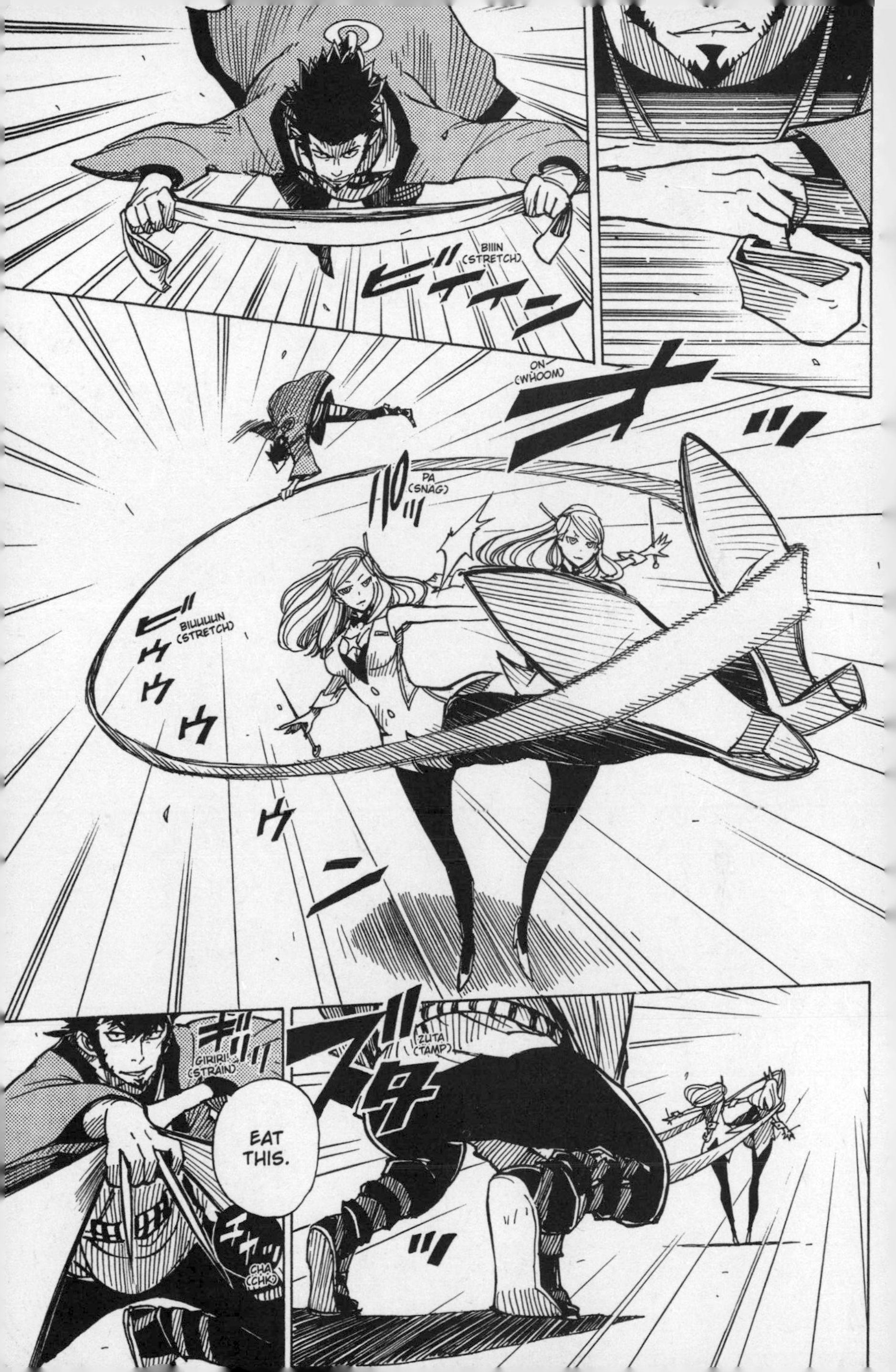
BIIIN
(STRETCH)
ON
(WHOOM)
PA
(SNAG)
BIUUUUUN
(STRETCH)
ZUTA
(TAMP)
GIRIRI
(STRAIN)
EAT THIS.
CHA
(CHK)

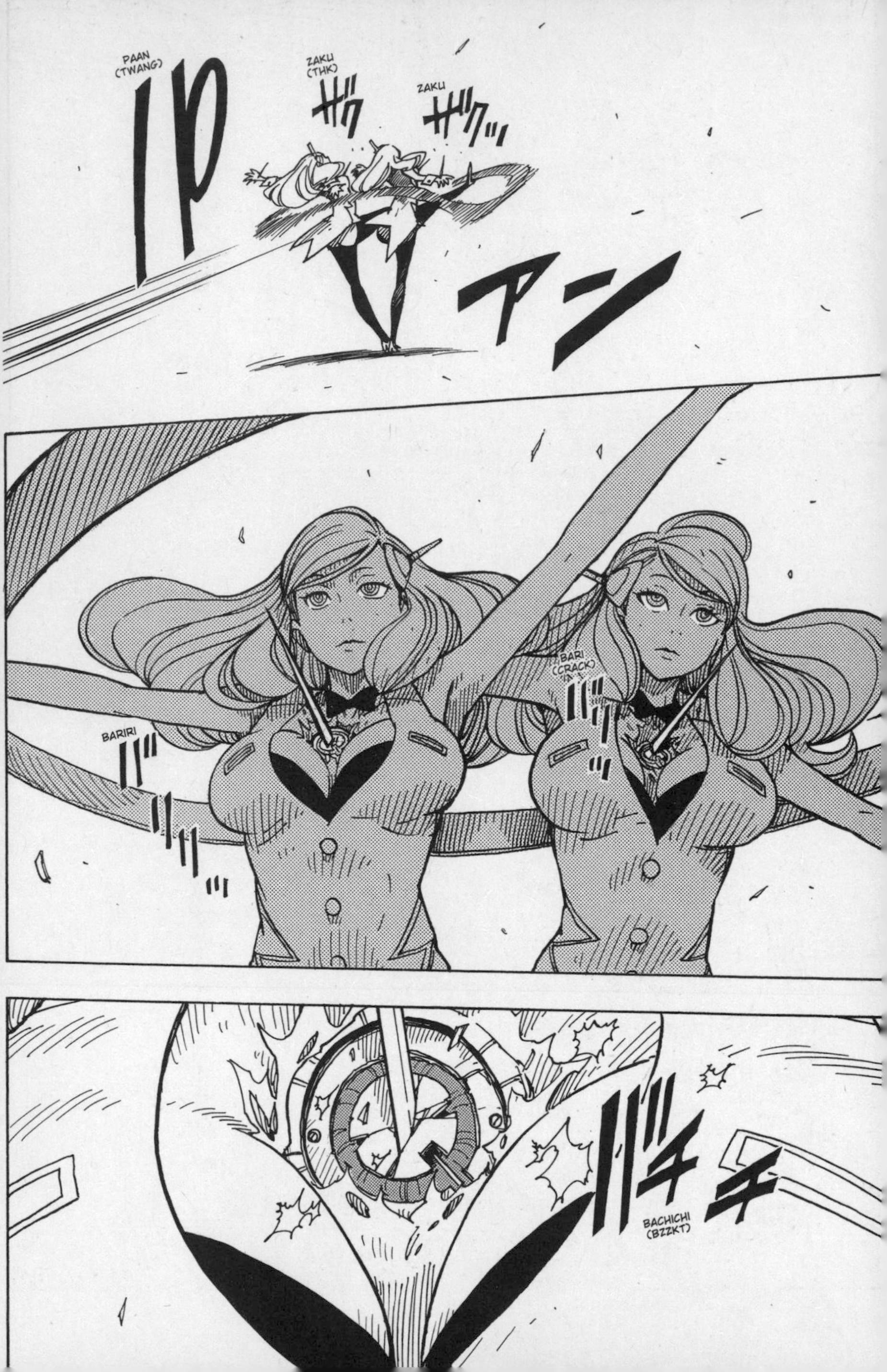

PAAN
(TWANG)
ZAKU
(THK)
ZAKU
BARI
(CRACK)
BARIRI
BACHICHI
(BZZKT)

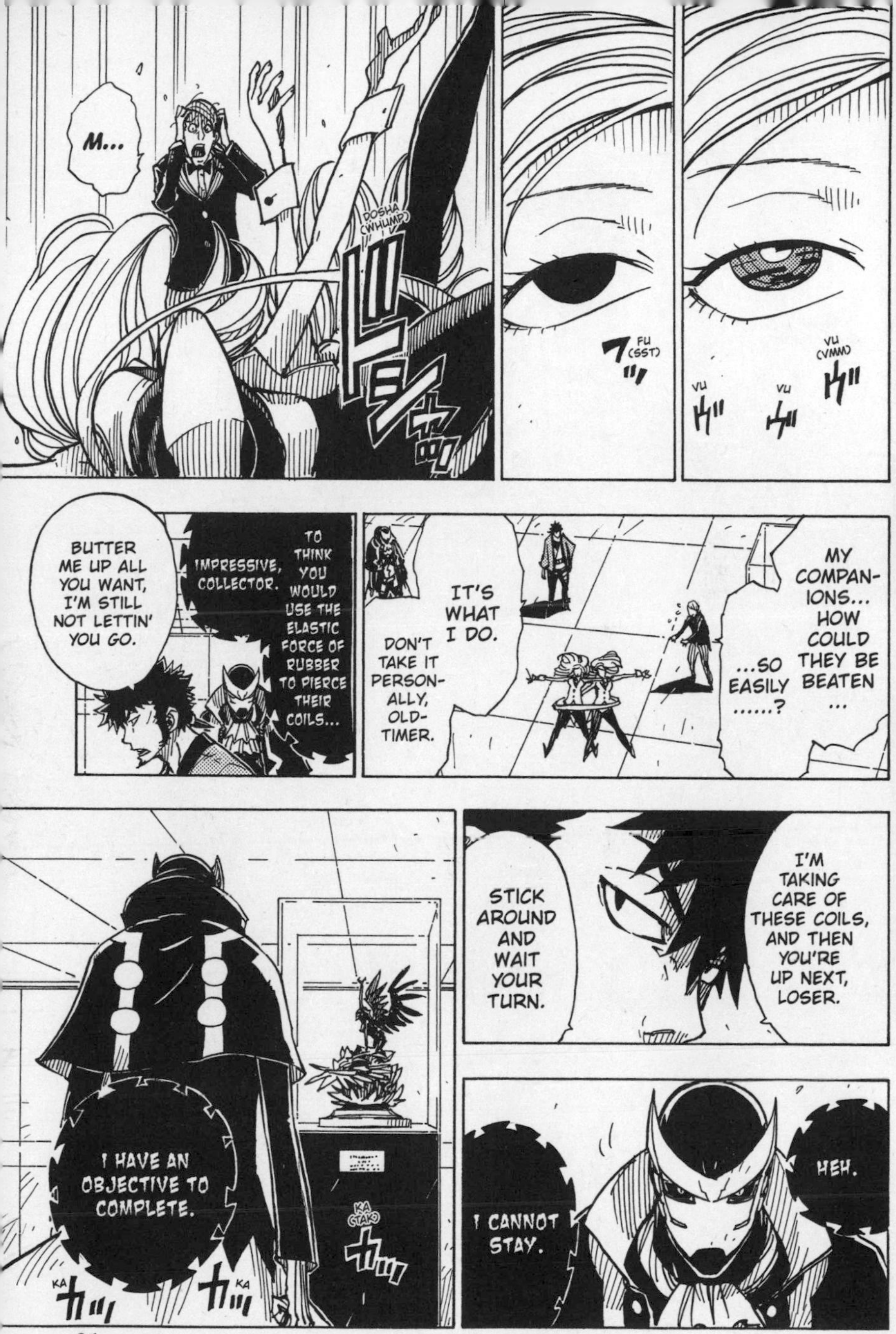
VU (VMM)
VU
VU
FU (SST)
M...
DOSHA (WHUMP)
MY COMPANIONS... HOW COULD THEY BE BEATEN ...
...SO EASILY ......?
IT'S WHAT I DO.
DON'T TAKE IT PERSONALLY, OLD-TIMER.
TO THINK YOU WOULD USE THE ELASTIC FORCE OF RUBBER TO PIERCE THEIR COILS...
IMPRESSIVE, COLLECTOR.
BUTTER ME UP ALL YOU WANT, I'M STILL NOT LETTIN' YOU GO.
I'M TAKING CARE OF THESE COILS, AND THEN YOU'RE UP NEXT, LOSER.
STICK AROUND AND WAIT YOUR TURN.
HEH.
I CANNOT STAY.
I HAVE AN OBJECTIVE TO COMPLETE.
KA (TAK)
KA
KA

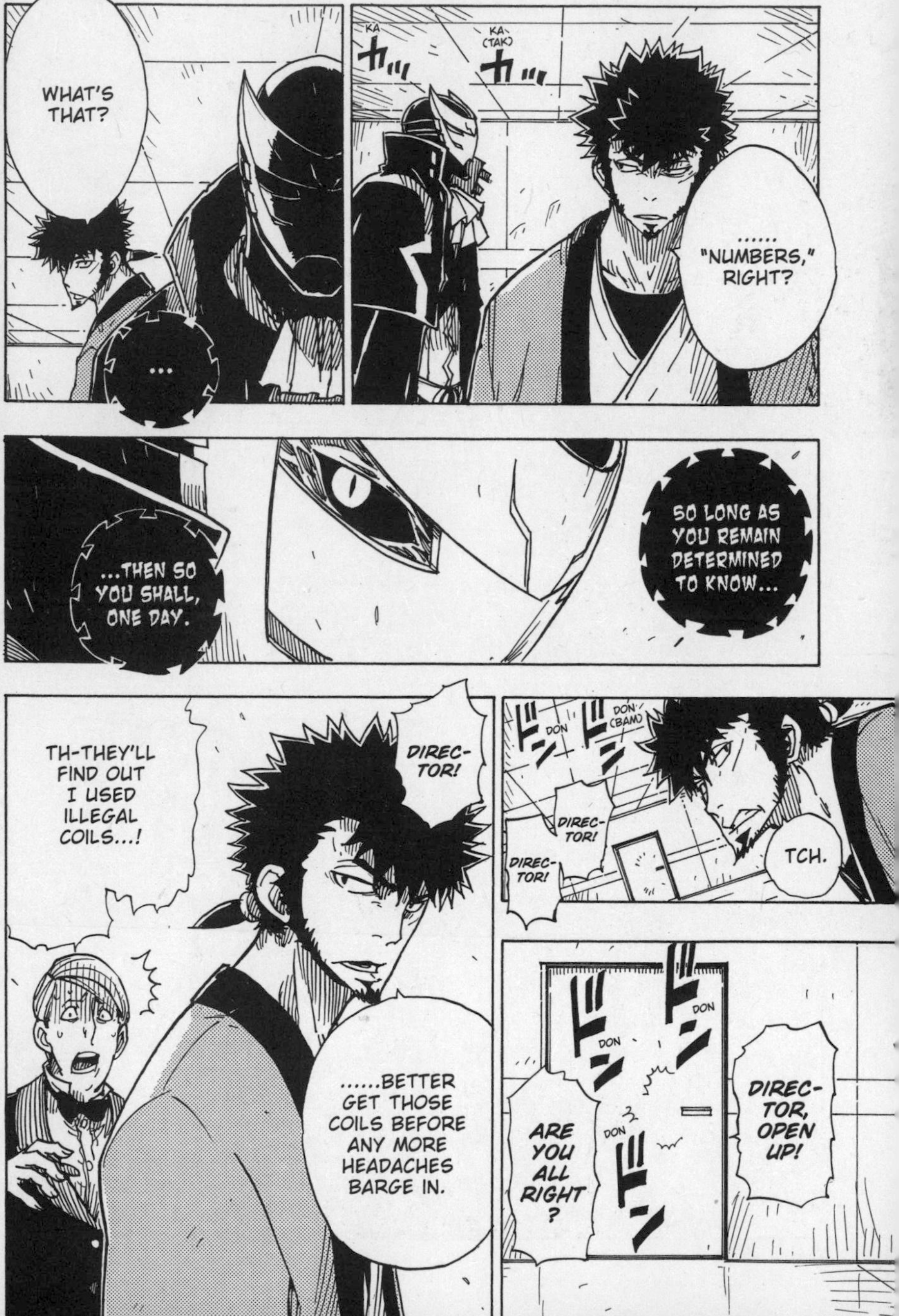

KA (TAK)
カッ
KA
カッ
......"NUMBERS," RIGHT?
WHAT'S THAT?
...
SO LONG AS YOU REMAIN DETERMINED TO KNOW...
...THEN SO YOU SHALL, ONE DAY.
DON (BAM)
ドン
DON
ドン
DIREC-TOR!
DIREC-TOR!
TCH.
DON
ドン
DON
ドン
DON
ドン
DIREC-TOR, OPEN UP!
ARE YOU ALL RIGHT?
DIREC-TOR!
TH-THEY'LL FIND OUT I USED ILLEGAL COILS...!
......BETTER GET THOSE COILS BEFORE ANY MORE HEADACHES BARGE IN.

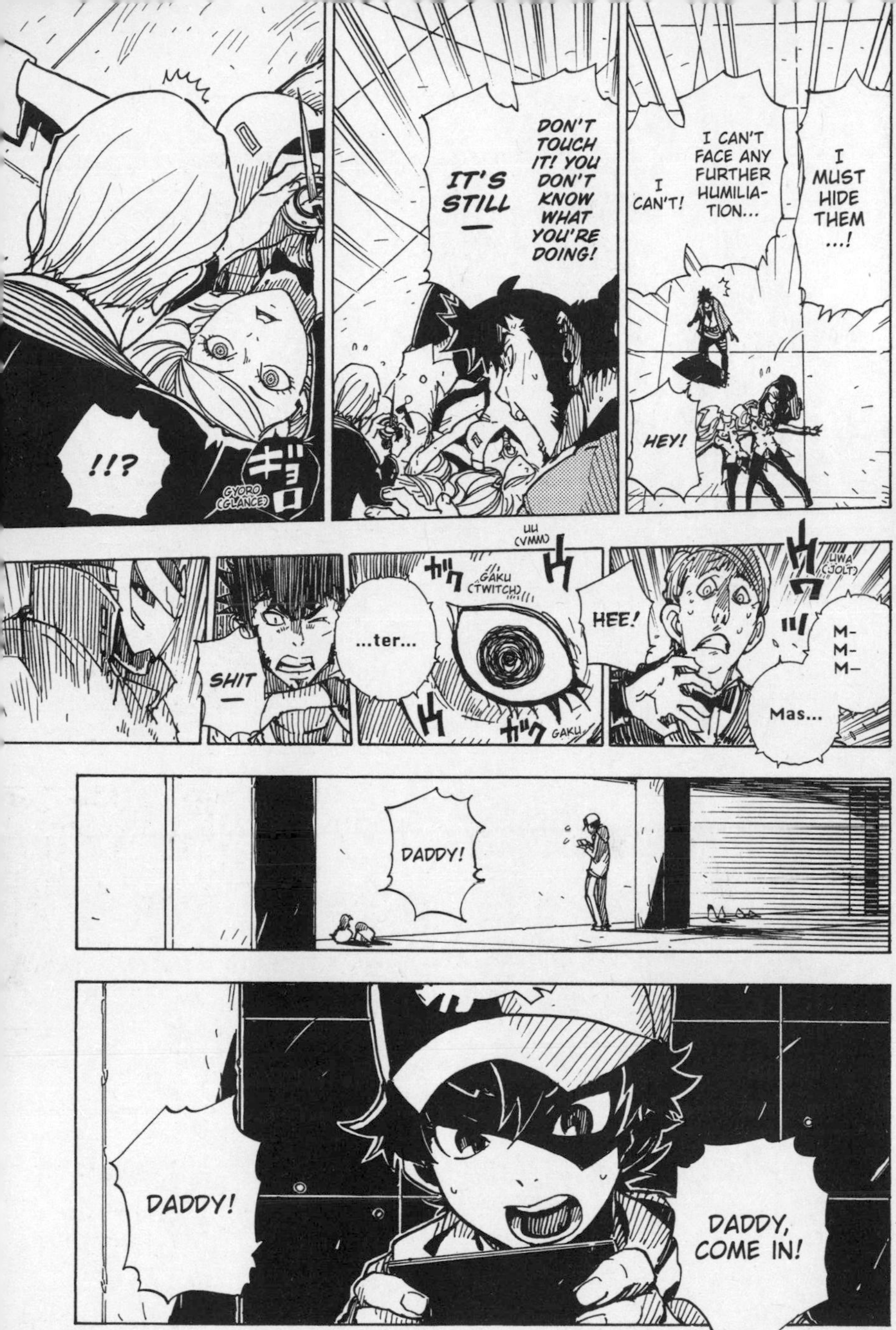
I MUST HIDE THEM ...!
I CAN'T FACE ANY FURTHER HUMILIA-TION...
I CAN'T!
HEY!
DON'T TOUCH IT! YOU DON'T KNOW WHAT YOU'RE DOING!
IT'S STILL —
!!?
ギョロ
GYORO (GLANCE)
ウワッ
UWA (JOLT)
M- M- M-
Mas...
HEE!
ウ
UU (VMM)
ガク
GAKU (TWITCH)
...ter...
ガク
GAKU
SHIT —
DADDY!
DADDY, COME IN!
DADDY!

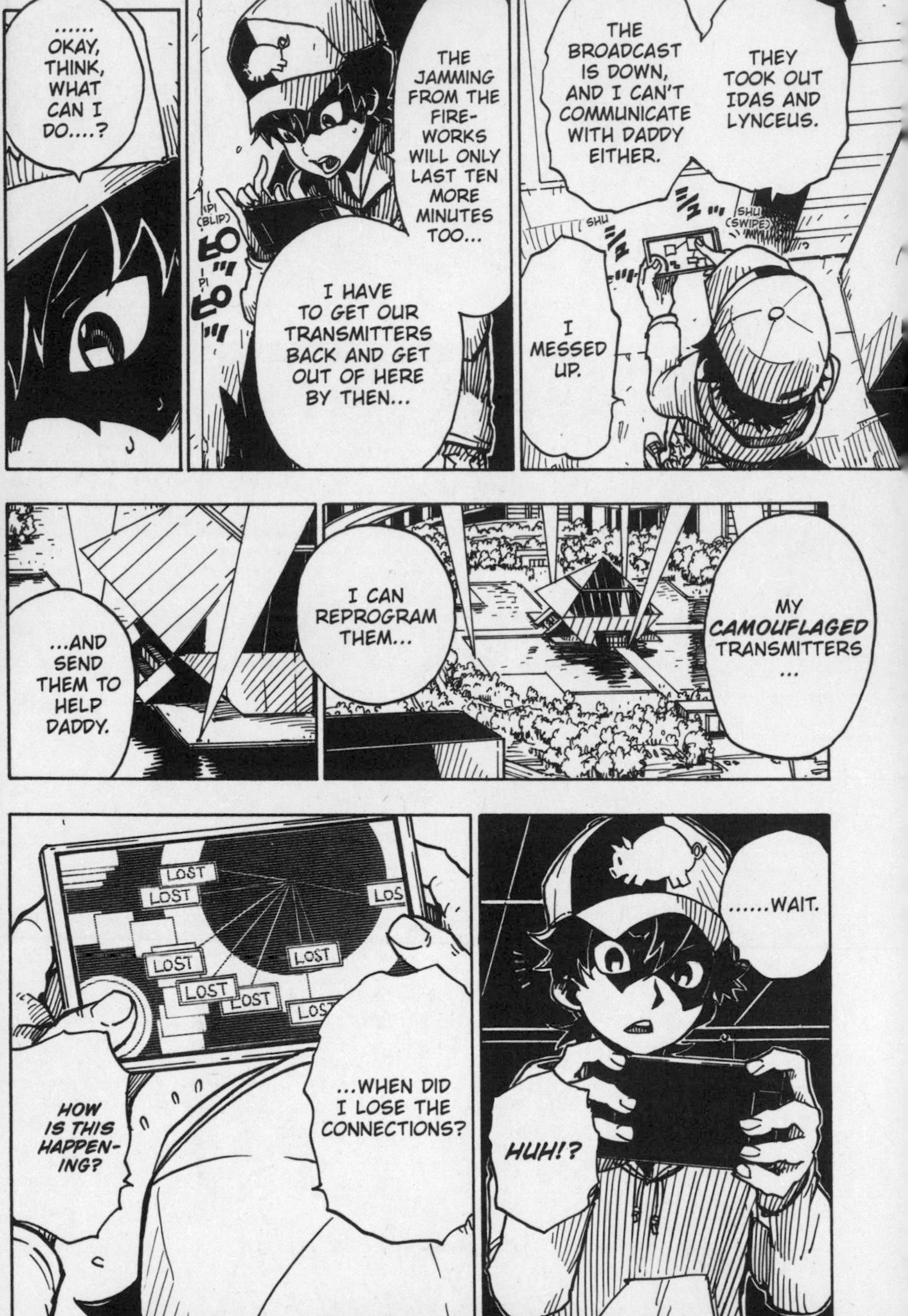
THEY TOOK OUT IDAS AND LYNCEUS.
THE BROADCAST IS DOWN, AND I CAN'T COMMUNICATE WITH DADDY EITHER.
SHU (SWIPE)
SHU
I MESSED UP.
THE JAMMING FROM THE FIRE-WORKS WILL ONLY LAST TEN MORE MINUTES TOO...
PI (BLIP)
PI
I HAVE TO GET OUR TRANSMITTERS BACK AND GET OUT OF HERE BY THEN...
......OKAY, THINK, WHAT CAN I DO....?
MY *CAMOUFLAGED* TRANSMITTERS ...
I CAN REPROGRAM THEM...
...AND SEND THEM TO HELP DADDY.
......WAIT.
HUH!?
LOST
LOST
LOST
LOST
LOST
LOST
...WHEN DID I LOSE THE CONNECTIONS?
HOW IS THIS HAPPENING?

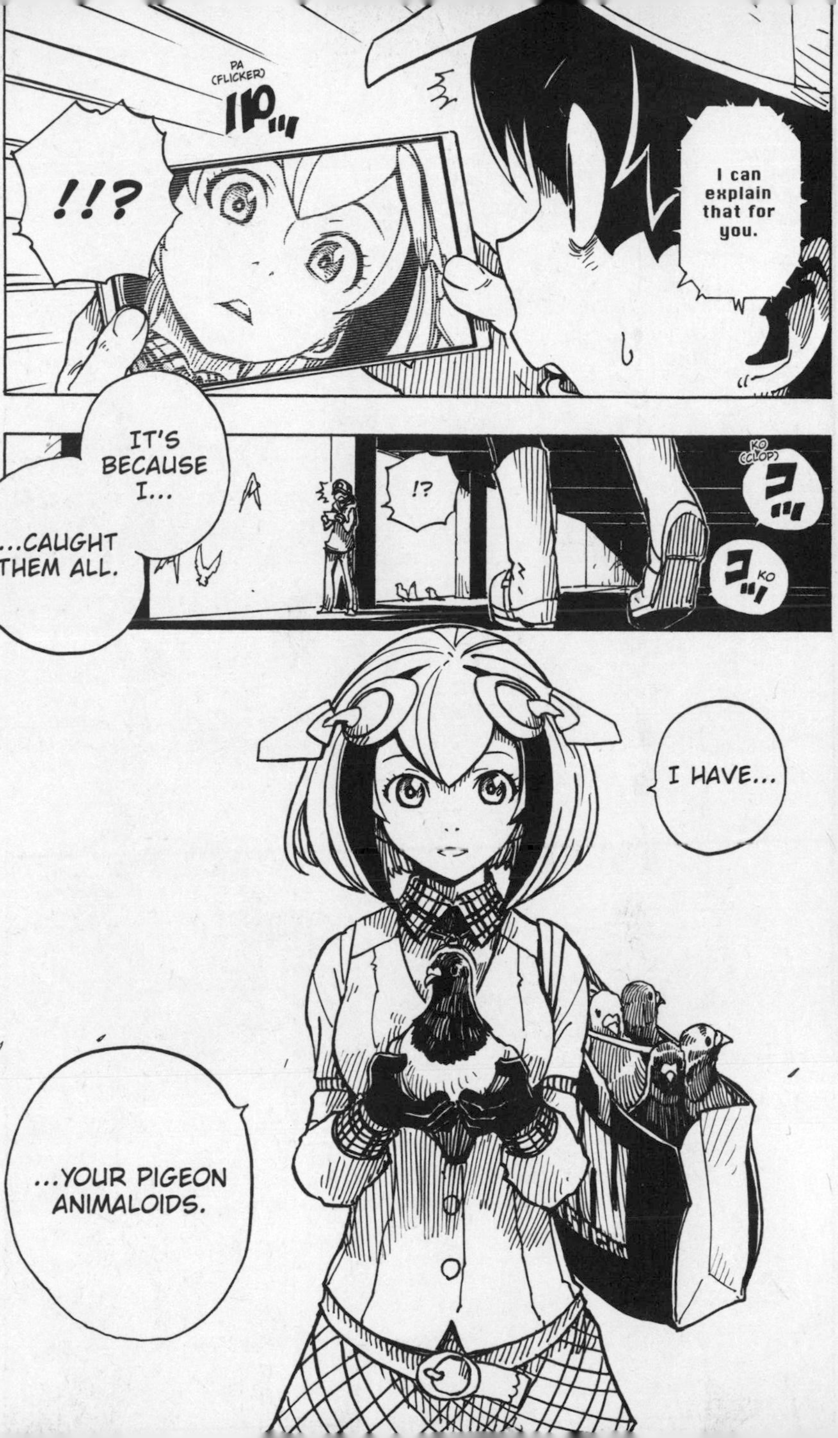
I can explain that for you.
PA (FLICKER)
!!?
KO (CLOP)
KO
!?
IT'S BECAUSE I...
...CAUGHT THEM ALL.
I HAVE...
...YOUR PIGEON ANIMALOIDS.

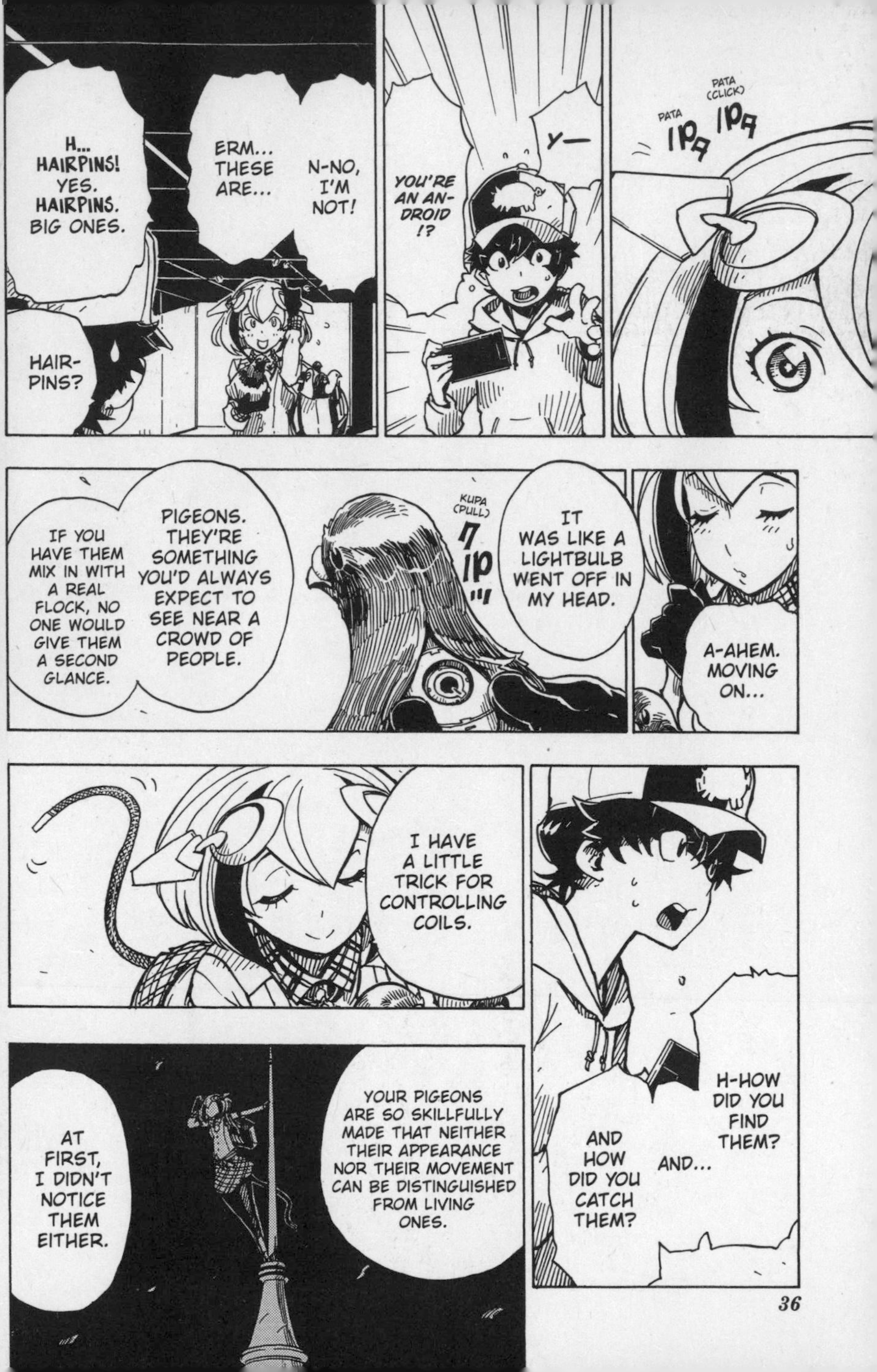
PATA (CLICK)
PATA
Y—
YOU'RE AN AN-DROID !?
N-NO, I'M NOT!
ERM... THESE ARE...
H... HAIRPINS! YES. HAIRPINS. BIG ONES.
HAIR-PINS?
A-AHEM. MOVING ON...
KUPA (PULL)
IT WAS LIKE A LIGHTBULB WENT OFF IN MY HEAD.
PIGEONS. THEY'RE SOMETHING YOU'D ALWAYS EXPECT TO SEE NEAR A CROWD OF PEOPLE.
IF YOU HAVE THEM MIX IN WITH A REAL FLOCK, NO ONE WOULD GIVE THEM A SECOND GLANCE.
H-HOW DID YOU FIND THEM?
AND...
AND HOW DID YOU CATCH THEM?
I HAVE A LITTLE TRICK FOR CONTROLLING COILS.
YOUR PIGEONS ARE SO SKILLFULLY MADE THAT NEITHER THEIR APPEARANCE NOR THEIR MOVEMENT CAN BE DISTINGUISHED FROM LIVING ONES.
AT FIRST, I DIDN'T NOTICE THEM EITHER.

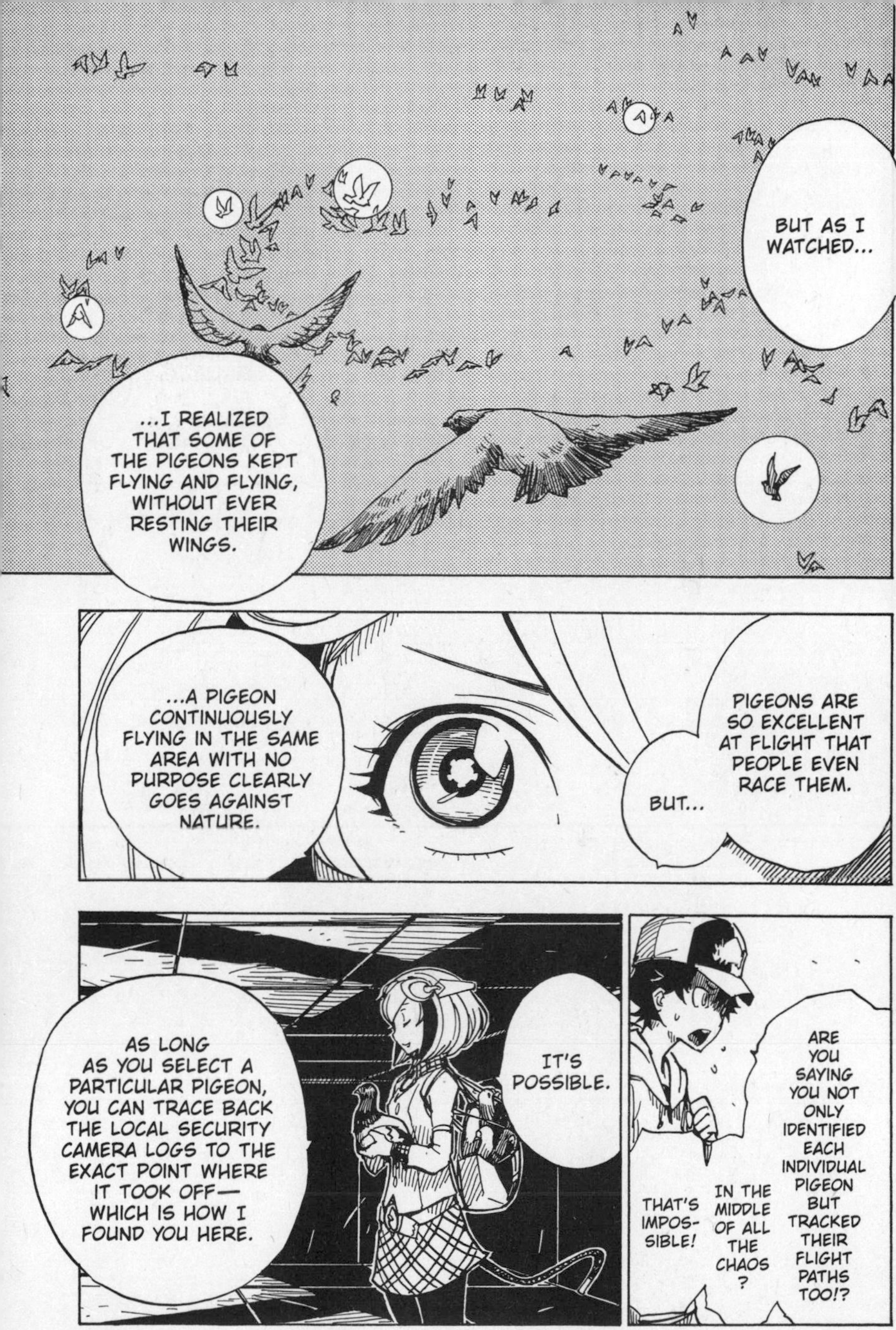
BUT AS I WATCHED...
...I REALIZED THAT SOME OF THE PIGEONS KEPT FLYING AND FLYING, WITHOUT EVER RESTING THEIR WINGS.
PIGEONS ARE SO EXCELLENT AT FLIGHT THAT PEOPLE EVEN RACE THEM.
BUT...
...A PIGEON CONTINUOUSLY FLYING IN THE SAME AREA WITH NO PURPOSE CLEARLY GOES AGAINST NATURE.
ARE YOU SAYING YOU NOT ONLY IDENTIFIED EACH INDIVIDUAL PIGEON BUT TRACKED THEIR FLIGHT PATHS TOO!?
IN THE MIDDLE OF ALL THE CHAOS?
THAT'S IMPOS-SIBLE!
IT'S POSSIBLE.
AS LONG AS YOU SELECT A PARTICULAR PIGEON, YOU CAN TRACE BACK THE LOCAL SECURITY CAMERA LOGS TO THE EXACT POINT WHERE IT TOOK OFF—WHICH IS HOW I FOUND YOU HERE.

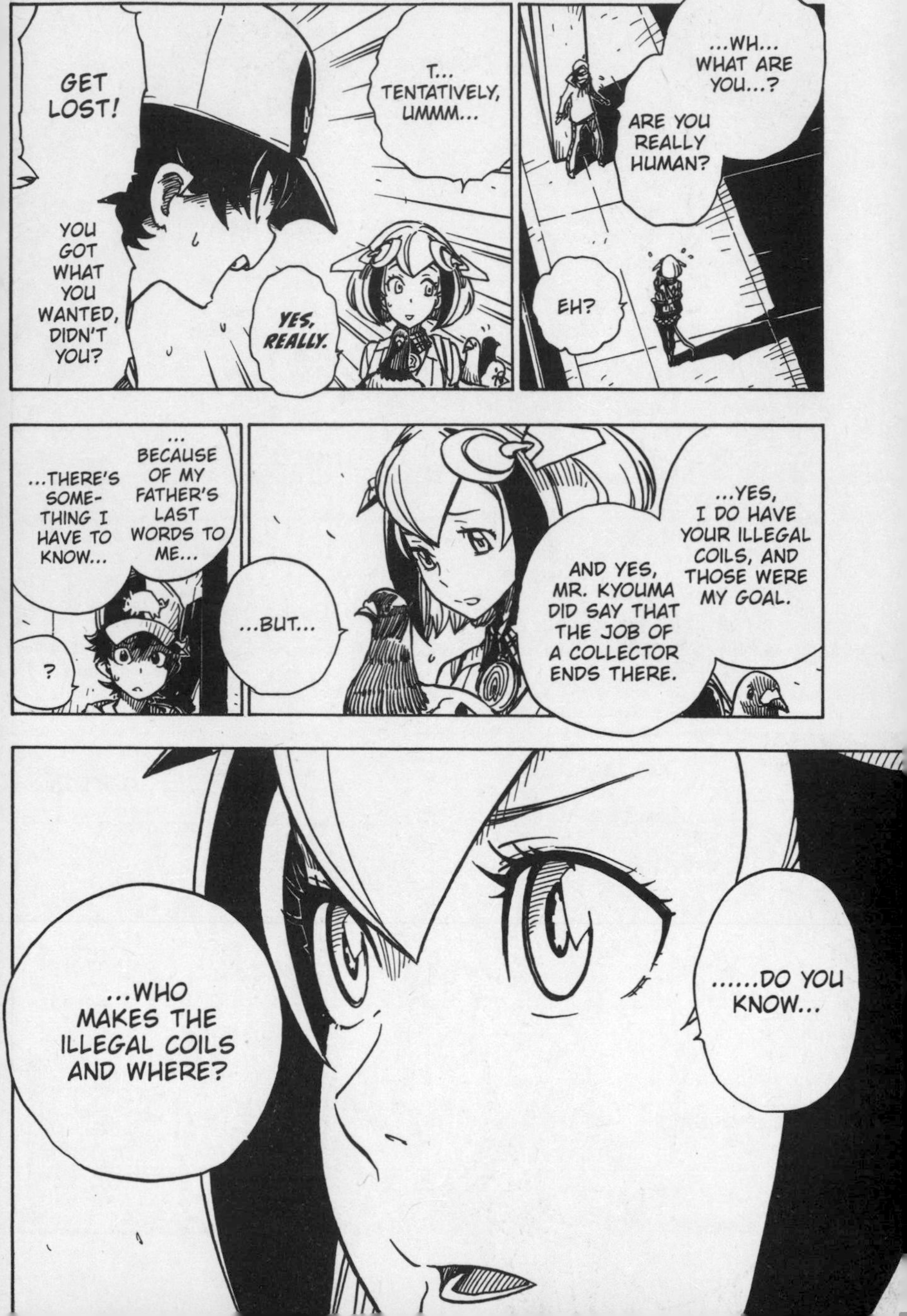
...WH... WHAT ARE YOU...?
ARE YOU REALLY HUMAN?
EH?
T... TENTATIVELY, UMMM...
GET LOST!
YOU GOT WHAT YOU WANTED, DIDN'T YOU?
YES, REALLY.
...YES, I DO HAVE YOUR ILLEGAL COILS, AND THOSE WERE MY GOAL.
AND YES, MR. KYOUMA DID SAY THAT THE JOB OF A COLLECTOR ENDS THERE.
...BUT...
...BECAUSE OF MY FATHER'S LAST WORDS TO ME...
...THERE'S SOME-THING I HAVE TO KNOW...
?
......DO YOU KNOW...
...WHO MAKES THE ILLEGAL COILS AND WHERE?

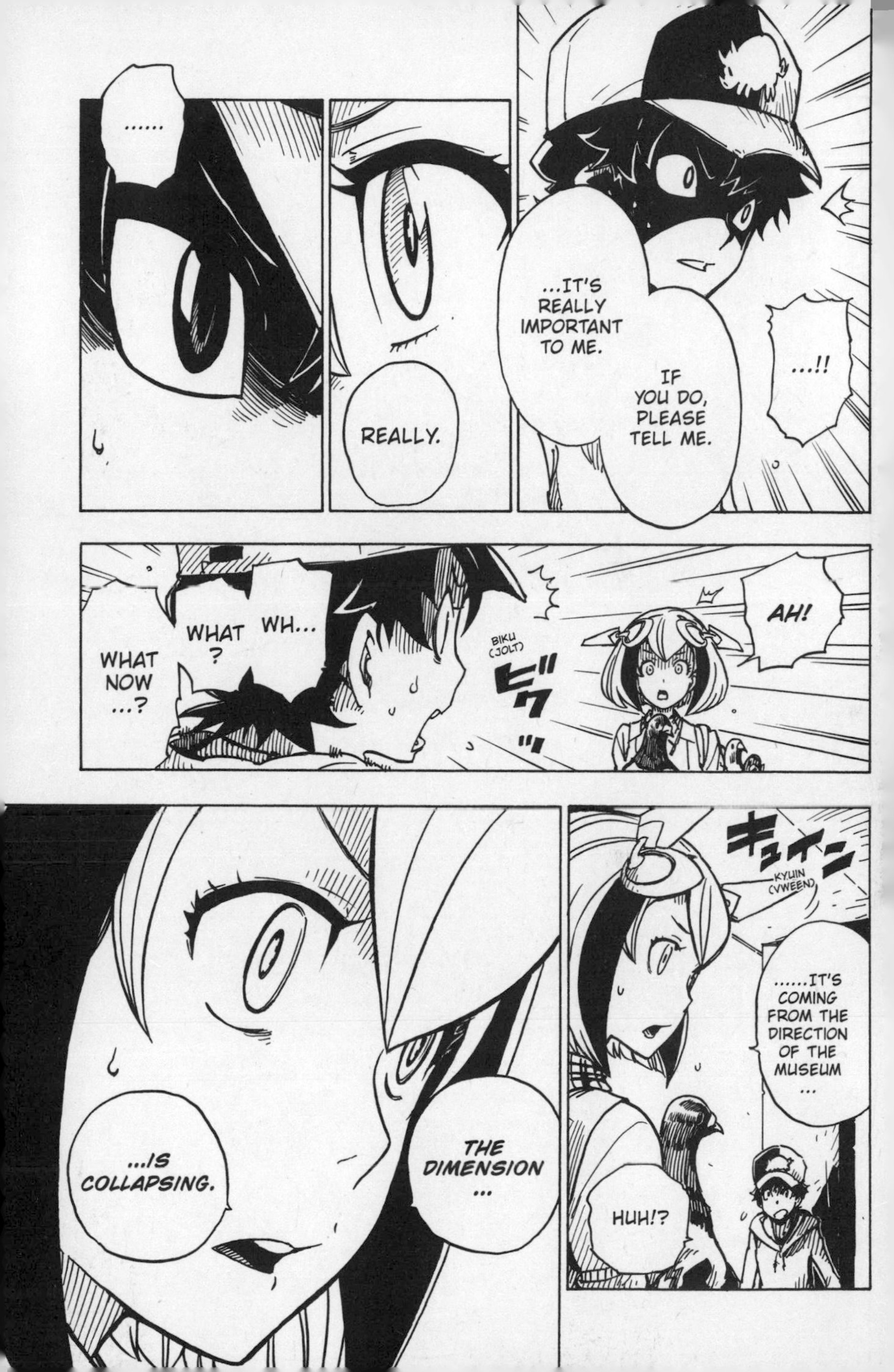

...!!
...IT'S REALLY IMPORTANT TO ME.
IF YOU DO, PLEASE TELL ME.
REALLY.
......
AH!
BIKU (JOLT)
WH...
WHAT ?
WHAT NOW ...?
KYUIN (VWEEN)
......IT'S COMING FROM THE DIRECTION OF THE MUSEUM ...
HUH!?
THE DIMENSION ...
...IS COLLAPSING.

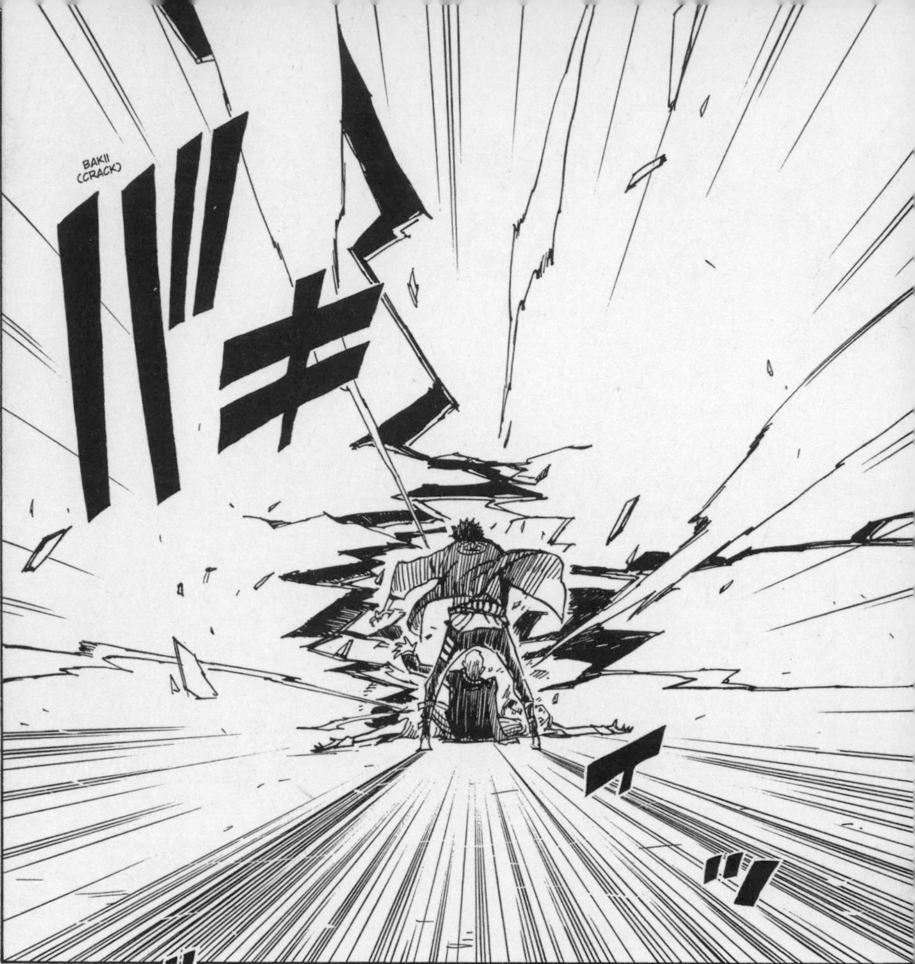
BAKII
(CRACK)
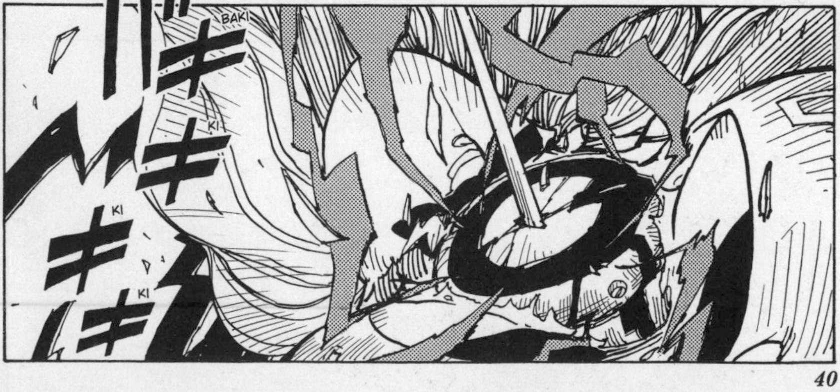
BAKI
KI
KI
KI

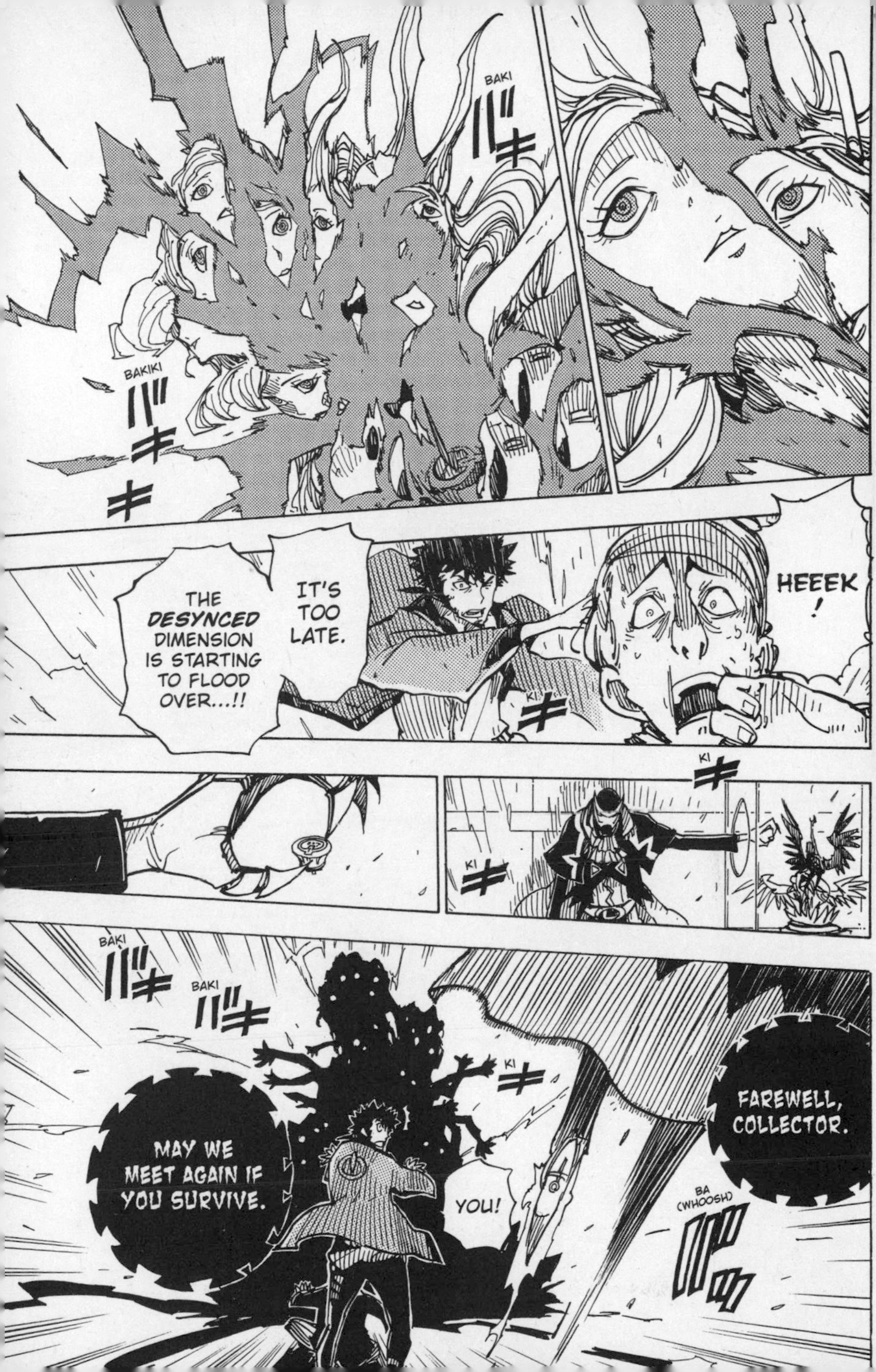
BAKI
BAKIKI
HEEEK!
KI
IT'S TOO LATE.
THE DESYNCED DIMENSION IS STARTING TO FLOOD OVER...!!
KI
KI
FAREWELL, COLLECTOR.
KI
BAKI
BAKI
BA (WHOOSH)
YOU!
MAY WE MEET AGAIN IF YOU SURVIVE.

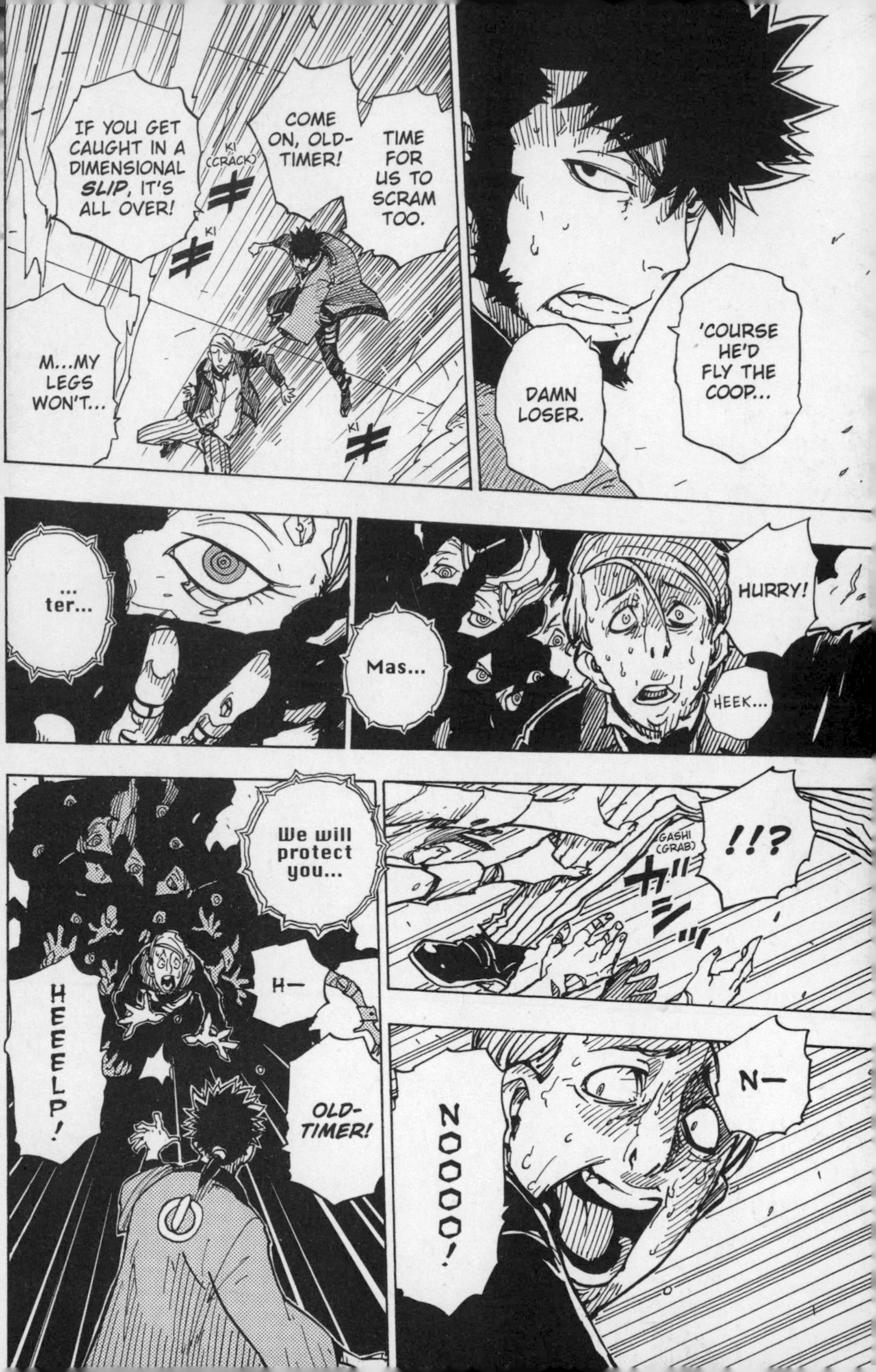
'COURSE HE'D FLY THE COOP...
DAMN LOSER.
TIME FOR US TO SCRAM TOO.
COME ON, OLD-TIMER!
KI (CRACK)
IF YOU GET CAUGHT IN A DIMENSIONAL SLIP, IT'S ALL OVER!
KI
M...MY LEGS WON'T...
KI
HURRY!
HEEK...
Mas...
...ter...
!!?
GASHI (GRAB)
N—
NOOOOO!
We will protect you...
H—
HEEELP!
OLD-TIMER!

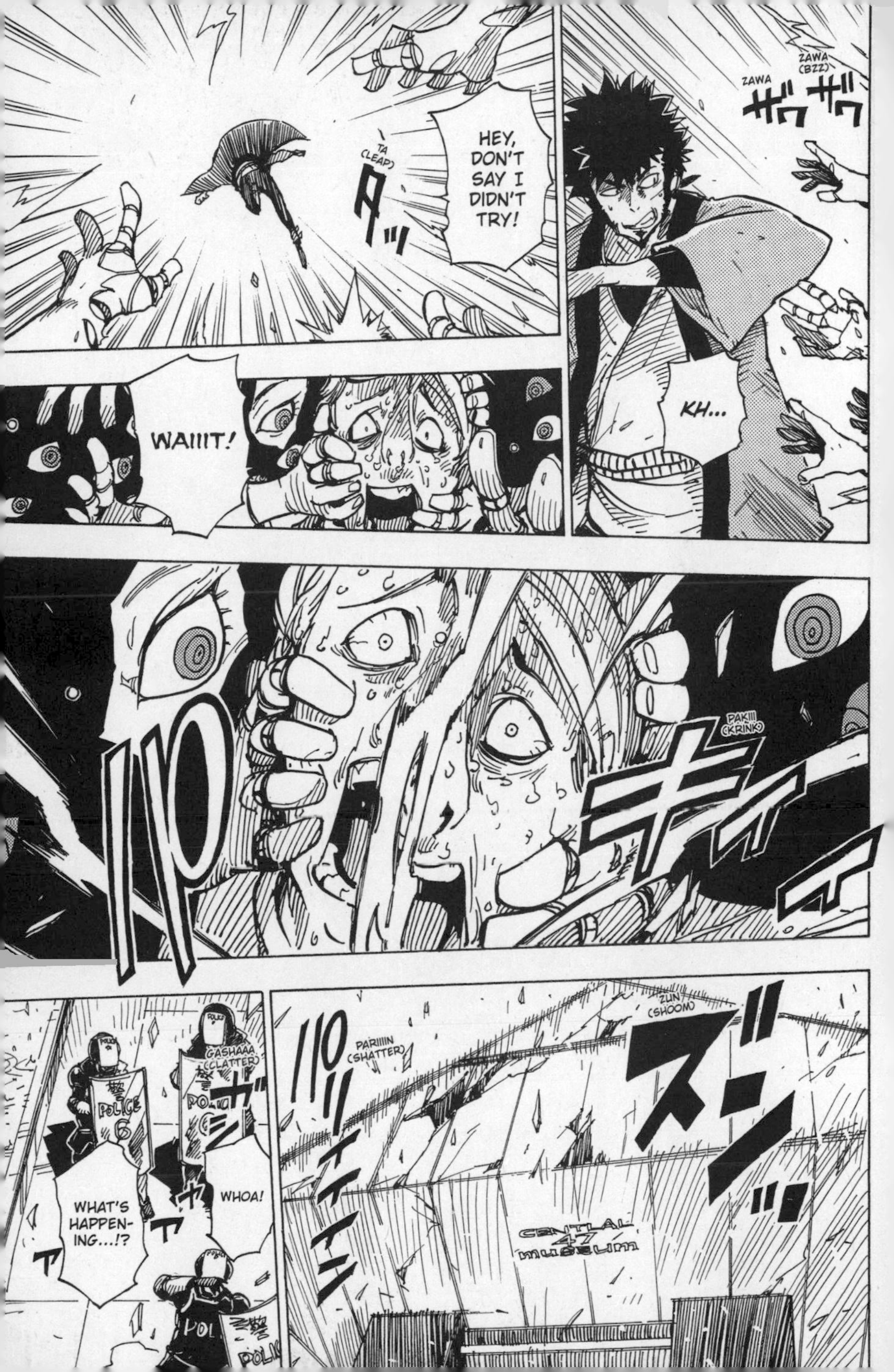

ZAWA (BZZ)
ZAWA
KH...
HEY, DON'T SAY I DIDN'T TRY!
TA (LEAP)
WAIIIT!
PAKIII (KRINK)
ZUN (SHOOM)
PARIIIIN (SHATTER)
CENTRAL 47 MUSEUM
GASHAAA (CLATTER)
POLICE 6
WHOA!
WHAT'S HAPPEN-ING...!?

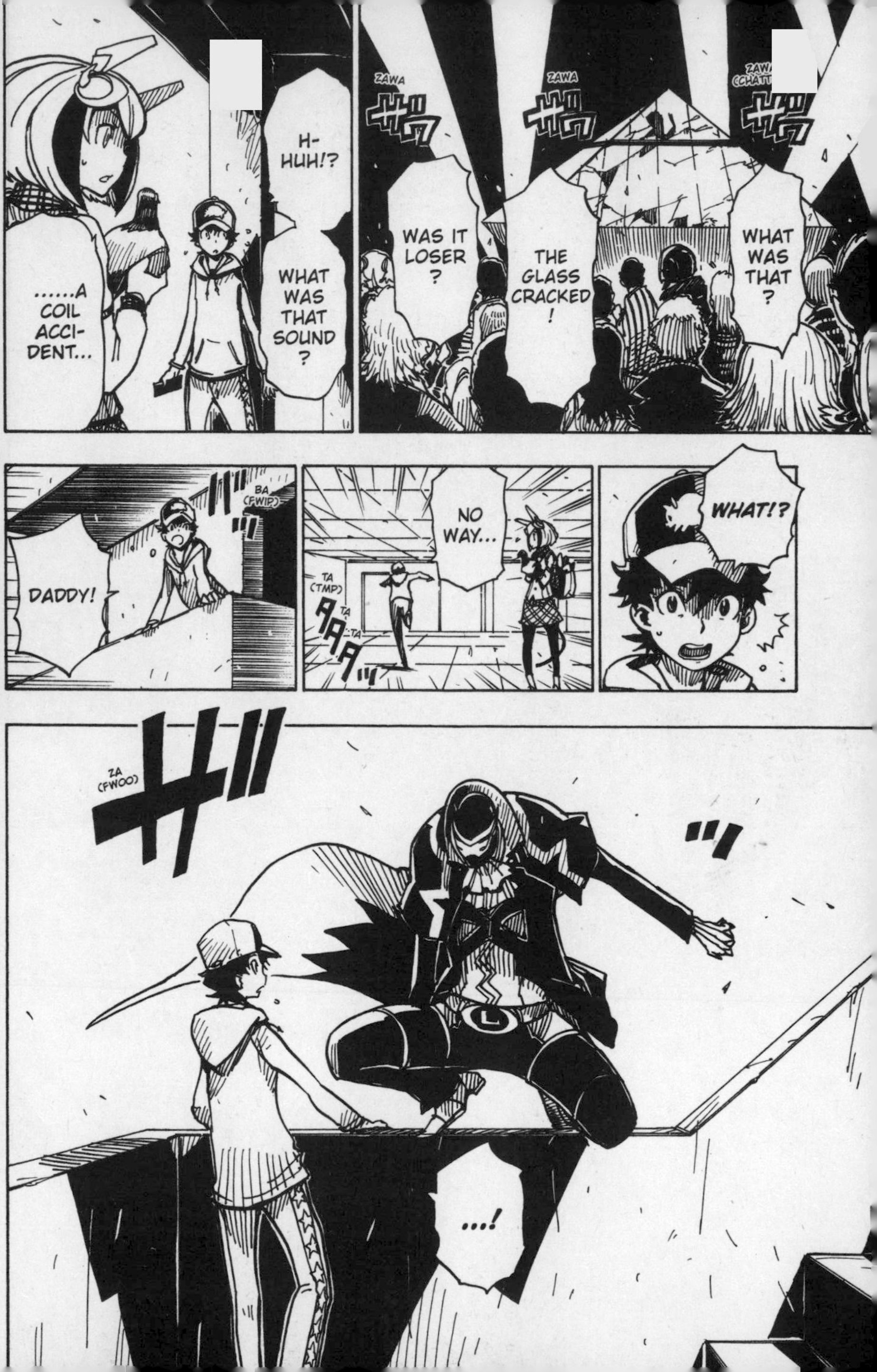
ZAWA
WHAT WAS THAT?
ZAWA
THE GLASS CRACKED!
ZAWA
WAS IT LOSER?
H-HUH!?
WHAT WAS THAT SOUND?
......A COIL ACCIDENT...
WHAT!?
NO WAY...
TA (TMP) TA TA
BA (FWIP)
DADDY!
ZA (FWOO)
...!

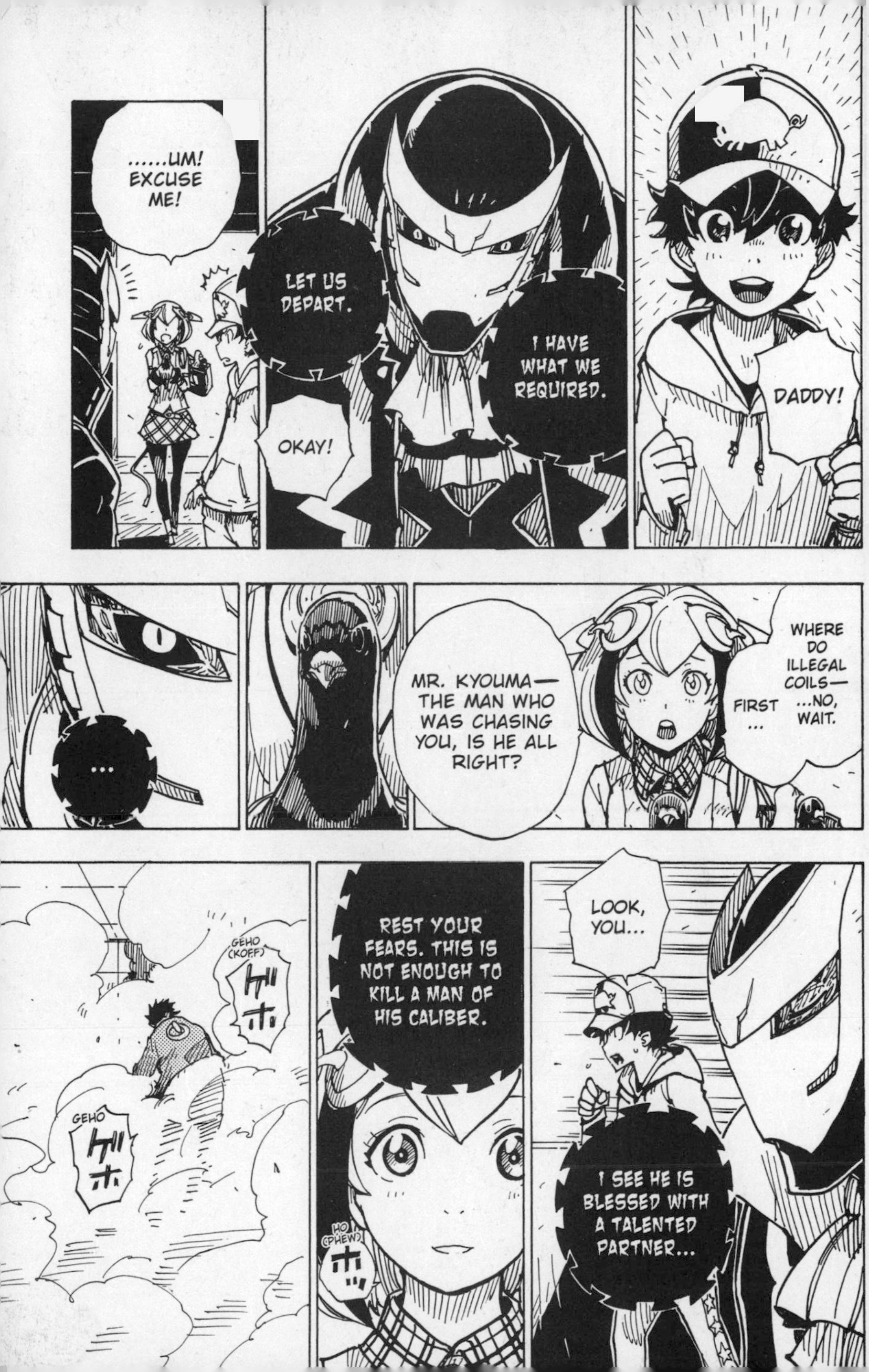
DADDY!
LET US DEPART.
I HAVE WHAT WE REQUIRED.
OKAY!
......UM! EXCUSE ME!
WHERE DO ILLEGAL COILS— ...NO, WAIT.
FIRST ...
MR. KYOUMA— THE MAN WHO WAS CHASING YOU, IS HE ALL RIGHT?
...
LOOK, YOU...
I SEE HE IS BLESSED WITH A TALENTED PARTNER...
REST YOUR FEARS. THIS IS NOT ENOUGH TO KILL A MAN OF HIS CALIBER.
HO (PHEW) ホッ
GEHO (KOFF) ゲホ
GEHO ゲホ

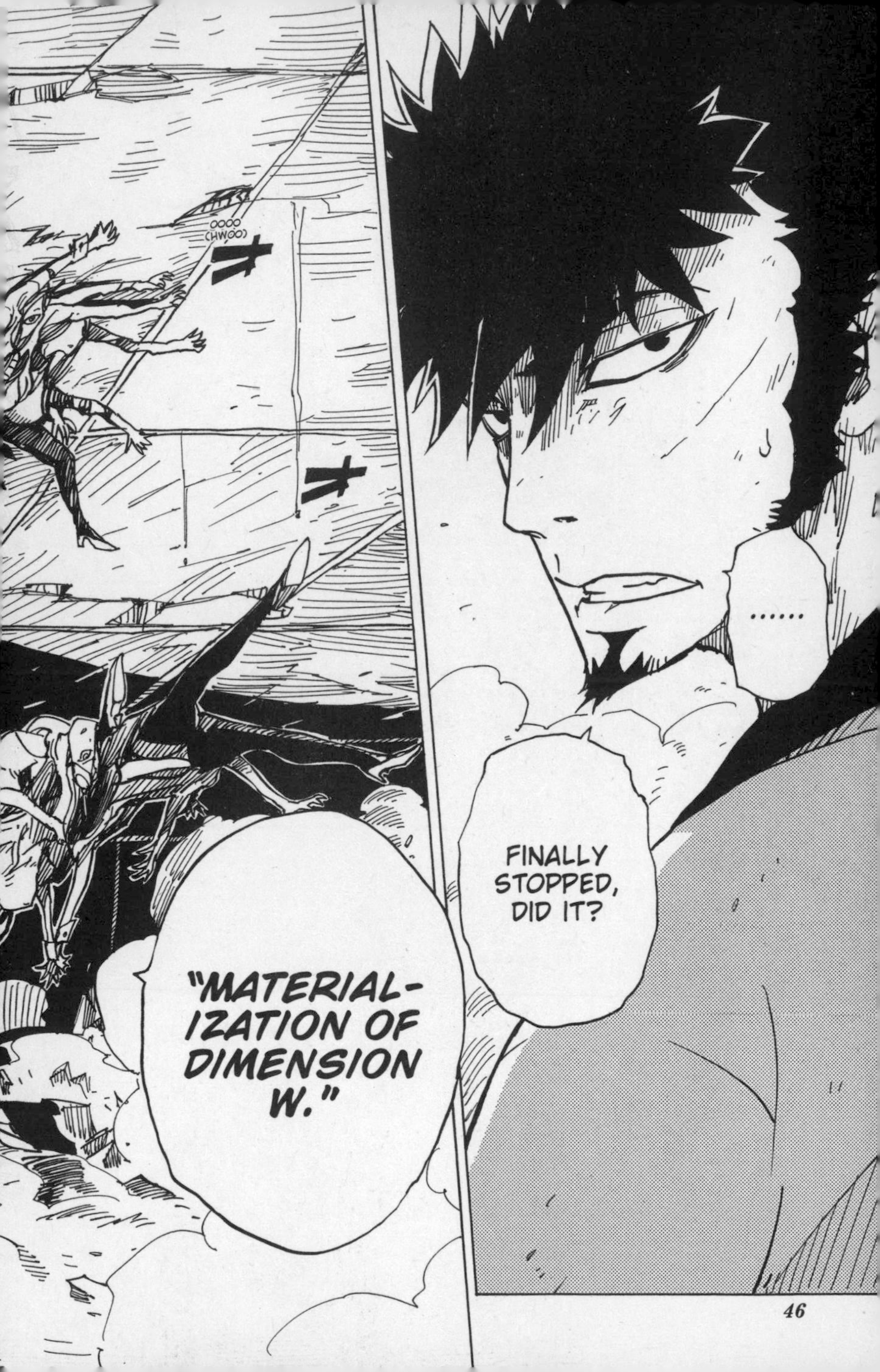
......
FINALLY STOPPED, DID IT?
(HWOOO)
"MATERIALIZATION OF DIMENSION W."

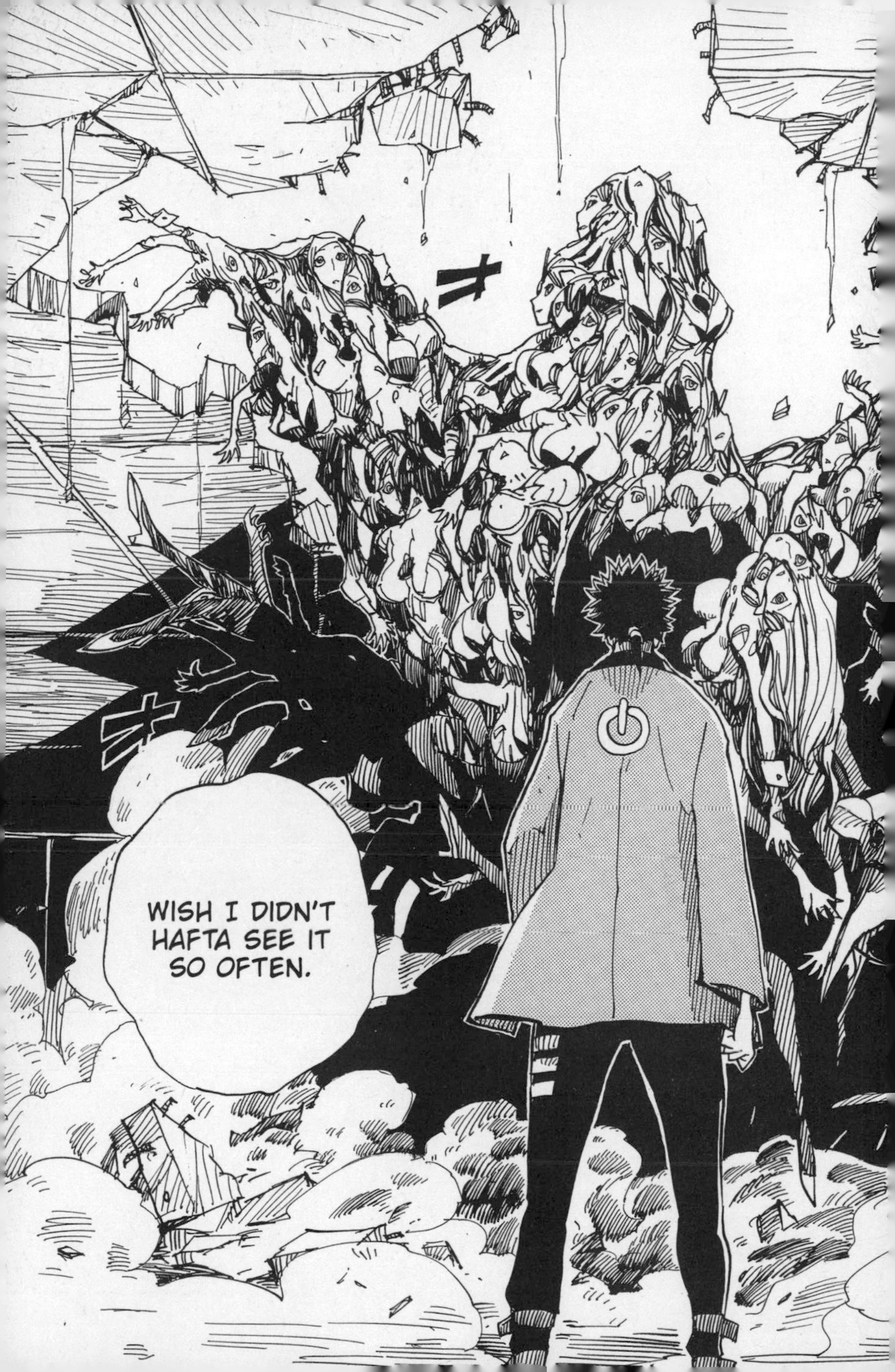
WISH I DIDN'T HAFTA SEE IT SO OFTEN.

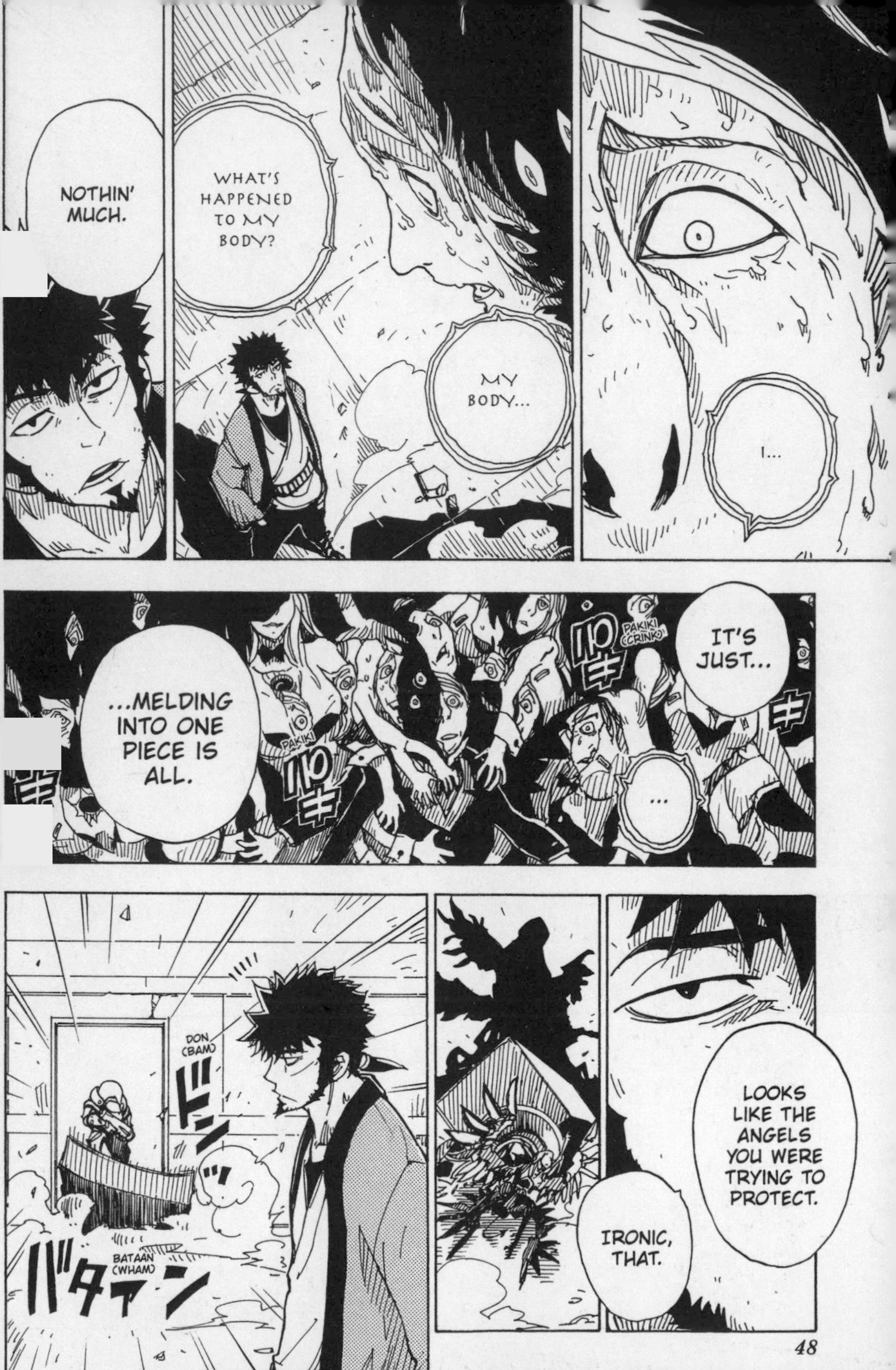
I...
WHAT'S HAPPENED TO MY BODY?
MY BODY...
NOTHIN' MUCH.
IT'S JUST...
PAKIKI (CRINK)
...
PAKIKI
...MELDING INTO ONE PIECE IS ALL.
LOOKS LIKE THE ANGELS YOU WERE TRYING TO PROTECT.
IRONIC, THAT.
DON (BAM)
BATAAN (WHAM)

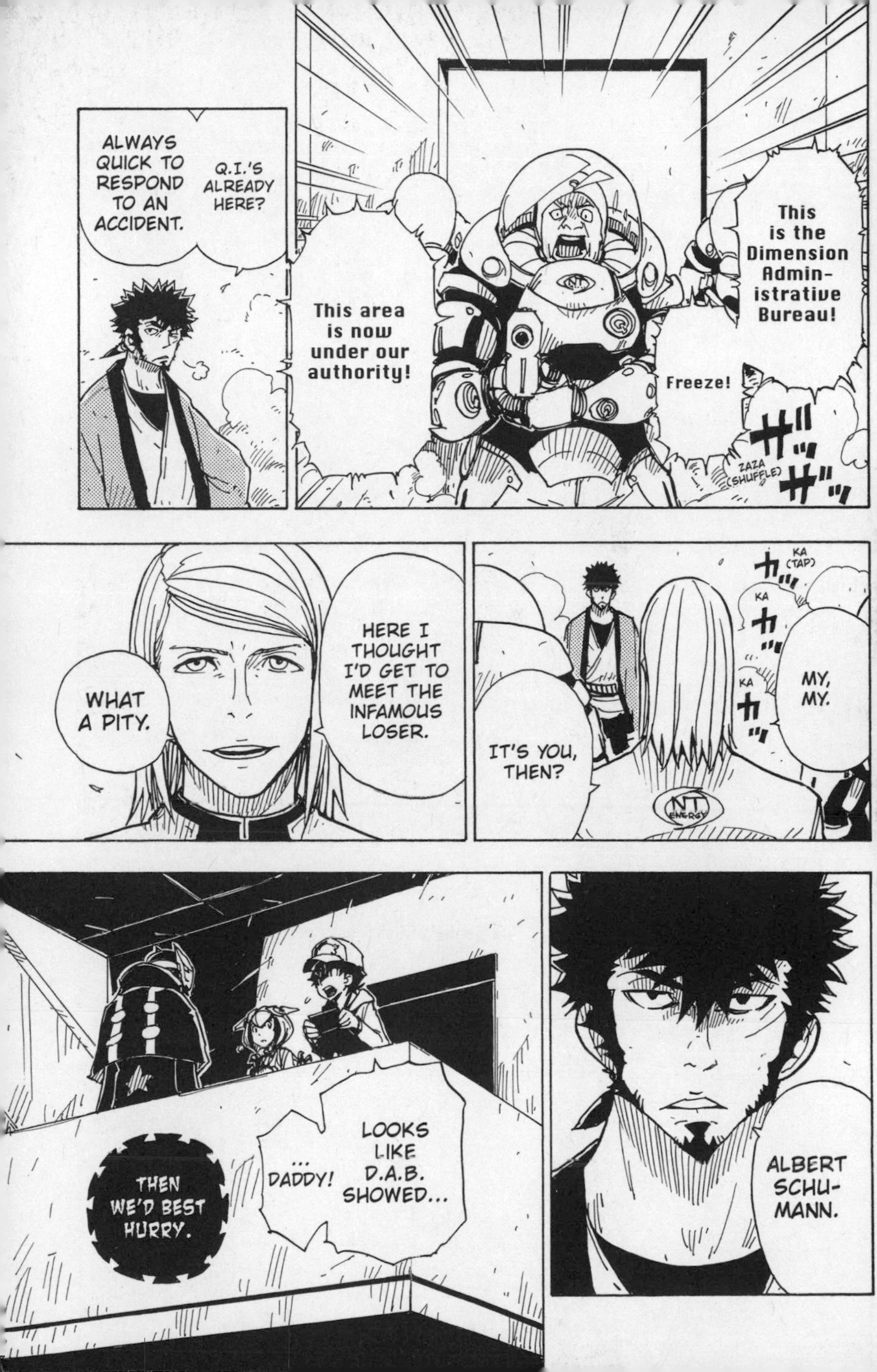
This is the Dimension Administrative Bureau!
Freeze!
This area is now under our authority!
ザッ ザッ
ZAZA (SHUFFLE)
Q.I.'S ALREADY HERE?
ALWAYS QUICK TO RESPOND TO AN ACCIDENT.
カッ
KA (TAP)
KA
カッ
KA
カッ
MY, MY.
IT'S YOU, THEN?
NT ENERGY
HERE I THOUGHT I'D GET TO MEET THE INFAMOUS LOSER.
WHAT A PITY.
ALBERT SCHUMANN.
LOOKS LIKE D.A.B. SHOWED...
...DADDY!
THEN WE'D BEST HURRY.

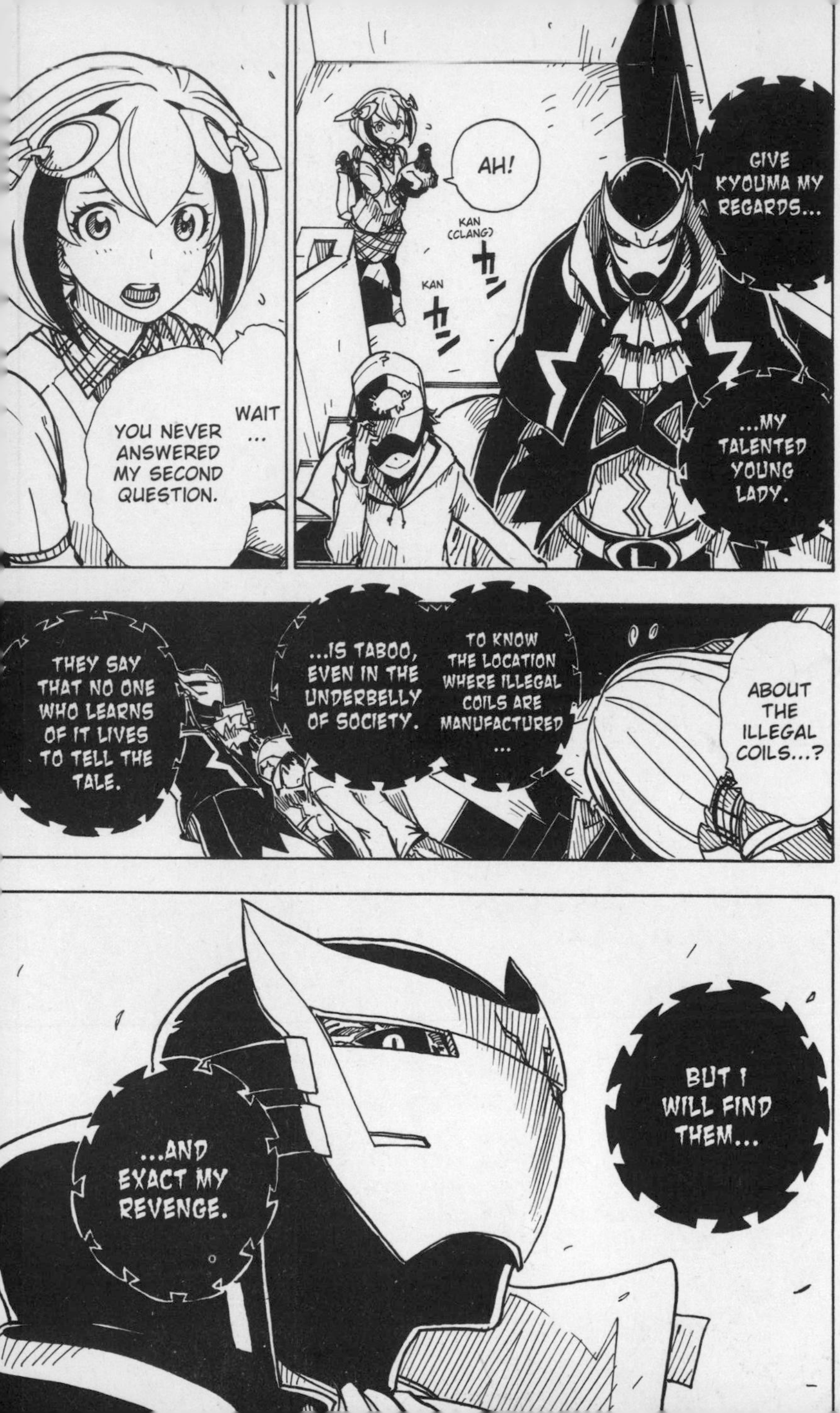
GIVE KYOUMA MY REGARDS...
...MY TALENTED YOUNG LADY.
AH!
KAN (CLANG)
カン
KAN
カン
WAIT...
YOU NEVER ANSWERED MY SECOND QUESTION.
ABOUT THE ILLEGAL COILS...?
TO KNOW THE LOCATION WHERE ILLEGAL COILS ARE MANUFACTURED...
...IS TABOO, EVEN IN THE UNDERBELLY OF SOCIETY.
THEY SAY THAT NO ONE WHO LEARNS OF IT LIVES TO TELL THE TALE.
BUT I WILL FIND THEM...
...AND EXACT MY REVENGE.

FILE.10 HOME

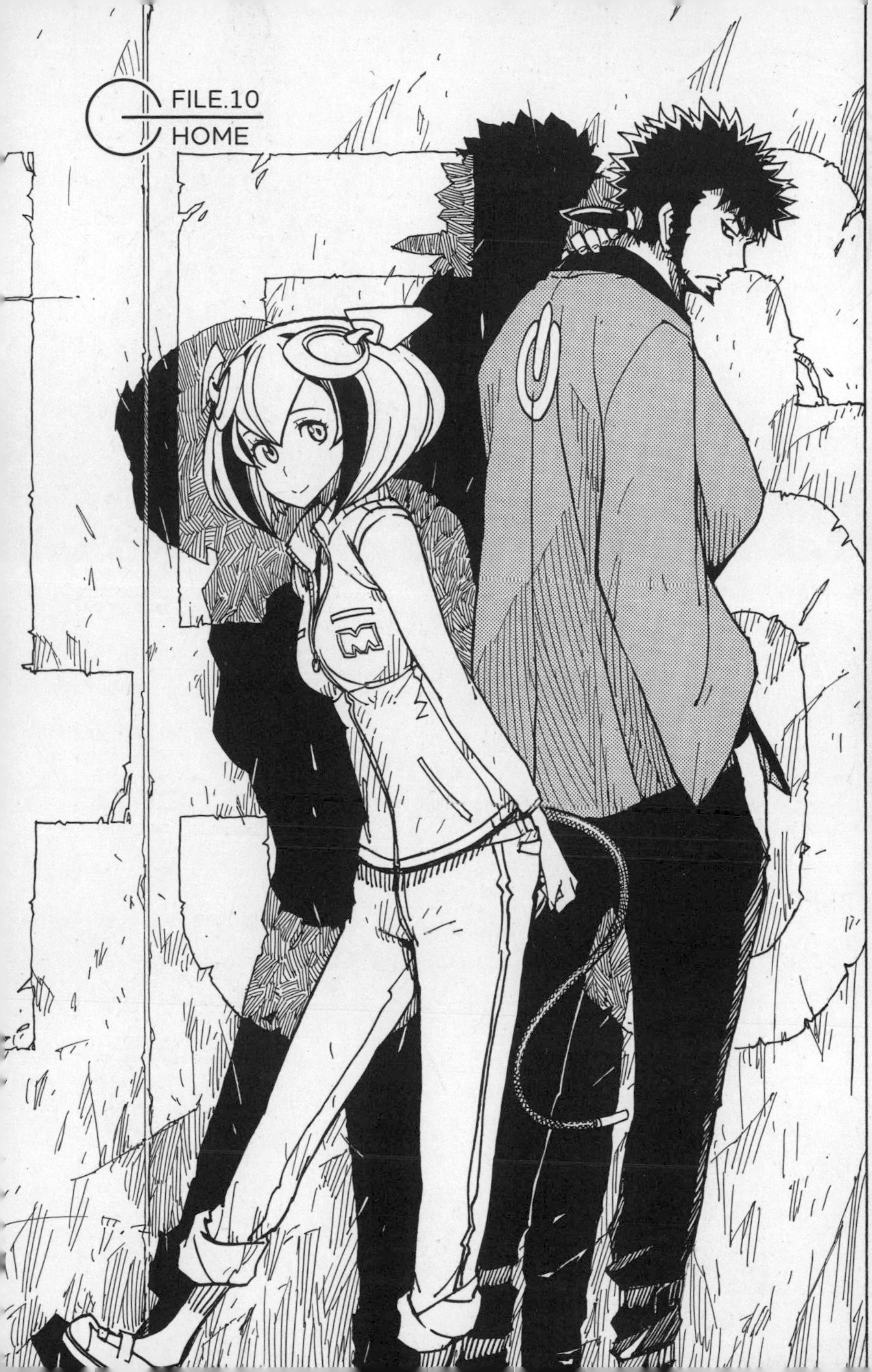

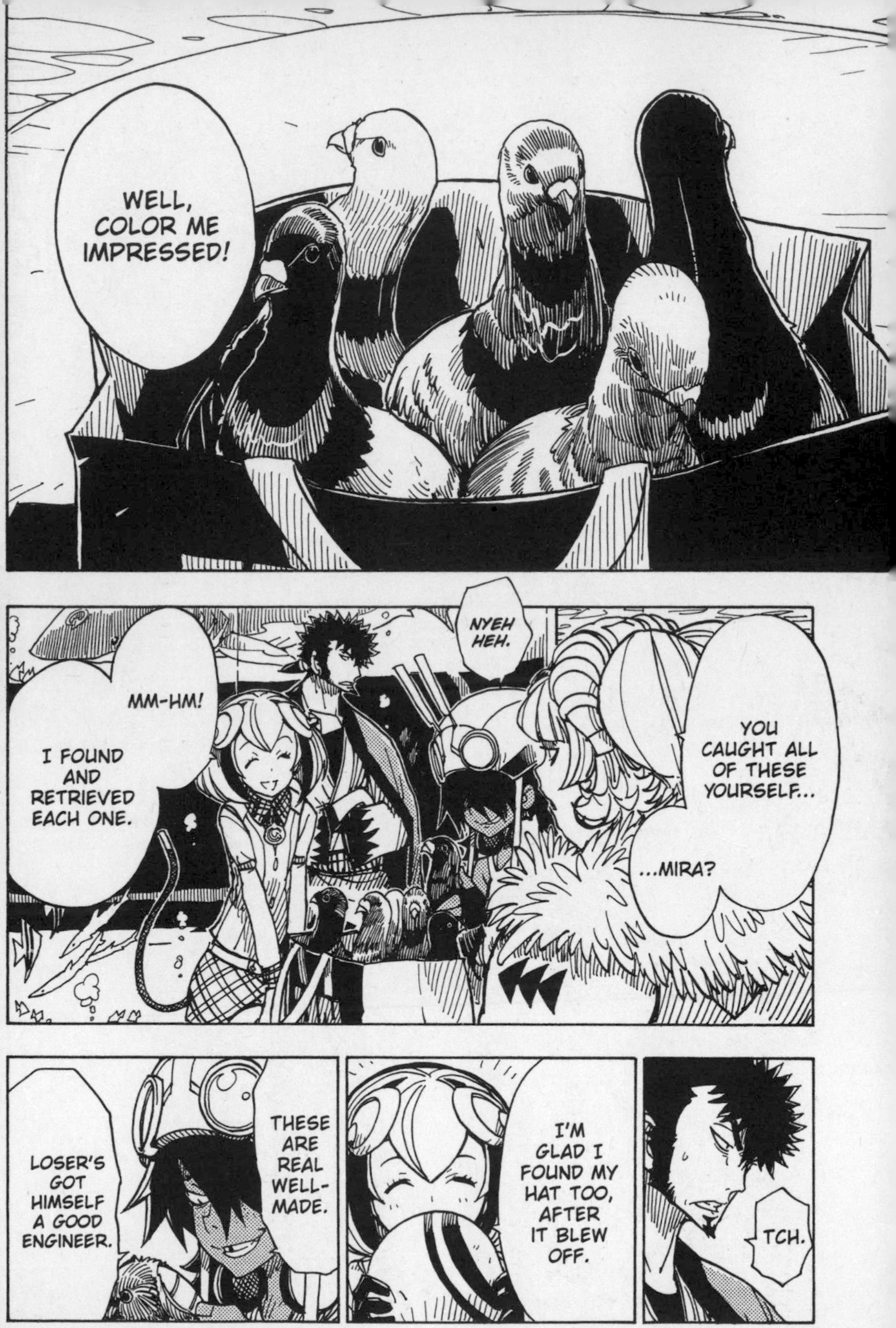
WELL, COLOR ME IMPRESSED!
YOU CAUGHT ALL OF THESE YOURSELF...
...MIRA?
NYEH HEH.
MM-HM!
I FOUND AND RETRIEVED EACH ONE.
TCH.
I'M GLAD I FOUND MY HAT TOO, AFTER IT BLEW OFF.
THESE ARE REAL WELL-MADE.
LOSER'S GOT HIMSELF A GOOD ENGINEER.

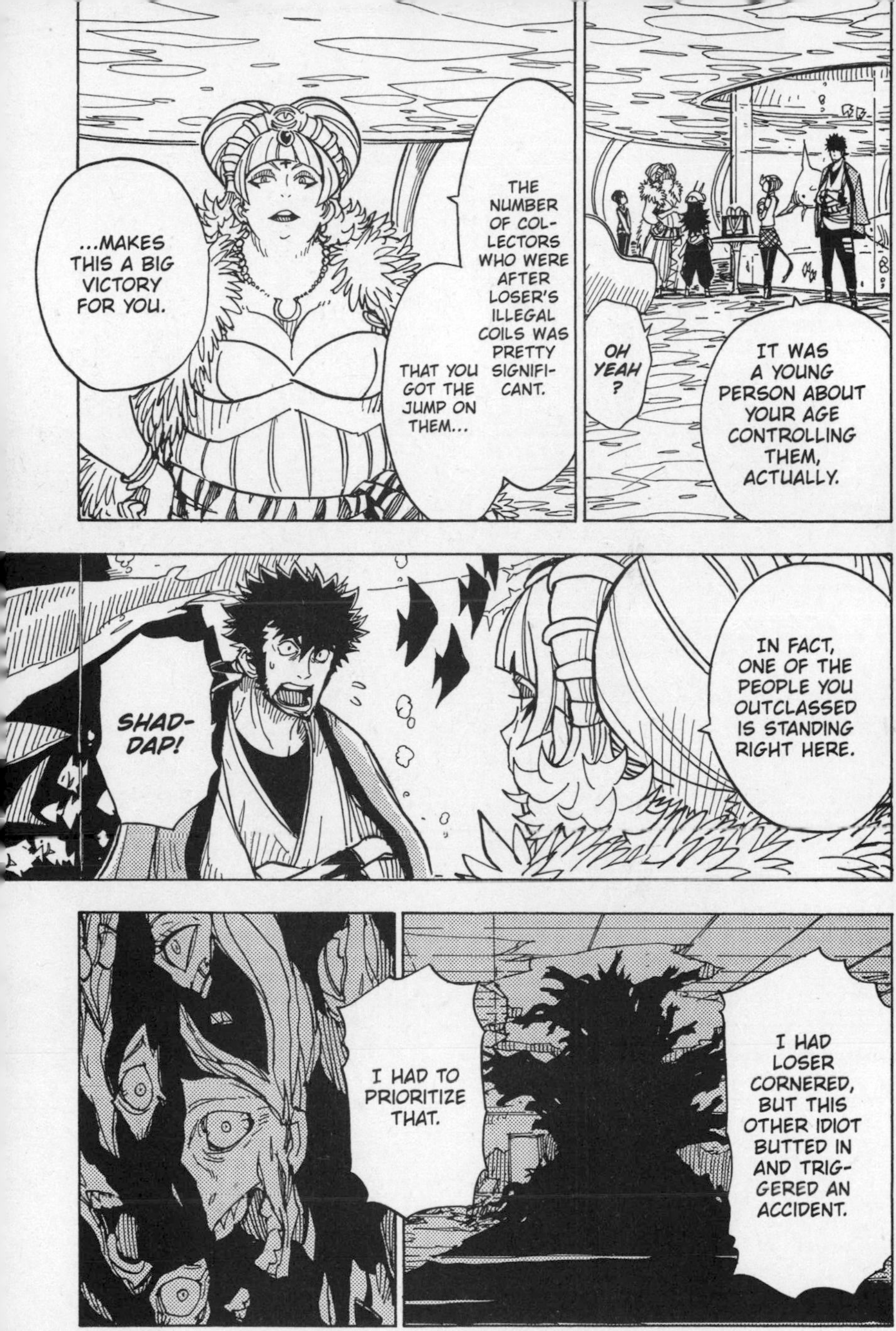
IT WAS A YOUNG PERSON ABOUT YOUR AGE CONTROLLING THEM, ACTUALLY.
OH YEAH ?
THE NUMBER OF COLLECTORS WHO WERE AFTER LOSER'S ILLEGAL COILS WAS PRETTY SIGNIFICANT.
THAT YOU GOT THE JUMP ON THEM...
...MAKES THIS A BIG VICTORY FOR YOU.
IN FACT, ONE OF THE PEOPLE YOU OUTCLASSED IS STANDING RIGHT HERE.
SHADDAP!
I HAD LOSER CORNERED, BUT THIS OTHER IDIOT BUTTED IN AND TRIGGERED AN ACCIDENT.
I HAD TO PRIORITIZE THAT.

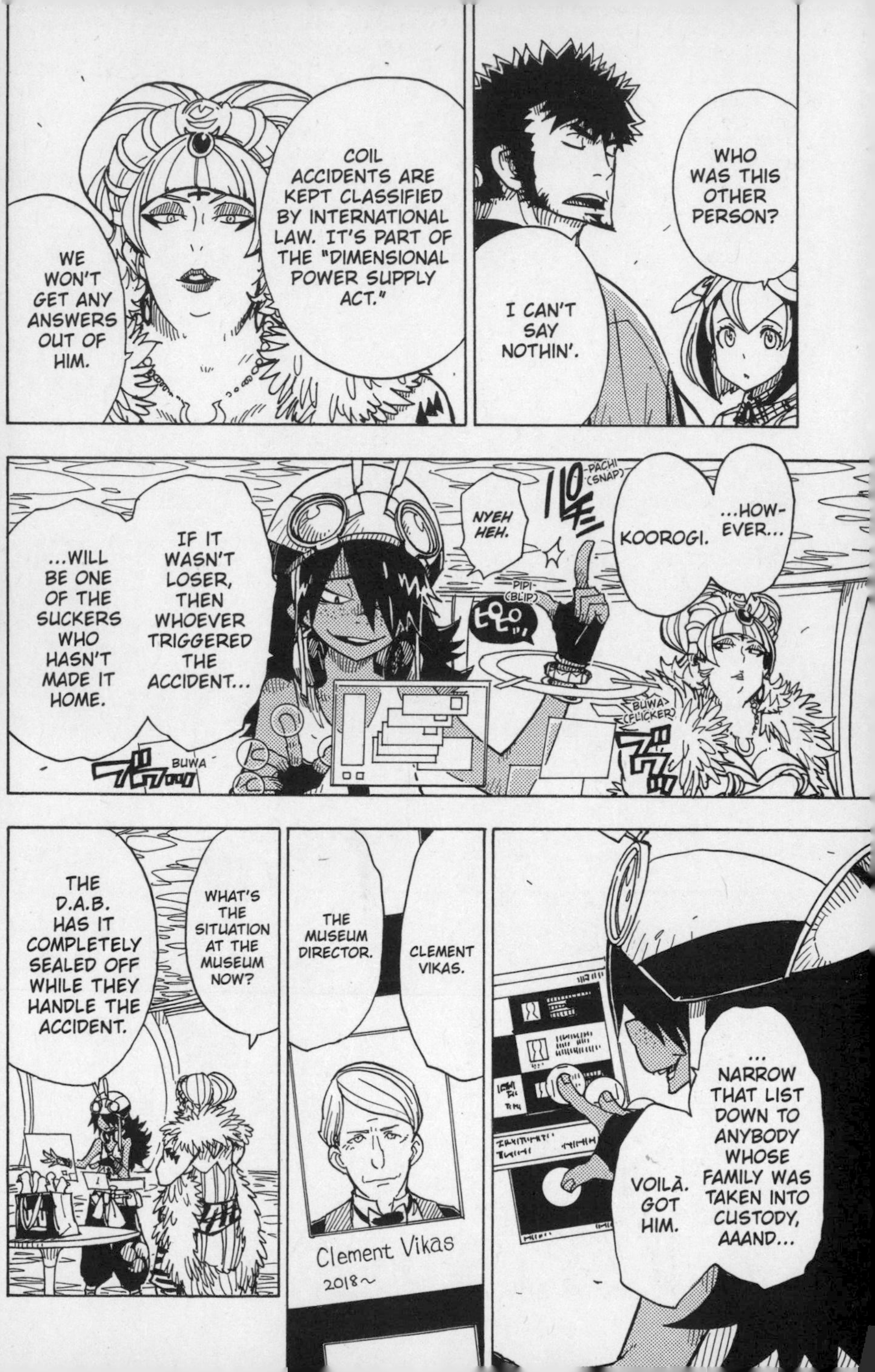
WHO WAS THIS OTHER PERSON?
I CAN'T SAY NOTHIN'.
COIL ACCIDENTS ARE KEPT CLASSIFIED BY INTERNATIONAL LAW. IT'S PART OF THE "DIMENSIONAL POWER SUPPLY ACT."
WE WON'T GET ANY ANSWERS OUT OF HIM.
...HOW-EVER...
KOOROGI.
PACHI (SNAP)
NYEH HEH.
PIPI (BLIP)
IF IT WASN'T LOSER, THEN WHOEVER TRIGGERED THE ACCIDENT...
...WILL BE ONE OF THE SUCKERS WHO HASN'T MADE IT HOME.
BUWA (FLICKER)
BUWA
...NARROW THAT LIST DOWN TO ANYBODY WHOSE FAMILY WAS TAKEN INTO CUSTODY, AAAND...
VOILÀ. GOT HIM.
CLEMENT VIKAS.
THE MUSEUM DIRECTOR.
Clement Vikas
2018～
WHAT'S THE SITUATION AT THE MUSEUM NOW?
THE D.A.B. HAS IT COMPLETELY SEALED OFF WHILE THEY HANDLE THE ACCIDENT.

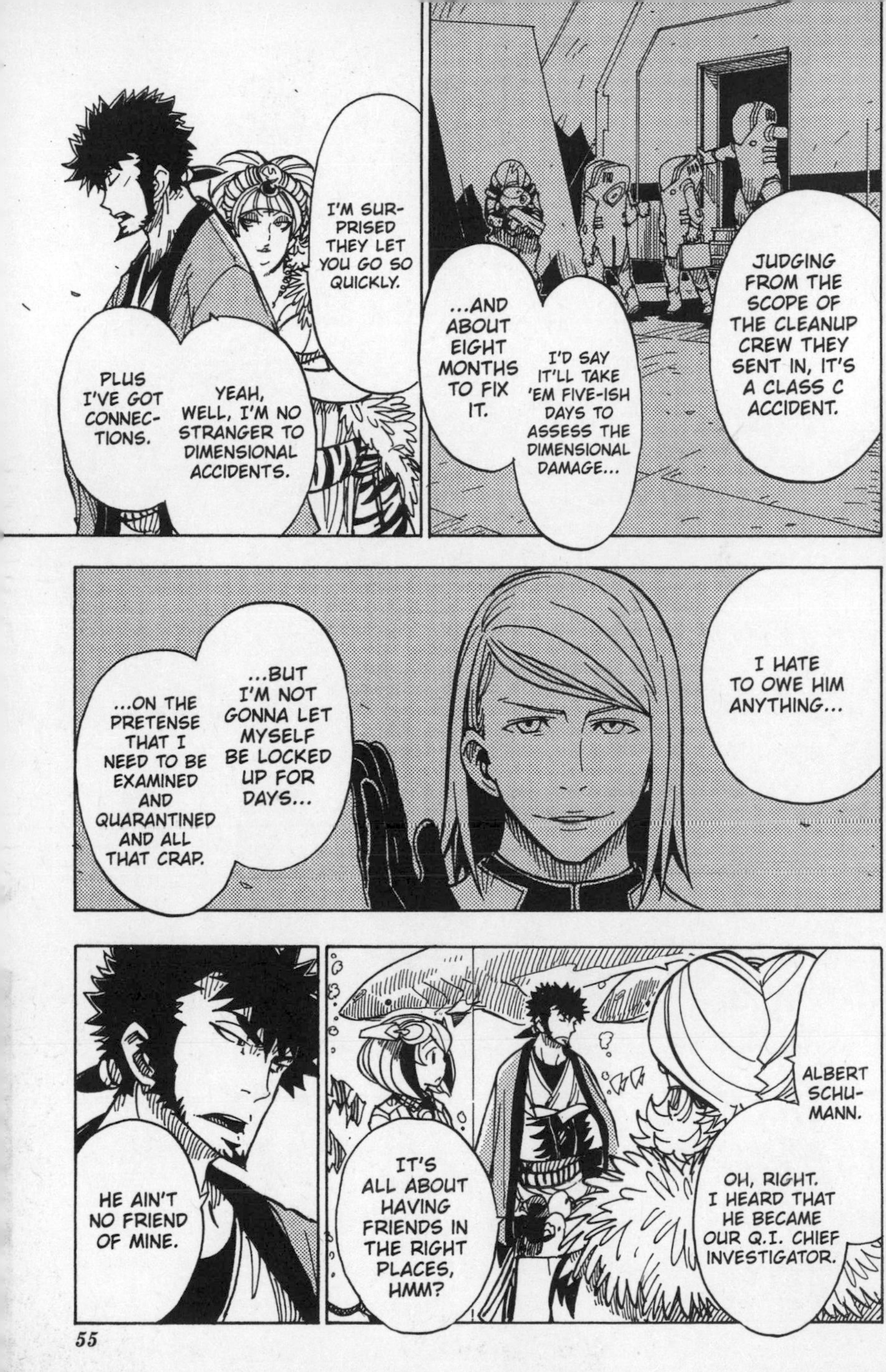
JUDGING FROM THE SCOPE OF THE CLEANUP CREW THEY SENT IN, IT'S A CLASS C ACCIDENT.
I'D SAY IT'LL TAKE 'EM FIVE-ISH DAYS TO ASSESS THE DIMENSIONAL DAMAGE...
...AND ABOUT EIGHT MONTHS TO FIX IT.
I'M SURPRISED THEY LET YOU GO SO QUICKLY.
YEAH, WELL, I'M NO STRANGER TO DIMENSIONAL ACCIDENTS.
PLUS I'VE GOT CONNECTIONS.
I HATE TO OWE HIM ANYTHING...
...BUT I'M NOT GONNA LET MYSELF BE LOCKED UP FOR DAYS...
...ON THE PRETENSE THAT I NEED TO BE EXAMINED AND QUARANTINED AND ALL THAT CRAP.
ALBERT SCHUMANN.
OH, RIGHT. I HEARD THAT HE BECAME OUR Q.I. CHIEF INVESTIGATOR.
IT'S ALL ABOUT HAVING FRIENDS IN THE RIGHT PLACES, HMM?
HE AIN'T NO FRIEND OF MINE.

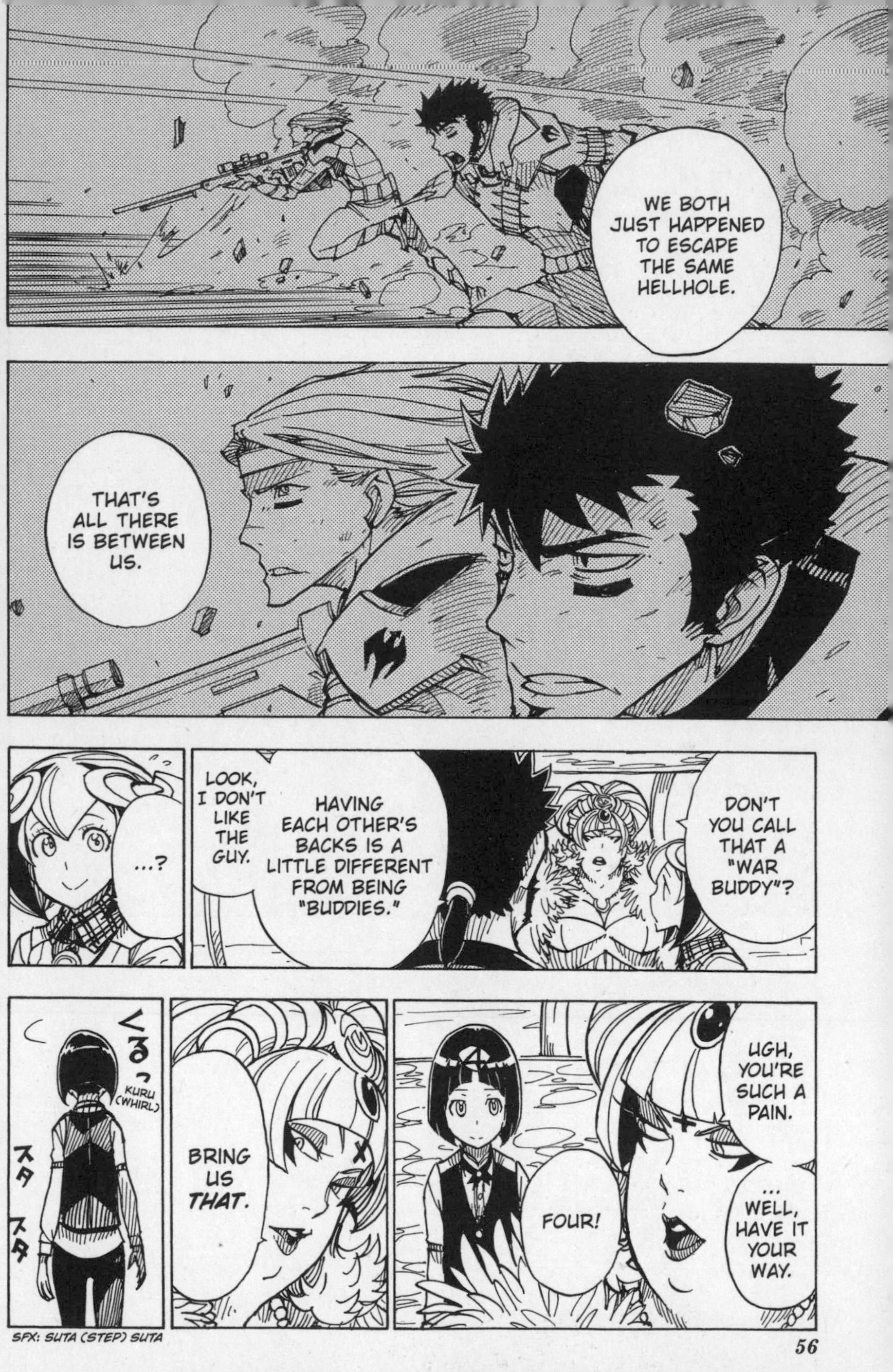
WE BOTH JUST HAPPENED TO ESCAPE THE SAME HELLHOLE.
THAT'S ALL THERE IS BETWEEN US.
DON'T YOU CALL THAT A "WAR BUDDY"?
HAVING EACH OTHER'S BACKS IS A LITTLE DIFFERENT FROM BEING "BUDDIES."
LOOK, I DON'T LIKE THE GUY.
...?
UGH, YOU'RE SUCH A PAIN.
... WELL, HAVE IT YOUR WAY.
FOUR!
BRING US *THAT*.
くるっ
KURU (WHIRL)
スタ
スタ

SFX: SUTA (STEP) SUTA

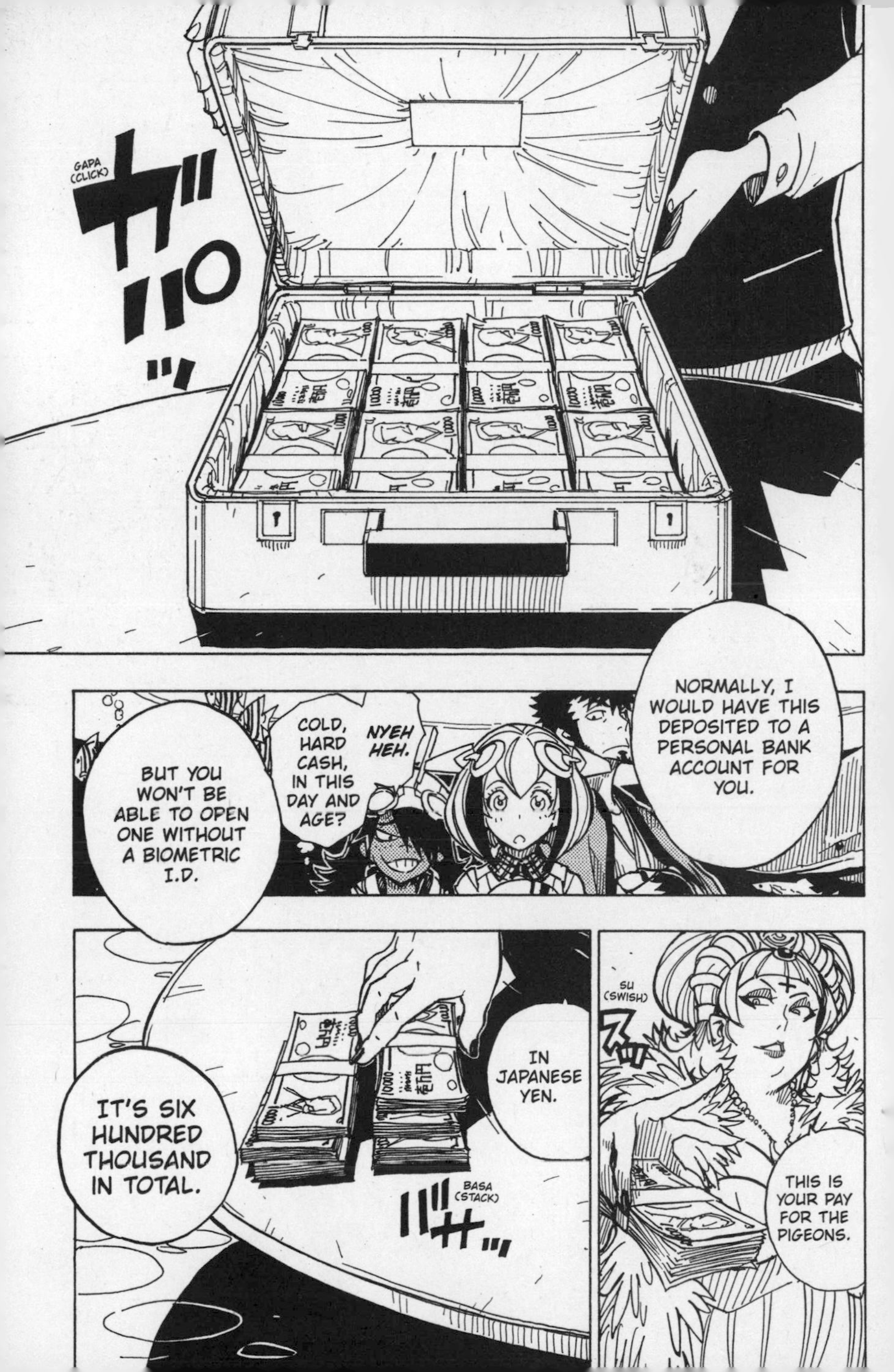
GAPA (CLICK)
NORMALLY, I WOULD HAVE THIS DEPOSITED TO A PERSONAL BANK ACCOUNT FOR YOU.
NYEH HEH.
COLD, HARD CASH, IN THIS DAY AND AGE?
BUT YOU WON'T BE ABLE TO OPEN ONE WITHOUT A BIOMETRIC I.D.
SU (SWISH)
THIS IS YOUR PAY FOR THE PIGEONS.
IN JAPANESE YEN.
IT'S SIX HUNDRED THOUSAND IN TOTAL.
BASA (STACK)

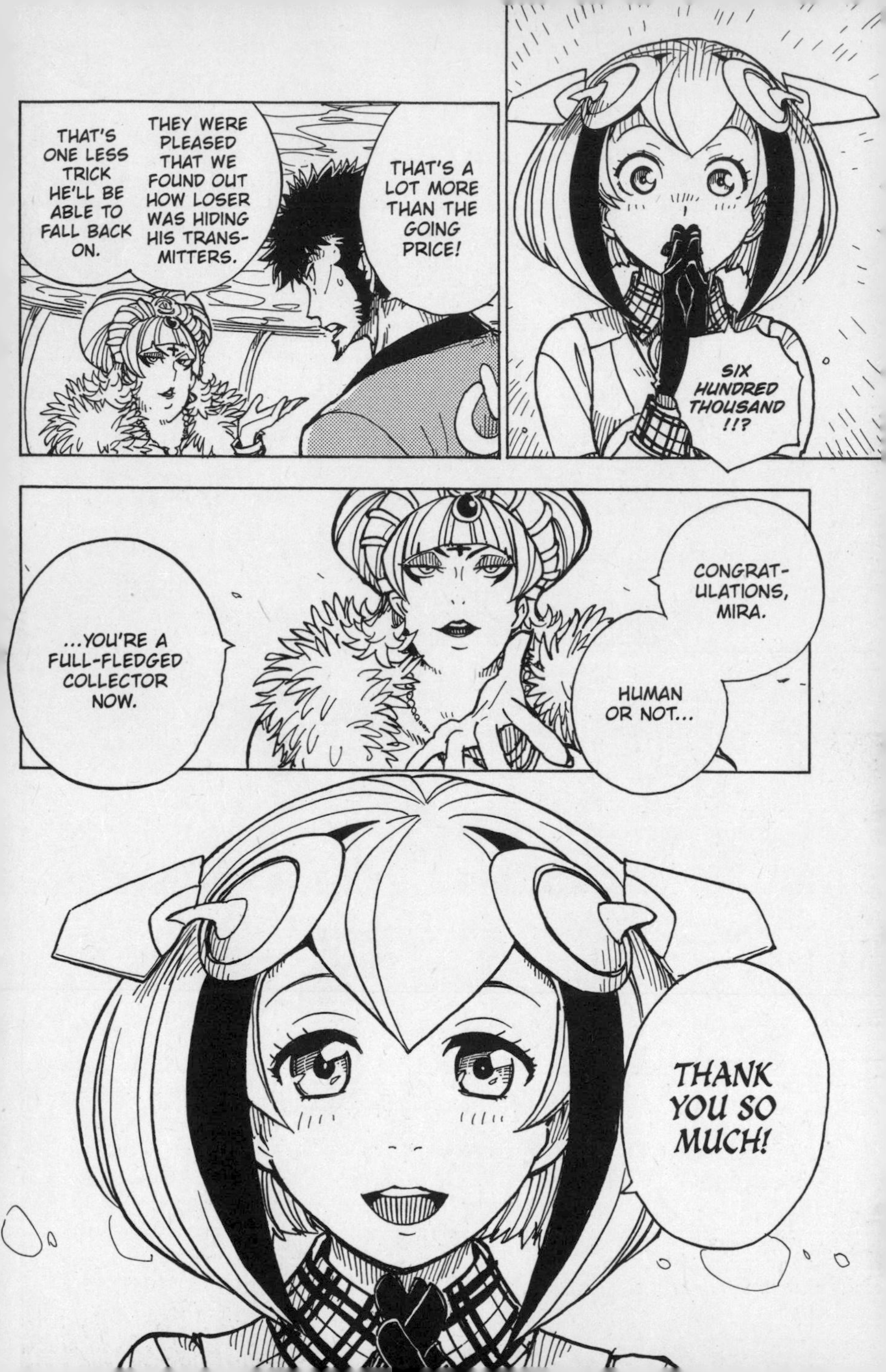
SIX HUNDRED THOUSAND!!?
THAT'S A LOT MORE THAN THE GOING PRICE!
THEY WERE PLEASED THAT WE FOUND OUT HOW LOSER WAS HIDING HIS TRANS-MITTERS.
THAT'S ONE LESS TRICK HE'LL BE ABLE TO FALL BACK ON.
CONGRAT-ULATIONS, MIRA.
HUMAN OR NOT...
...YOU'RE A FULL-FLEDGED COLLECTOR NOW.
THANK YOU SO MUCH!

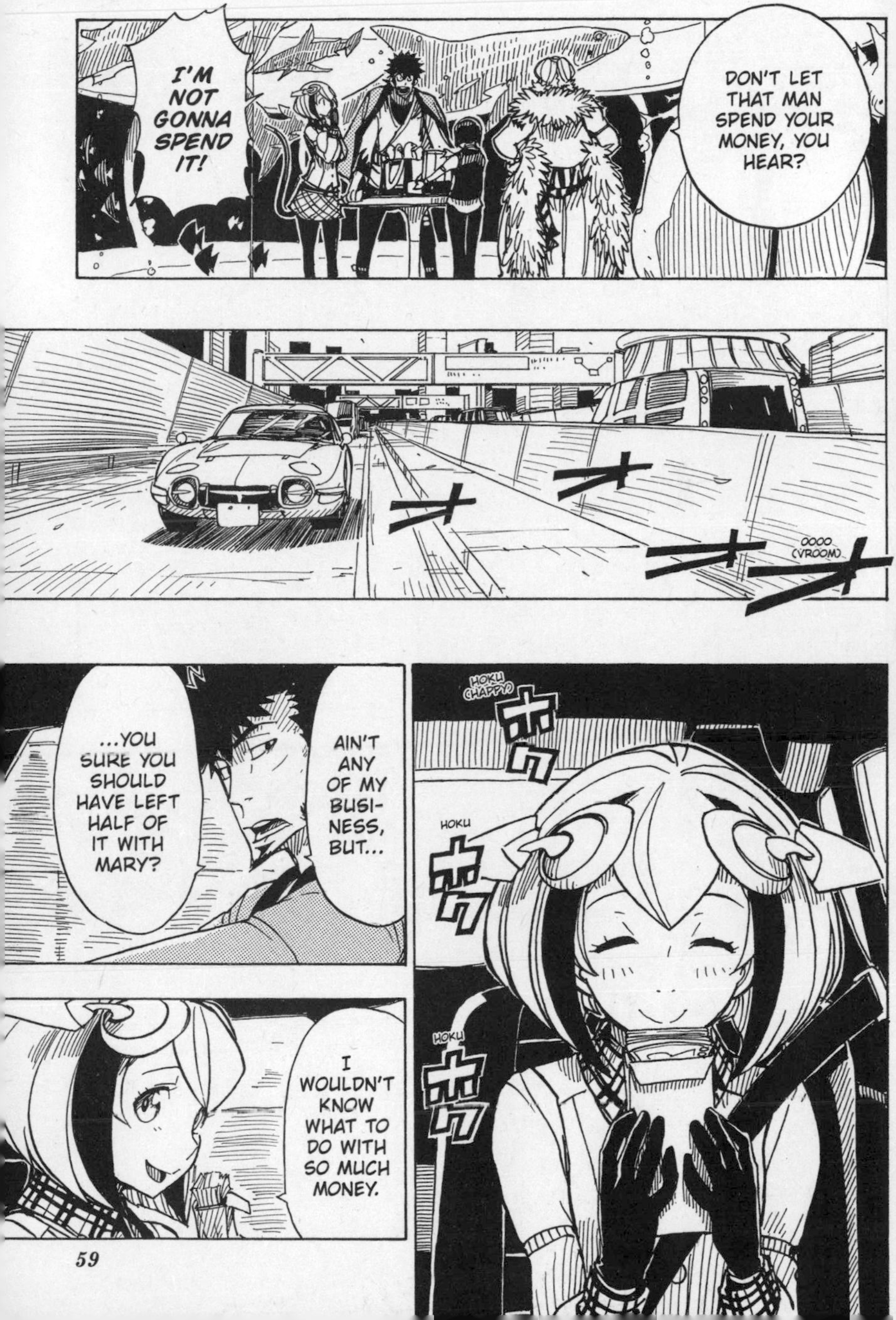
DON'T LET THAT MAN SPEND YOUR MONEY, YOU HEAR?
I'M NOT GONNA SPEND IT!
OOOO (VROOM)
HOKU (HAPPY)
HOKU
HOKU
AIN'T ANY OF MY BUSI- NESS, BUT...
...YOU SURE YOU SHOULD HAVE LEFT HALF OF IT WITH MARY?
I WOULDN'T KNOW WHAT TO DO WITH SO MUCH MONEY.

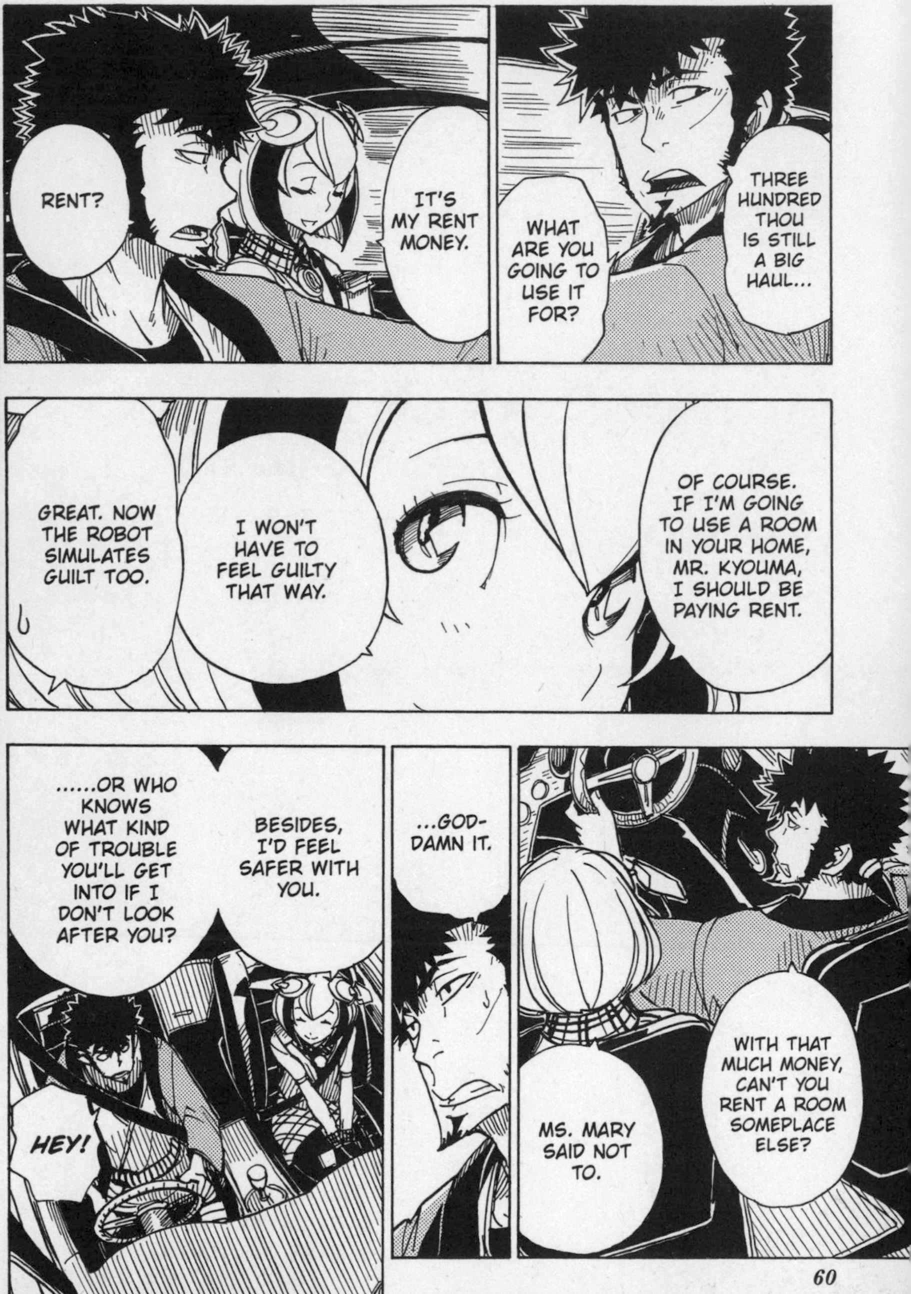
THREE HUNDRED THOU IS STILL A BIG HAUL...
WHAT ARE YOU GOING TO USE IT FOR?
IT'S MY RENT MONEY.
RENT?
OF COURSE. IF I'M GOING TO USE A ROOM IN YOUR HOME, MR. KYOUMA, I SHOULD BE PAYING RENT.
I WON'T HAVE TO FEEL GUILTY THAT WAY.
GREAT. NOW THE ROBOT SIMULATES GUILT TOO.
WITH THAT MUCH MONEY, CAN'T YOU RENT A ROOM SOMEPLACE ELSE?
MS. MARY SAID NOT TO.
...GOD-DAMN IT.
BESIDES, I'D FEEL SAFER WITH YOU.
......OR WHO KNOWS WHAT KIND OF TROUBLE YOU'LL GET INTO IF I DON'T LOOK AFTER YOU?
HEY!

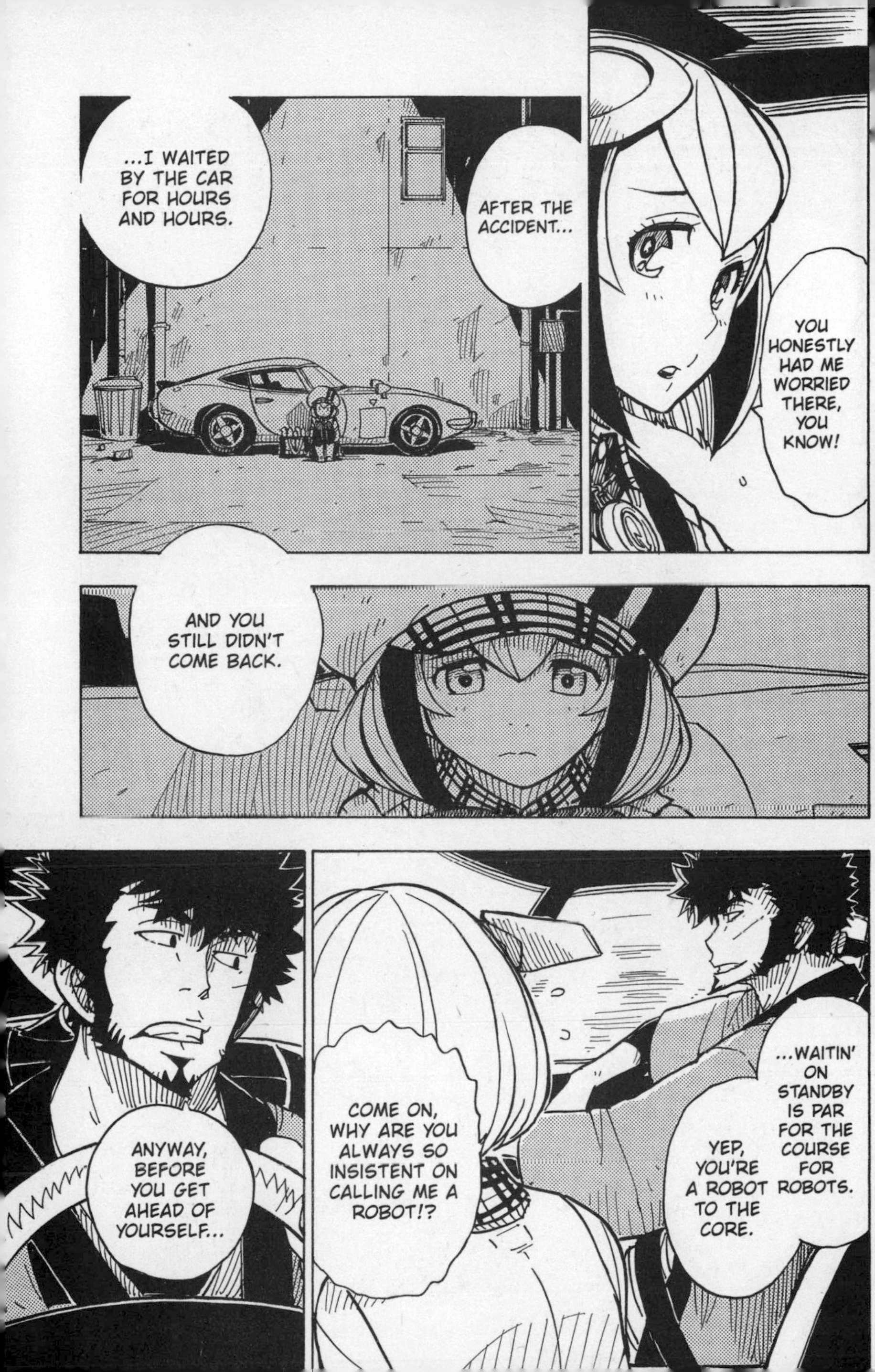
YOU HONESTLY HAD ME WORRIED THERE, YOU KNOW!
AFTER THE ACCIDENT...
...I WAITED BY THE CAR FOR HOURS AND HOURS.
AND YOU STILL DIDN'T COME BACK.
...WAITIN' ON STANDBY IS PAR FOR THE COURSE FOR ROBOTS.
YEP, YOU'RE A ROBOT TO THE CORE.
COME ON, WHY ARE YOU ALWAYS SO INSISTENT ON CALLING ME A ROBOT!?
ANYWAY, BEFORE YOU GET AHEAD OF YOURSELF...

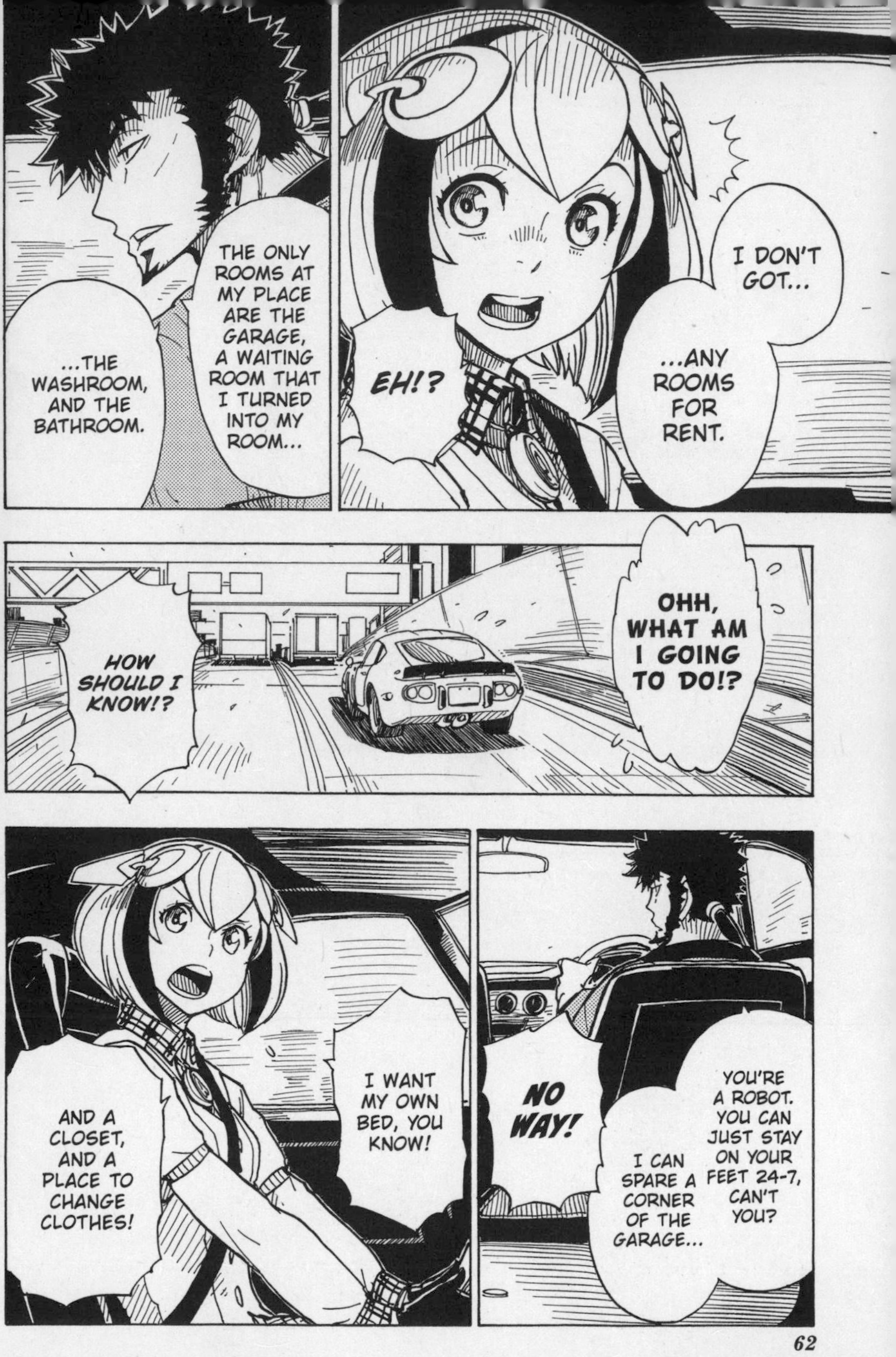
I DON'T GOT...
...ANY ROOMS FOR RENT.
EH!?
THE ONLY ROOMS AT MY PLACE ARE THE GARAGE, A WAITING ROOM THAT I TURNED INTO MY ROOM...
...THE WASHROOM, AND THE BATHROOM.
OHH, WHAT AM I GOING TO DO!?
HOW SHOULD I KNOW!?
YOU'RE A ROBOT. YOU CAN JUST STAY ON YOUR FEET 24-7, CAN'T YOU?
I CAN SPARE A CORNER OF THE GARAGE...
NO WAY!
I WANT MY OWN BED, YOU KNOW!
AND A CLOSET, AND A PLACE TO CHANGE CLOTHES!

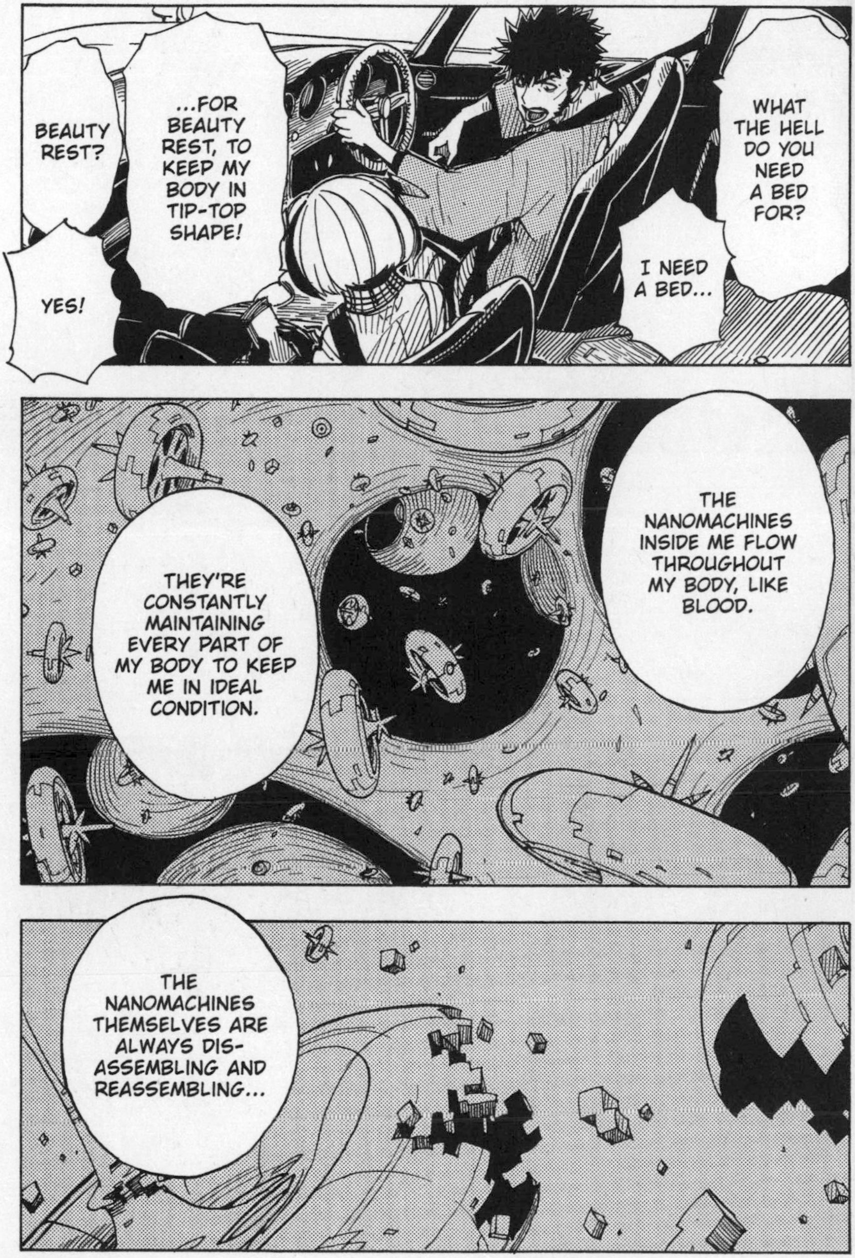
WHAT THE HELL DO YOU NEED A BED FOR?
I NEED A BED...
...FOR BEAUTY REST, TO KEEP MY BODY IN TIP-TOP SHAPE!
BEAUTY REST?
YES!
THE NANOMACHINES INSIDE ME FLOW THROUGHOUT MY BODY, LIKE BLOOD.
THEY'RE CONSTANTLY MAINTAINING EVERY PART OF MY BODY TO KEEP ME IN IDEAL CONDITION.
THE NANOMACHINES THEMSELVES ARE ALWAYS DIS-ASSEMBLING AND REASSEMBLING...

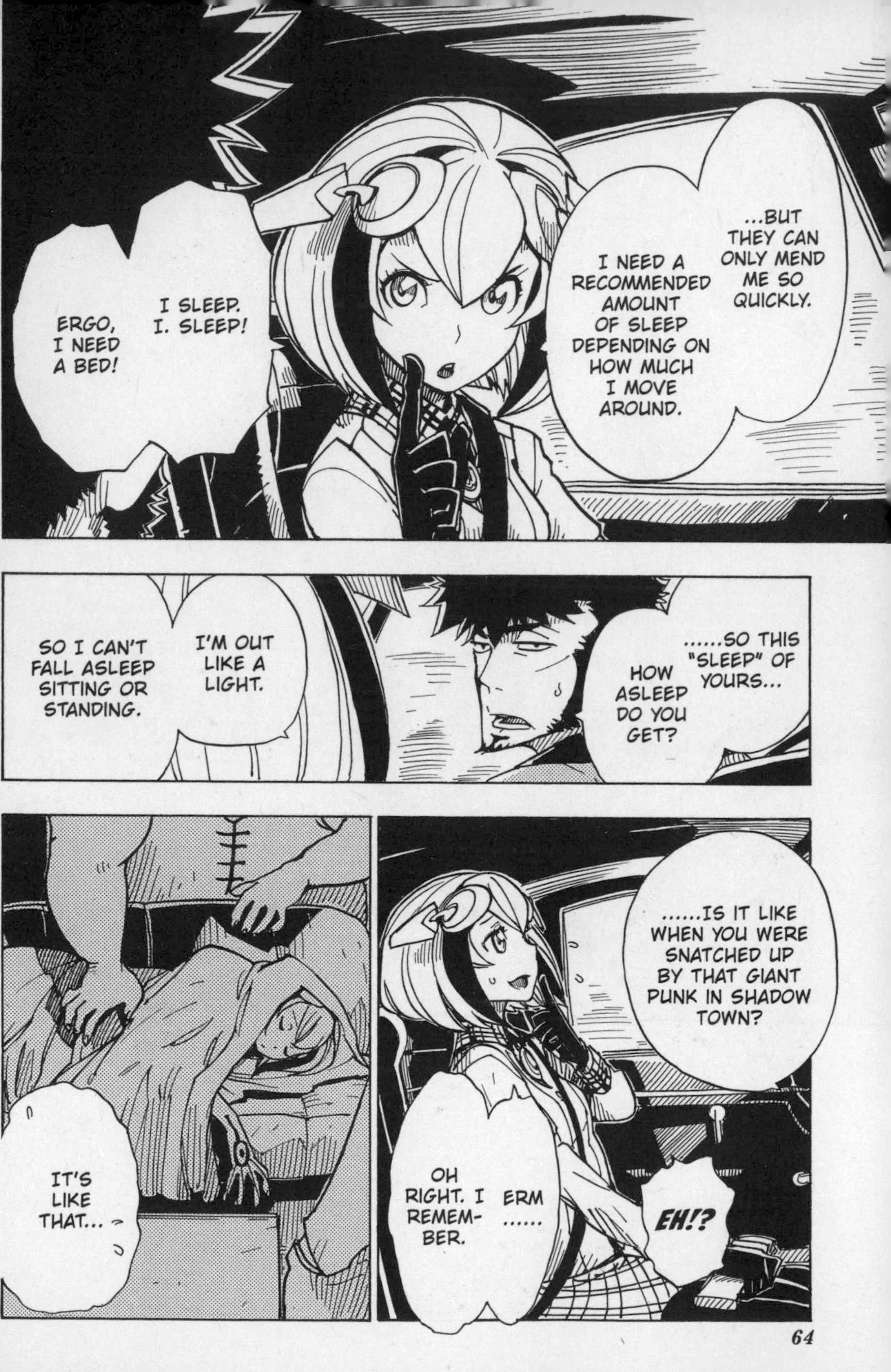
...BUT THEY CAN ONLY MEND ME SO QUICKLY.
I NEED A RECOMMENDED AMOUNT OF SLEEP DEPENDING ON HOW MUCH I MOVE AROUND.
I SLEEP. I. SLEEP!
ERGO, I NEED A BED!
......SO THIS "SLEEP" OF YOURS...
HOW ASLEEP DO YOU GET?
I'M OUT LIKE A LIGHT.
SO I CAN'T FALL ASLEEP SITTING OR STANDING.
......IS IT LIKE WHEN YOU WERE SNATCHED UP BY THAT GIANT PUNK IN SHADOW TOWN?
EH!?
ERM ......
OH RIGHT. I REMEMBER.
IT'S LIKE THAT...

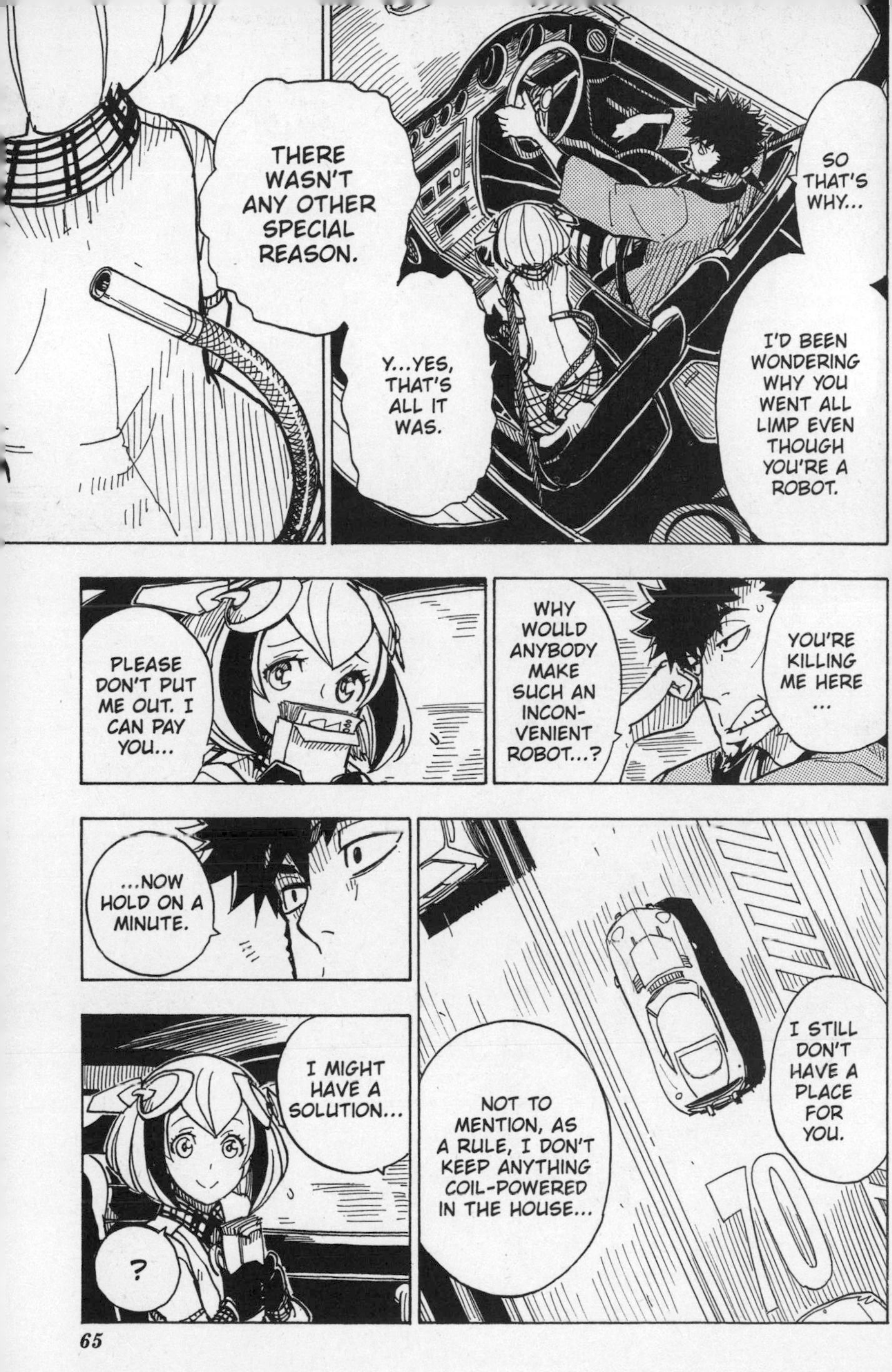
SO THAT'S WHY...
I'D BEEN WONDERING WHY YOU WENT ALL LIMP EVEN THOUGH YOU'RE A ROBOT.
THERE WASN'T ANY OTHER SPECIAL REASON.
Y...YES, THAT'S ALL IT WAS.
YOU'RE KILLING ME HERE ...
WHY WOULD ANYBODY MAKE SUCH AN INCON-VENIENT ROBOT...?
PLEASE DON'T PUT ME OUT. I CAN PAY YOU...
I STILL DON'T HAVE A PLACE FOR YOU.
NOT TO MENTION, AS A RULE, I DON'T KEEP ANYTHING COIL-POWERED IN THE HOUSE...
...NOW HOLD ON A MINUTE.
I MIGHT HAVE A SOLUTION...
?

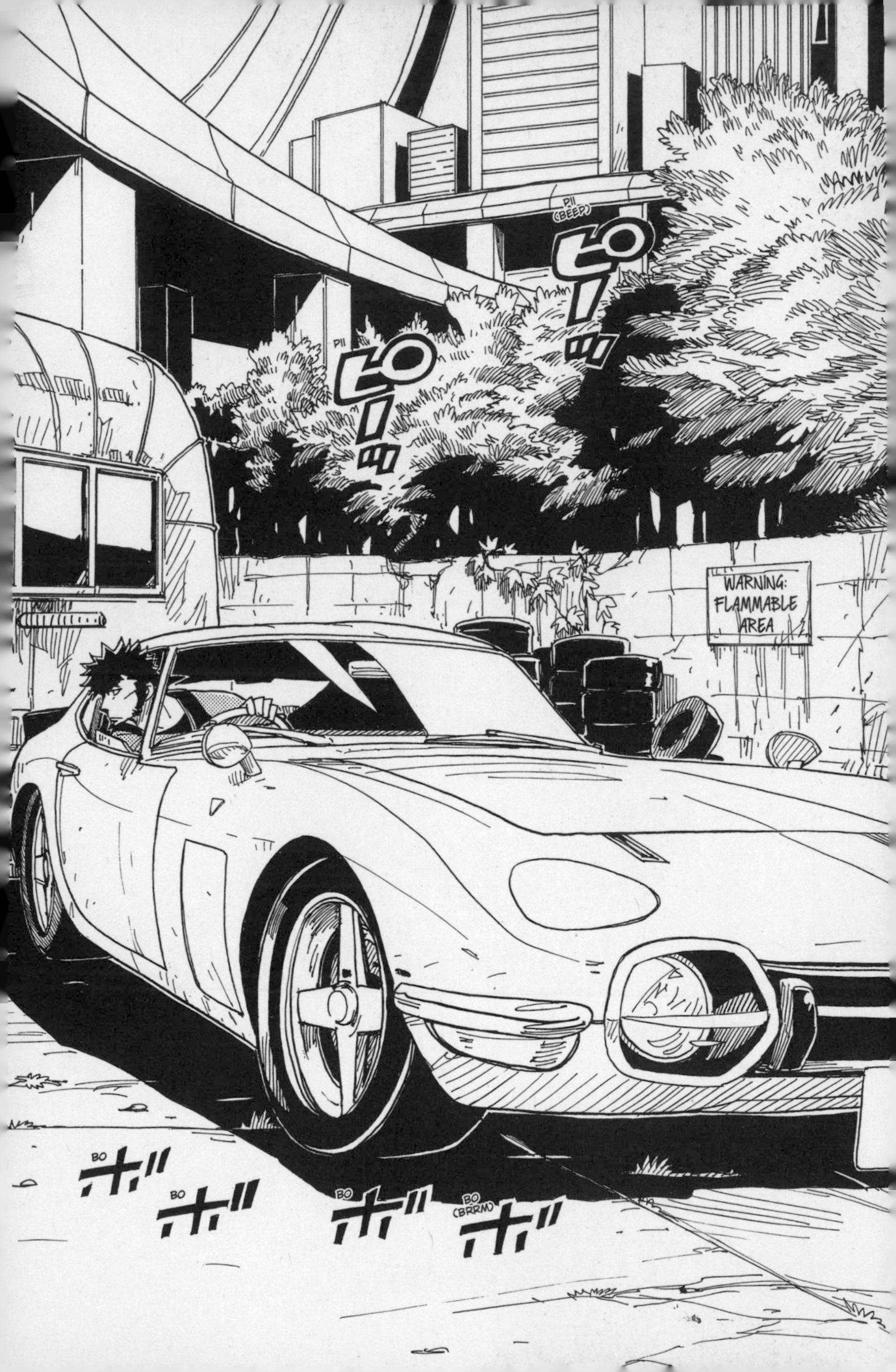
PII (BEEP)
ピーッ
PII
ピーッ
WARNING: FLAMMABLE AREA
BO (BRRM)
ボ
BO
ボ
BO
ボ
BO
ボ

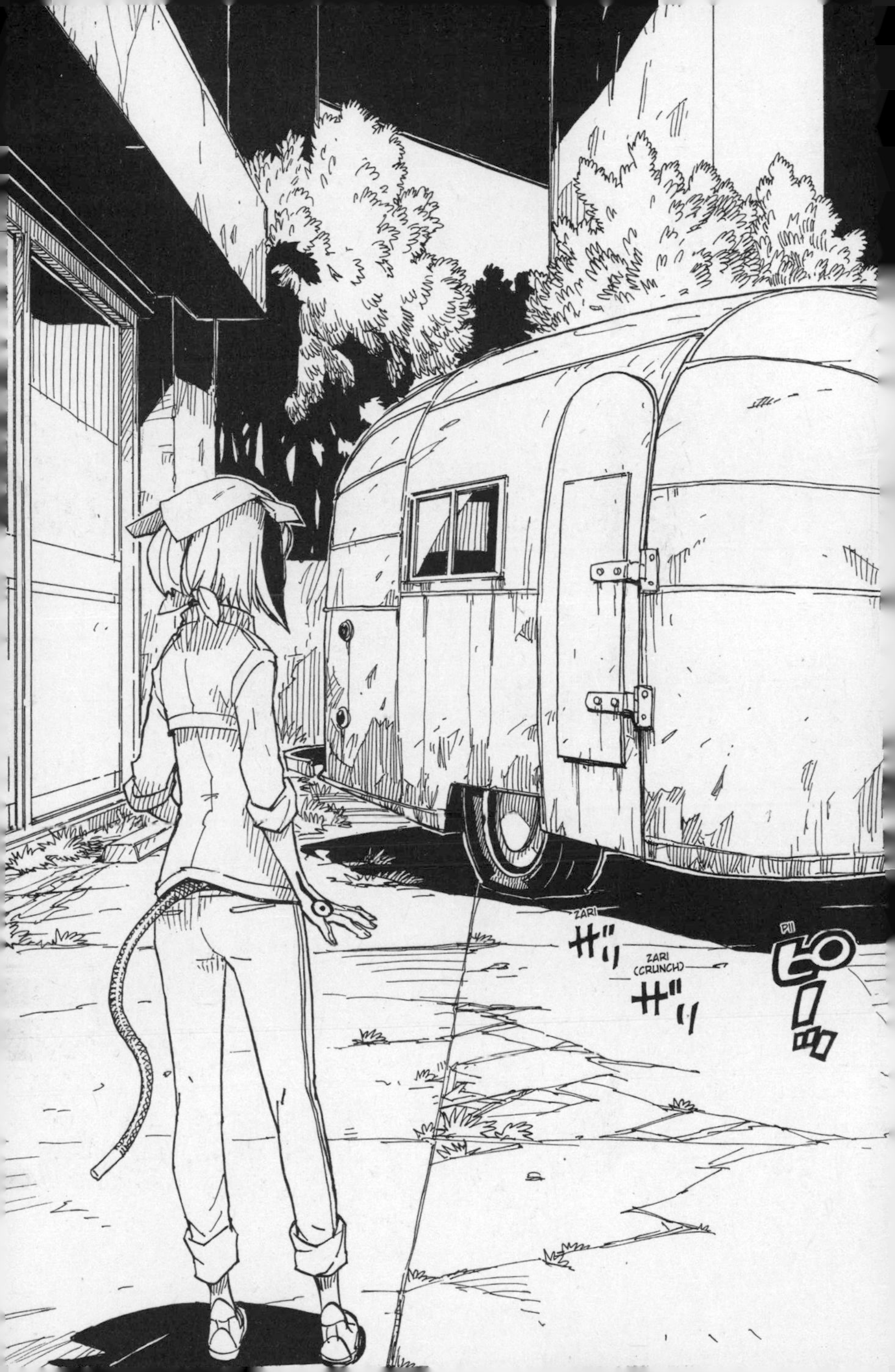
PII
ZARI
ザリ
ZARI (CRUNCH)
ザリ

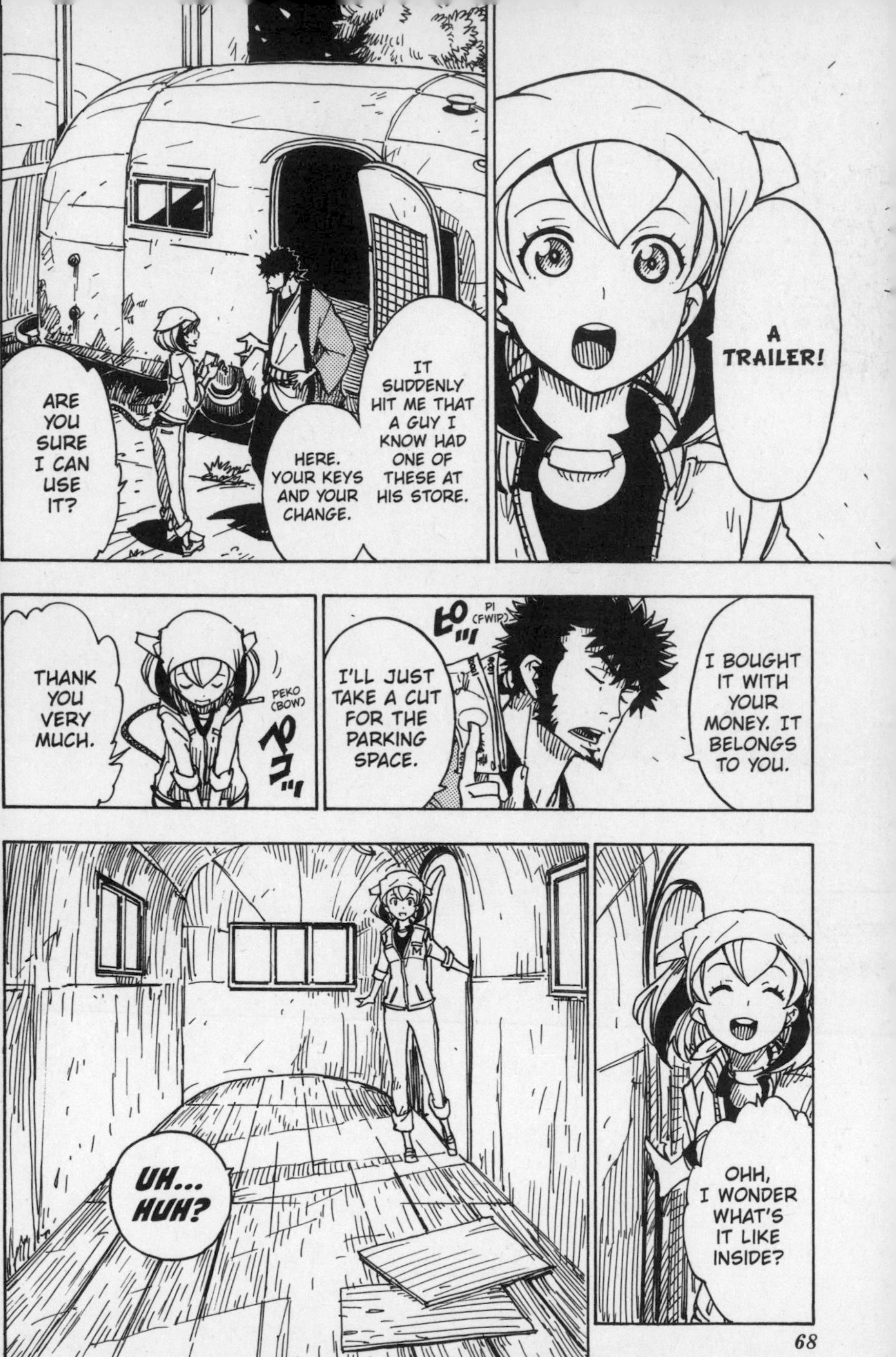
A TRAILER!
IT SUDDENLY HIT ME THAT A GUY I KNOW HAD ONE OF THESE AT HIS STORE.
HERE. YOUR KEYS AND YOUR CHANGE.
ARE YOU SURE I CAN USE IT?
I BOUGHT IT WITH YOUR MONEY. IT BELONGS TO YOU.
PI (FWIP)
I'LL JUST TAKE A CUT FOR THE PARKING SPACE.
PEKO (BOW)
THANK YOU VERY MUCH.
OHH, I WONDER WHAT'S IT LIKE INSIDE?
UH... HUH?

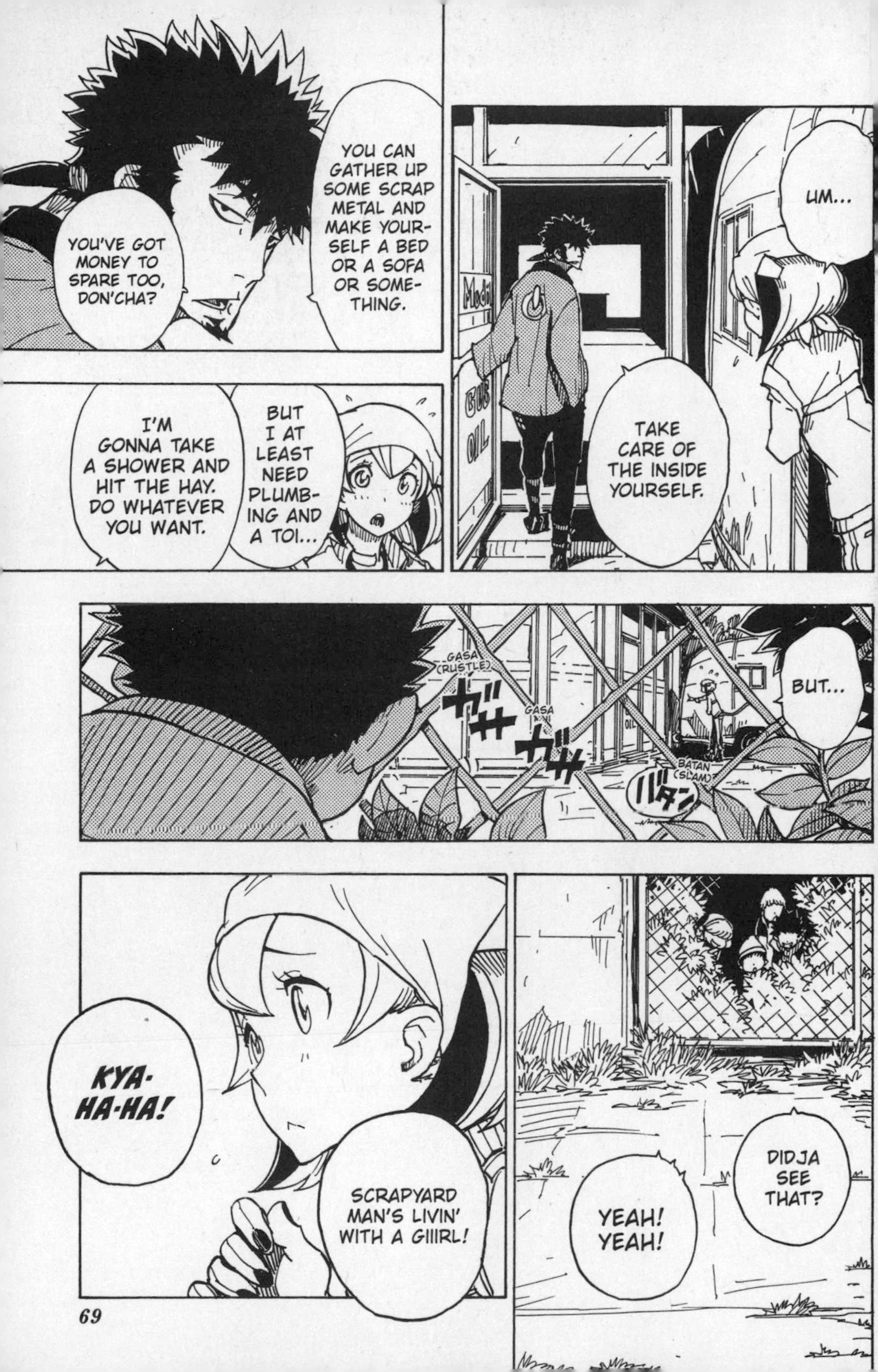
UM...
TAKE CARE OF THE INSIDE YOURSELF.
YOU CAN GATHER UP SOME SCRAP METAL AND MAKE YOURSELF A BED OR A SOFA OR SOMETHING.
YOU'VE GOT MONEY TO SPARE TOO, DON'CHA?
BUT I AT LEAST NEED PLUMBING AND A TOI...
I'M GONNA TAKE A SHOWER AND HIT THE HAY. DO WHATEVER YOU WANT.
BUT...
GASA (RUSTLE)
GASA
BATAN (SLAM)
DIDJA SEE THAT?
YEAH! YEAH!
SCRAPYARD MAN'S LIVIN' WITH A GIIIRL!
KYA-HA-HA!

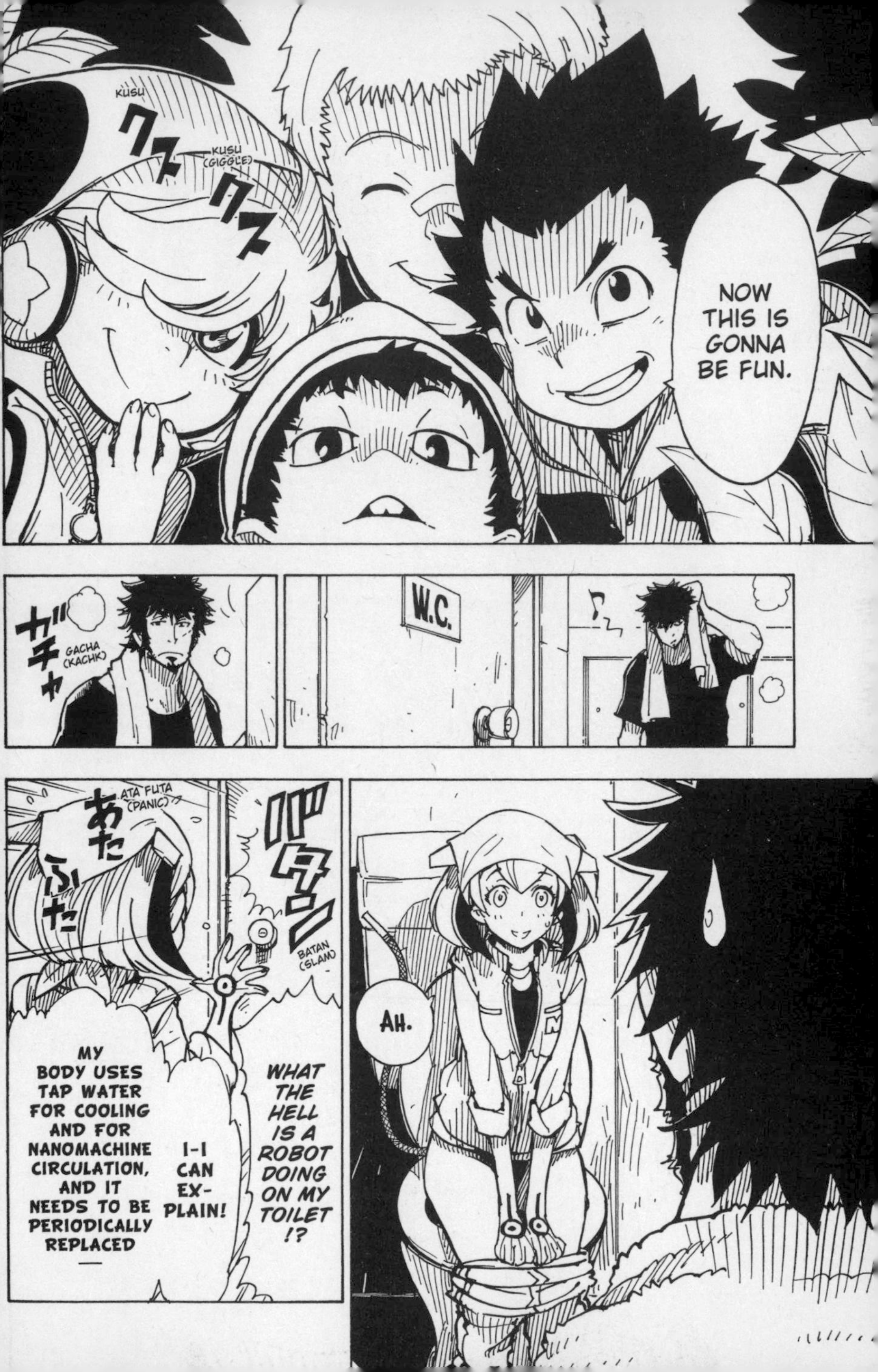
NOW THIS IS GONNA BE FUN.
KUSU (GIGGLE)
KUSU
クスクス
W.C.
GACHA (KACHK)
ガチャ
AH.
BATAN (SLAM)
バタン
WHAT THE HELL IS A ROBOT DOING ON MY TOILET!?
ATA FUTA (PANIC)
あたふた
I-I CAN EX-PLAIN!
MY BODY USES TAP WATER FOR COOLING AND FOR NANOMACHINE CIRCULATION, AND IT NEEDS TO BE PERIODICALLY REPLACED —

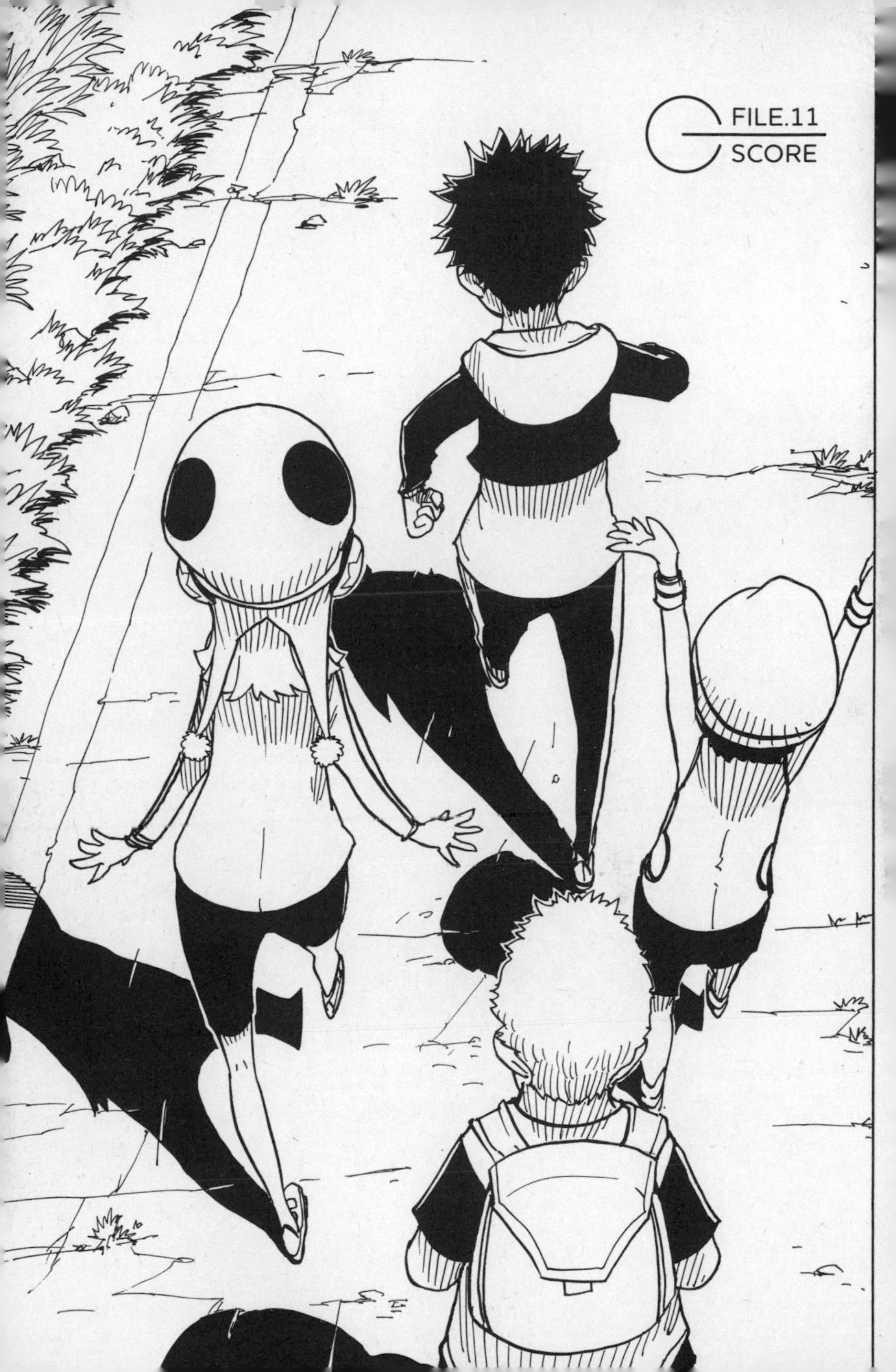
FILE.11
SCORE

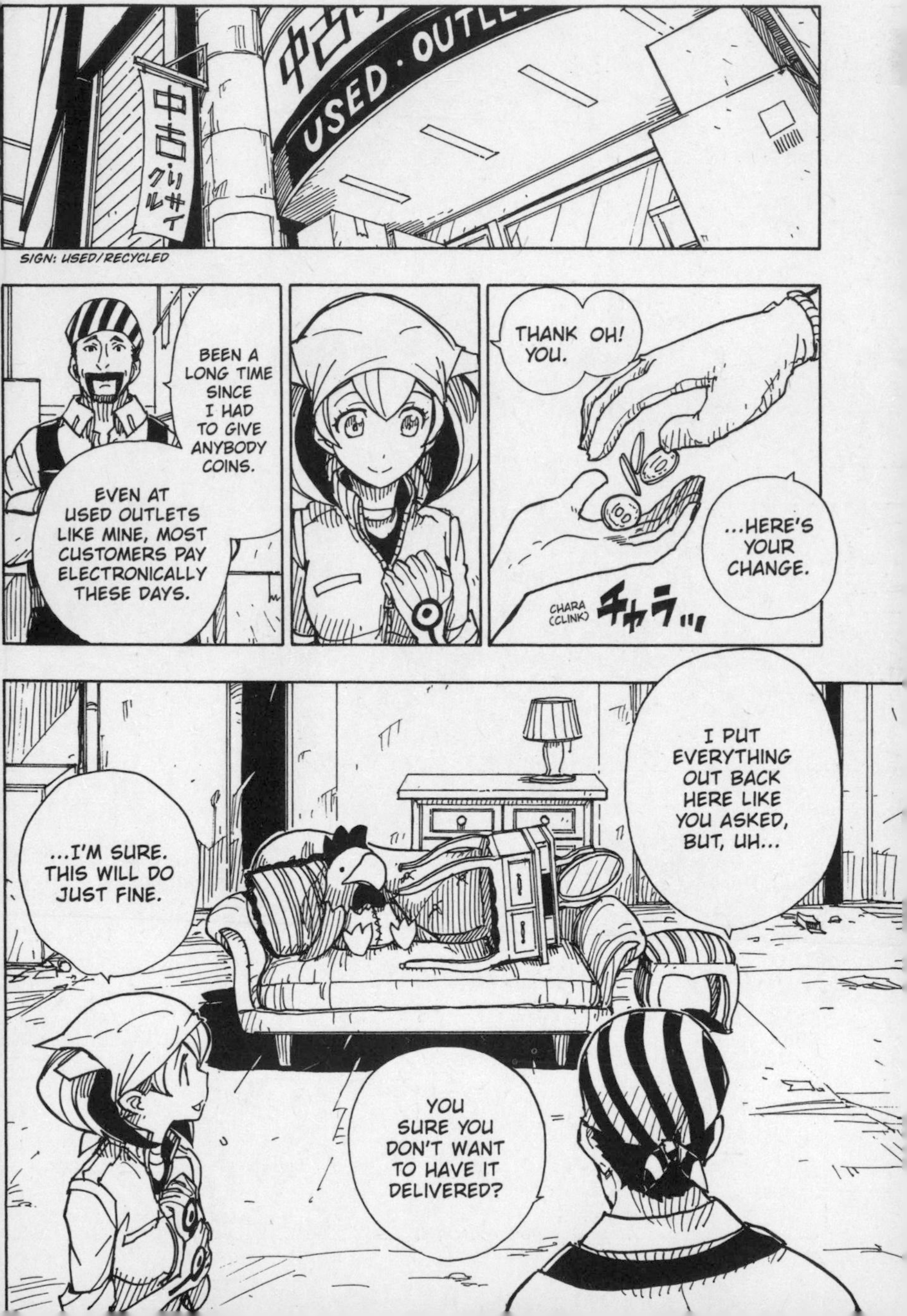
USED · OUTLET
SIGN: USED/RECYCLED
OH!
THANK YOU.
...HERE'S YOUR CHANGE.
CHARA (CLINK)
BEEN A LONG TIME SINCE I HAD TO GIVE ANYBODY COINS.
EVEN AT USED OUTLETS LIKE MINE, MOST CUSTOMERS PAY ELECTRONICALLY THESE DAYS.
I PUT EVERYTHING OUT BACK HERE LIKE YOU ASKED, BUT, UH...
...I'M SURE. THIS WILL DO JUST FINE.
YOU SURE YOU DON'T WANT TO HAVE IT DELIVERED?

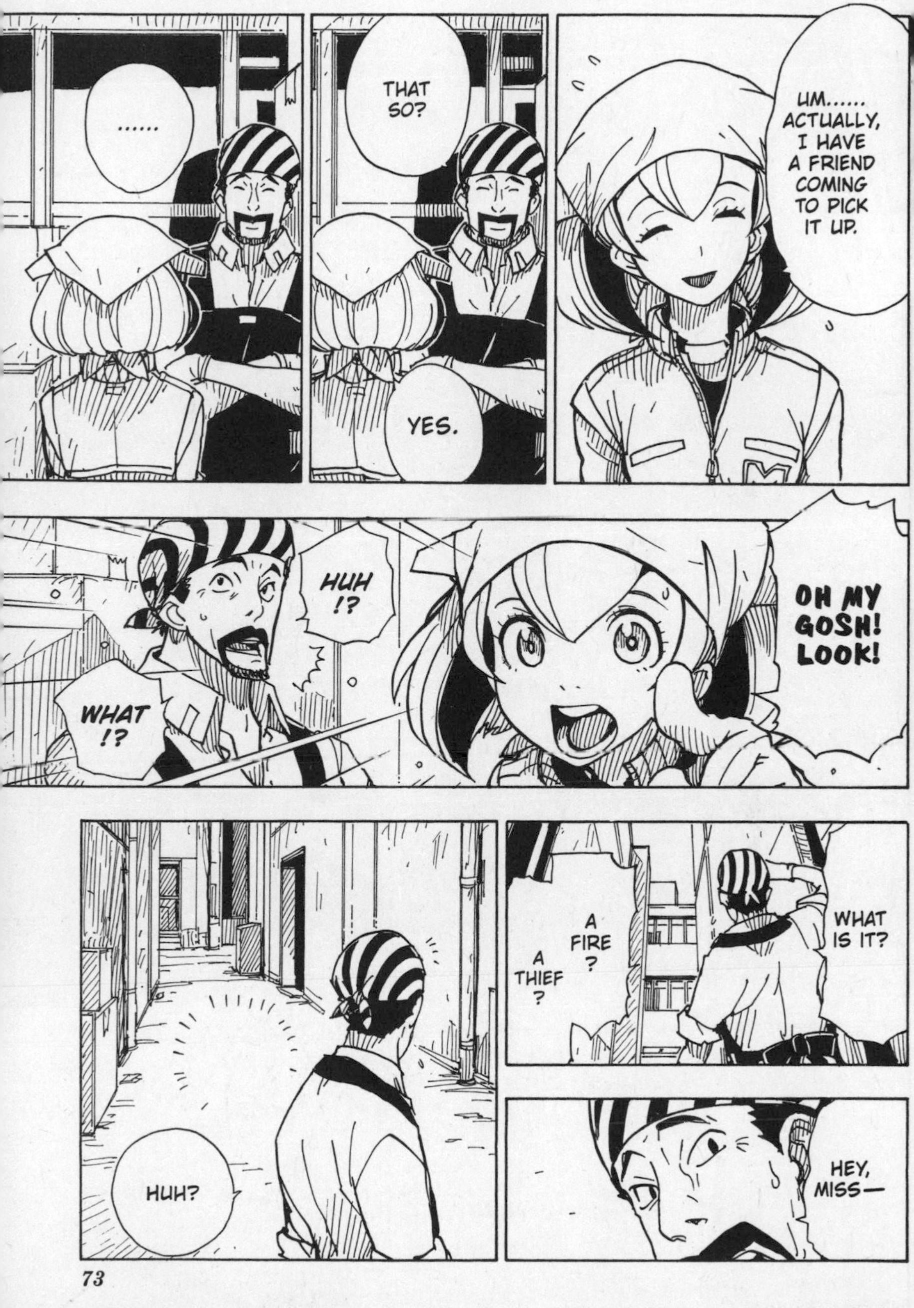
UM...... ACTUALLY, I HAVE A FRIEND COMING TO PICK IT UP.
THAT SO?
YES.
......
OH MY GOSH! LOOK!
HUH !?
WHAT !?
WHAT IS IT?
A FIRE ?
A THIEF ?
HEY, MISS—
HUH?

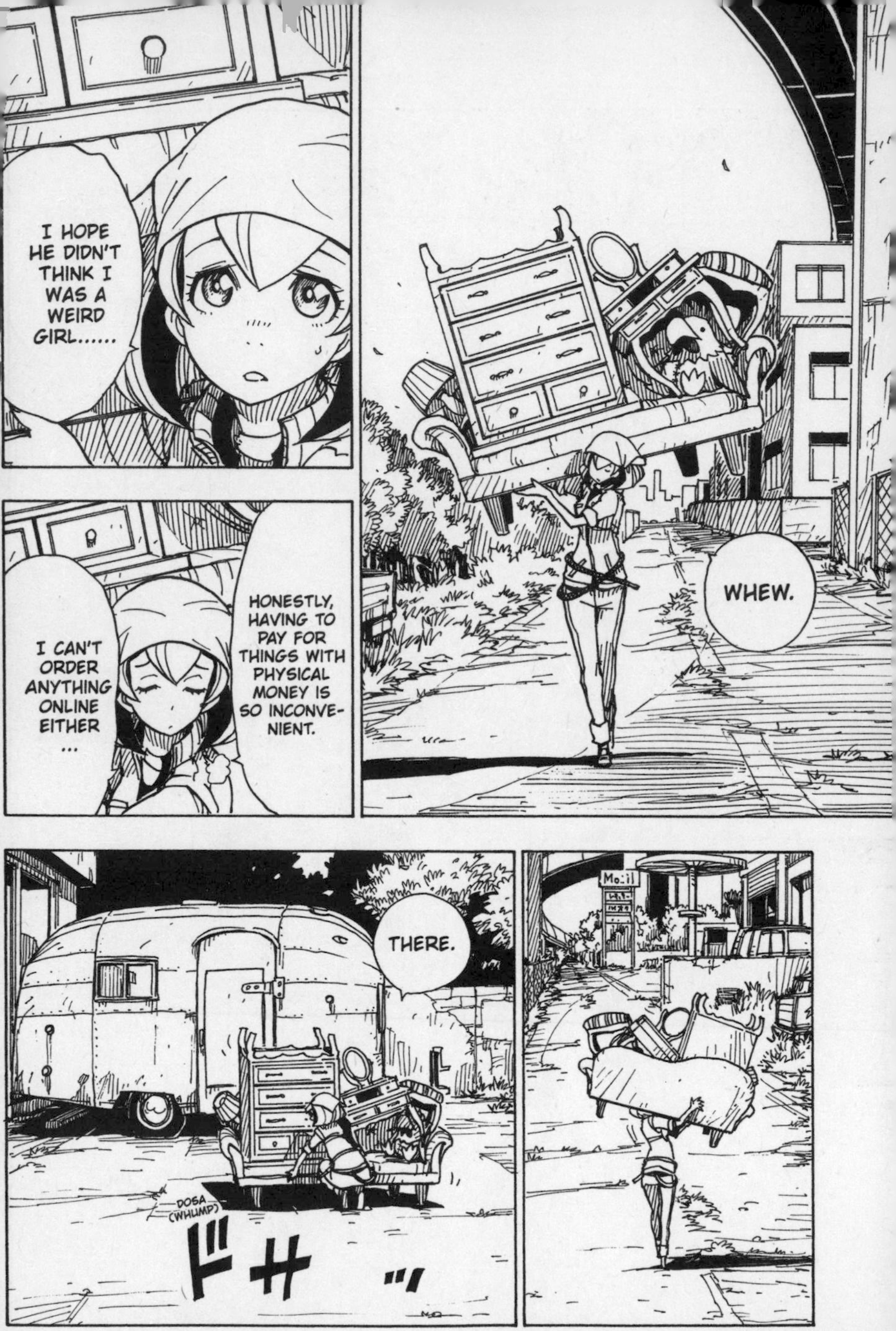
WHEW.
I HOPE HE DIDN'T THINK I WAS A WEIRD GIRL......
HONESTLY, HAVING TO PAY FOR THINGS WITH PHYSICAL MONEY IS SO INCONVE- NIENT.
I CAN'T ORDER ANYTHING ONLINE EITHER ...
THERE.
DOSA (WHUMP)
ドサッ

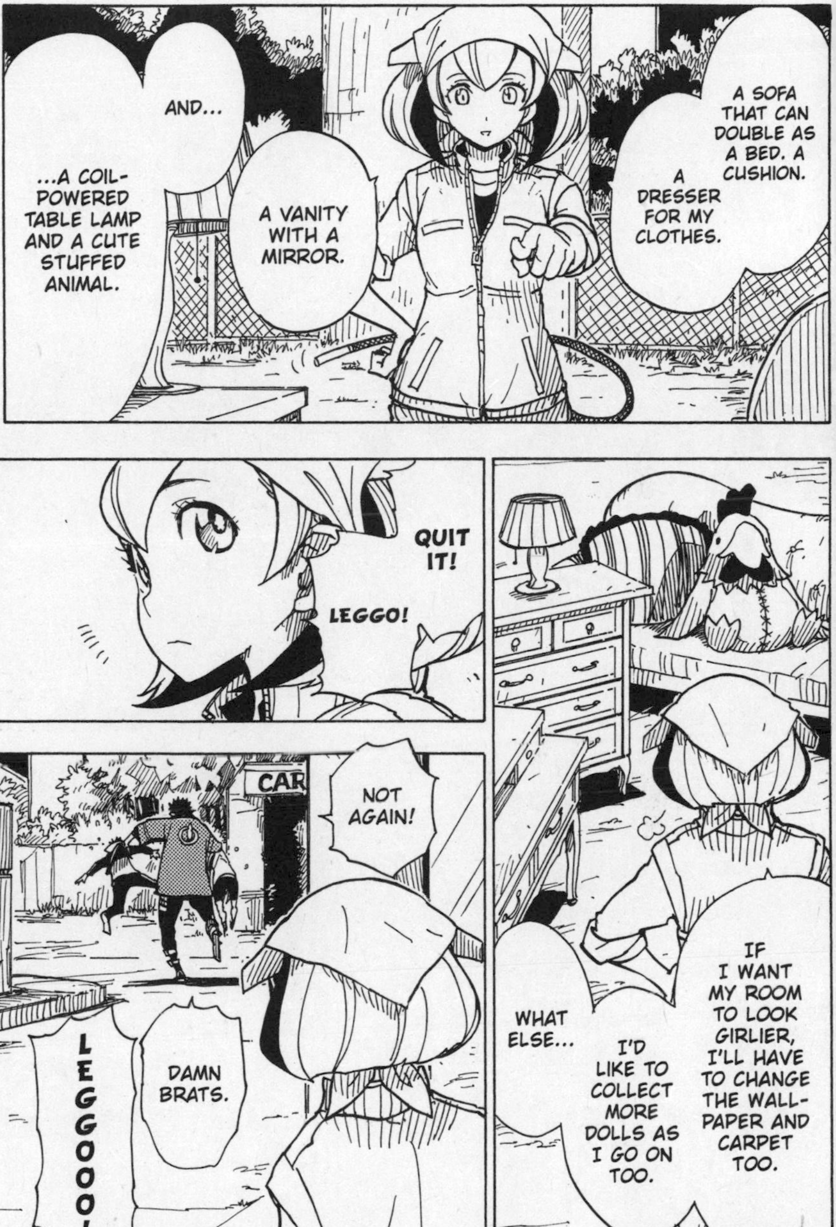
A SOFA THAT CAN DOUBLE AS A BED. A CUSHION.
A DRESSER FOR MY CLOTHES.
A VANITY WITH A MIRROR.
AND...
...A COIL-POWERED TABLE LAMP AND A CUTE STUFFED ANIMAL.
IF I WANT MY ROOM TO LOOK GIRLIER, I'LL HAVE TO CHANGE THE WALL-PAPER AND CARPET TOO.
I'D LIKE TO COLLECT MORE DOLLS AS I GO ON TOO.
WHAT ELSE...
QUIT IT!
LEGGO!
NOT AGAIN!
DAMN BRATS.
LEGGOOOO!

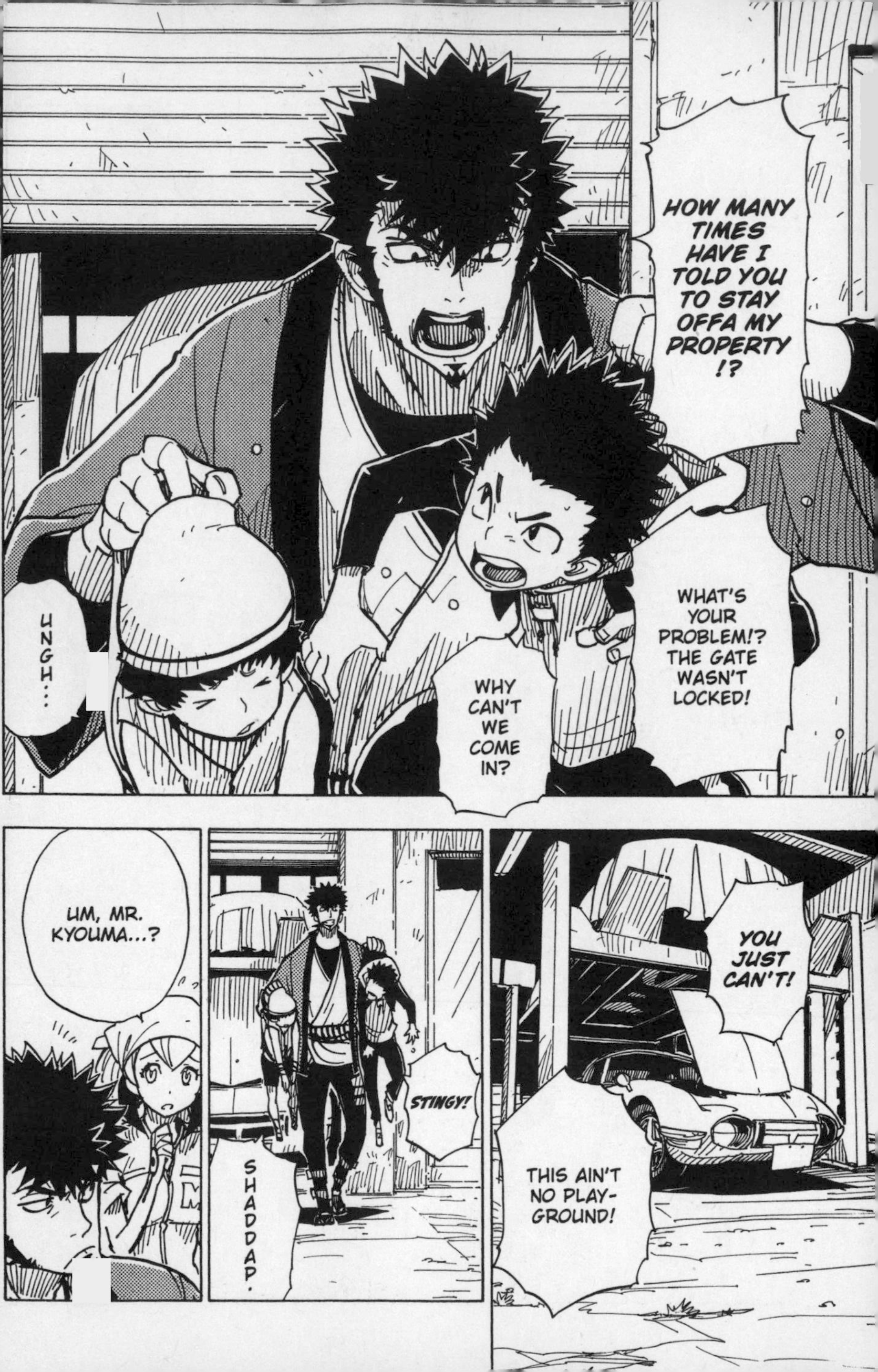
HOW MANY TIMES HAVE I TOLD YOU TO STAY OFFA MY PROPERTY !?
WHAT'S YOUR PROBLEM!? THE GATE WASN'T LOCKED!
WHY CAN'T WE COME IN?
UNGH...
YOU JUST CAN'T!
THIS AIN'T NO PLAY-GROUND!
STINGY!
SHADDAP.
UM, MR. KYOUMA...?

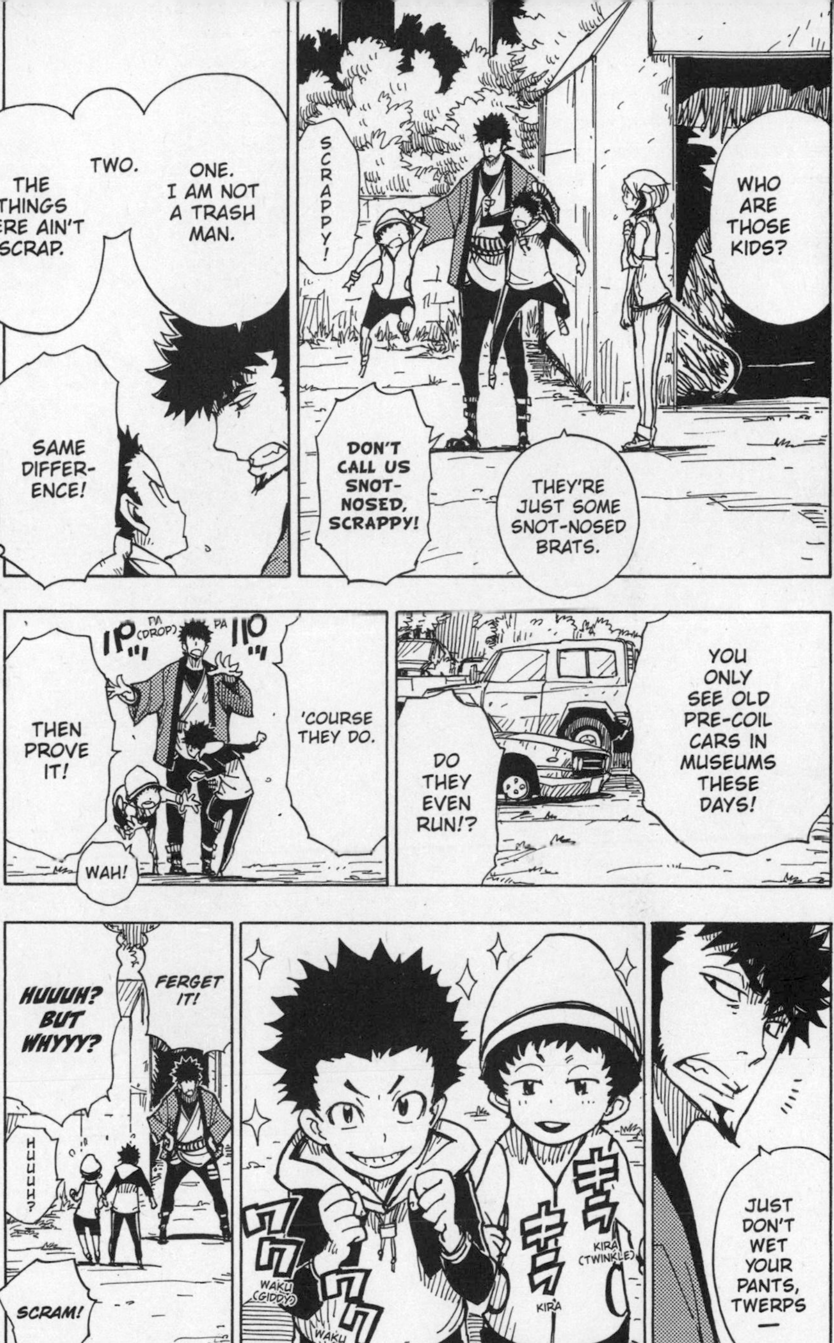
WHO ARE THOSE KIDS?
SCRAPPY!
THEY'RE JUST SOME SNOT-NOSED BRATS.
DON'T CALL US SNOT-NOSED, SCRAPPY!
ONE. I AM NOT A TRASH MAN.
TWO.
THE THINGS HERE AIN'T SCRAP.
SAME DIFFERENCE!
YOU ONLY SEE OLD PRE-COIL CARS IN MUSEUMS THESE DAYS!
DO THEY EVEN RUN!?
'COURSE THEY DO.
PA
PA (DROP)
THEN PROVE IT!
WAH!
JUST DON'T WET YOUR PANTS, TWERPS —
KIRA (TWINKLE)
KIRA
WAKU (GIDDY)
WAKU
FERGET IT!
HUUUH? BUT WHYYY?
HUUUH?
SCRAM!

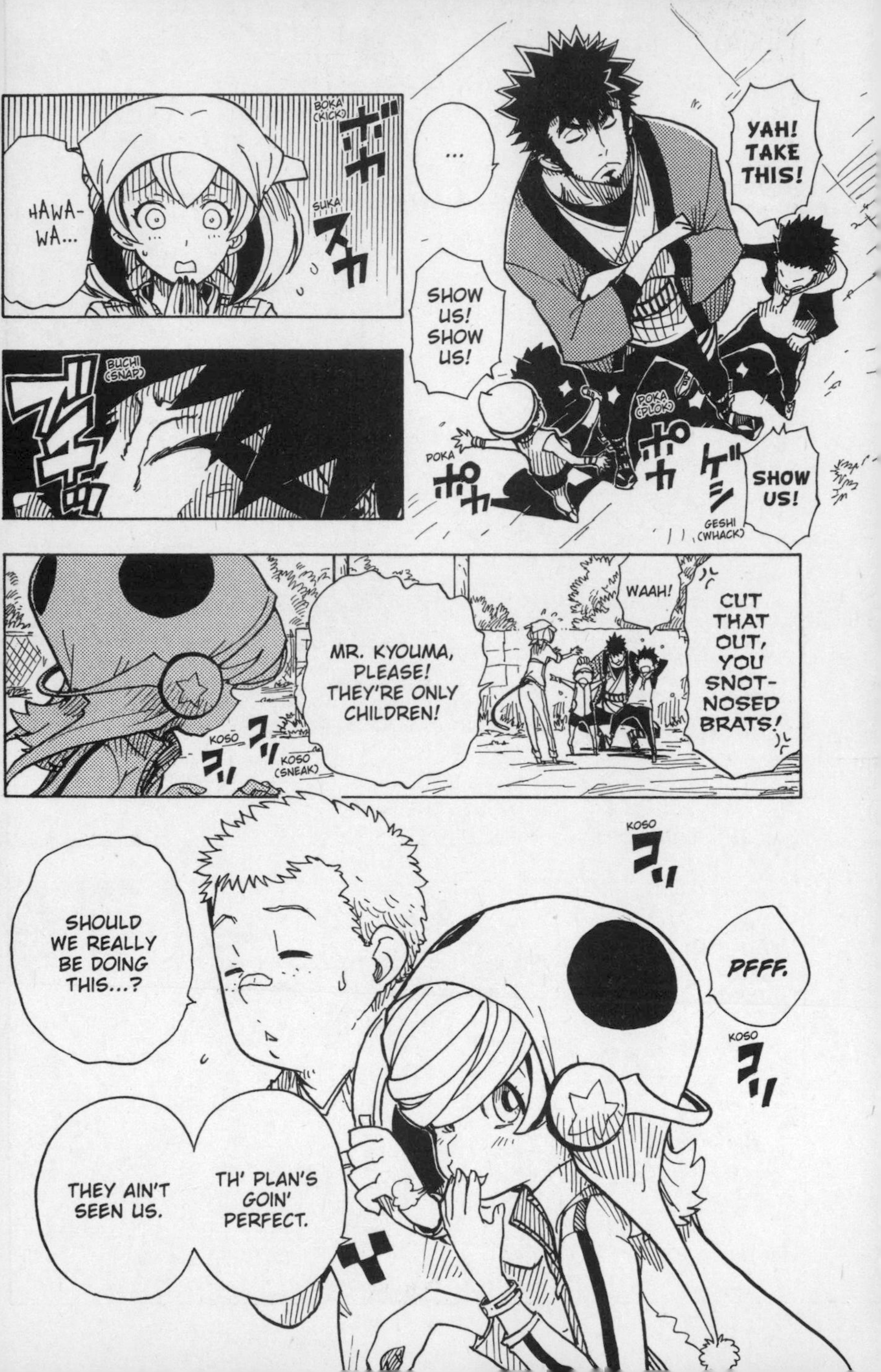
YAH! TAKE THIS!
...
SHOW US! SHOW US!
POKA (PLOK)
GESHI (WHACK)
SHOW US!
POKA
BOKA (KICK)
SUKA
HAWA-WA...
BUCHI (SNAP)
CUT THAT OUT, YOU SNOT-NOSED BRATS!
WAAH!
MR. KYOUMA, PLEASE! THEY'RE ONLY CHILDREN!
KOSO
KOSO (SNEAK)
KOSO
PFFF.
KOSO
SHOULD WE REALLY BE DOING THIS...?
TH' PLAN'S GOIN' PERFECT.
THEY AIN'T SEEN US.

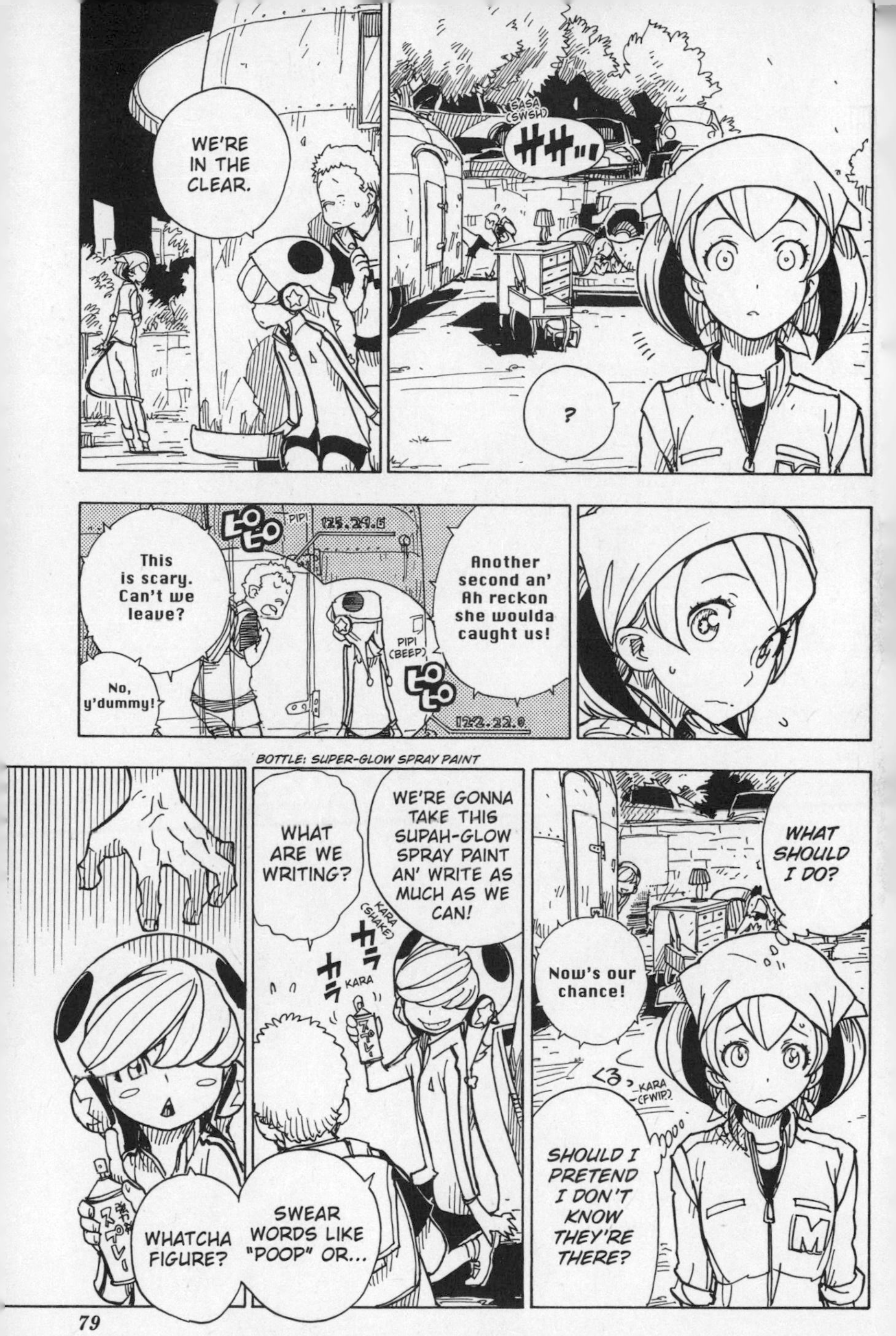
SASA (SWSH)
ササッ
?
WE'RE IN THE CLEAR.
Another second an' Ah reckon she woulda caught us!
PIPI (BEEP)
PIPI
This is scary. Can't we leave?
No, y'dummy!
BOTTLE: SUPER-GLOW SPRAY PAINT
WHAT SHOULD I DO?
Now's our chance!
KARA (FWIP)
SHOULD I PRETEND I DON'T KNOW THEY'RE THERE?
WE'RE GONNA TAKE THIS SUPAH-GLOW SPRAY PAINT AN' WRITE AS MUCH AS WE CAN!
WHAT ARE WE WRITING?
KARA (SHAKE)
KARA
SWEAR WORDS LIKE "POOP" OR...
WHATCHA FIGURE?

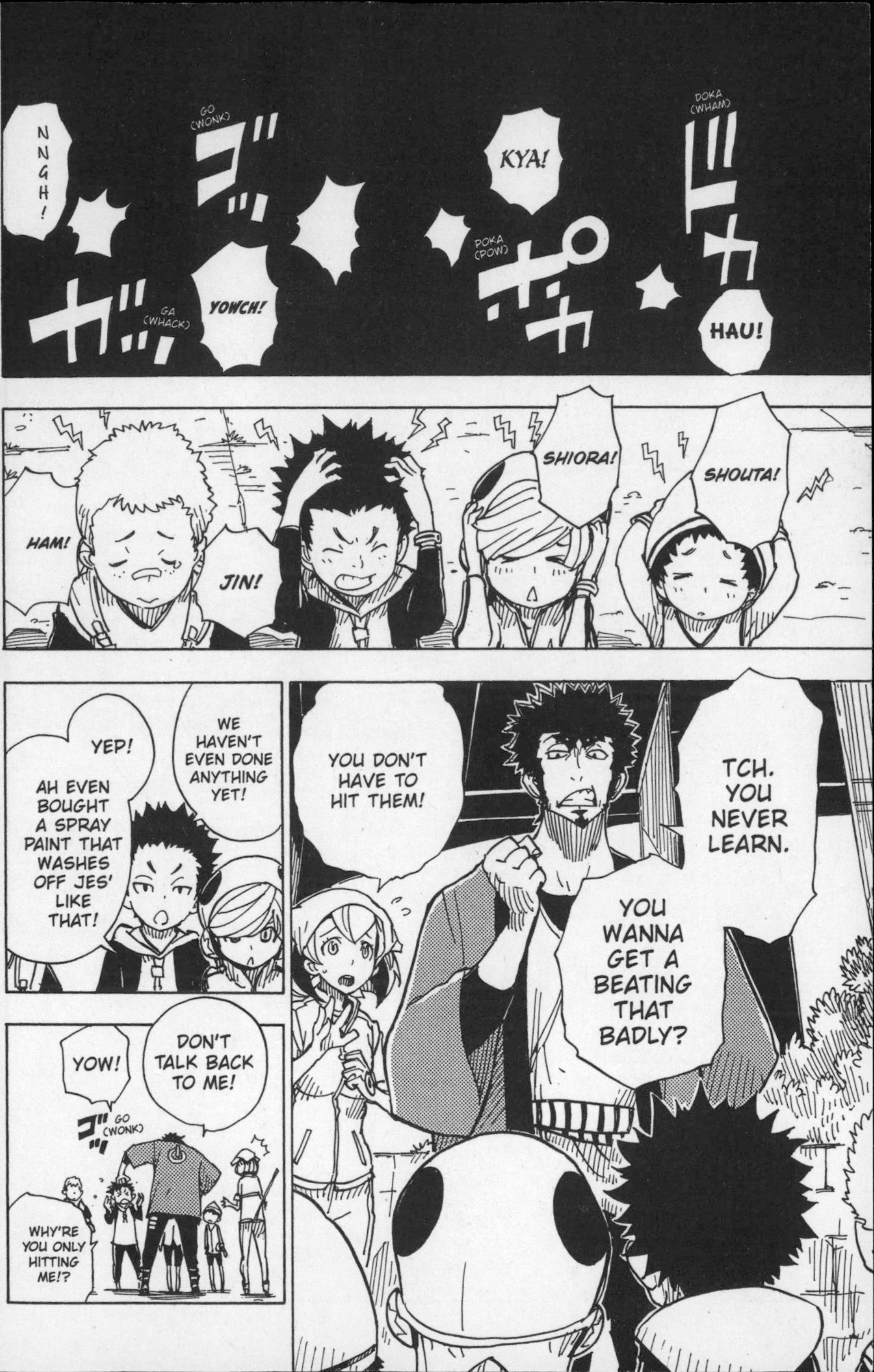
DOKA (WHAM)
HAU!
POKA (POW)
KYA!
GO (WONK)
NNGH!
YOWCH!
GA (WHACK)
SHOUTA!
SHIORA!
JIN!
HAM!
TCH. YOU NEVER LEARN.
YOU WANNA GET A BEATING THAT BADLY?
YOU DON'T HAVE TO HIT THEM!
WE HAVEN'T EVEN DONE ANYTHING YET!
YEP!
AH EVEN BOUGHT A SPRAY PAINT THAT WASHES OFF JES' LIKE THAT!
DON'T TALK BACK TO ME!
YOW!
GO (WONK)
WHY'RE YOU ONLY HITTING ME!?

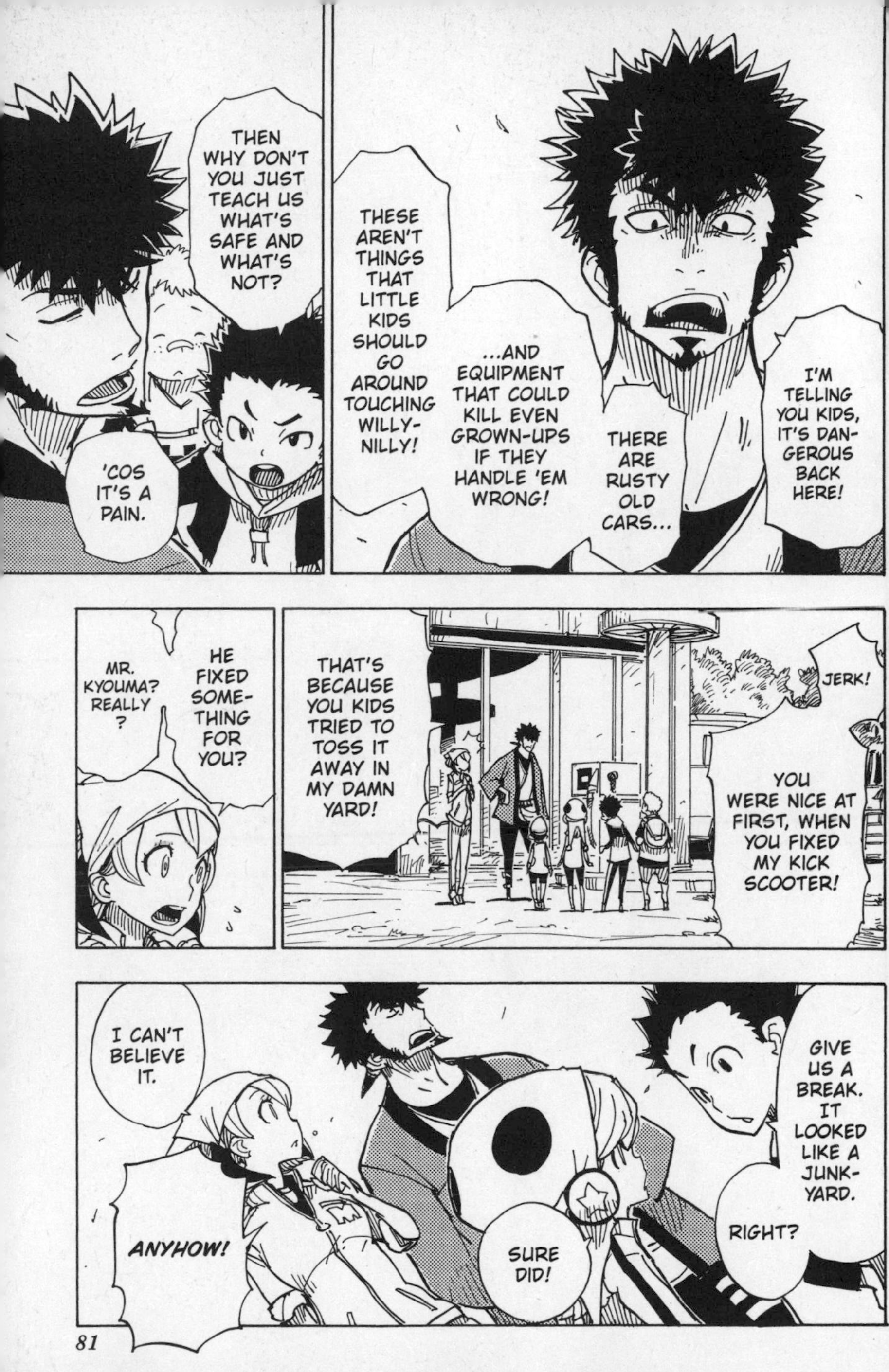
I'M TELLING YOU KIDS, IT'S DAN-GEROUS BACK HERE!
THERE ARE RUSTY OLD CARS...
...AND EQUIPMENT THAT COULD KILL EVEN GROWN-UPS IF THEY HANDLE 'EM WRONG!
THESE AREN'T THINGS THAT LITTLE KIDS SHOULD GO AROUND TOUCHING WILLY-NILLY!
THEN WHY DON'T YOU JUST TEACH US WHAT'S SAFE AND WHAT'S NOT?
'COS IT'S A PAIN.
JERK!
YOU WERE NICE AT FIRST, WHEN YOU FIXED MY KICK SCOOTER!
THAT'S BECAUSE YOU KIDS TRIED TO TOSS IT AWAY IN MY DAMN YARD!
HE FIXED SOME-THING FOR YOU?
MR. KYOUMA? REALLY?
GIVE US A BREAK. IT LOOKED LIKE A JUNK-YARD.
RIGHT?
SURE DID!
I CAN'T BELIEVE IT.
ANYHOW!

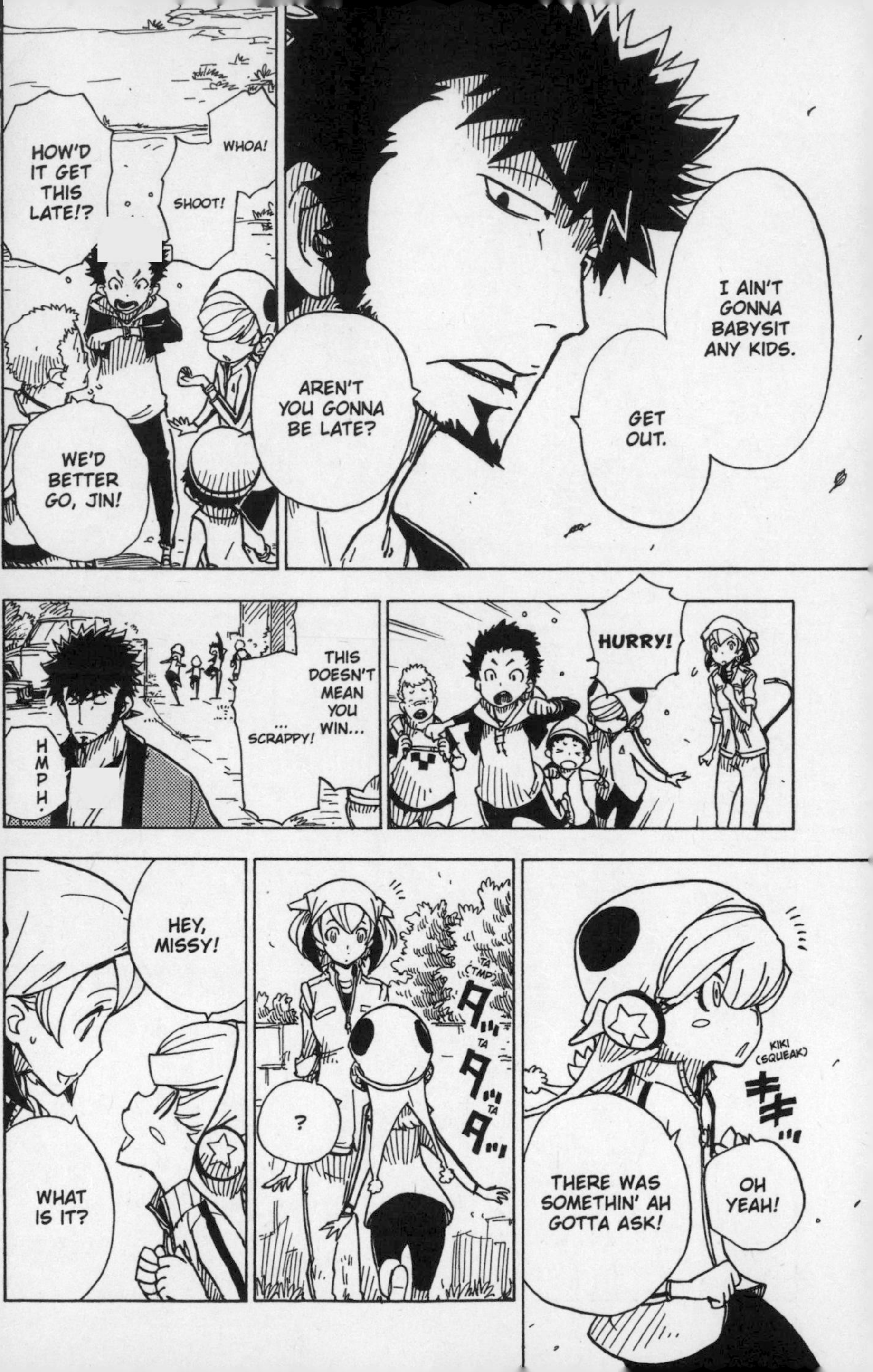
I AIN'T GONNA BABYSIT ANY KIDS.
GET OUT.
AREN'T YOU GONNA BE LATE?
WHOA!
HOW'D IT GET THIS LATE!?
SHOOT!
WE'D BETTER GO, JIN!
HURRY!
THIS DOESN'T MEAN YOU WIN...
...SCRAPPY!
HMPH.
KIKI (SQUEAK)
キキッ
OH YEAH!
THERE WAS SOMETHIN' AH GOTTA ASK!
TA (TMP)
タッ
TA
タッ
TA
タッ
?
HEY, MISSY!
WHAT IS IT?

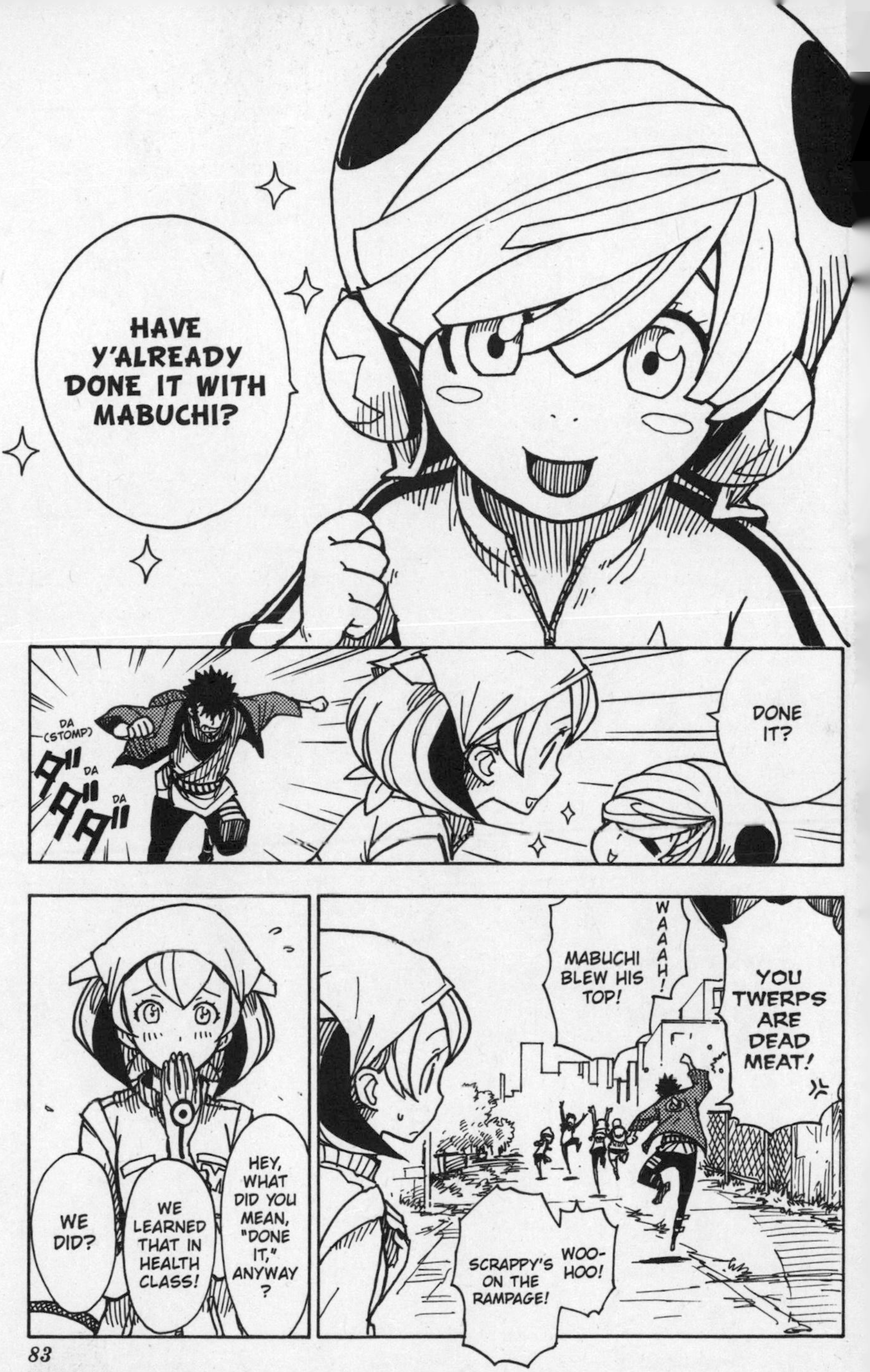
HAVE Y'ALREADY DONE IT WITH MABUCHI?
DONE IT?
DA (STOMP)
DA
DA
YOU TWERPS ARE DEAD MEAT!
WAAAAH!
MABUCHI BLEW HIS TOP!
WOO-HOO!
SCRAPPY'S ON THE RAMPAGE!
HEY, WHAT DID YOU MEAN, "DONE IT," ANYWAY?
WE LEARNED THAT IN HEALTH CLASS!
WE DID?

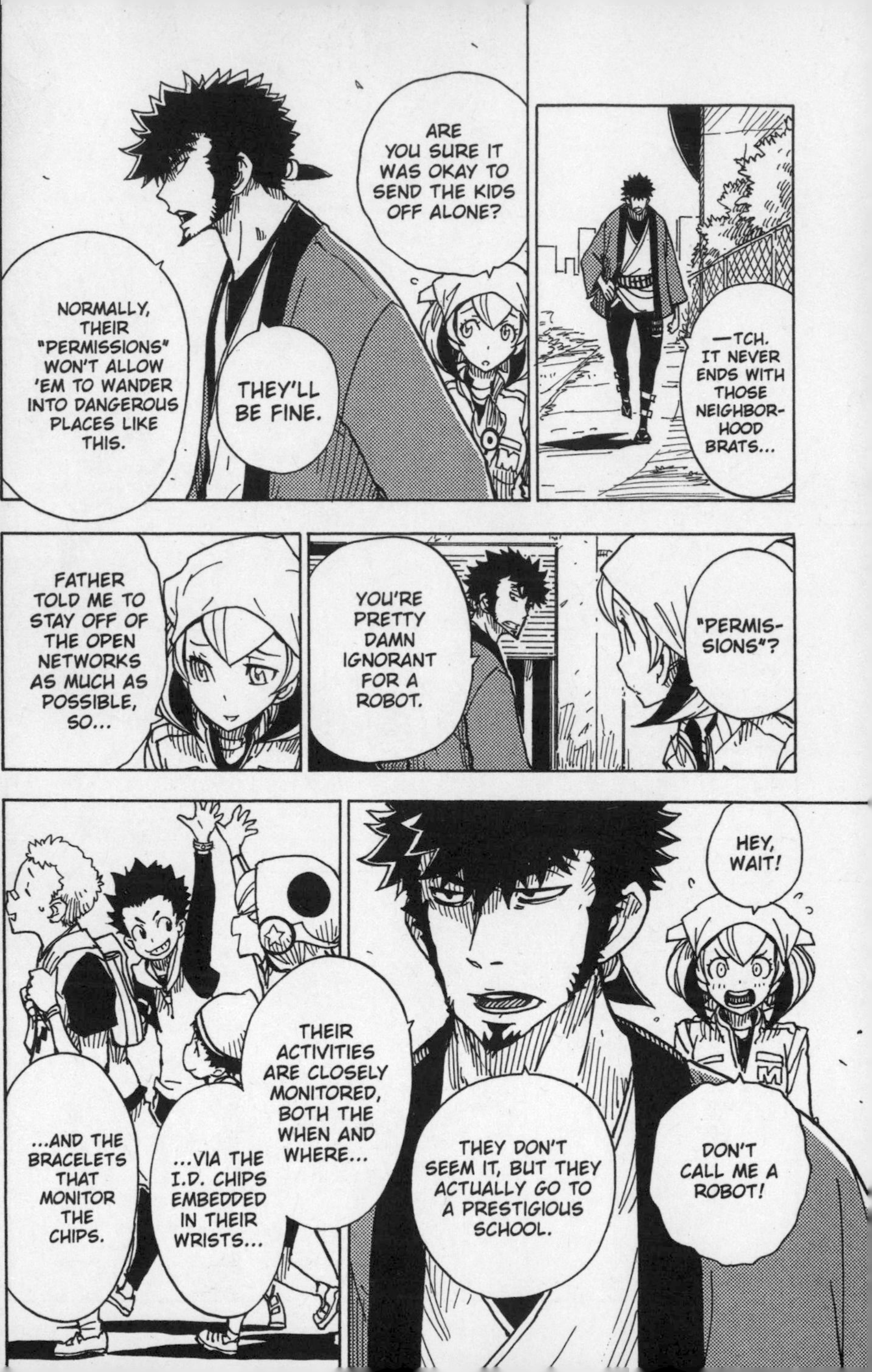
—TCH. IT NEVER ENDS WITH THOSE NEIGHBOR-HOOD BRATS...
ARE YOU SURE IT WAS OKAY TO SEND THE KIDS OFF ALONE?
THEY'LL BE FINE.
NORMALLY, THEIR "PERMISSIONS" WON'T ALLOW 'EM TO WANDER INTO DANGEROUS PLACES LIKE THIS.
"PERMIS-SIONS"?
YOU'RE PRETTY DAMN IGNORANT FOR A ROBOT.
FATHER TOLD ME TO STAY OFF OF THE OPEN NETWORKS AS MUCH AS POSSIBLE, SO...
HEY, WAIT!
DON'T CALL ME A ROBOT!
THEY DON'T SEEM IT, BUT THEY ACTUALLY GO TO A PRESTIGIOUS SCHOOL.
THEIR ACTIVITIES ARE CLOSELY MONITORED, BOTH THE WHEN AND WHERE...
...VIA THE I.D. CHIPS EMBEDDED IN THEIR WRISTS...
...AND THE BRACELETS THAT MONITOR THE CHIPS.

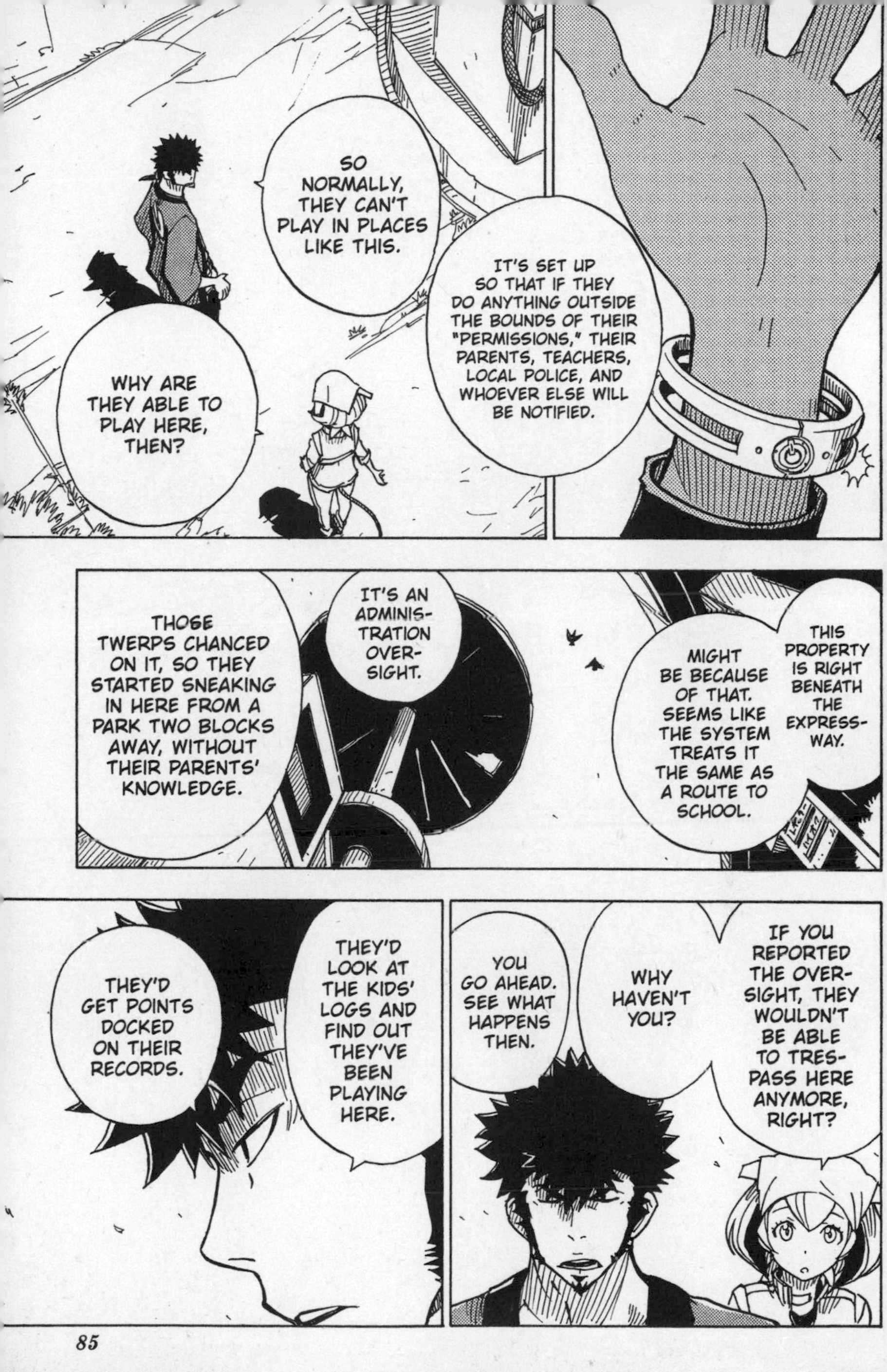
IT'S SET UP SO THAT IF THEY DO ANYTHING OUTSIDE THE BOUNDS OF THEIR "PERMISSIONS," THEIR PARENTS, TEACHERS, LOCAL POLICE, AND WHOEVER ELSE WILL BE NOTIFIED.
SO NORMALLY, THEY CAN'T PLAY IN PLACES LIKE THIS.
WHY ARE THEY ABLE TO PLAY HERE, THEN?
THIS PROPERTY IS RIGHT BENEATH THE EXPRESS-WAY.
MIGHT BE BECAUSE OF THAT. SEEMS LIKE THE SYSTEM TREATS IT THE SAME AS A ROUTE TO SCHOOL.
IT'S AN ADMINIS-TRATION OVER-SIGHT.
THOSE TWERPS CHANCED ON IT, SO THEY STARTED SNEAKING IN HERE FROM A PARK TWO BLOCKS AWAY, WITHOUT THEIR PARENTS' KNOWLEDGE.
IF YOU REPORTED THE OVER-SIGHT, THEY WOULDN'T BE ABLE TO TRES-PASS HERE ANYMORE, RIGHT?
WHY HAVEN'T YOU?
YOU GO AHEAD. SEE WHAT HAPPENS THEN.
THEY'D LOOK AT THE KIDS' LOGS AND FIND OUT THEY'VE BEEN PLAYING HERE.
THEY'D GET POINTS DOCKED ON THEIR RECORDS.

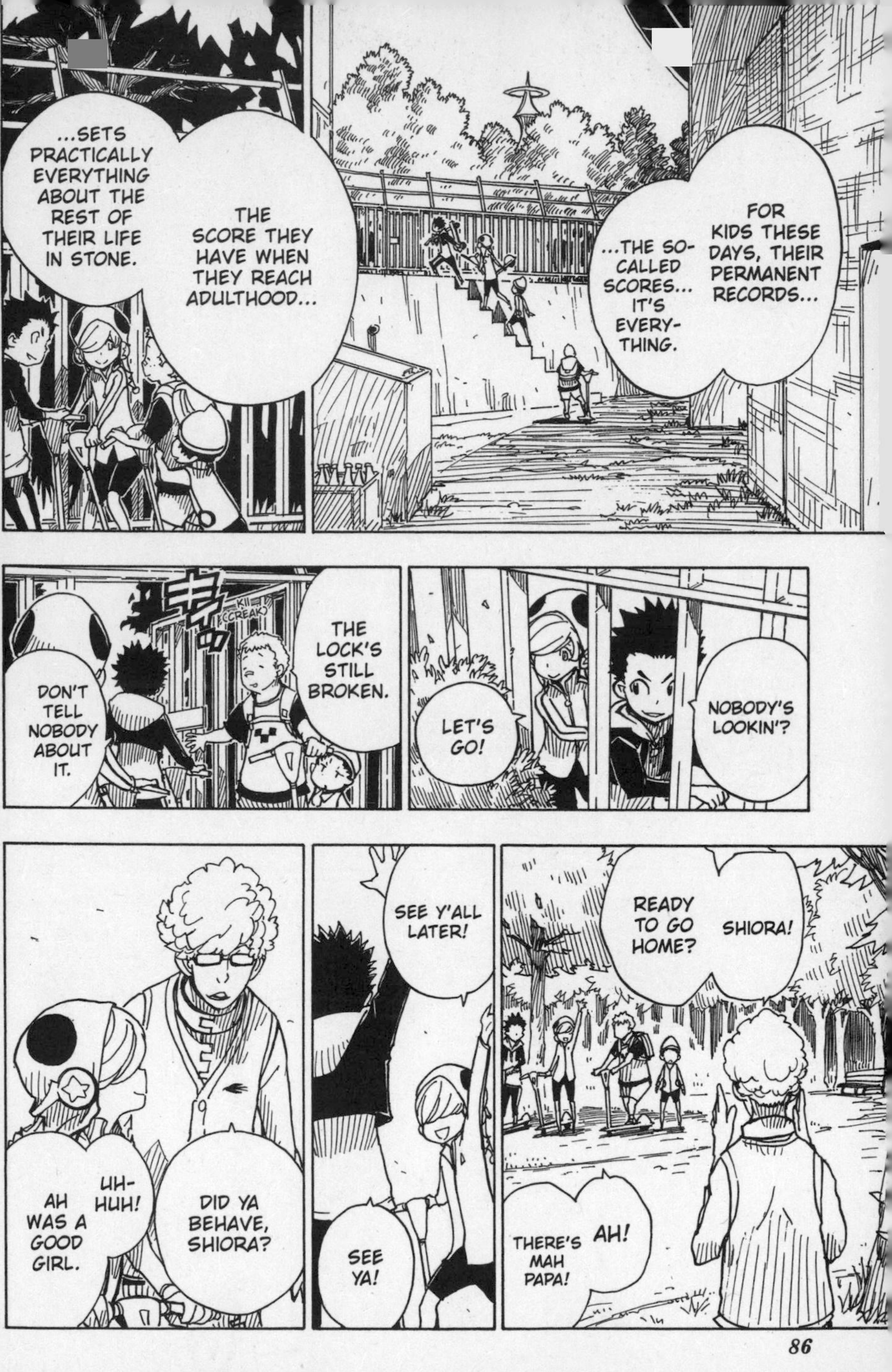
FOR KIDS THESE DAYS, THEIR PERMANENT RECORDS...
...THE SO-CALLED SCORES... IT'S EVERYTHING.
THE SCORE THEY HAVE WHEN THEY REACH ADULTHOOD...
...SETS PRACTICALLY EVERYTHING ABOUT THE REST OF THEIR LIFE IN STONE.
NOBODY'S LOOKIN'?
LET'S GO!
KI (CREAK)
THE LOCK'S STILL BROKEN.
DON'T TELL NOBODY ABOUT IT.
SHIORA!
READY TO GO HOME?
AH!
THERE'S MAH PAPA!
SEE Y'ALL LATER!
SEE YA!
DID YA BEHAVE, SHIORA?
UH-HUH!
AH WAS A GOOD GIRL.

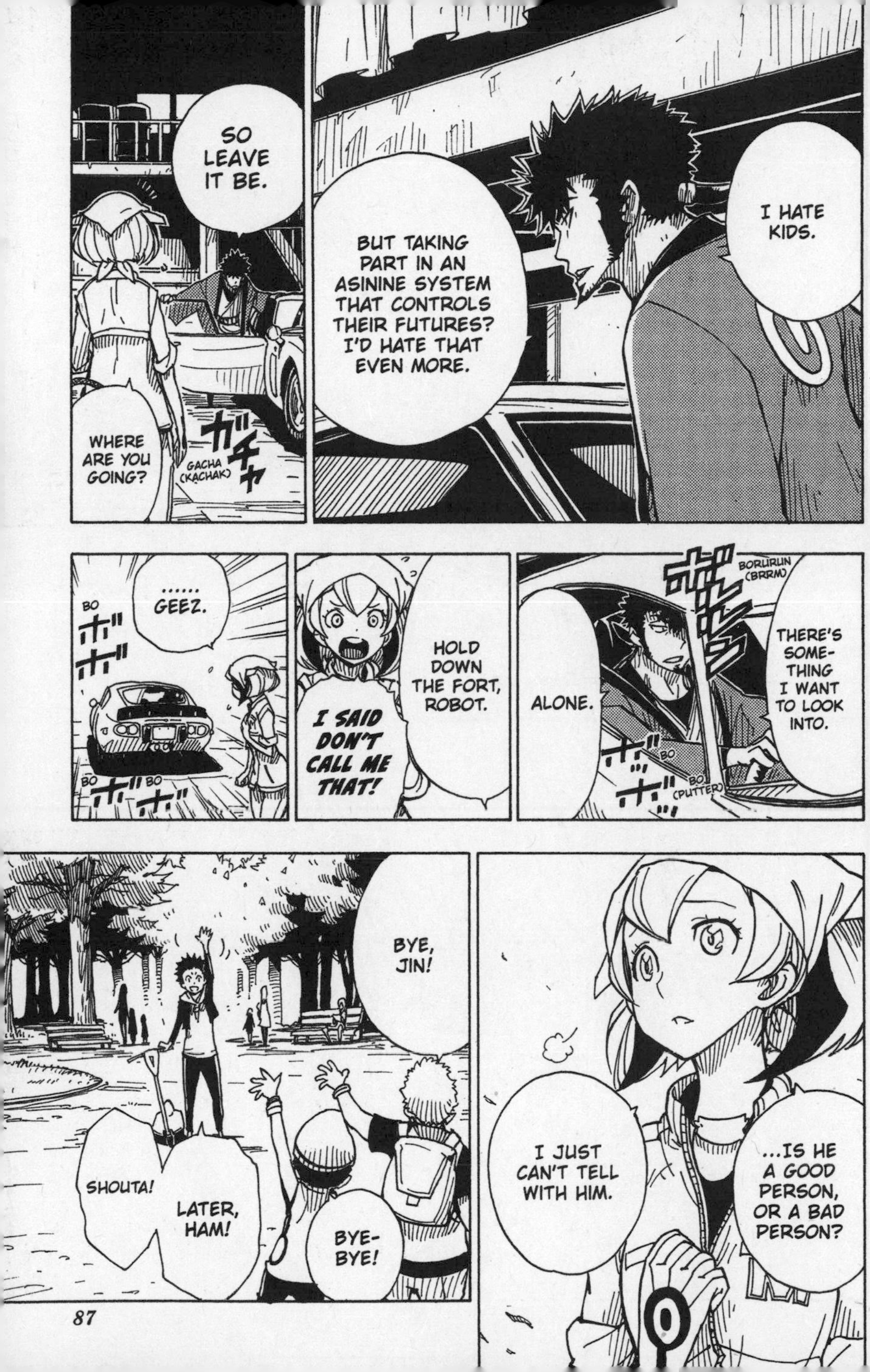
I HATE KIDS.
BUT TAKING PART IN AN ASININE SYSTEM THAT CONTROLS THEIR FUTURES? I'D HATE THAT EVEN MORE.
SO LEAVE IT BE.
GACHA (KACHAK)
WHERE ARE YOU GOING?
BORURUN (BRRM)
THERE'S SOME-THING I WANT TO LOOK INTO.
ALONE.
BO BO (PUTTER)
HOLD DOWN THE FORT, ROBOT.
I SAID DON'T CALL ME THAT!
...... GEEZ.
BO
BO BO
...IS HE A GOOD PERSON, OR A BAD PERSON?
I JUST CAN'T TELL WITH HIM.
BYE, JIN!
LATER, HAM!
SHOUTA!
BYE-BYE!

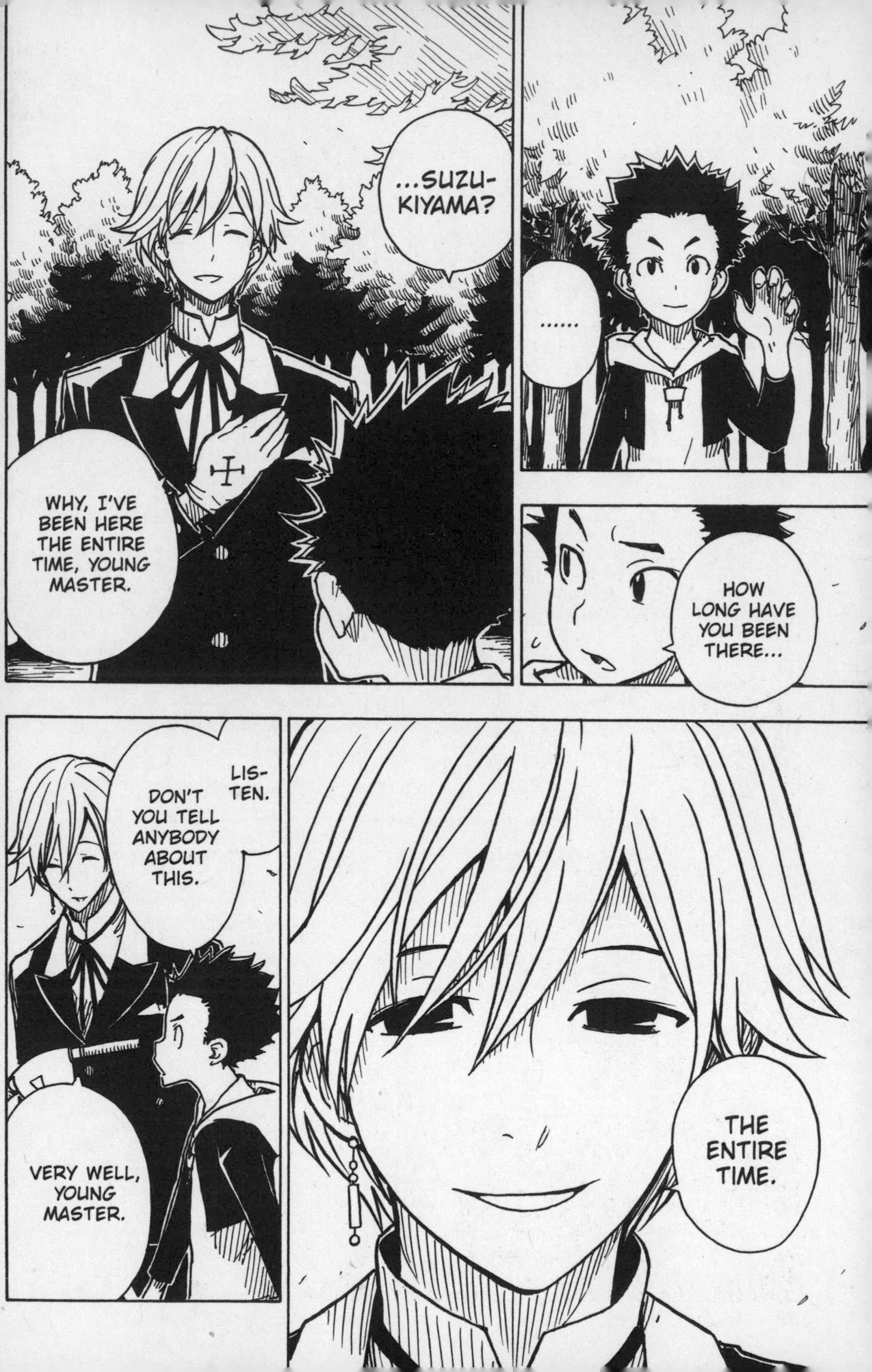
......
HOW LONG HAVE YOU BEEN THERE...
...SUZU-KIYAMA?
WHY, I'VE BEEN HERE THE ENTIRE TIME, YOUNG MASTER.
THE ENTIRE TIME.
LIS-TEN.
DON'T YOU TELL ANYBODY ABOUT THIS.
VERY WELL, YOUNG MASTER.

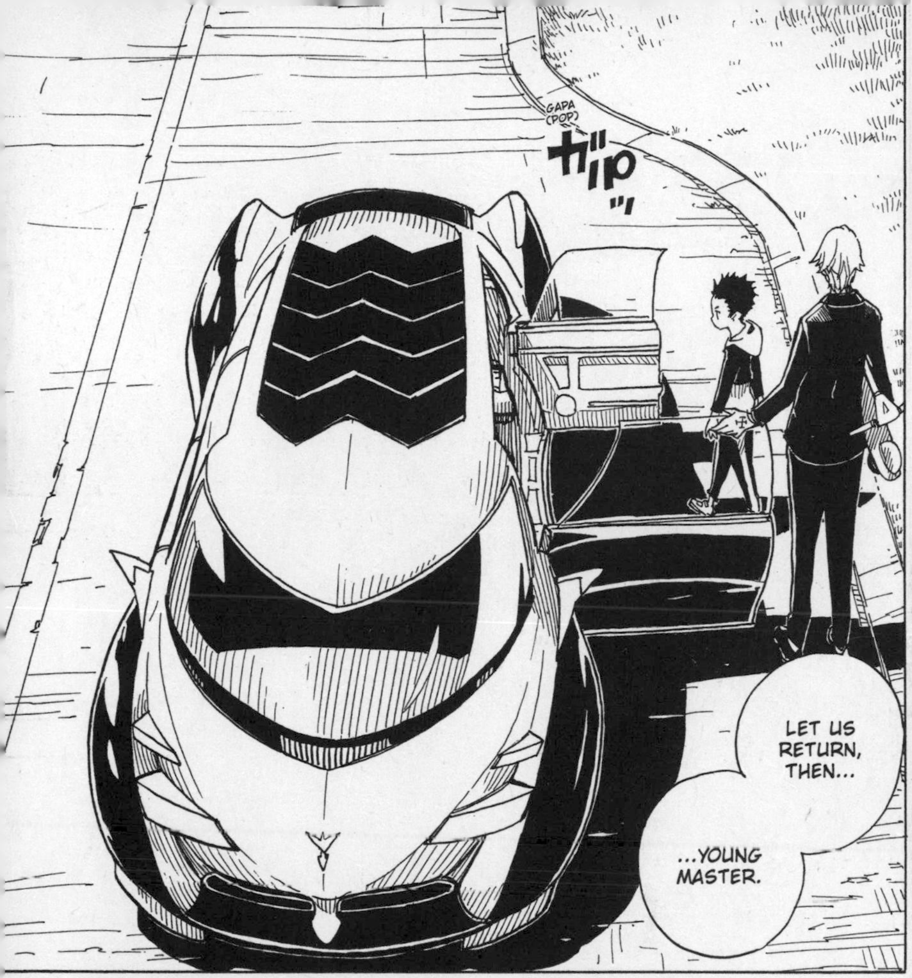
GAPA (POP)
ガパッ
LET US RETURN, THEN...
...YOUNG MASTER.

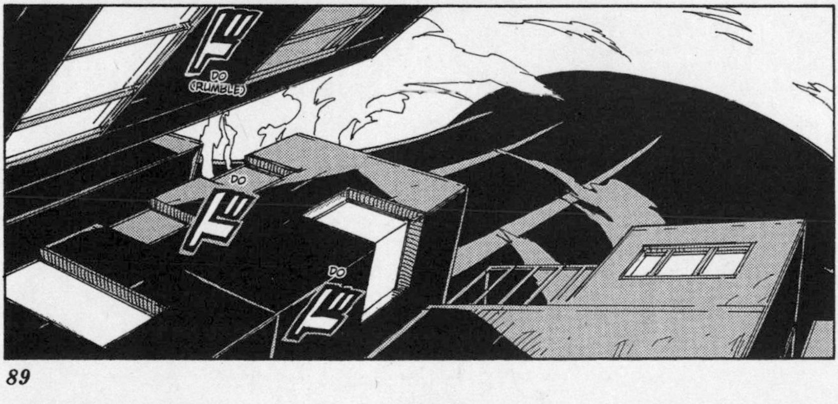
ド
DO (RUMBLE)
DO
ド
DO
ド

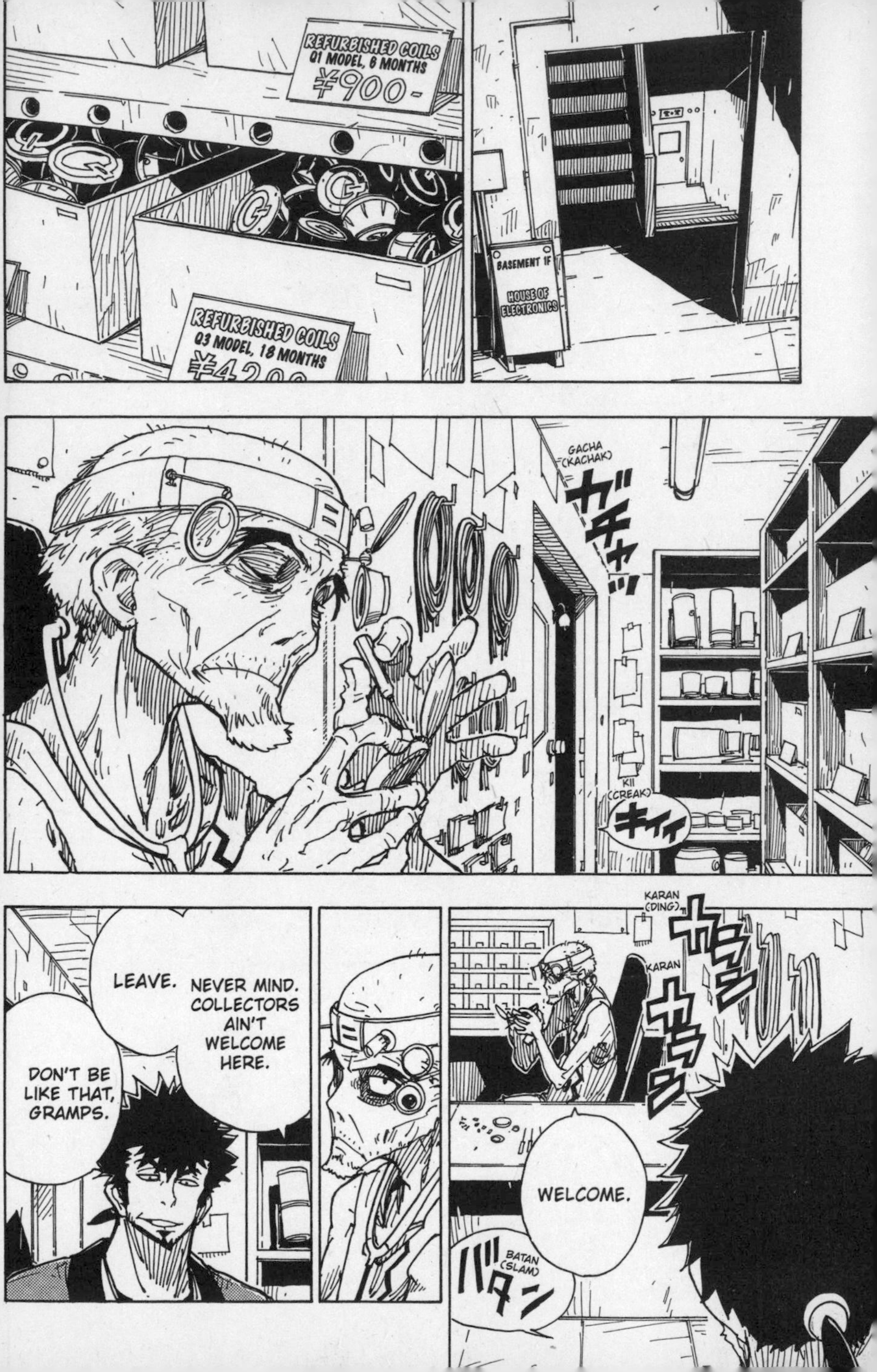
BASEMENT 1F
HOUSE OF ELECTRONICS
REFURBISHED COILS
Q1 MODEL, 6 MONTHS
¥900-
REFURBISHED COILS
Q3 MODEL, 18 MONTHS
¥4200
GACHA (KACHAK)
ガチャッ
KII (CREAK)
キイイ
KARAN (DING)
カラン
KARAN
カラン
WELCOME.
BATAN (SLAM)
バタン
NEVER MIND. COLLECTORS AIN'T WELCOME HERE.
LEAVE.
DON'T BE LIKE THAT, GRAMPS.

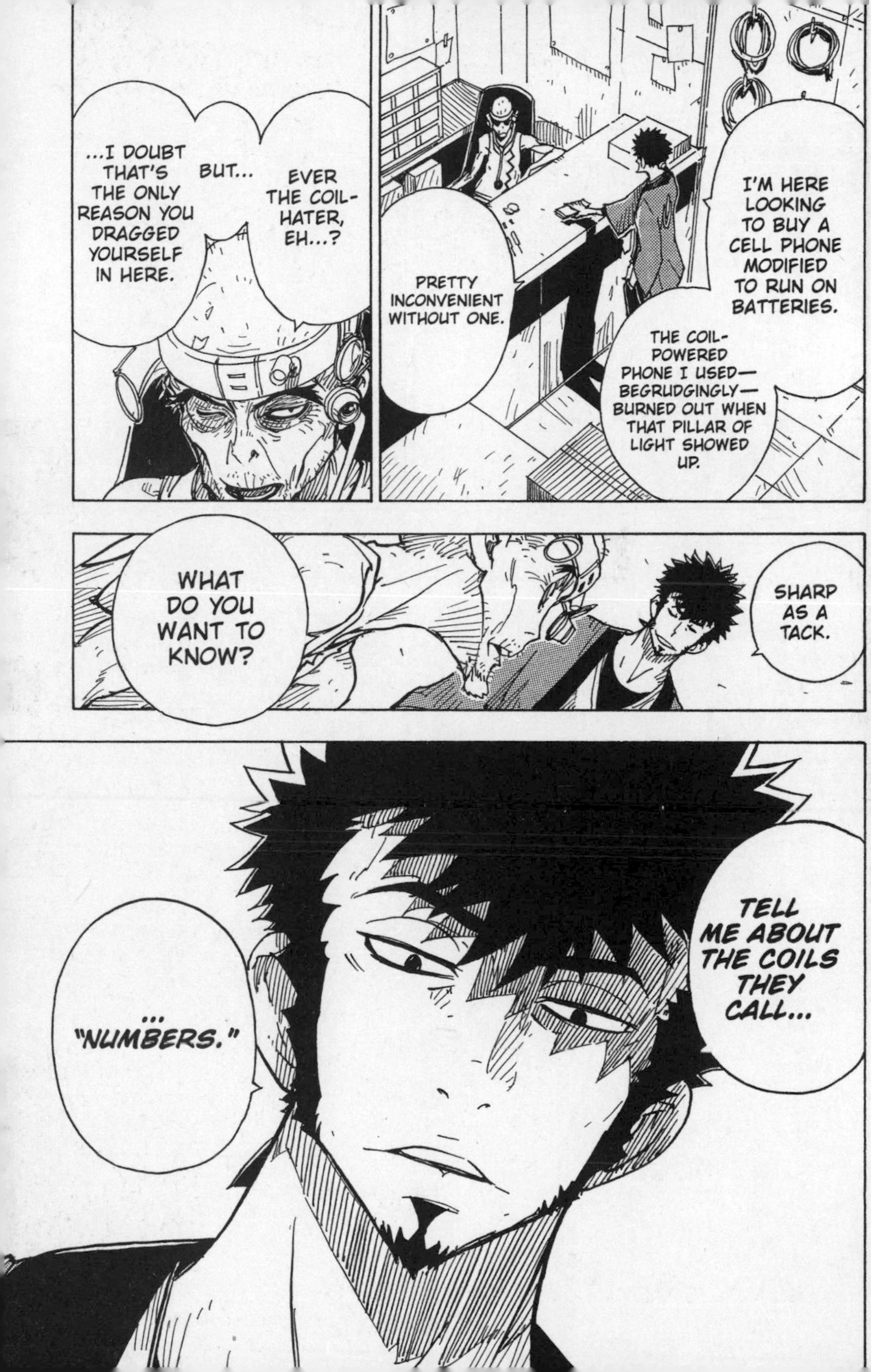

I'M HERE LOOKING TO BUY A CELL PHONE MODIFIED TO RUN ON BATTERIES.
THE COIL-POWERED PHONE I USED—BEGRUDGINGLY—BURNED OUT WHEN THAT PILLAR OF LIGHT SHOWED UP.
PRETTY INCONVENIENT WITHOUT ONE.
EVER THE COIL-HATER, EH...?
BUT...
...I DOUBT THAT'S THE ONLY REASON YOU DRAGGED YOURSELF IN HERE.
SHARP AS A TACK.
WHAT DO YOU WANT TO KNOW?
TELL ME ABOUT THE COILS THEY CALL...
... "NUMBERS."

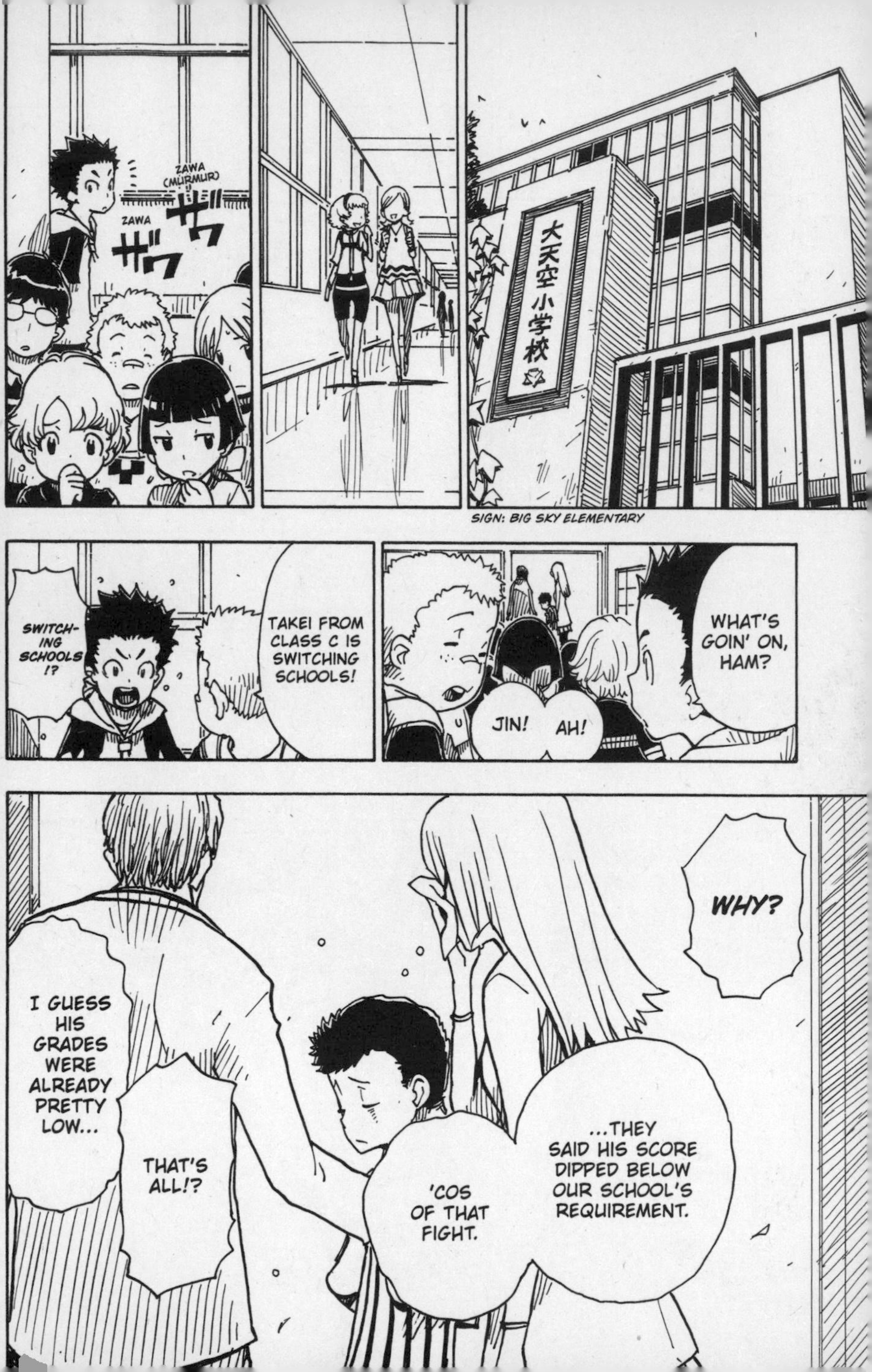
大天空小学校
SIGN: BIG SKY ELEMENTARY
ZAWA (MURMUR)
ザワ
ZAWA
ザワ
WHAT'S GOIN' ON, HAM?
AH!
JIN!
TAKEI FROM CLASS C IS SWITCHING SCHOOLS!
SWITCHING SCHOOLS!?
WHY?
I GUESS HIS GRADES WERE ALREADY PRETTY LOW...
...THEY SAID HIS SCORE DIPPED BELOW OUR SCHOOL'S REQUIREMENT.
'COS OF THAT FIGHT.
THAT'S ALL!?

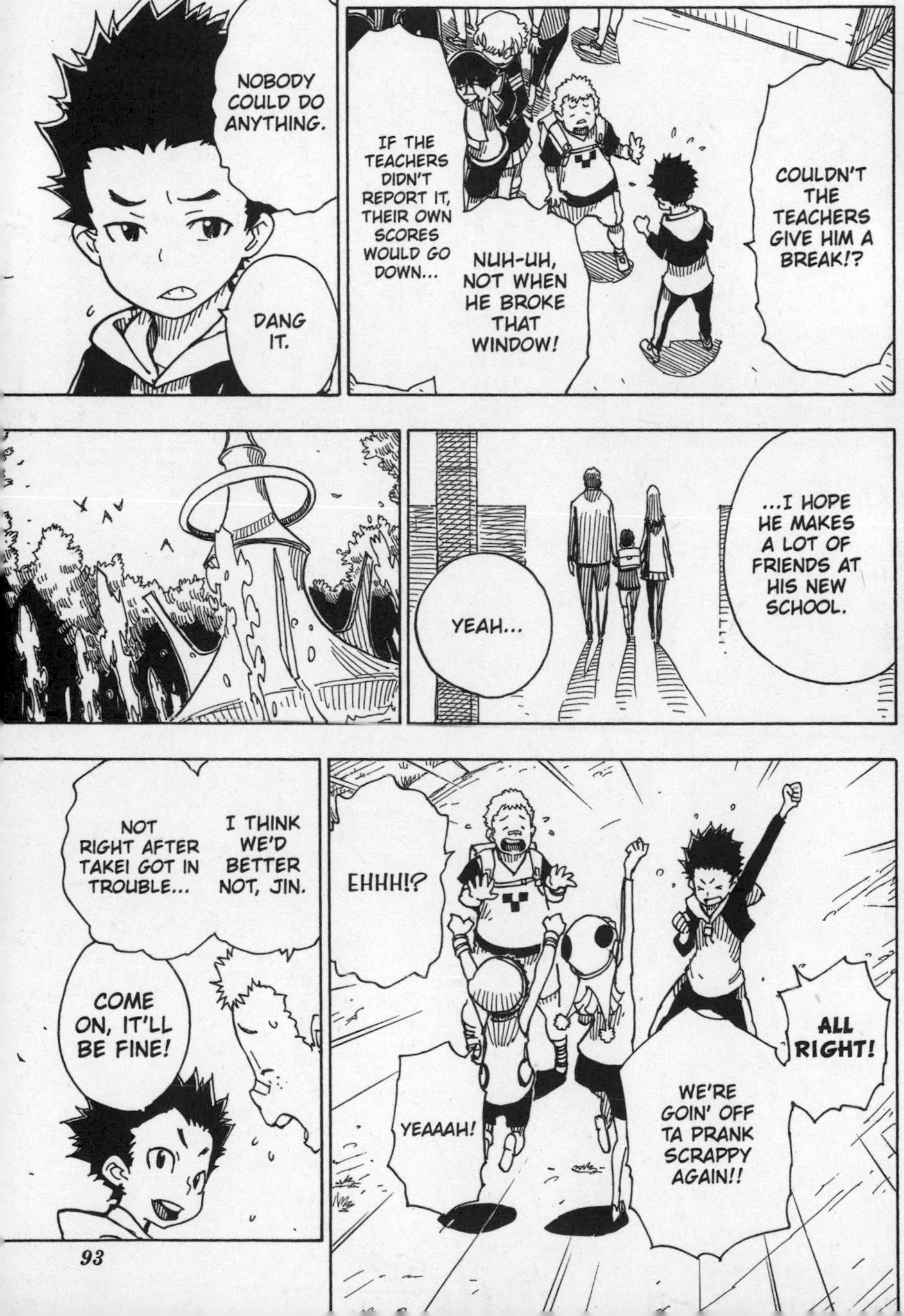
COULDN'T THE TEACHERS GIVE HIM A BREAK!?
NUH-UH, NOT WHEN HE BROKE THAT WINDOW!
IF THE TEACHERS DIDN'T REPORT IT, THEIR OWN SCORES WOULD GO DOWN...
NOBODY COULD DO ANYTHING.
DANG IT.
...I HOPE HE MAKES A LOT OF FRIENDS AT HIS NEW SCHOOL.
YEAH...
ALL RIGHT!
WE'RE GOIN' OFF TA PRANK SCRAPPY AGAIN!!
EHHH!?
YEAAAH!
I THINK WE'D BETTER NOT, JIN.
NOT RIGHT AFTER TAKEI GOT IN TROUBLE...
COME ON, IT'LL BE FINE!

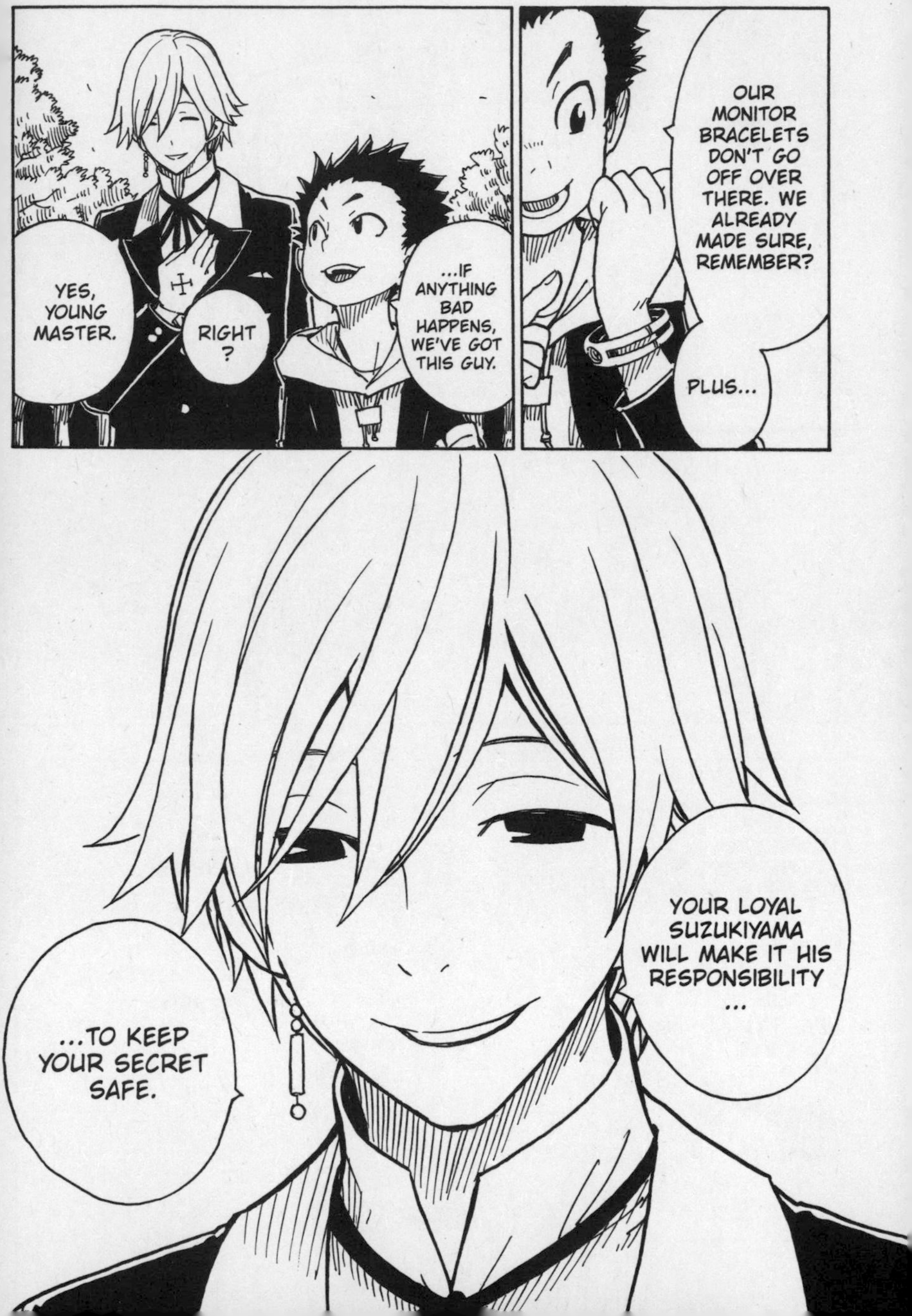
OUR MONITOR BRACELETS DON'T GO OFF OVER THERE. WE ALREADY MADE SURE, REMEMBER?
PLUS...
...IF ANYTHING BAD HAPPENS, WE'VE GOT THIS GUY.
RIGHT?
YES, YOUNG MASTER.
YOUR LOYAL SUZUKIYAMA WILL MAKE IT HIS RESPONSIBILITY ...
...TO KEEP YOUR SECRET SAFE.

FILE.12
SORROW

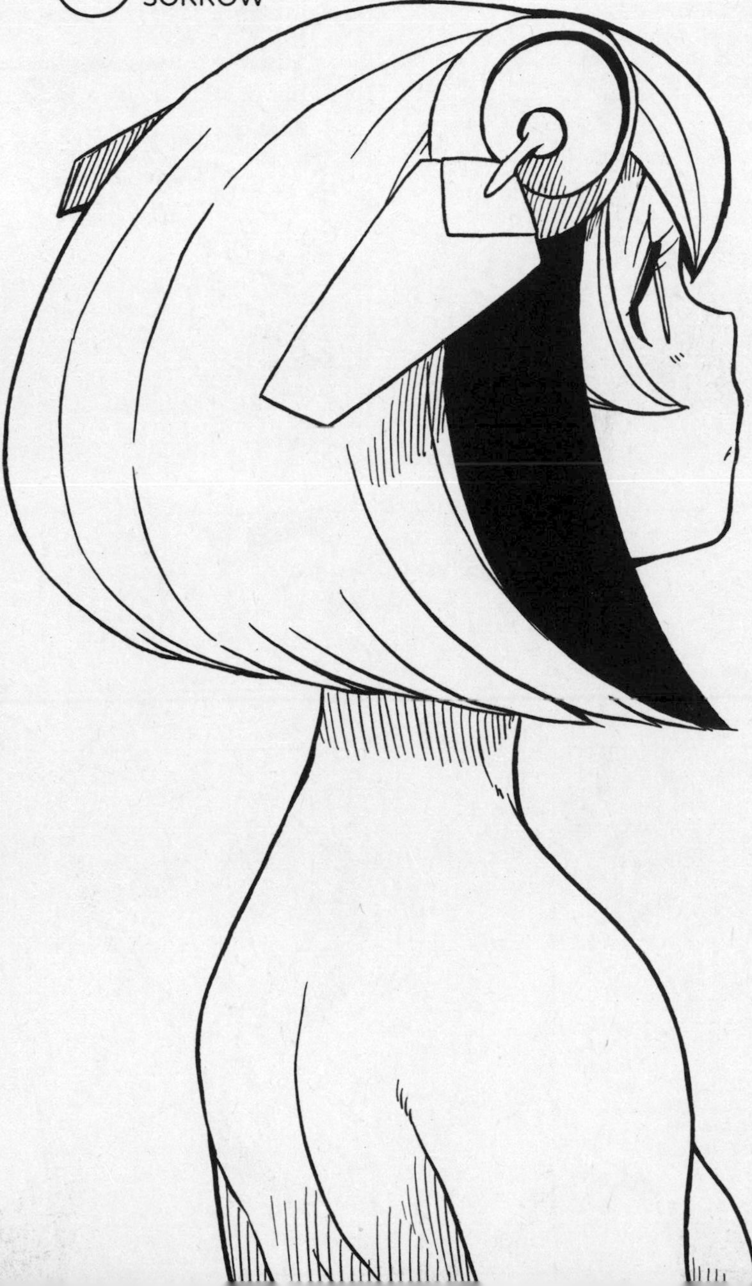

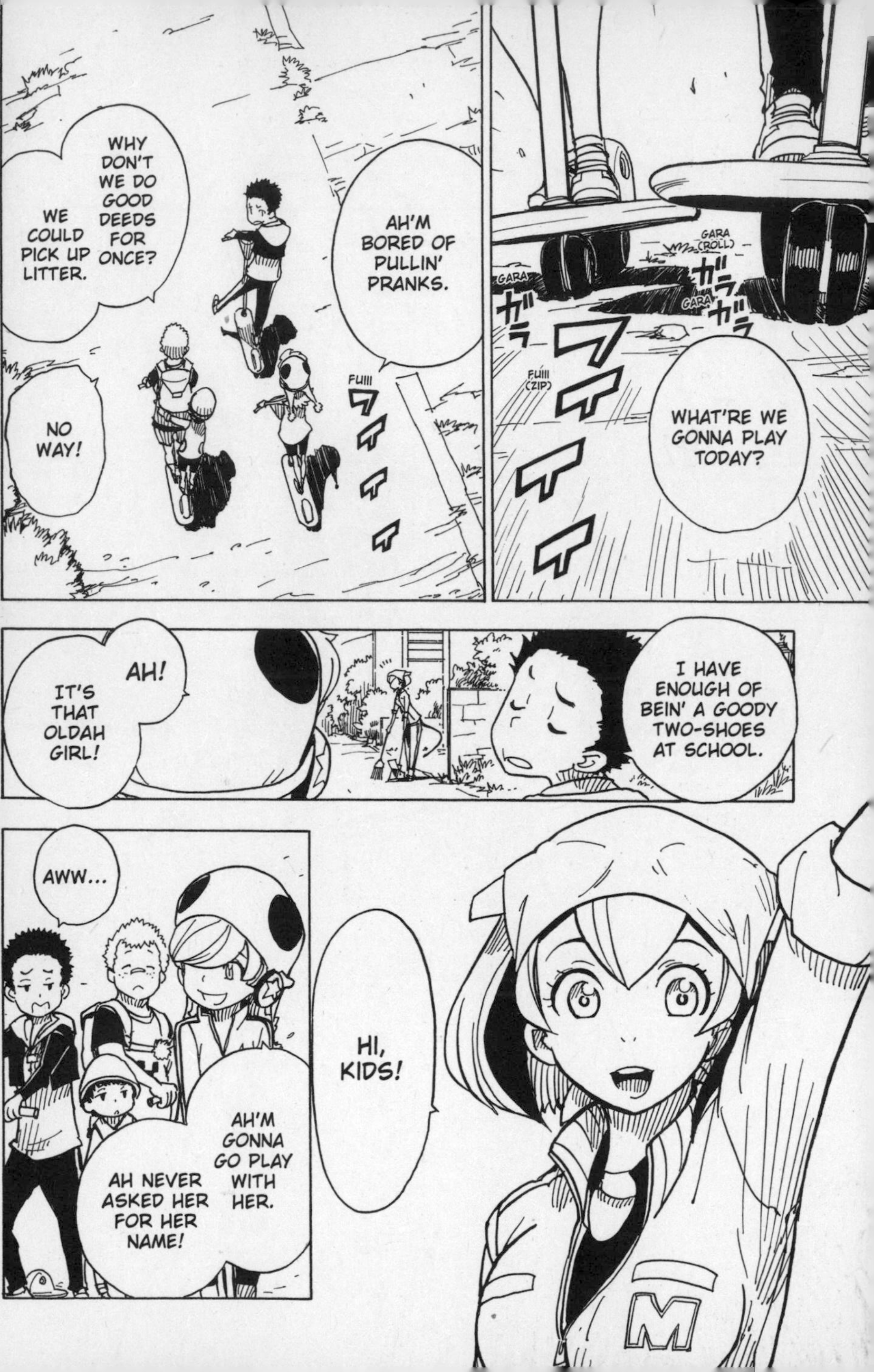
GARA (ROLL)
GARA
GARA
FUIII (ZIP)
WHAT'RE WE GONNA PLAY TODAY?
AH'M BORED OF PULLIN' PRANKS.
FUIII
WHY DON'T WE DO GOOD DEEDS FOR ONCE?
WE COULD PICK UP LITTER.
NO WAY!
I HAVE ENOUGH OF BEIN' A GOODY TWO-SHOES AT SCHOOL.
AH!
IT'S THAT OLDAH GIRL!
HI, KIDS!
AWW...
AH'M GONNA GO PLAY WITH HER.
AH NEVER ASKED HER FOR HER NAME!

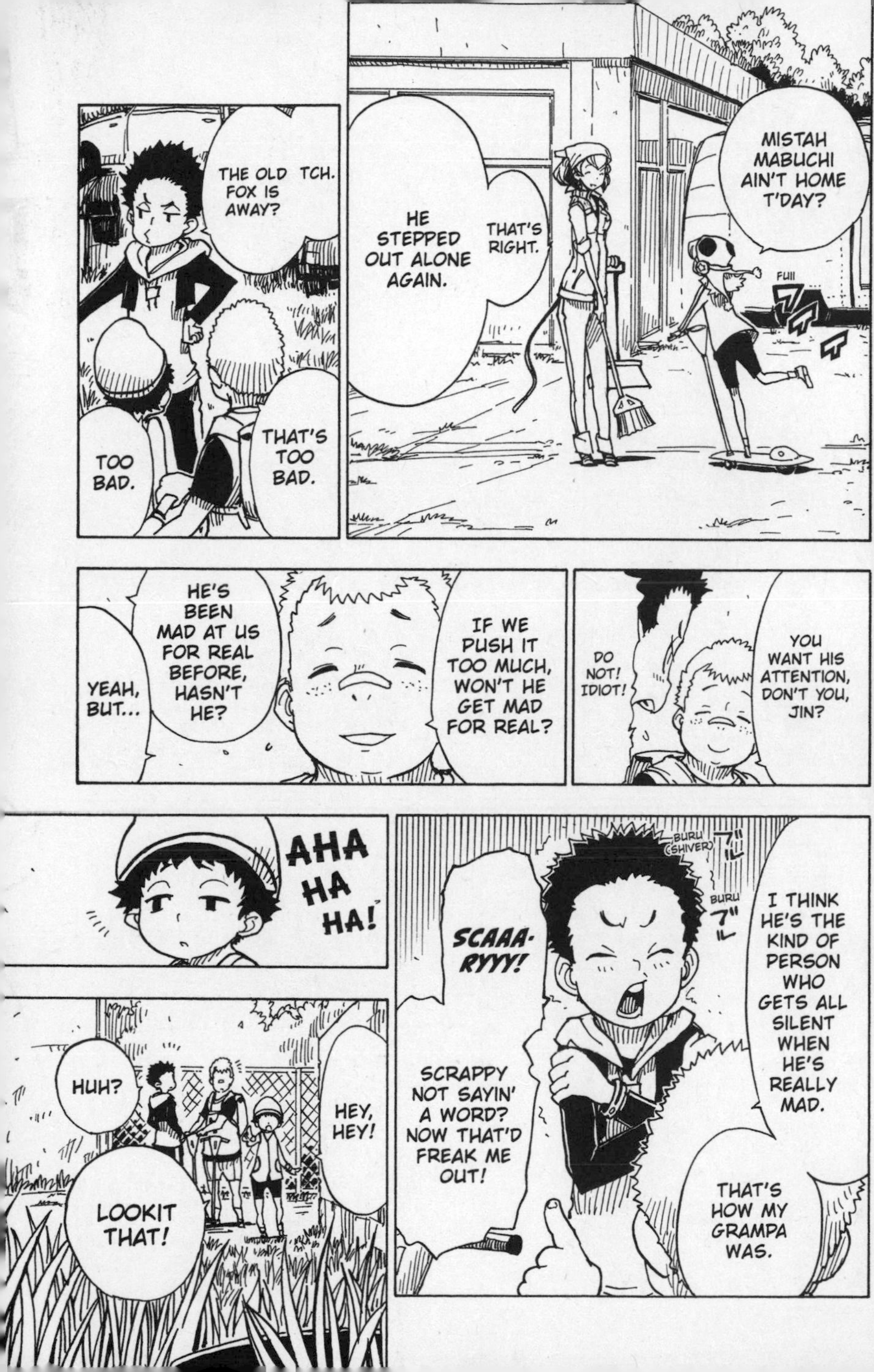
MISTAH MABUCHI AIN'T HOME T'DAY?
FUII
THAT'S RIGHT.
HE STEPPED OUT ALONE AGAIN.
THE OLD FOX IS AWAY?
TCH.
THAT'S TOO BAD.
TOO BAD.
YOU WANT HIS ATTENTION, DON'T YOU, JIN?
DO NOT! IDIOT!
IF WE PUSH IT TOO MUCH, WON'T HE GET MAD FOR REAL?
HE'S BEEN MAD AT US FOR REAL BEFORE, HASN'T HE?
YEAH, BUT...
I THINK HE'S THE KIND OF PERSON WHO GETS ALL SILENT WHEN HE'S REALLY MAD.
BURU (SHIVER)
BURU
SCAAA-RYYY!
THAT'S HOW MY GRAMPA WAS.
SCRAPPY NOT SAYIN' A WORD? NOW THAT'D FREAK ME OUT!
AHA HA HA!
HEY, HEY!
HUH?
LOOKIT THAT!

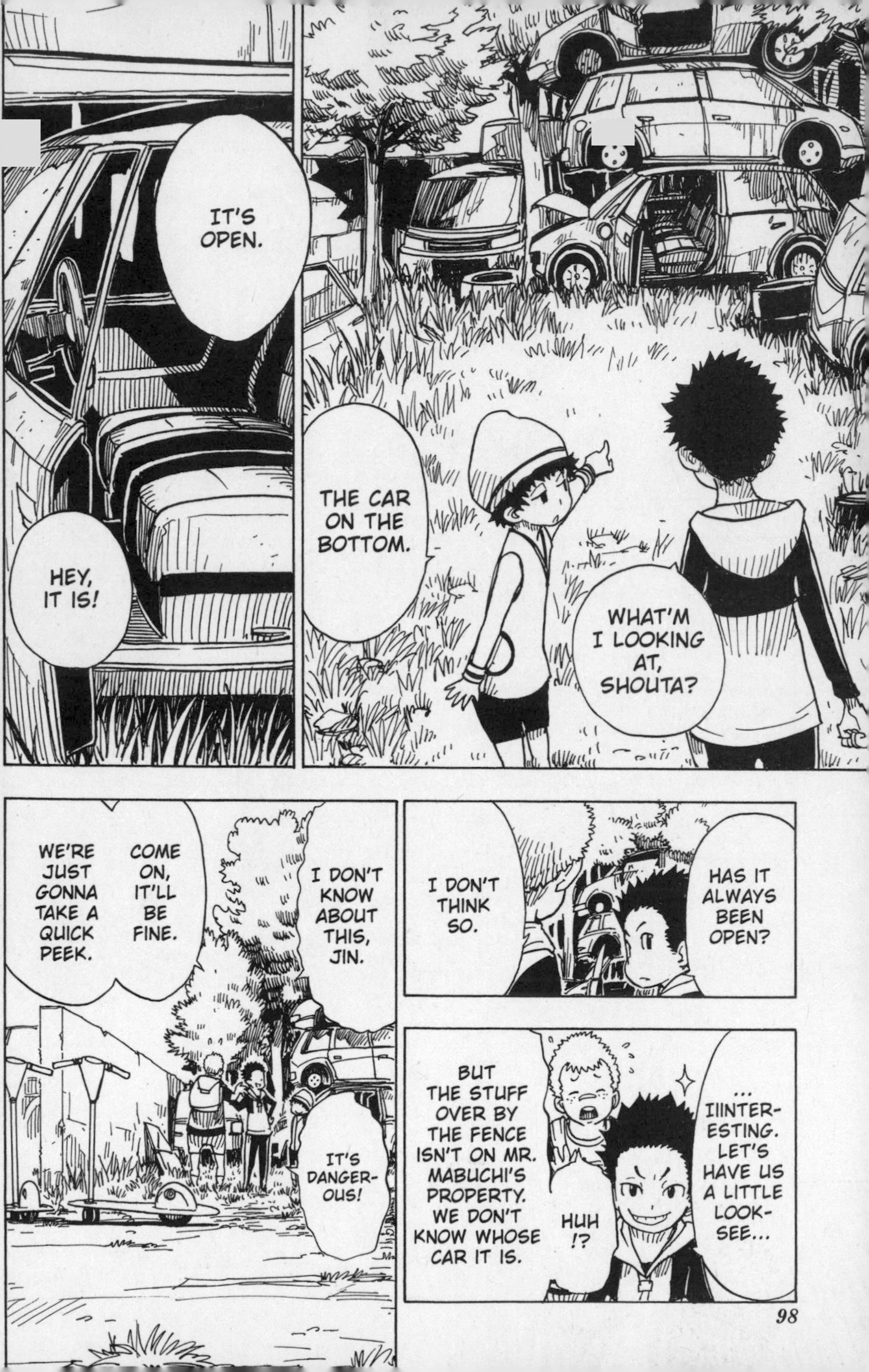

WHAT'M I LOOKING AT, SHOUTA?
THE CAR ON THE BOTTOM.
IT'S OPEN.
HEY, IT IS!
HAS IT ALWAYS BEEN OPEN?
I DON'T THINK SO.
...IIINTER-ESTING. LET'S HAVE US A LITTLE LOOK-SEE...
HUH!?
BUT THE STUFF OVER BY THE FENCE ISN'T ON MR. MABUCHI'S PROPERTY. WE DON'T KNOW WHOSE CAR IT IS.
I DON'T KNOW ABOUT THIS, JIN.
COME ON, IT'LL BE FINE.
WE'RE JUST GONNA TAKE A QUICK PEEK.
IT'S DANGEROUS!

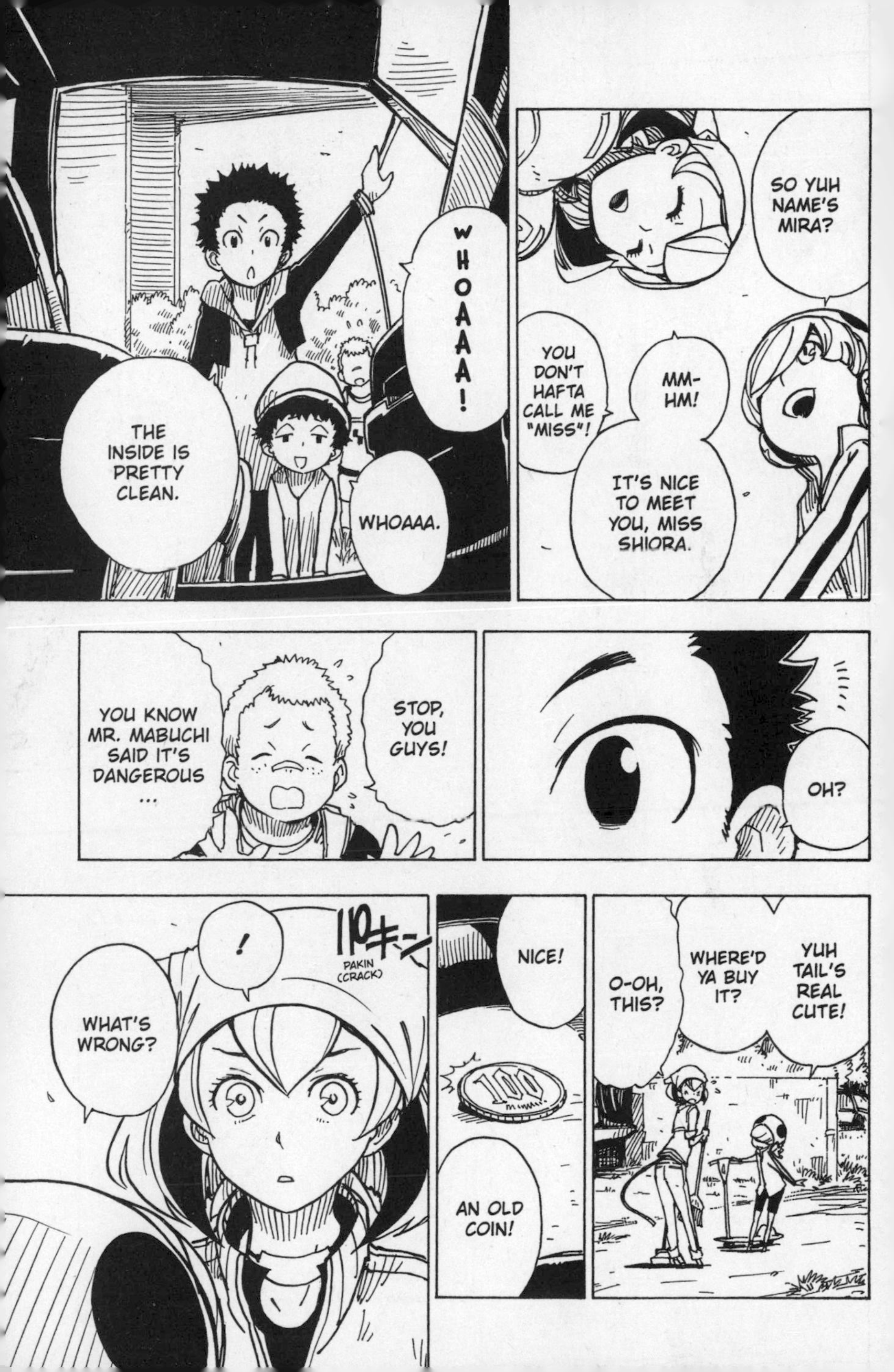
SO YUH NAME'S MIRA?
MM-HM!
IT'S NICE TO MEET YOU, MISS SHIORA.
YOU DON'T HAFTA CALL ME "MISS"!
WHOAAAA!
WHOAAA.
THE INSIDE IS PRETTY CLEAN.
OH?
STOP, YOU GUYS!
YOU KNOW MR. MABUCHI SAID IT'S DANGEROUS ...
YUH TAIL'S REAL CUTE!
WHERE'D YA BUY IT?
O-OH, THIS?
NICE!
AN OLD COIN!
PAKIN (CRACK)
!
WHAT'S WRONG?

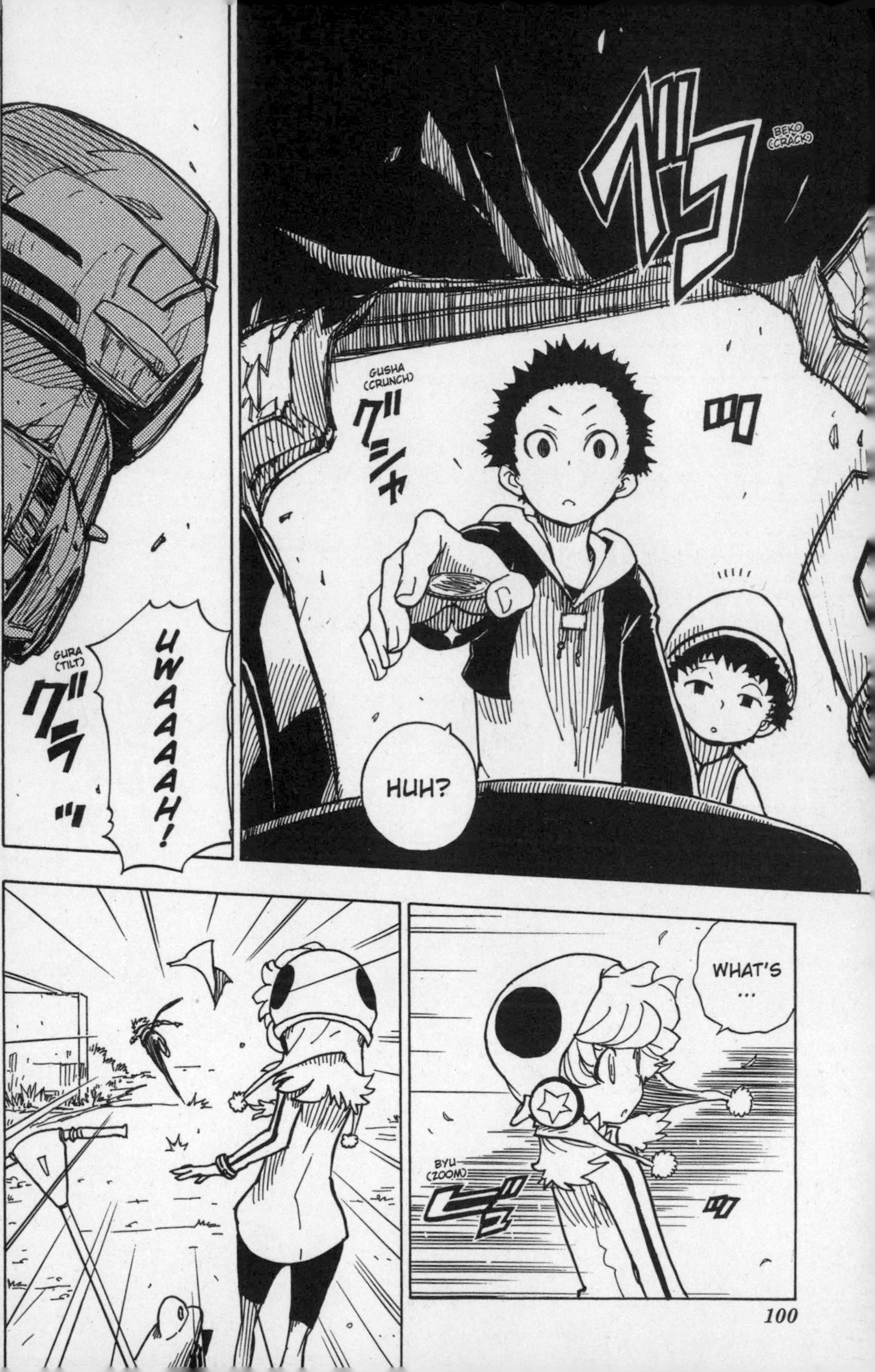
BEKO (CRACK)
GUSHA (CRUNCH)
HUH?
GURA (TILT)
UWAAAAAH!
WHAT'S ...
BYU (ZOOM)

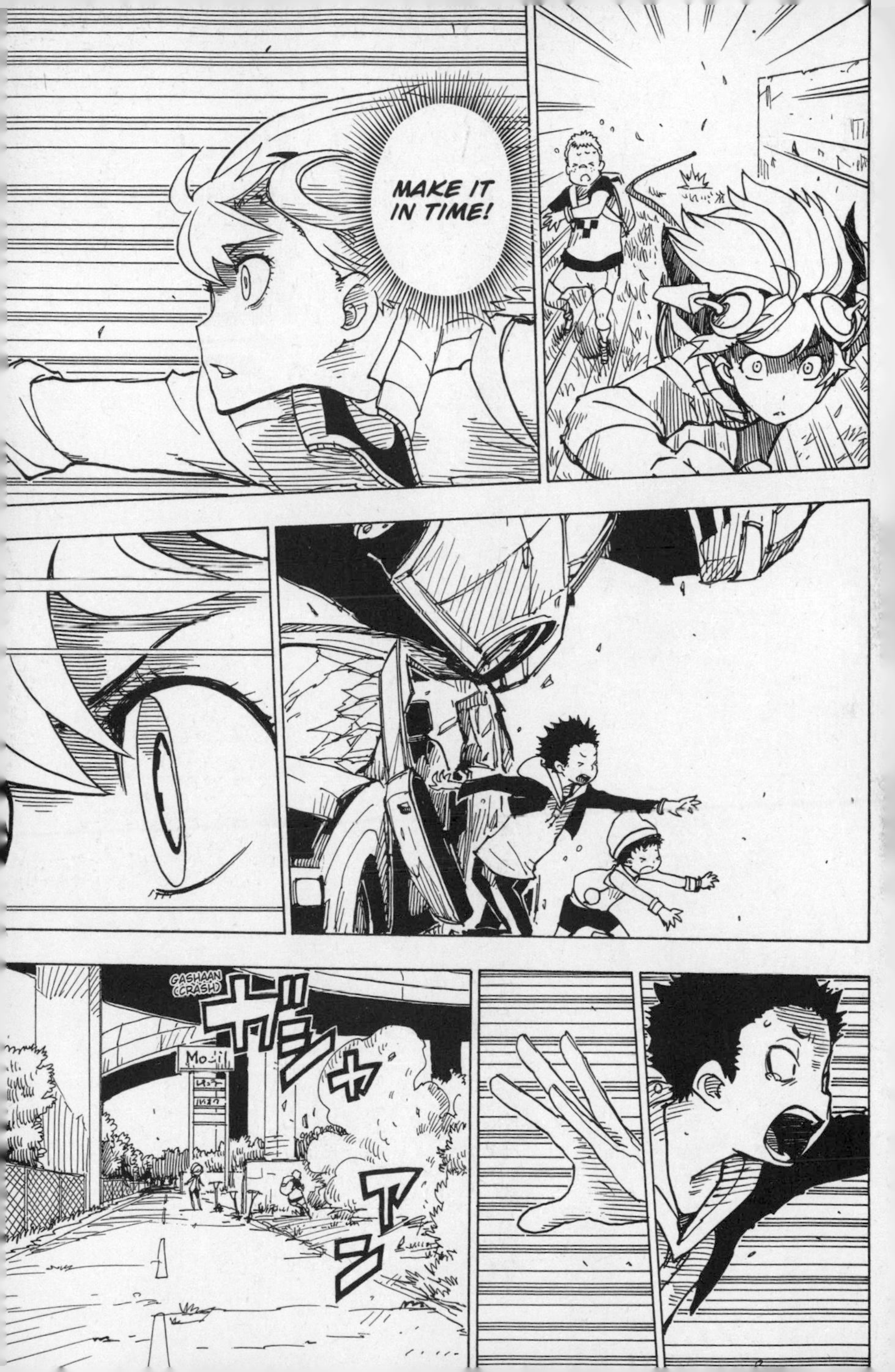
MAKE IT IN TIME!
GASHAAN (CRASH)

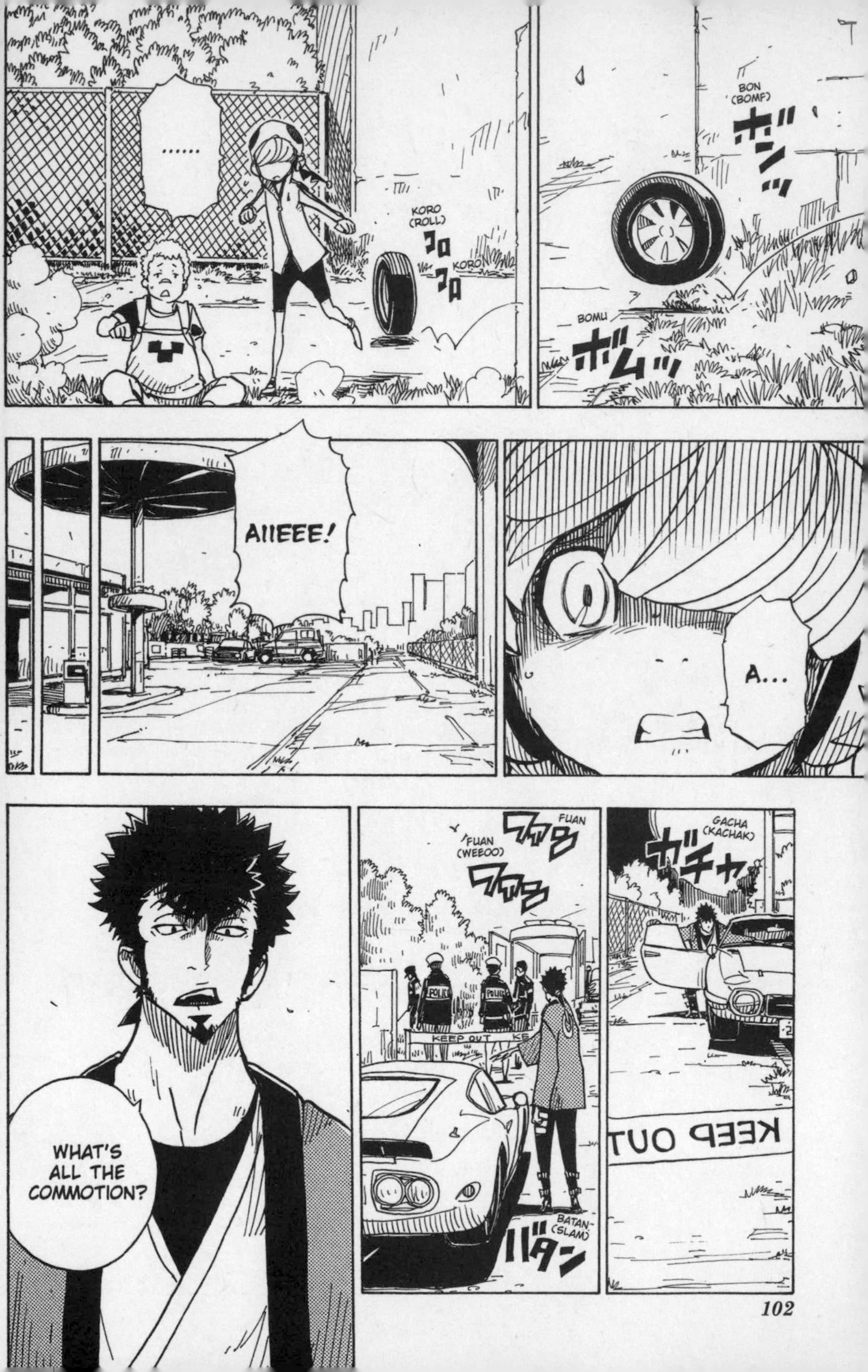
BON (BOMF)
ボンッ
BOMU
ボムッ
......
KORO (ROLL)
コロ
KORO
コロ
A...
AIIEEE!
GACHA (KACHAK)
ガチャ
KEEP OUT
FUAN
ファン
FUAN (WEEOO)
ファン
KEEP OUT KE
POLICE
POLICE
BATAN (SLAM)
バタン
WHAT'S ALL THE COMMOTION?

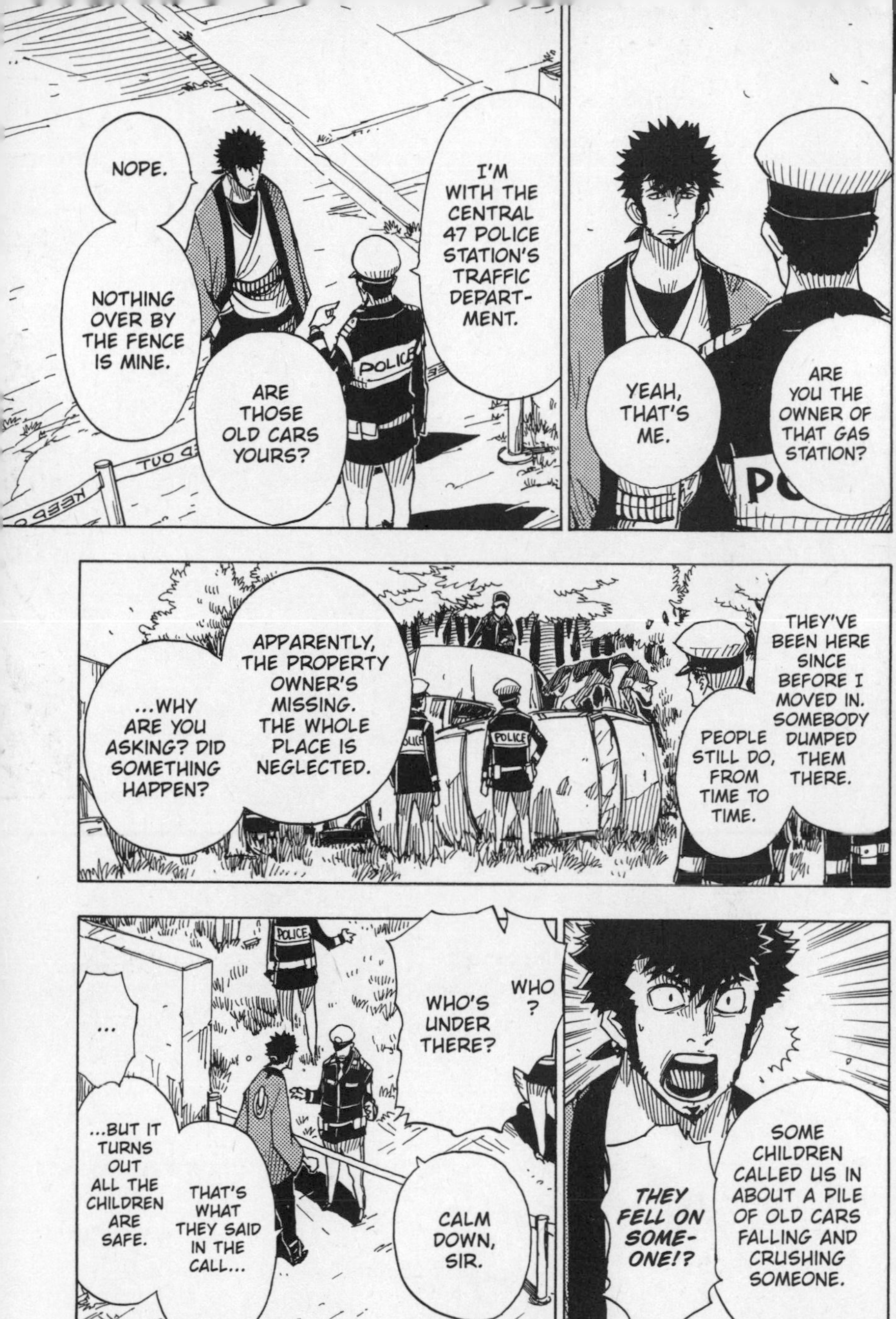
ARE YOU THE OWNER OF THAT GAS STATION?
YEAH, THAT'S ME.
I'M WITH THE CENTRAL 47 POLICE STATION'S TRAFFIC DEPART-MENT.
ARE THOSE OLD CARS YOURS?
NOPE.
NOTHING OVER BY THE FENCE IS MINE.
THEY'VE BEEN HERE SINCE BEFORE I MOVED IN. SOMEBODY DUMPED THEM THERE.
PEOPLE STILL DO, FROM TIME TO TIME.
APPARENTLY, THE PROPERTY OWNER'S MISSING. THE WHOLE PLACE IS NEGLECTED.
...WHY ARE YOU ASKING? DID SOMETHING HAPPEN?
SOME CHILDREN CALLED US IN ABOUT A PILE OF OLD CARS FALLING AND CRUSHING SOMEONE.
THEY FELL ON SOME-ONE!?
WHO?
WHO'S UNDER THERE?
CALM DOWN, SIR.
THAT'S WHAT THEY SAID IN THE CALL...
...BUT IT TURNS OUT ALL THE CHILDREN ARE SAFE.
...

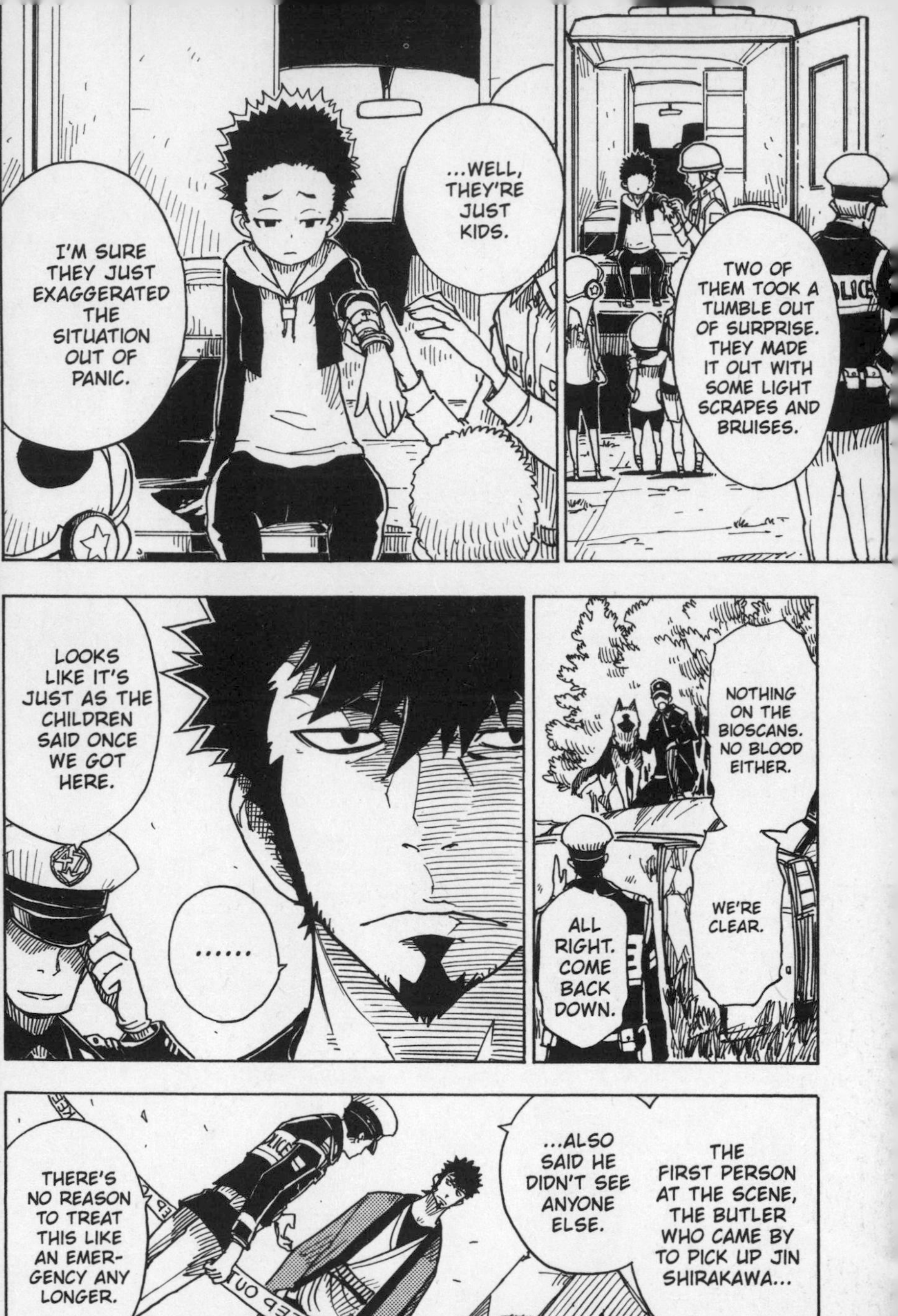
TWO OF THEM TOOK A TUMBLE OUT OF SURPRISE. THEY MADE IT OUT WITH SOME LIGHT SCRAPES AND BRUISES.
...WELL, THEY'RE JUST KIDS.
I'M SURE THEY JUST EXAGGERATED THE SITUATION OUT OF PANIC.
NOTHING ON THE BIOSCANS. NO BLOOD EITHER.
WE'RE CLEAR.
ALL RIGHT. COME BACK DOWN.
LOOKS LIKE IT'S JUST AS THE CHILDREN SAID ONCE WE GOT HERE.
......
THE FIRST PERSON AT THE SCENE, THE BUTLER WHO CAME BY TO PICK UP JIN SHIRAKAWA...
...ALSO SAID HE DIDN'T SEE ANYONE ELSE.
THERE'S NO REASON TO TREAT THIS LIKE AN EMER-GENCY ANY LONGER.

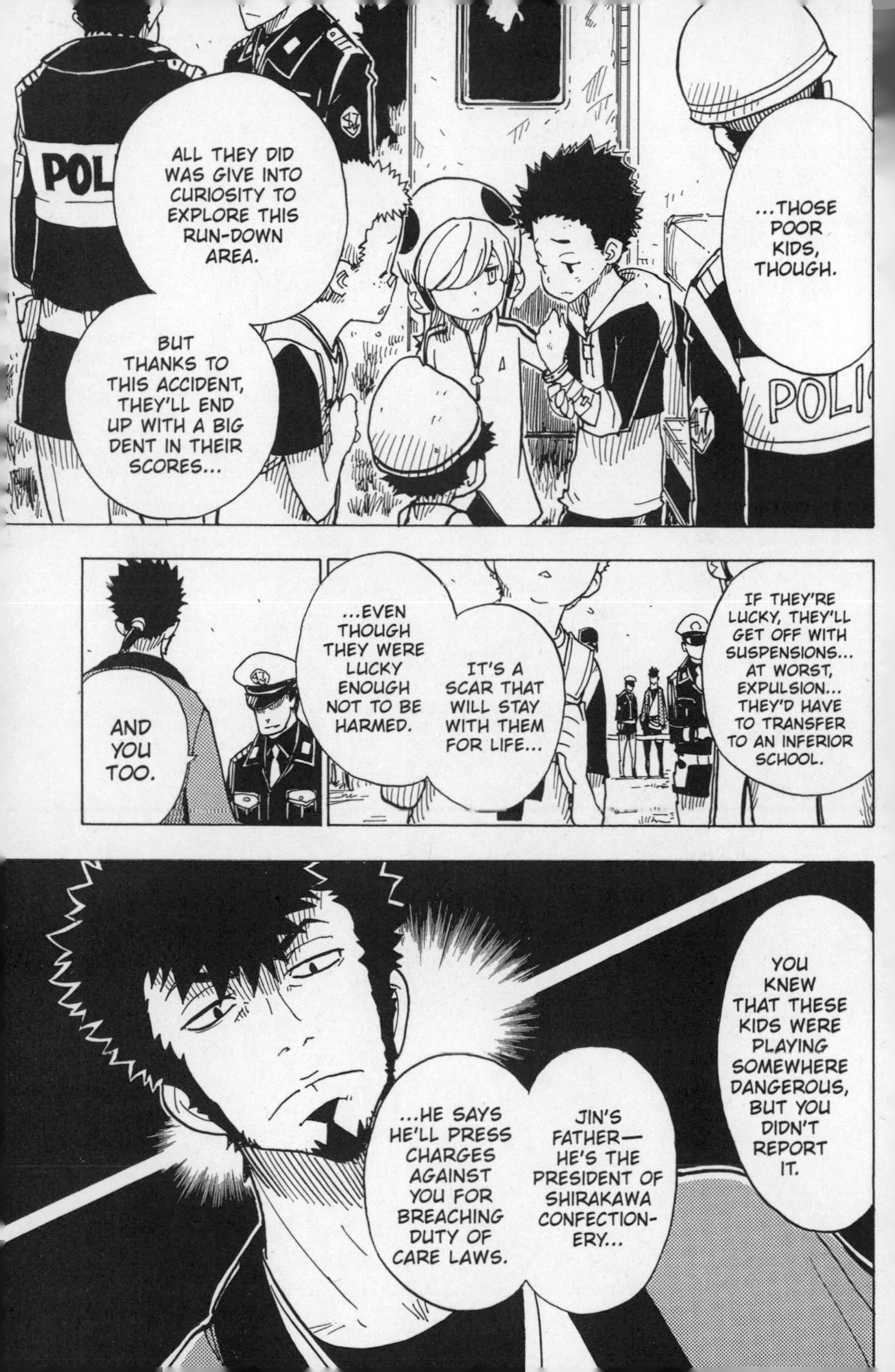

...THOSE POOR KIDS, THOUGH.
ALL THEY DID WAS GIVE INTO CURIOSITY TO EXPLORE THIS RUN-DOWN AREA.
BUT THANKS TO THIS ACCIDENT, THEY'LL END UP WITH A BIG DENT IN THEIR SCORES...
IF THEY'RE LUCKY, THEY'LL GET OFF WITH SUSPENSIONS... AT WORST, EXPULSION... THEY'D HAVE TO TRANSFER TO AN INFERIOR SCHOOL.
IT'S A SCAR THAT WILL STAY WITH THEM FOR LIFE...
...EVEN THOUGH THEY WERE LUCKY ENOUGH NOT TO BE HARMED.
AND YOU TOO.
YOU KNEW THAT THESE KIDS WERE PLAYING SOMEWHERE DANGEROUS, BUT YOU DIDN'T REPORT IT.
JIN'S FATHER—HE'S THE PRESIDENT OF SHIRAKAWA CONFECTION-ERY...
...HE SAYS HE'LL PRESS CHARGES AGAINST YOU FOR BREACHING DUTY OF CARE LAWS.

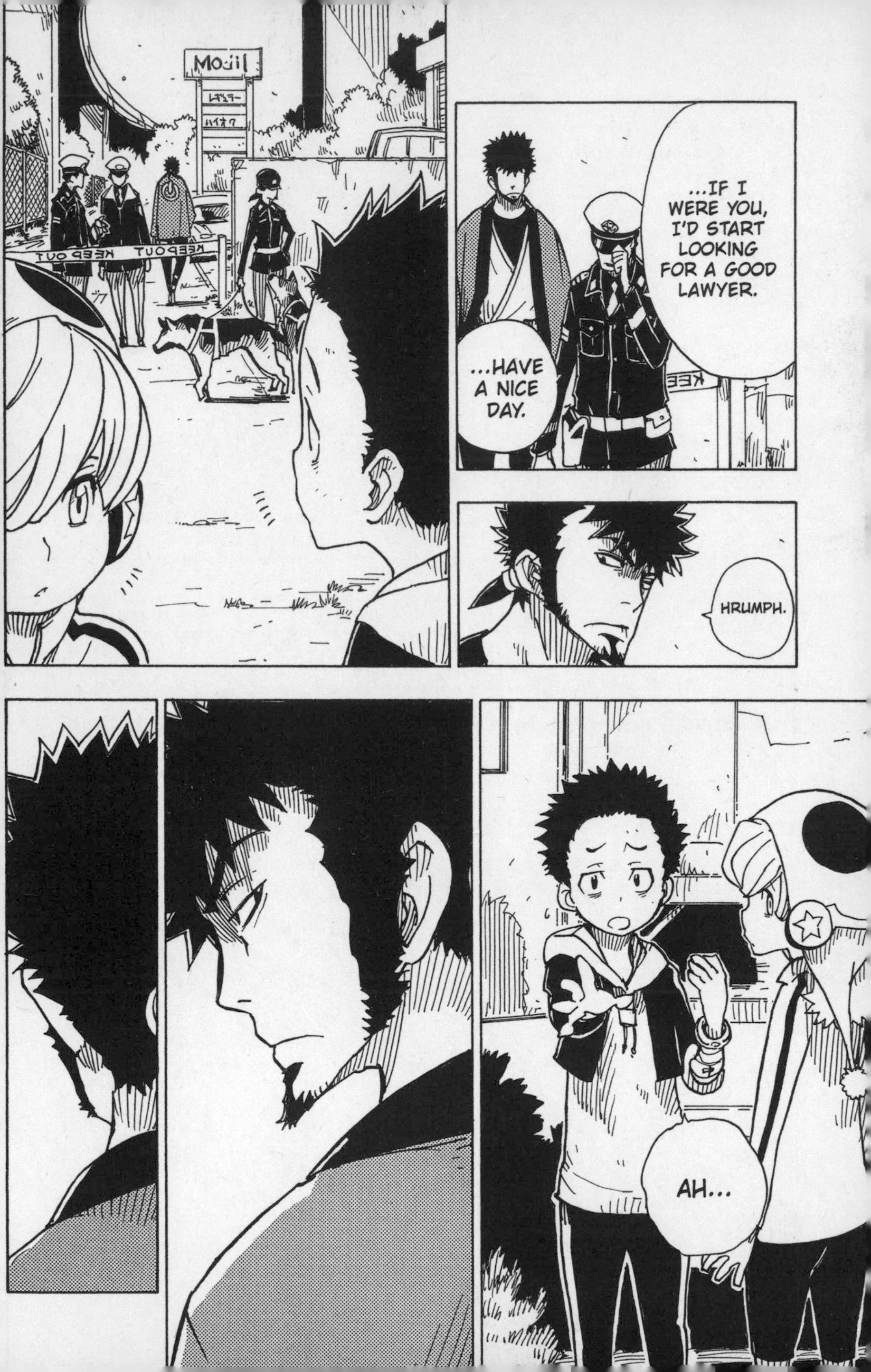
...IF I WERE YOU, I'D START LOOKING FOR A GOOD LAWYER.
...HAVE A NICE DAY.
HRUMPH.
KEEP OUT
AH...

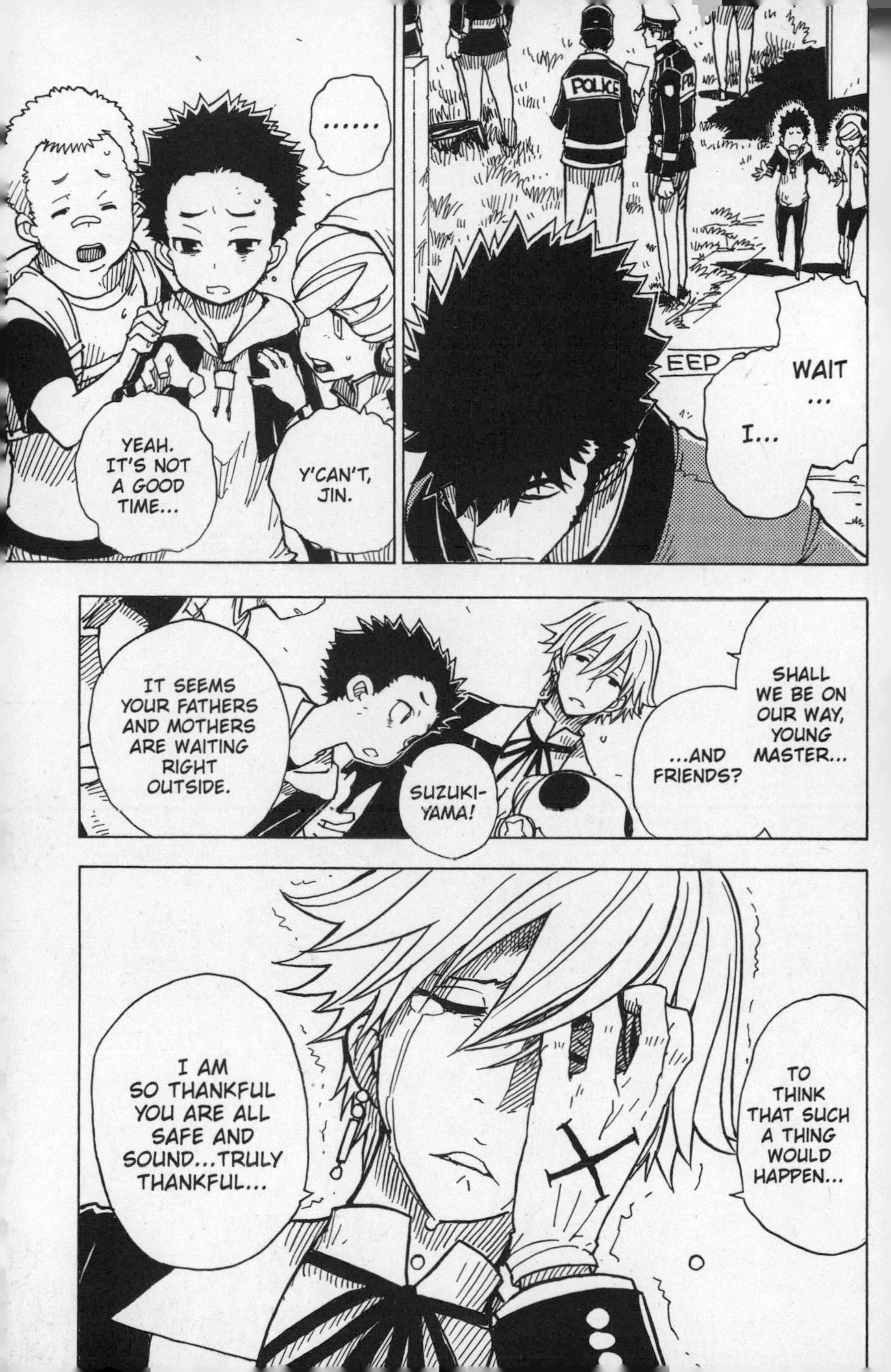
POLICE
EEP
WAIT ... I...
......
Y'CAN'T, JIN.
YEAH. IT'S NOT A GOOD TIME...
SHALL WE BE ON OUR WAY, YOUNG MASTER...
...AND FRIENDS?
SUZUKI-YAMA!
IT SEEMS YOUR FATHERS AND MOTHERS ARE WAITING RIGHT OUTSIDE.
TO THINK THAT SUCH A THING WOULD HAPPEN...
I AM SO THANKFUL YOU ARE ALL SAFE AND SOUND...TRULY THANKFUL...

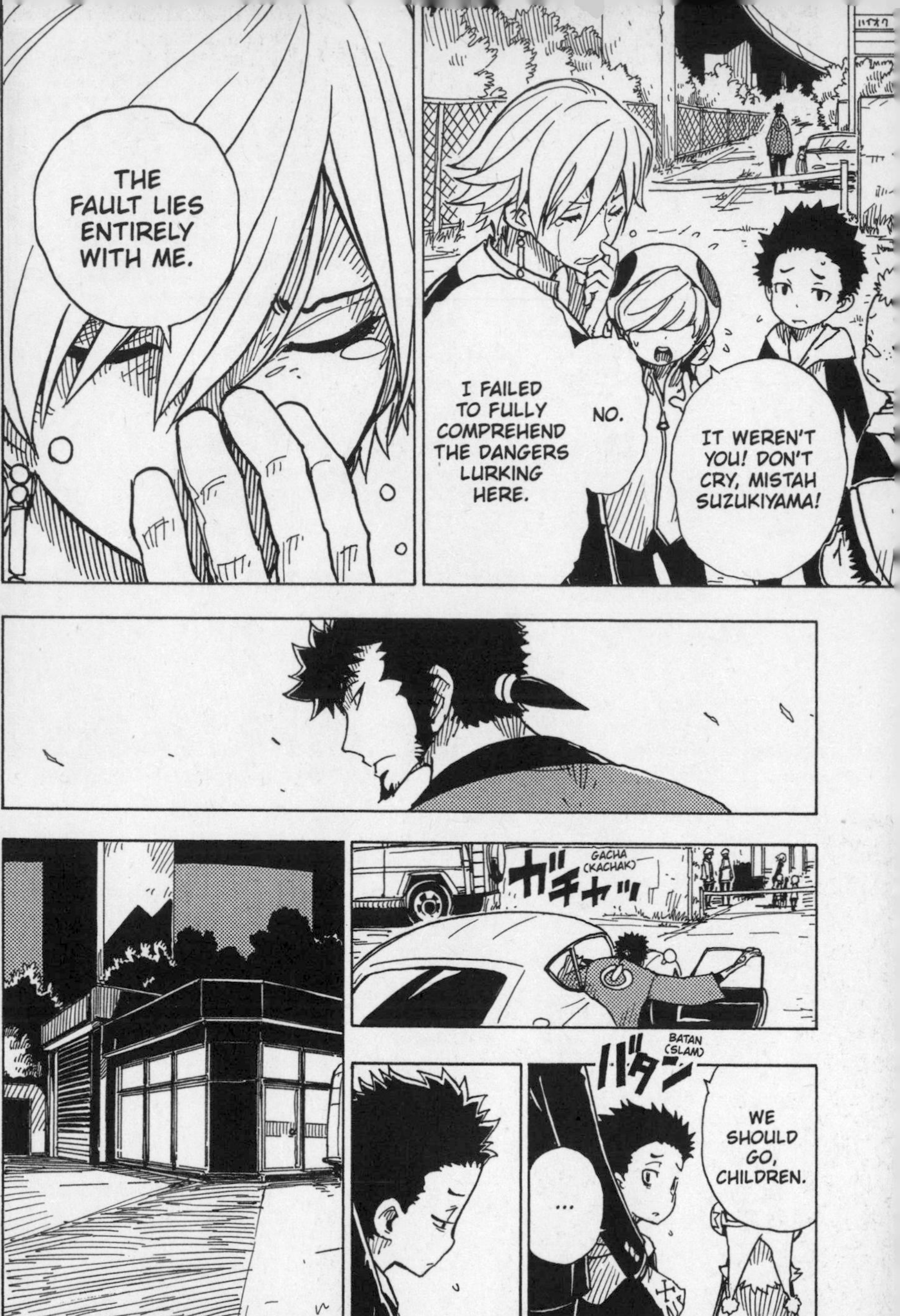
IT WEREN'T YOU! DON'T CRY, MISTAH SUZUKIYAMA!
NO.
I FAILED TO FULLY COMPREHEND THE DANGERS LURKING HERE.
THE FAULT LIES ENTIRELY WITH ME.
ガチャッ
GACHA (KACHAK)
バタン
BATAN (SLAM)
WE SHOULD GO, CHILDREN.
...

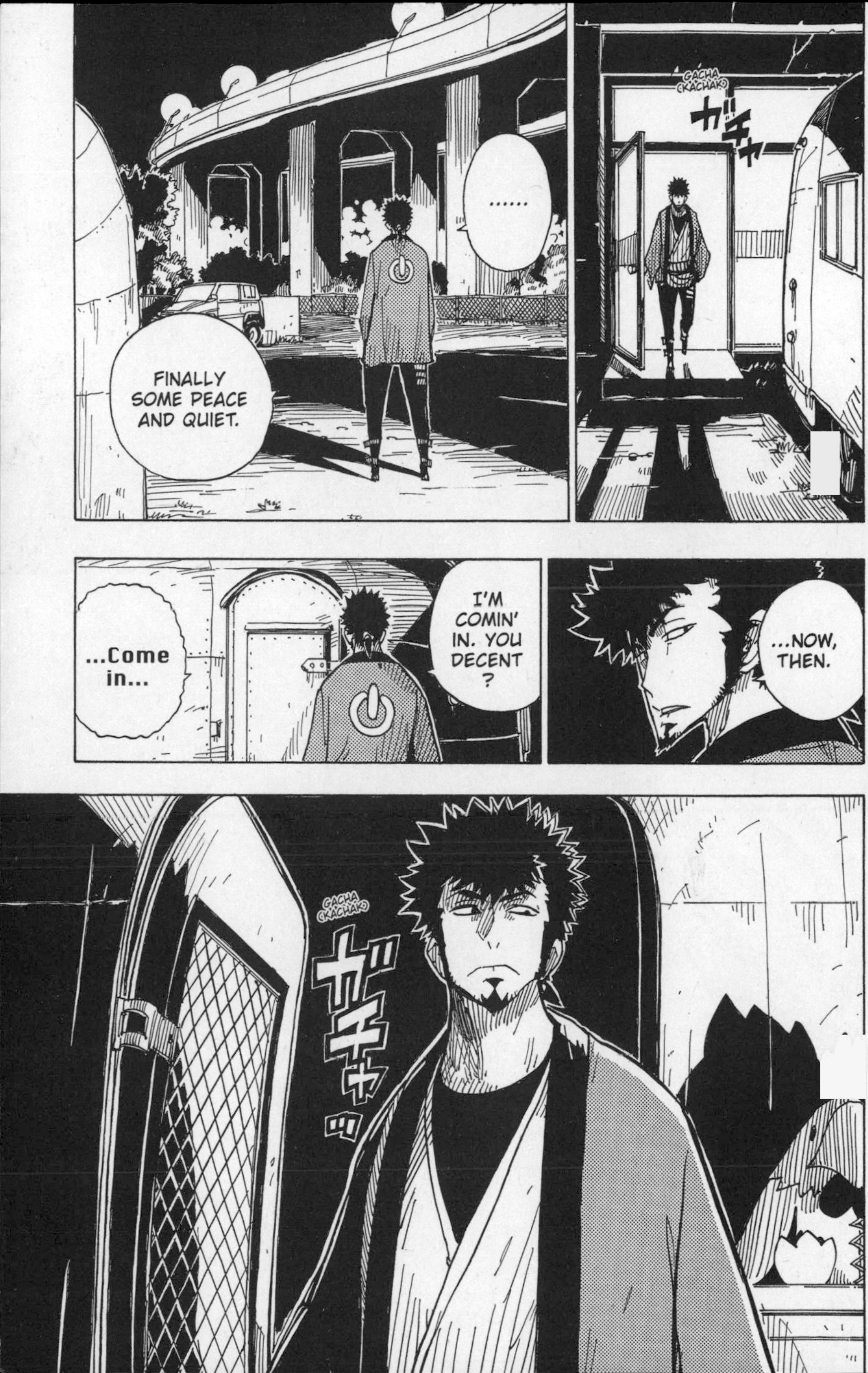
GACHA (KACHAK)
ガチャ
......
FINALLY SOME PEACE AND QUIET.
...NOW, THEN.
I'M COMIN' IN. YOU DECENT?
...Come in...
GACHA (KACHAK)
ガチャッ

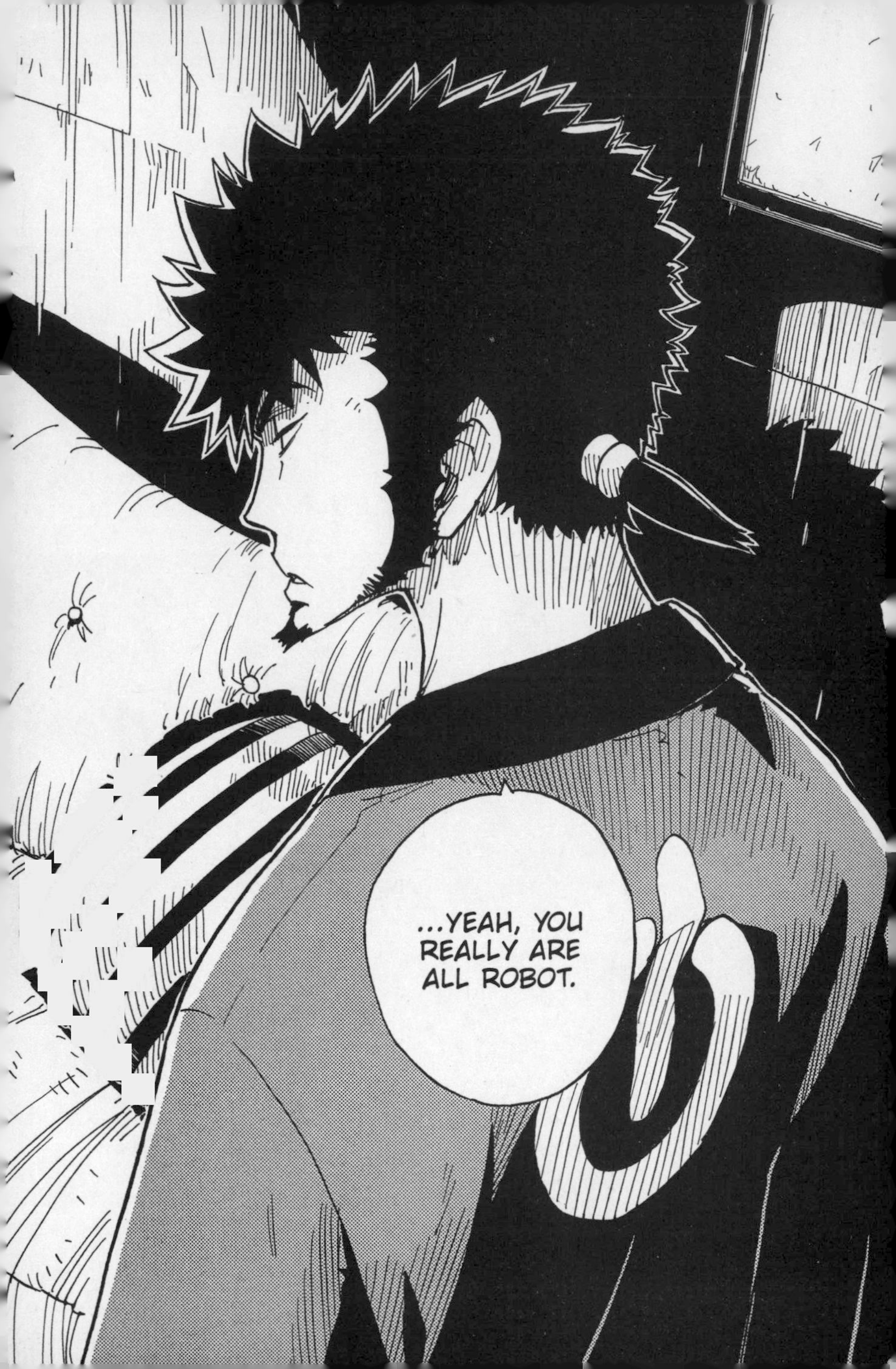
...YEAH, YOU REALLY ARE ALL ROBOT.

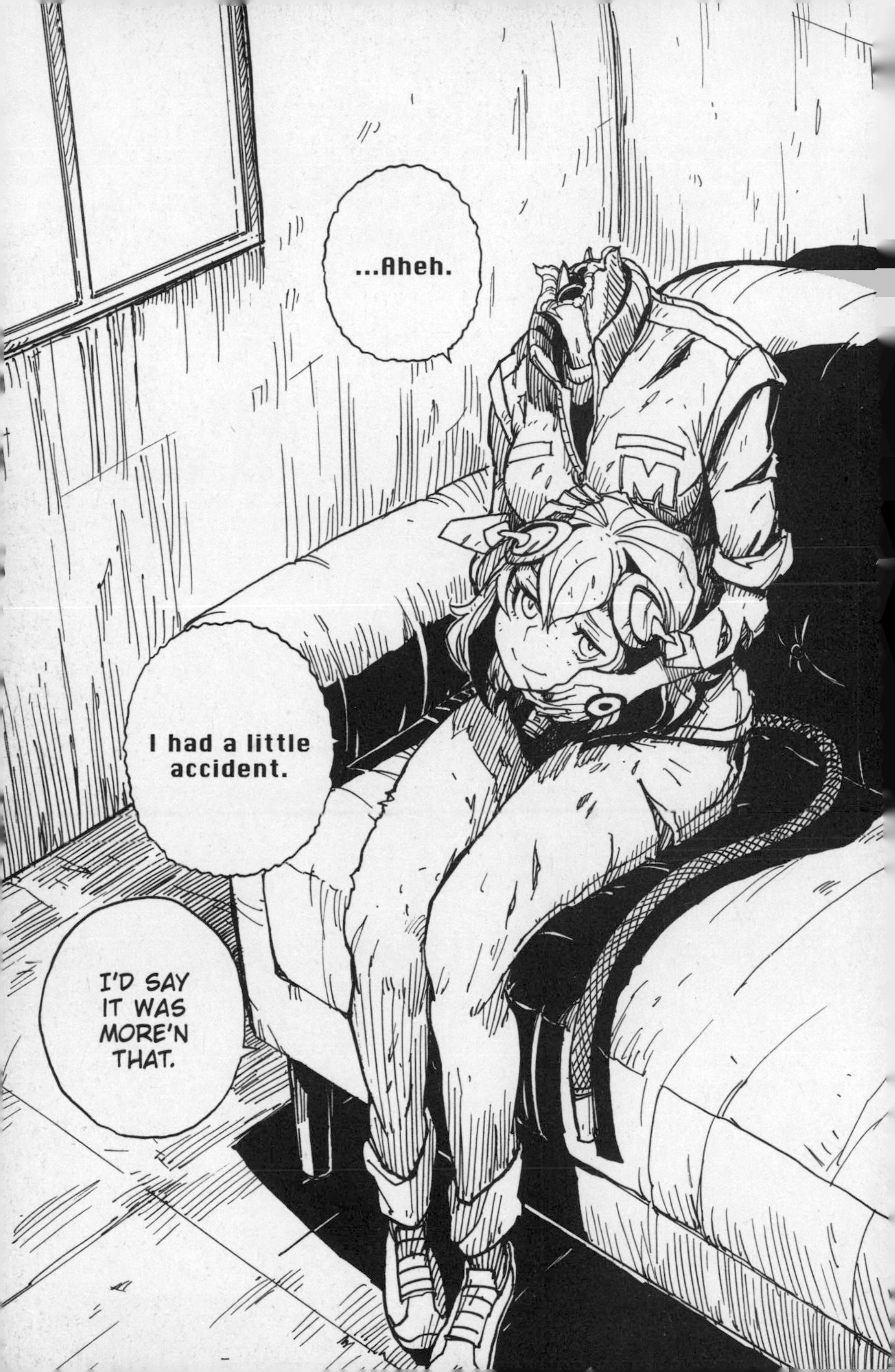
...Aheh.
I had a little accident.
I'D SAY IT WAS MORE'N THAT.

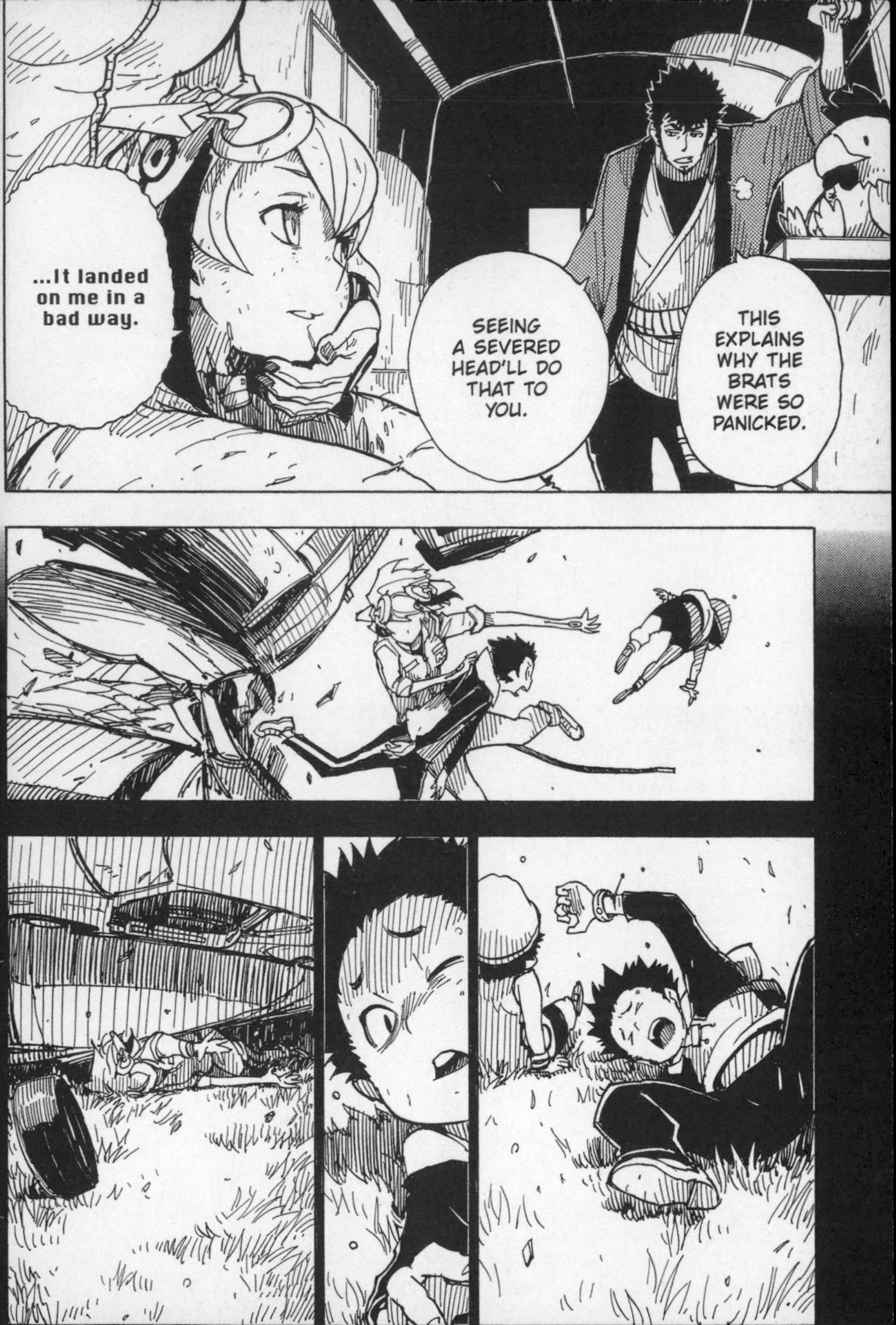
THIS EXPLAINS WHY THE BRATS WERE SO PANICKED.
SEEING A SEVERED HEAD'LL DO THAT TO YOU.
...It landed on me in a bad way.

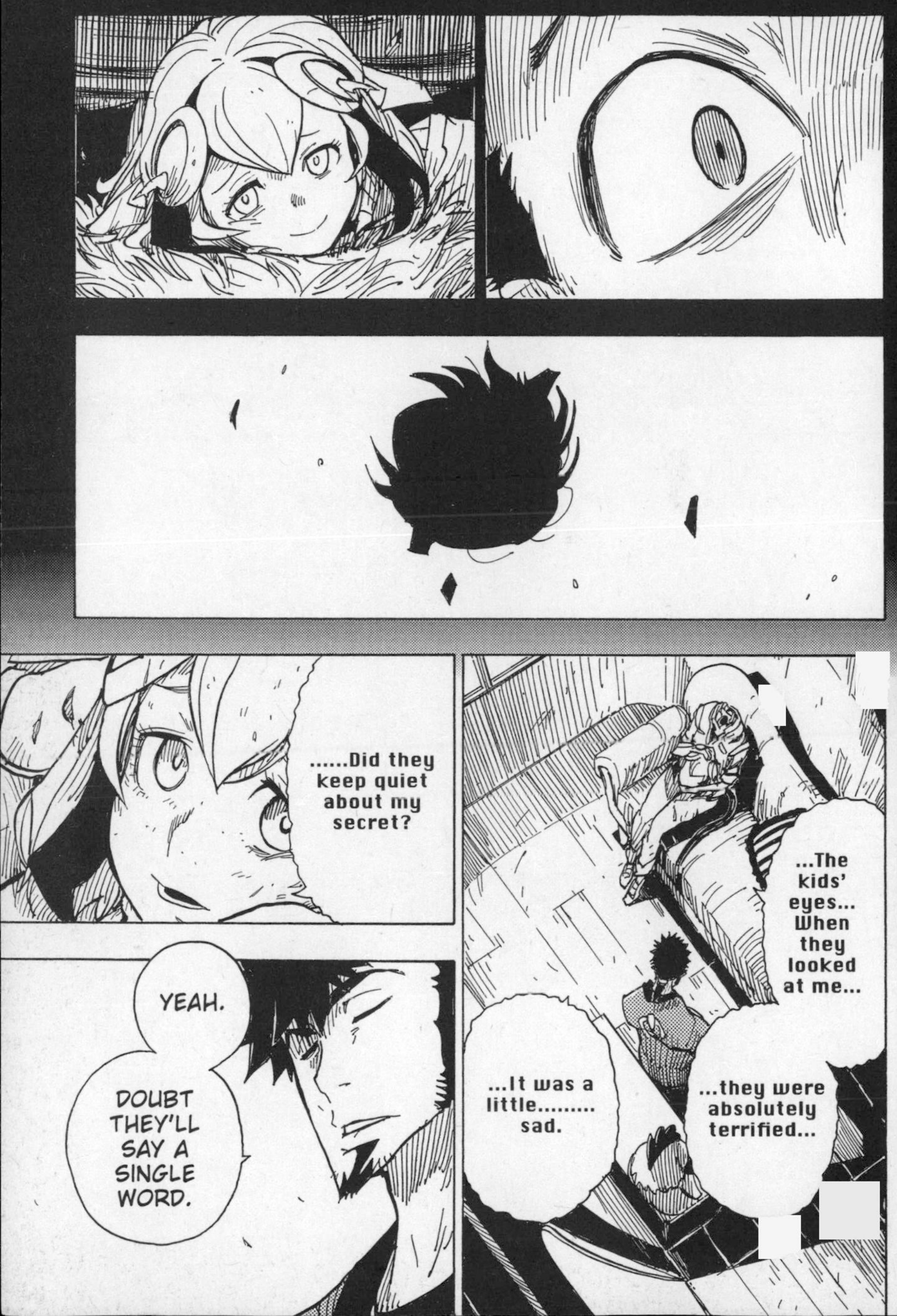
...The kids' eyes... When they looked at me...
...they were absolutely terrified...
...It was a little......... sad.
......Did they keep quiet about my secret?
YEAH.
DOUBT THEY'LL SAY A SINGLE WORD.

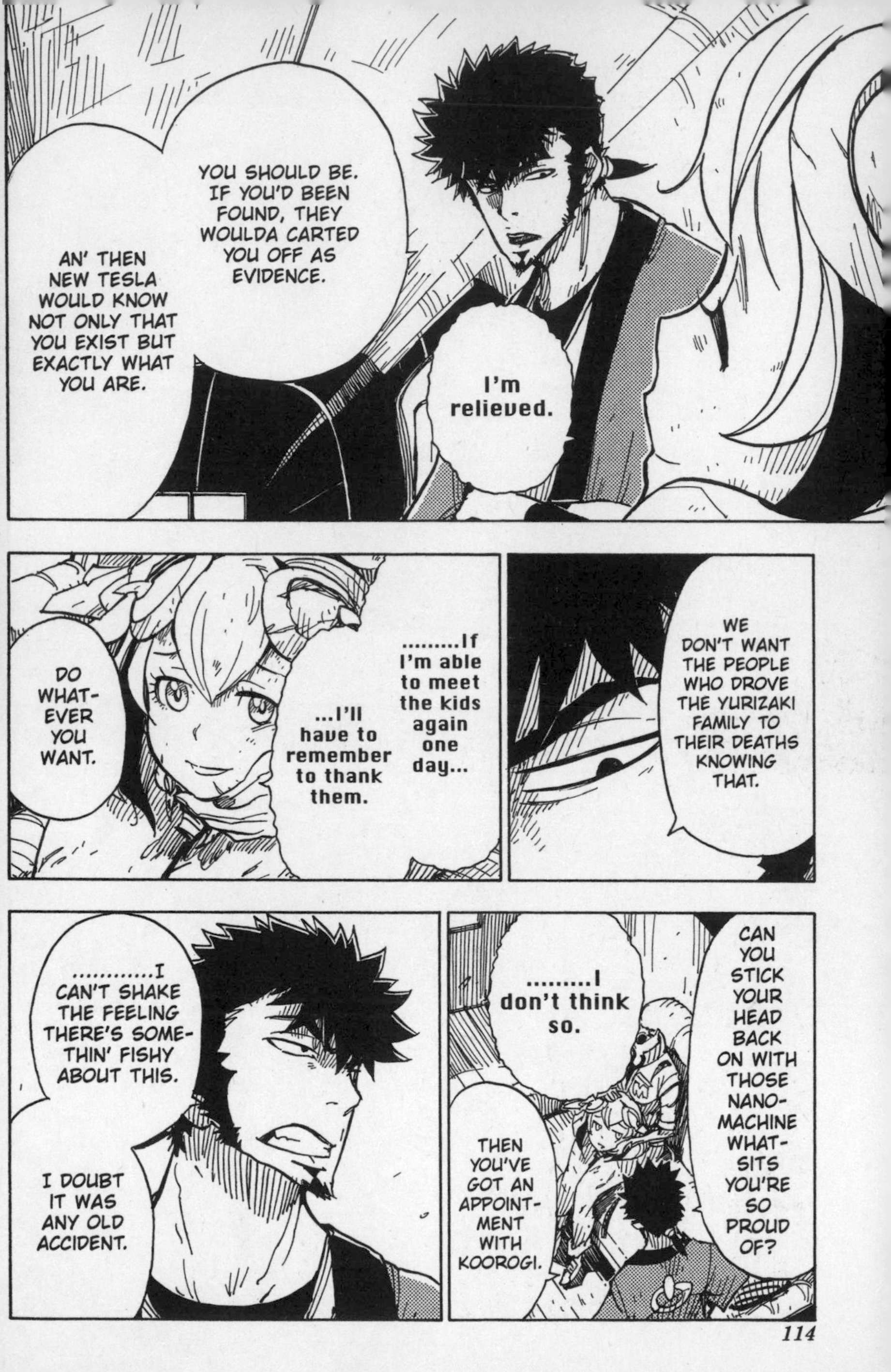
I'm relieved.
YOU SHOULD BE. IF YOU'D BEEN FOUND, THEY WOULDA CARTED YOU OFF AS EVIDENCE.
AN' THEN NEW TESLA WOULD KNOW NOT ONLY THAT YOU EXIST BUT EXACTLY WHAT YOU ARE.
WE DON'T WANT THE PEOPLE WHO DROVE THE YURIZAKI FAMILY TO THEIR DEATHS KNOWING THAT.
.........If I'm able to meet the kids again one day...
...I'll have to remember to thank them.
DO WHAT-EVER YOU WANT.
CAN YOU STICK YOUR HEAD BACK ON WITH THOSE NANO-MACHINE WHAT-SITS YOU'RE SO PROUD OF?
.........I don't think so.
THEN YOU'VE GOT AN APPOINT-MENT WITH KOOROGI.
............I CAN'T SHAKE THE FEELING THERE'S SOME-THIN' FISHY ABOUT THIS.
I DOUBT IT WAS ANY OLD ACCIDENT.

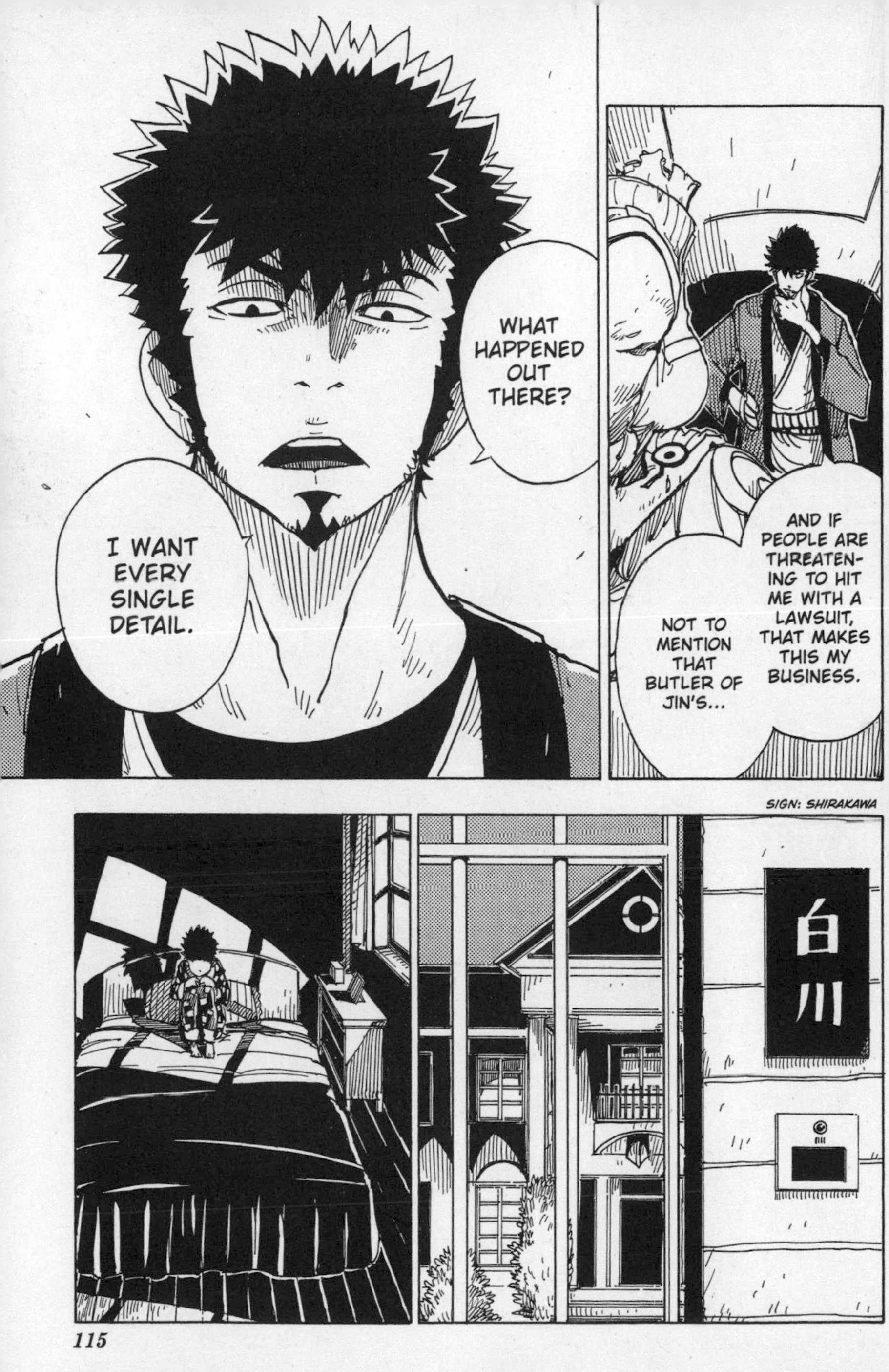
AND IF PEOPLE ARE THREATENING TO HIT ME WITH A LAWSUIT, THAT MAKES THIS MY BUSINESS.
NOT TO MENTION THAT BUTLER OF JIN'S...
WHAT HAPPENED OUT THERE?
I WANT EVERY SINGLE DETAIL.
SIGN: SHIRAKAWA
白川

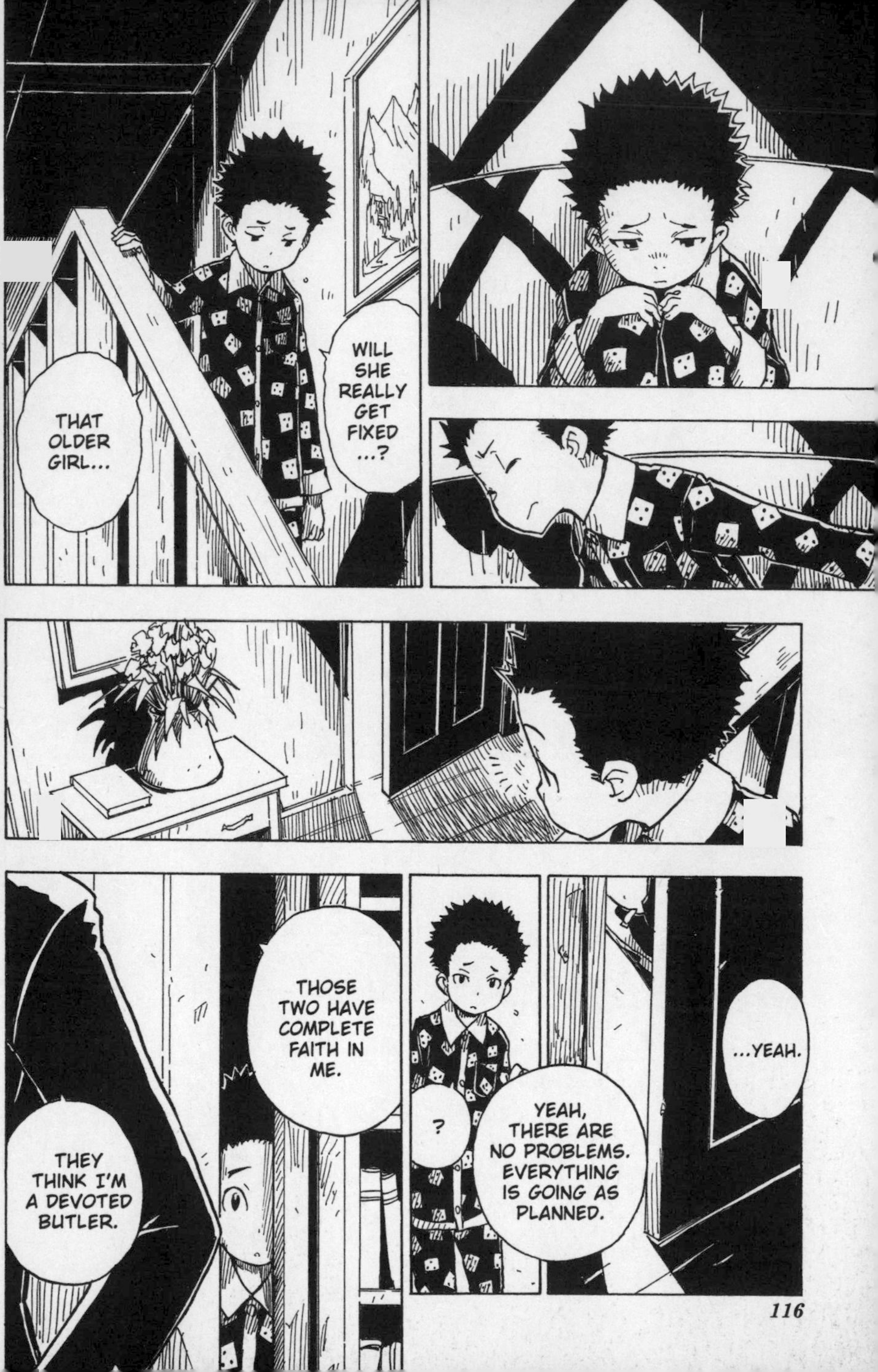
WILL SHE REALLY GET FIXED ...?
THAT OLDER GIRL...
...YEAH.
YEAH, THERE ARE NO PROBLEMS. EVERYTHING IS GOING AS PLANNED.
?
THOSE TWO HAVE COMPLETE FAITH IN ME.
THEY THINK I'M A DEVOTED BUTLER.

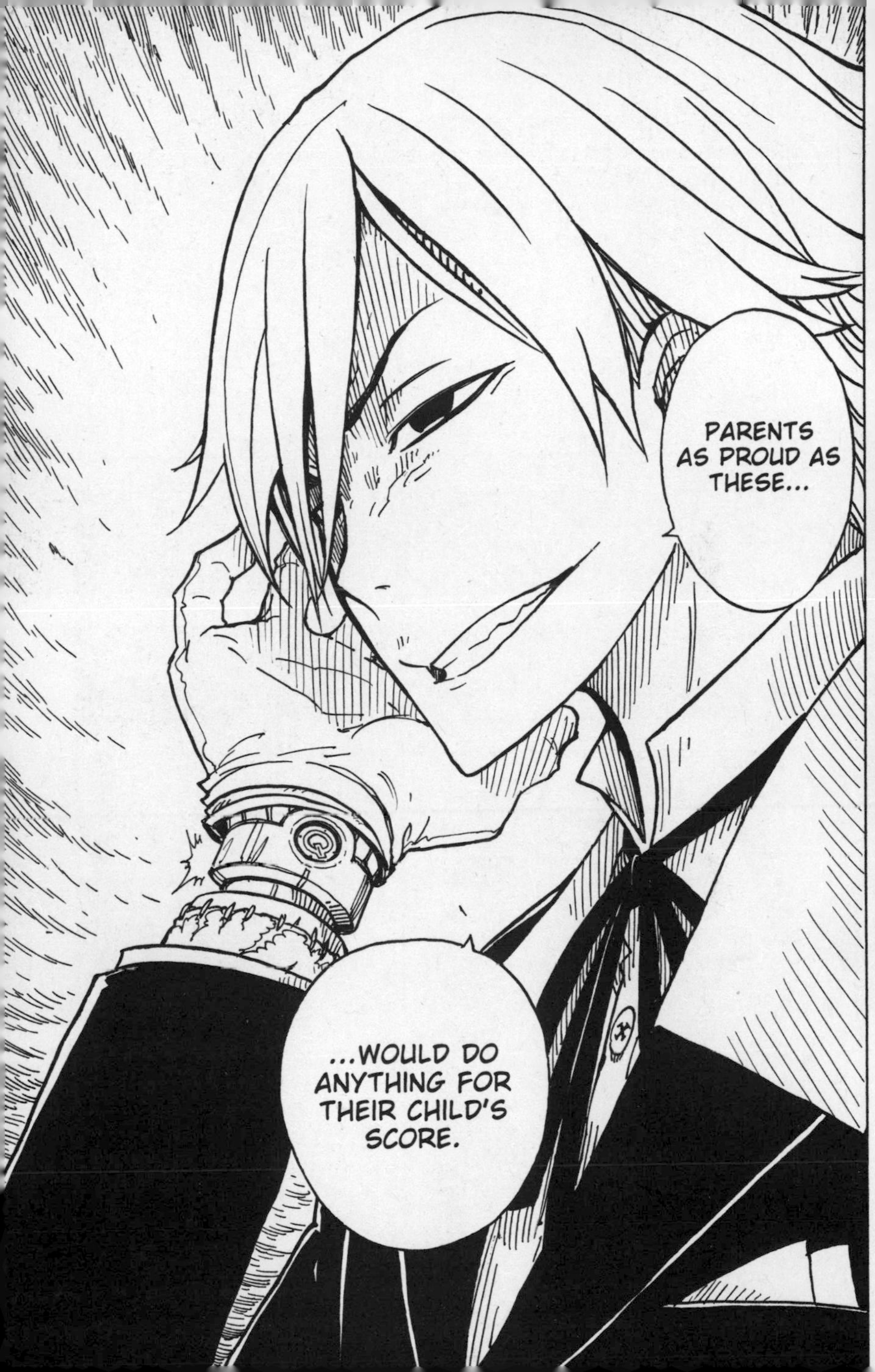
PARENTS AS PROUD AS THESE...
...WOULD DO ANYTHING FOR THEIR CHILD'S SCORE.

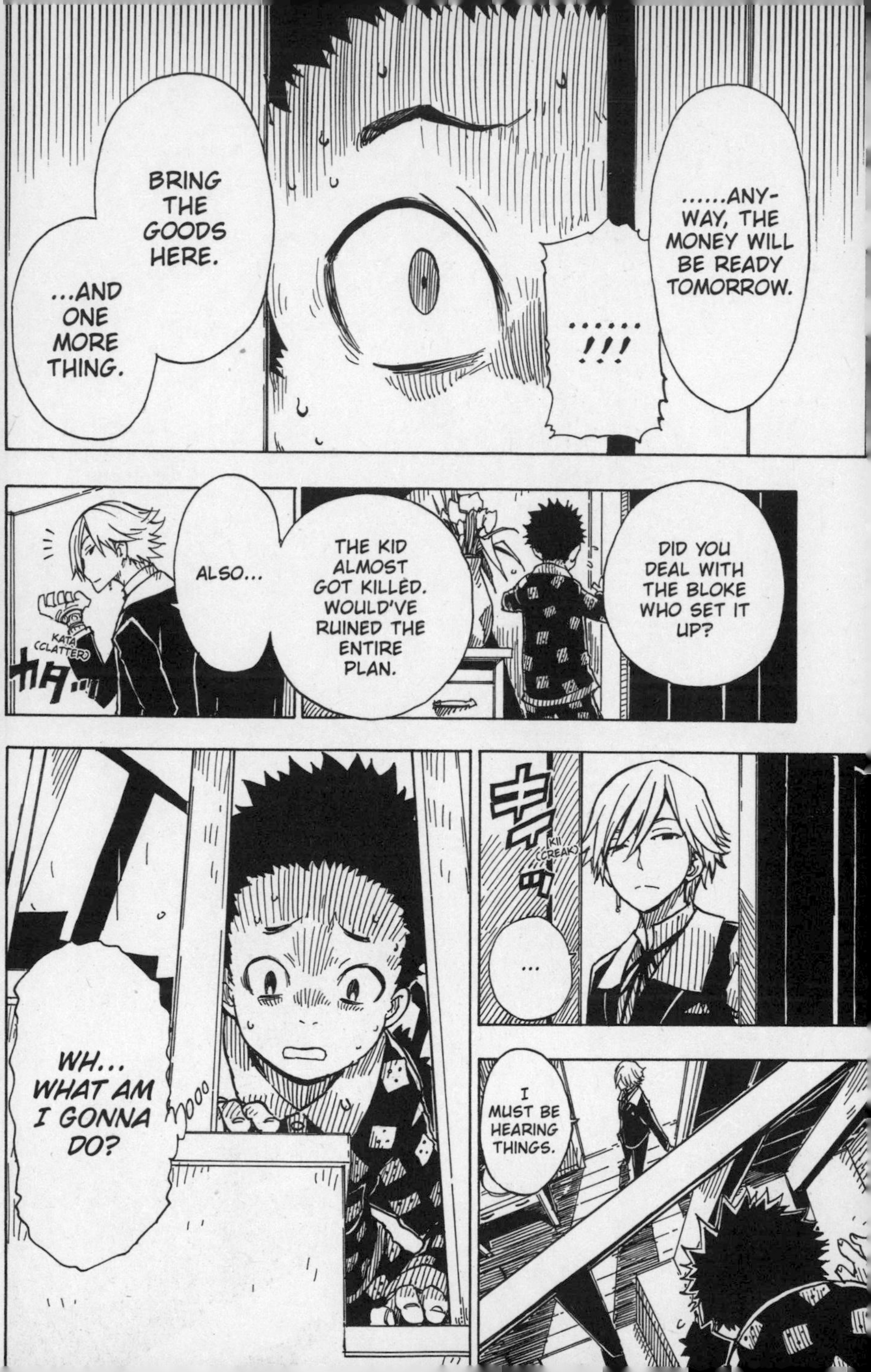
......ANY-WAY, THE MONEY WILL BE READY TOMORROW.
......!!!
BRING THE GOODS HERE.
...AND ONE MORE THING.
DID YOU DEAL WITH THE BLOKE WHO SET IT UP?
THE KID ALMOST GOT KILLED. WOULD'VE RUINED THE ENTIRE PLAN.
ALSO...
KATA (CLATTER)
KII (CREAK)
...
I MUST BE HEARING THINGS.
WH... WHAT AM I GONNA DO?

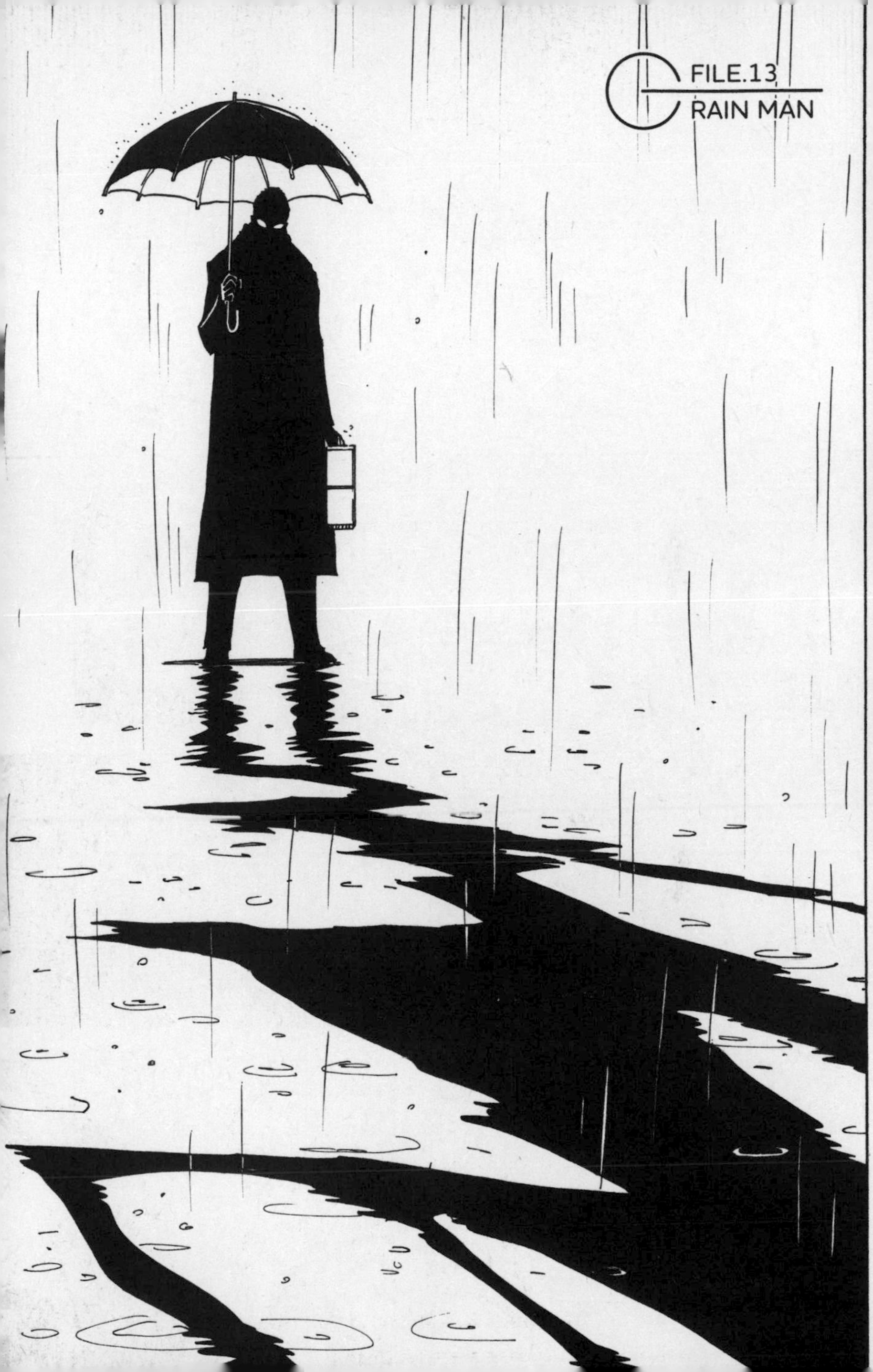
FILE.13
RAIN MAN

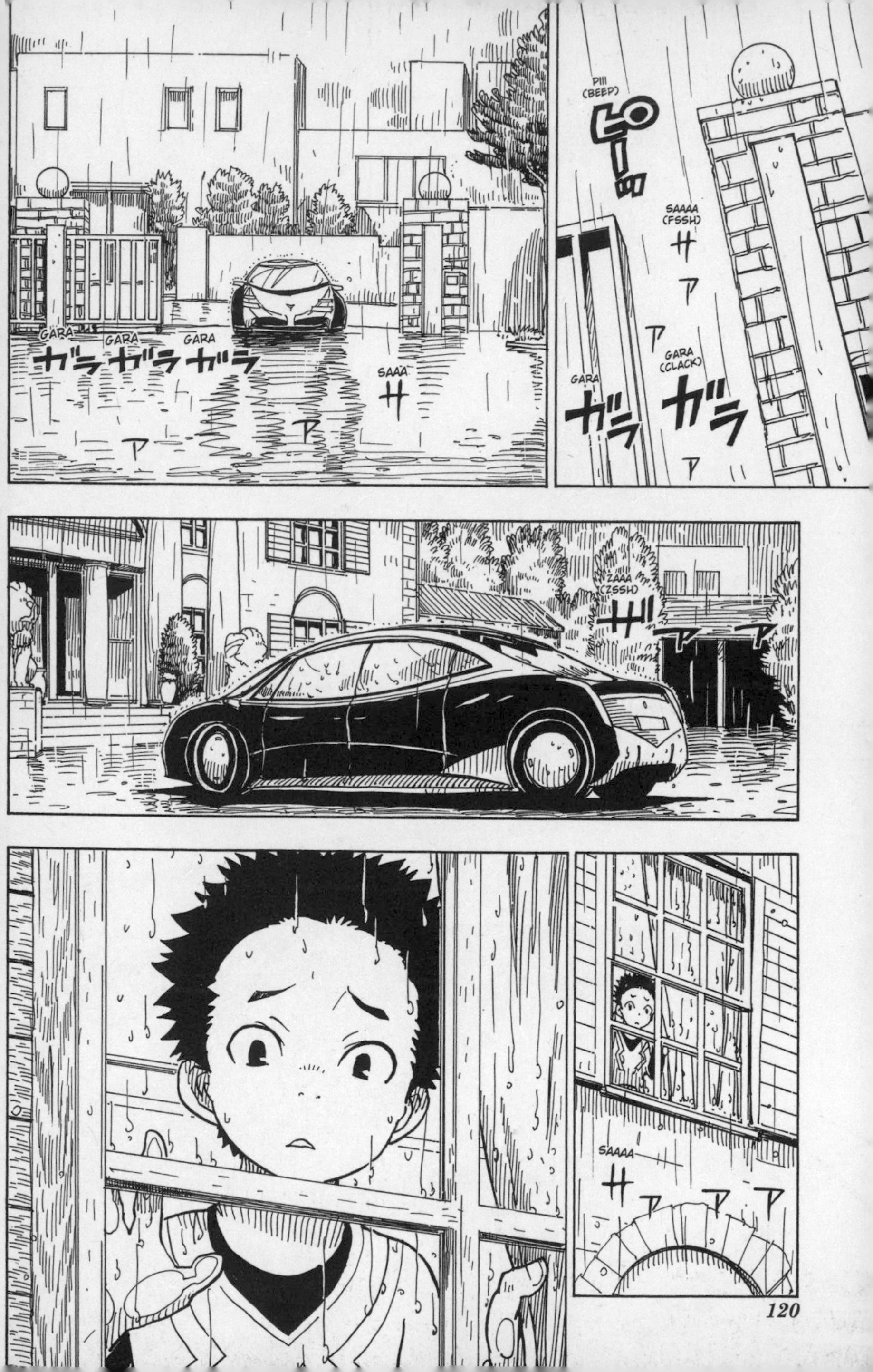
PIII (BEEP)
ピーッ
SAAAA (FSSH)
サァァァ
GARA (CLACK)
ガラ
GARA
ガラ
GARA GARA GARA
ガラガラガラ
SAAA
サァァ
ZAAA (ZSSH)
ザァァ
SAAAA
サァァァ

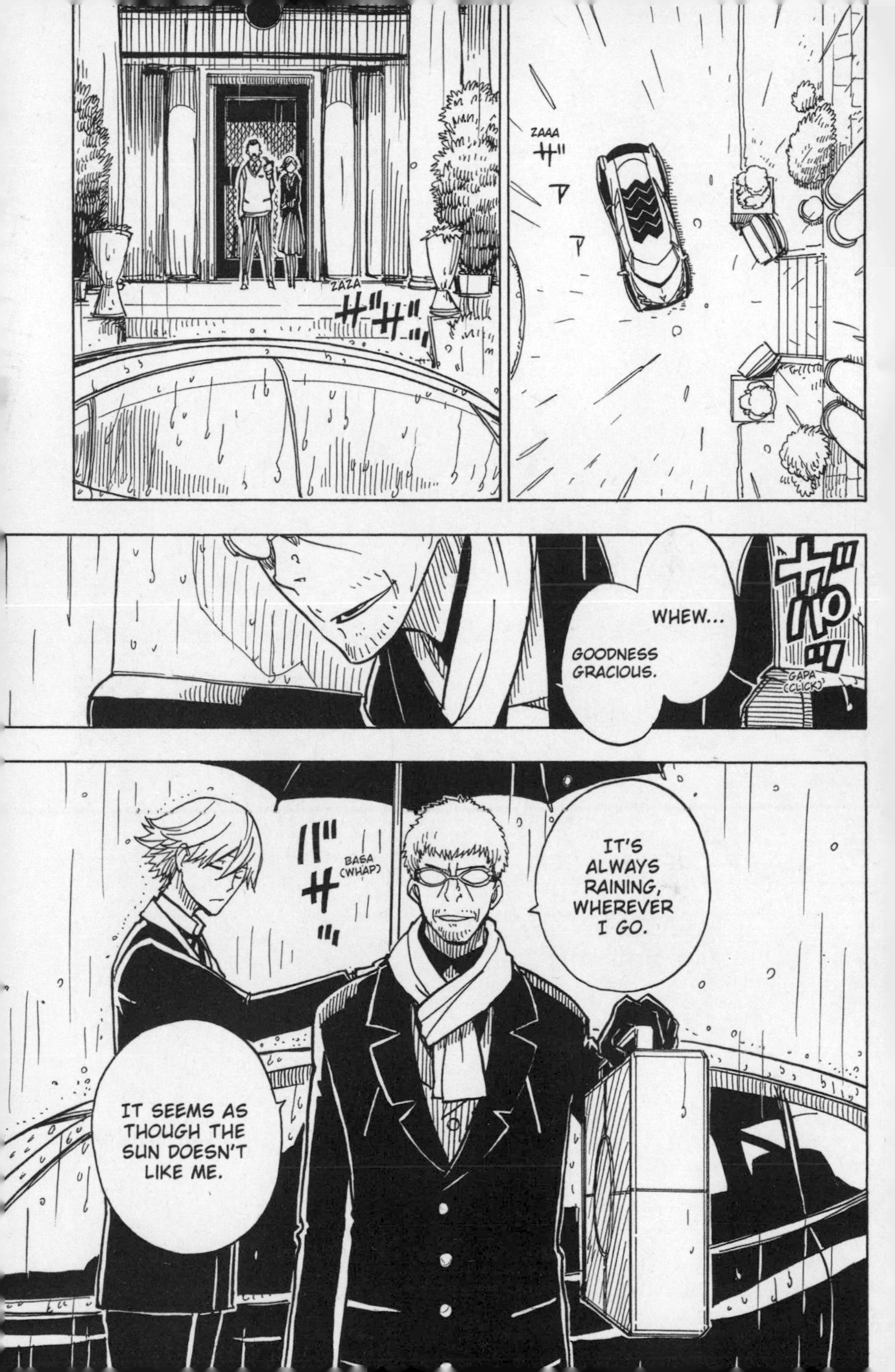
ZAAA
ZAZA
GAPA (CLICK)
WHEW...
GOODNESS GRACIOUS.
IT'S ALWAYS RAINING, WHEREVER I GO.
BASA (WHAP)
IT SEEMS AS THOUGH THE SUN DOESN'T LIKE ME.

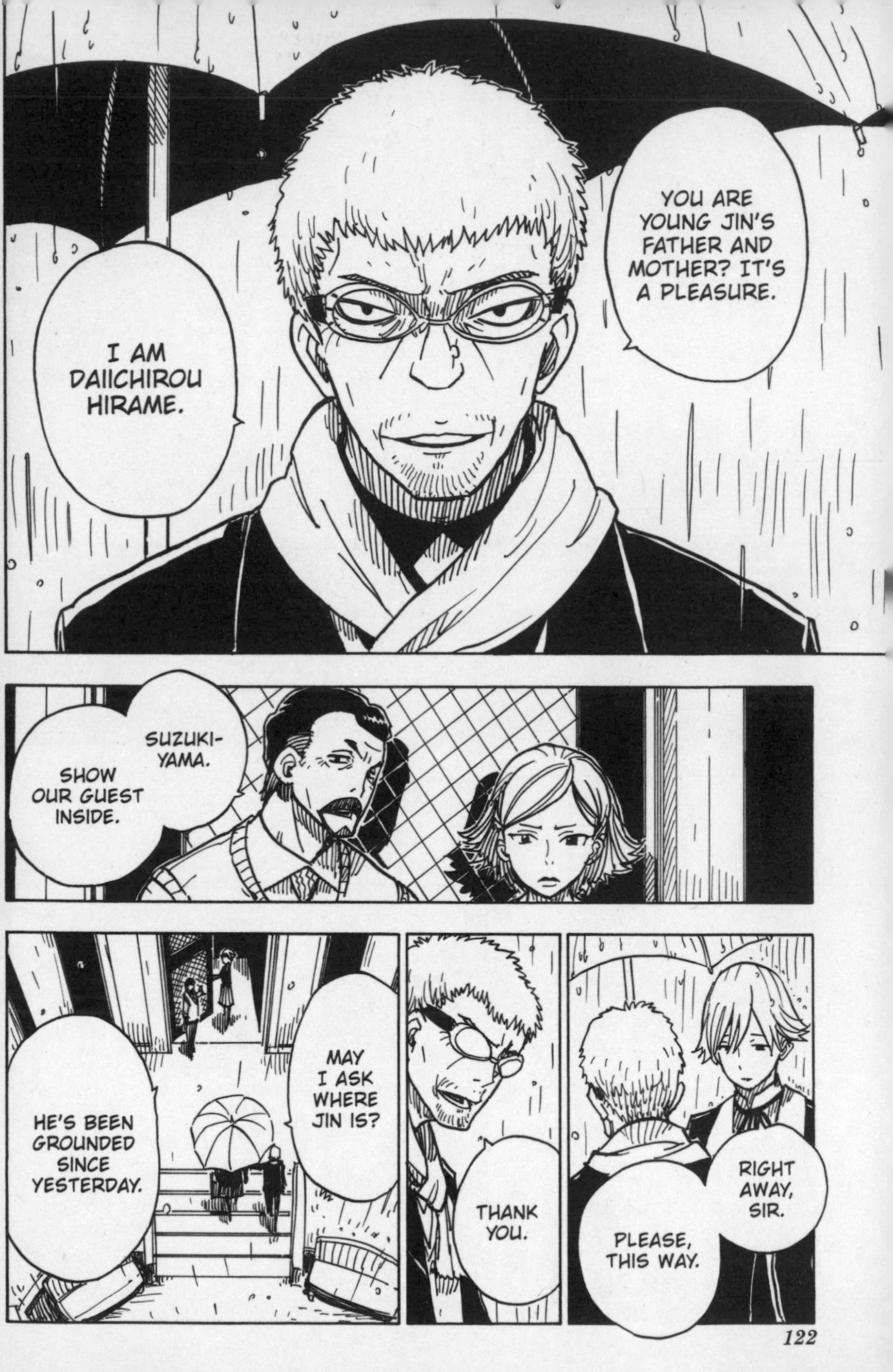
YOU ARE YOUNG JIN'S FATHER AND MOTHER? IT'S A PLEASURE.
I AM DAIICHIROU HIRAME.
SUZUKI-YAMA.
SHOW OUR GUEST INSIDE.
RIGHT AWAY, SIR.
PLEASE, THIS WAY.
THANK YOU.
MAY I ASK WHERE JIN IS?
HE'S BEEN GROUNDED SINCE YESTERDAY.

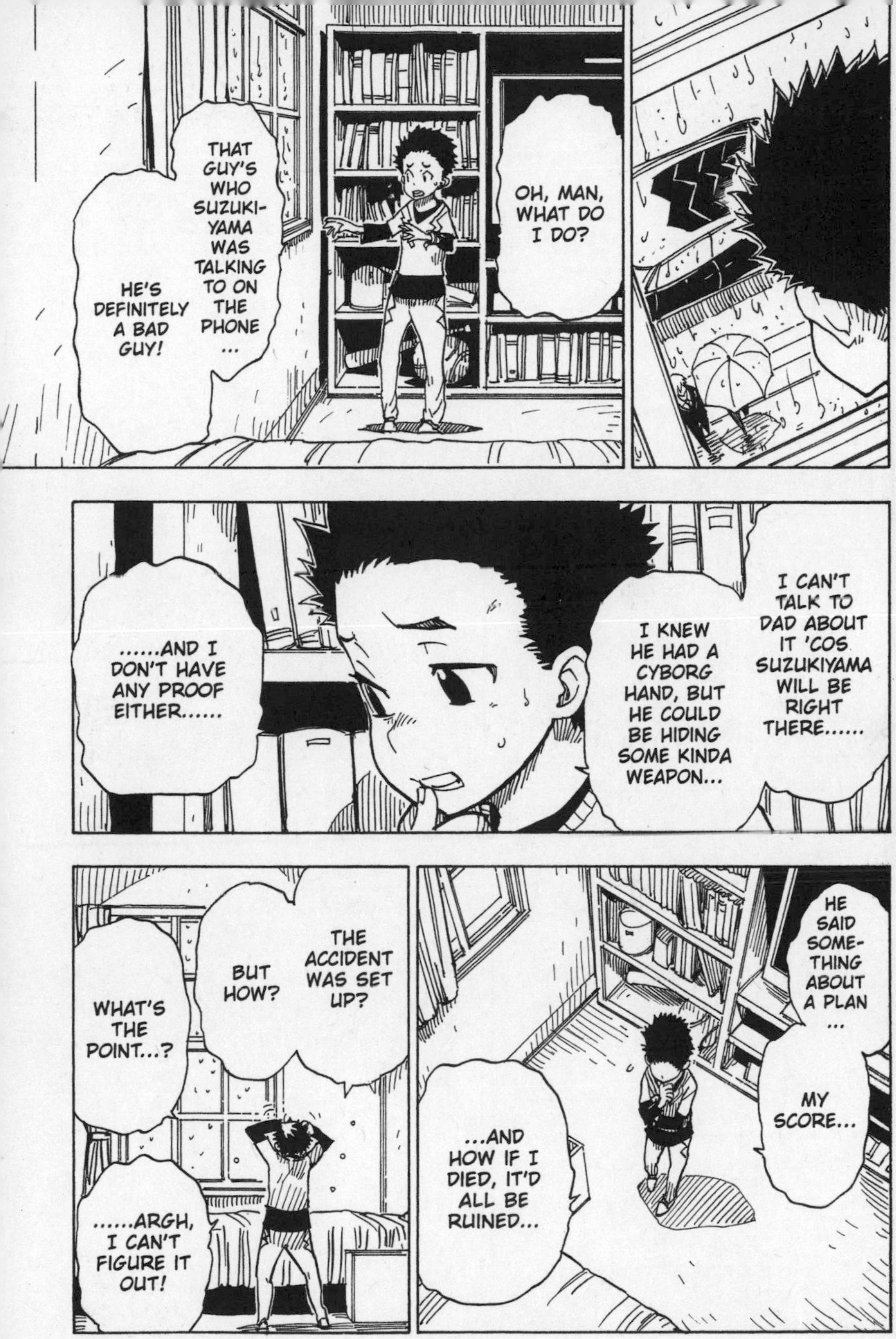
OH, MAN, WHAT DO I DO?
THAT GUY'S WHO SUZUKI-YAMA WAS TALKING TO ON THE PHONE ...
HE'S DEFINITELY A BAD GUY!
I CAN'T TALK TO DAD ABOUT IT 'COS SUZUKIYAMA WILL BE RIGHT THERE......
I KNEW HE HAD A CYBORG HAND, BUT HE COULD BE HIDING SOME KINDA WEAPON...
......AND I DON'T HAVE ANY PROOF EITHER......
HE SAID SOME-THING ABOUT A PLAN ...
MY SCORE...
...AND HOW IF I DIED, IT'D ALL BE RUINED...
THE ACCIDENT WAS SET UP?
BUT HOW?
WHAT'S THE POINT...?
......ARGH, I CAN'T FIGURE IT OUT!

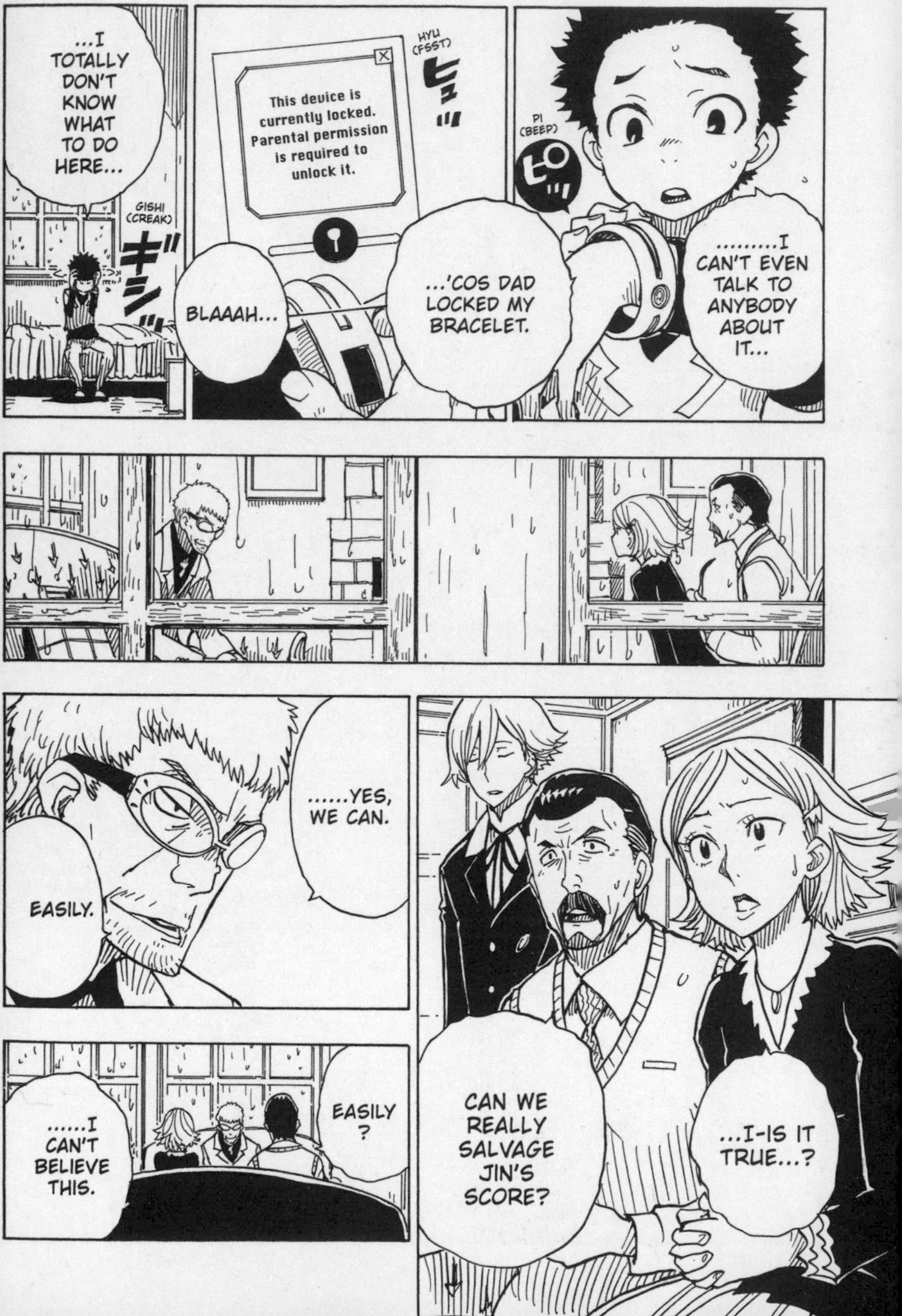
.........I CAN'T EVEN TALK TO ANYBODY ABOUT IT...
PI (BEEP)
...'COS DAD LOCKED MY BRACELET.
HYU (FSST)
This device is currently locked. Parental permission is required to unlock it.
BLAAAH...
...I TOTALLY DON'T KNOW WHAT TO DO HERE...
GISHI (CREAK)
...I-IS IT TRUE...?
CAN WE REALLY SALVAGE JIN'S SCORE?
......YES, WE CAN.
EASILY.
EASILY?
.....I CAN'T BELIEVE THIS.

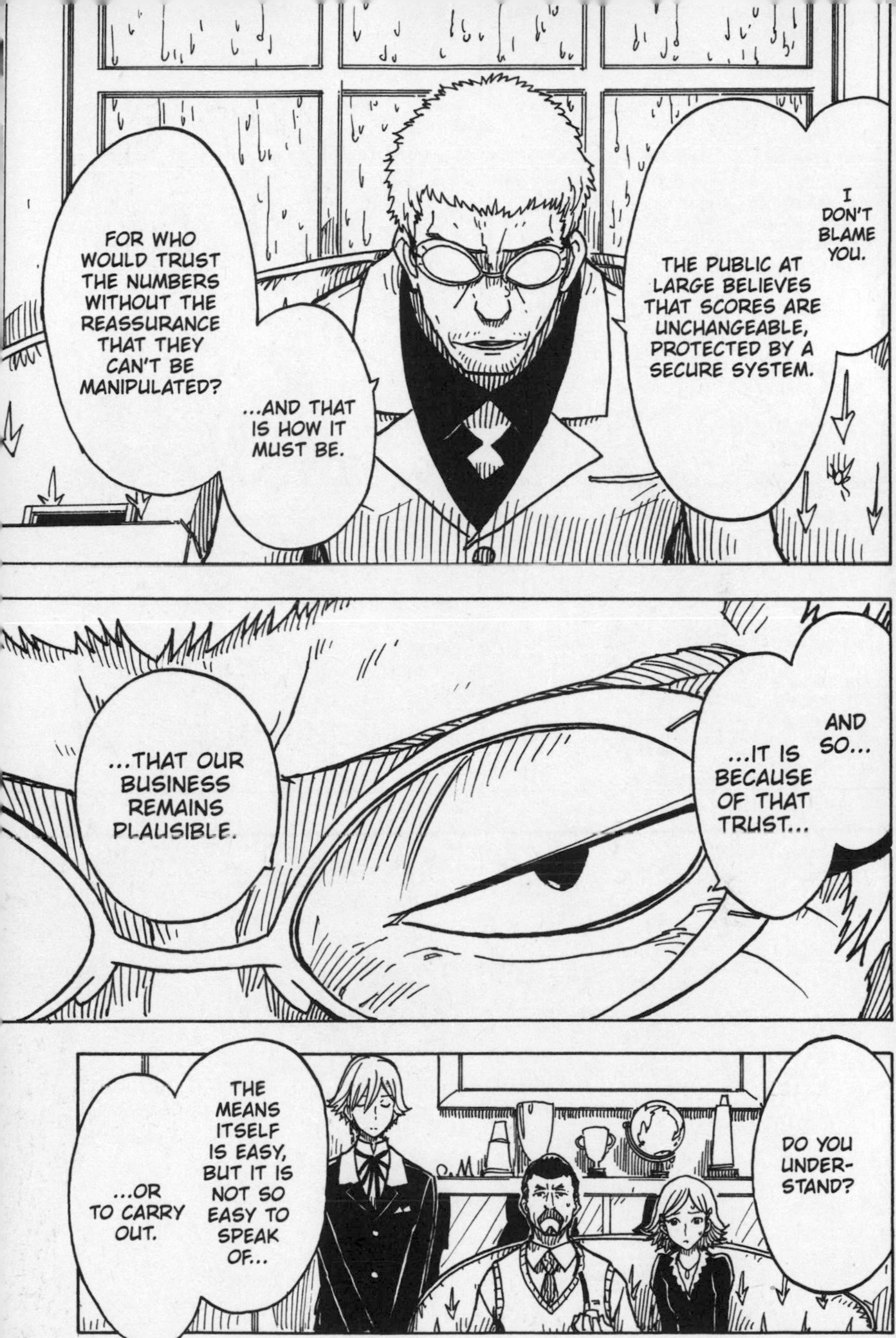
I DON'T BLAME YOU.
THE PUBLIC AT LARGE BELIEVES THAT SCORES ARE UNCHANGEABLE, PROTECTED BY A SECURE SYSTEM.
...AND THAT IS HOW IT MUST BE.
FOR WHO WOULD TRUST THE NUMBERS WITHOUT THE REASSURANCE THAT THEY CAN'T BE MANIPULATED?
AND SO...
...IT IS BECAUSE OF THAT TRUST...
...THAT OUR BUSINESS REMAINS PLAUSIBLE.
DO YOU UNDER-STAND?
THE MEANS ITSELF IS EASY, BUT IT IS NOT SO EASY TO SPEAK OF...
...OR TO CARRY OUT.

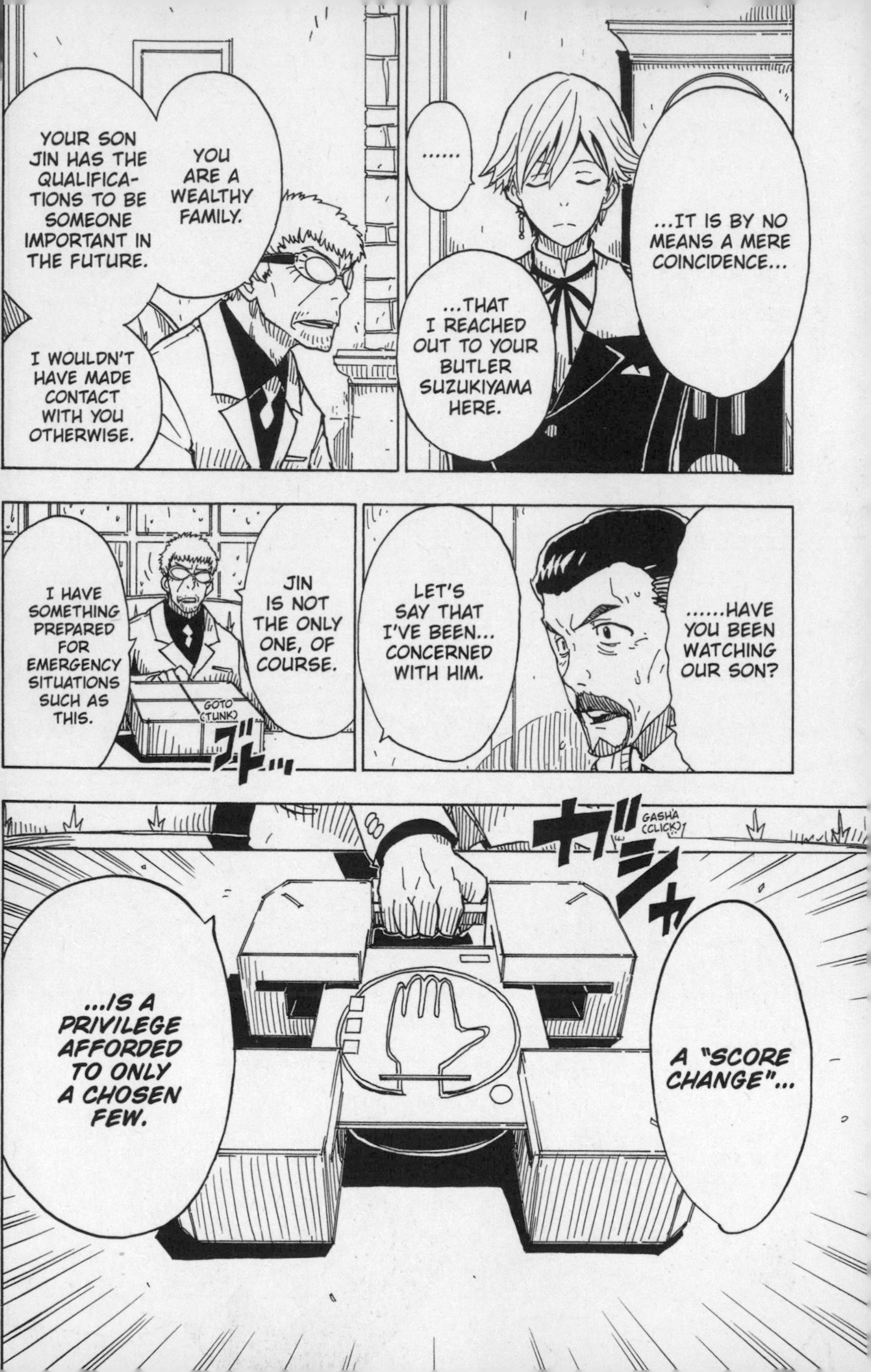
...IT IS BY NO MEANS A MERE COINCIDENCE...
...THAT I REACHED OUT TO YOUR BUTLER SUZUKIYAMA HERE.
......
YOU ARE A WEALTHY FAMILY.
YOUR SON JIN HAS THE QUALIFICATIONS TO BE SOMEONE IMPORTANT IN THE FUTURE.
I WOULDN'T HAVE MADE CONTACT WITH YOU OTHERWISE.
......HAVE YOU BEEN WATCHING OUR SON?
LET'S SAY THAT I'VE BEEN... CONCERNED WITH HIM.
JIN IS NOT THE ONLY ONE, OF COURSE.
I HAVE SOMETHING PREPARED FOR EMERGENCY SITUATIONS SUCH AS THIS.
GOTO (TUNK)
GASHA (CLICK)
A "SCORE CHANGE"...
...IS A PRIVILEGE AFFORDED TO ONLY A CHOSEN FEW.

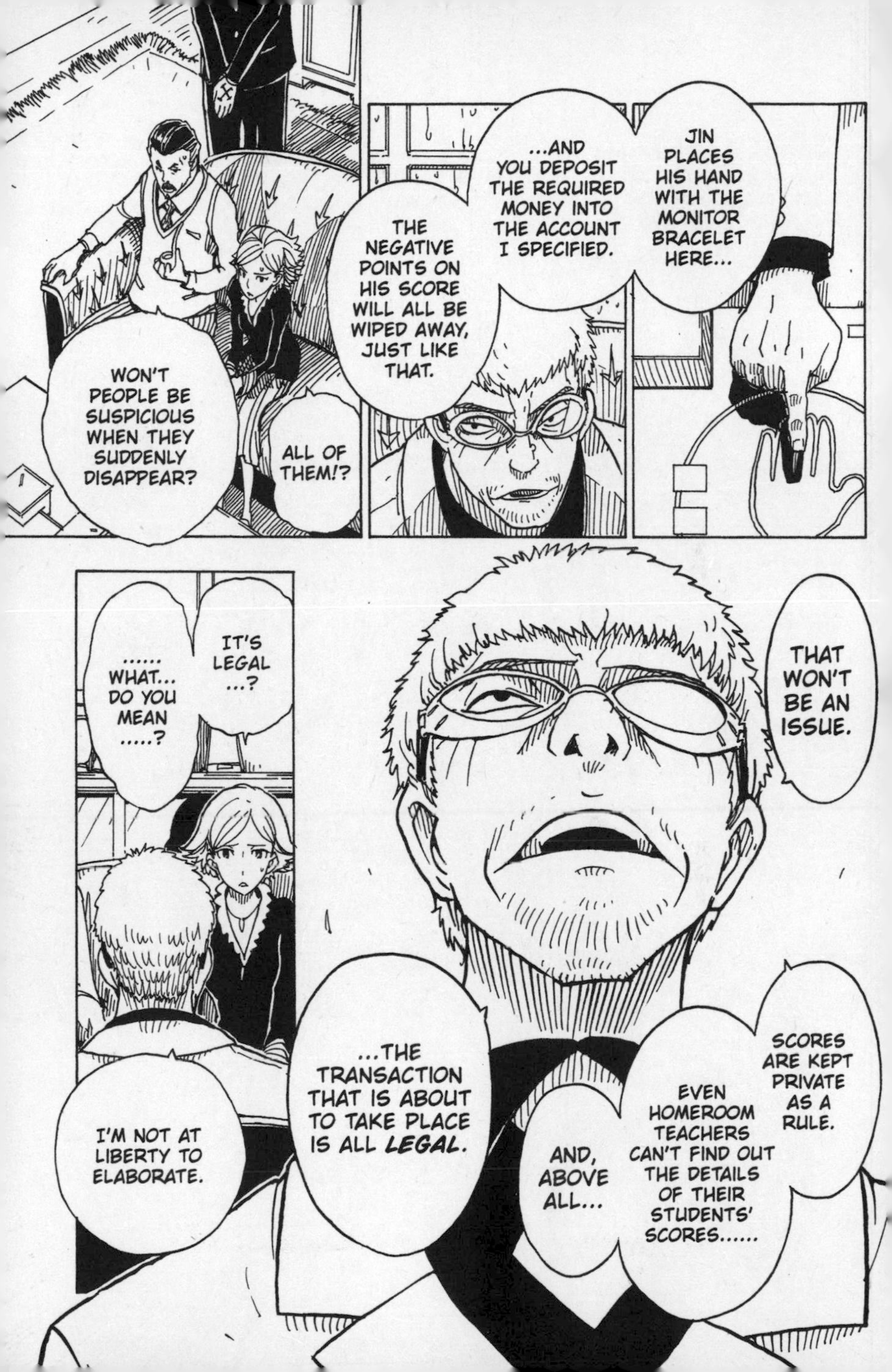

JIN PLACES HIS HAND WITH THE MONITOR BRACELET HERE...
...AND YOU DEPOSIT THE REQUIRED MONEY INTO THE ACCOUNT I SPECIFIED.
THE NEGATIVE POINTS ON HIS SCORE WILL ALL BE WIPED AWAY, JUST LIKE THAT.
ALL OF THEM!?
WON'T PEOPLE BE SUSPICIOUS WHEN THEY SUDDENLY DISAPPEAR?
THAT WON'T BE AN ISSUE.
SCORES ARE KEPT PRIVATE AS A RULE.
EVEN HOMEROOM TEACHERS CAN'T FIND OUT THE DETAILS OF THEIR STUDENTS' SCORES......
AND, ABOVE ALL...
...THE TRANSACTION THAT IS ABOUT TO TAKE PLACE IS ALL *LEGAL*.
IT'S LEGAL...?
...... WHAT... DO YOU MEAN.....?
I'M NOT AT LIBERTY TO ELABORATE.

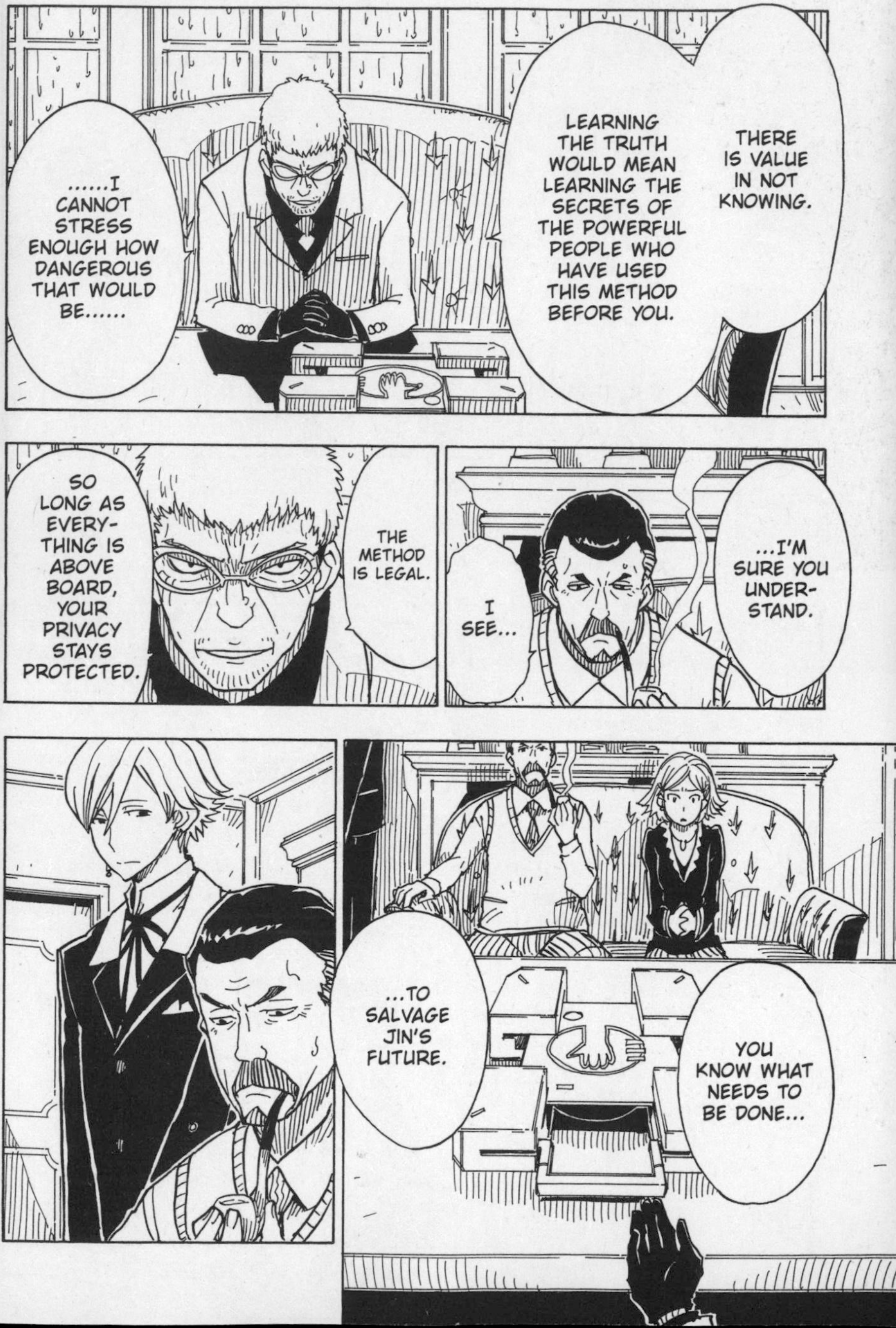
THERE IS VALUE IN NOT KNOWING.
LEARNING THE TRUTH WOULD MEAN LEARNING THE SECRETS OF THE POWERFUL PEOPLE WHO HAVE USED THIS METHOD BEFORE YOU.
......I CANNOT STRESS ENOUGH HOW DANGEROUS THAT WOULD BE......
...I'M SURE YOU UNDER-STAND.
I SEE...
THE METHOD IS LEGAL.
SO LONG AS EVERY-THING IS ABOVE BOARD, YOUR PRIVACY STAYS PROTECTED.
YOU KNOW WHAT NEEDS TO BE DONE...
...TO SALVAGE JIN'S FUTURE.

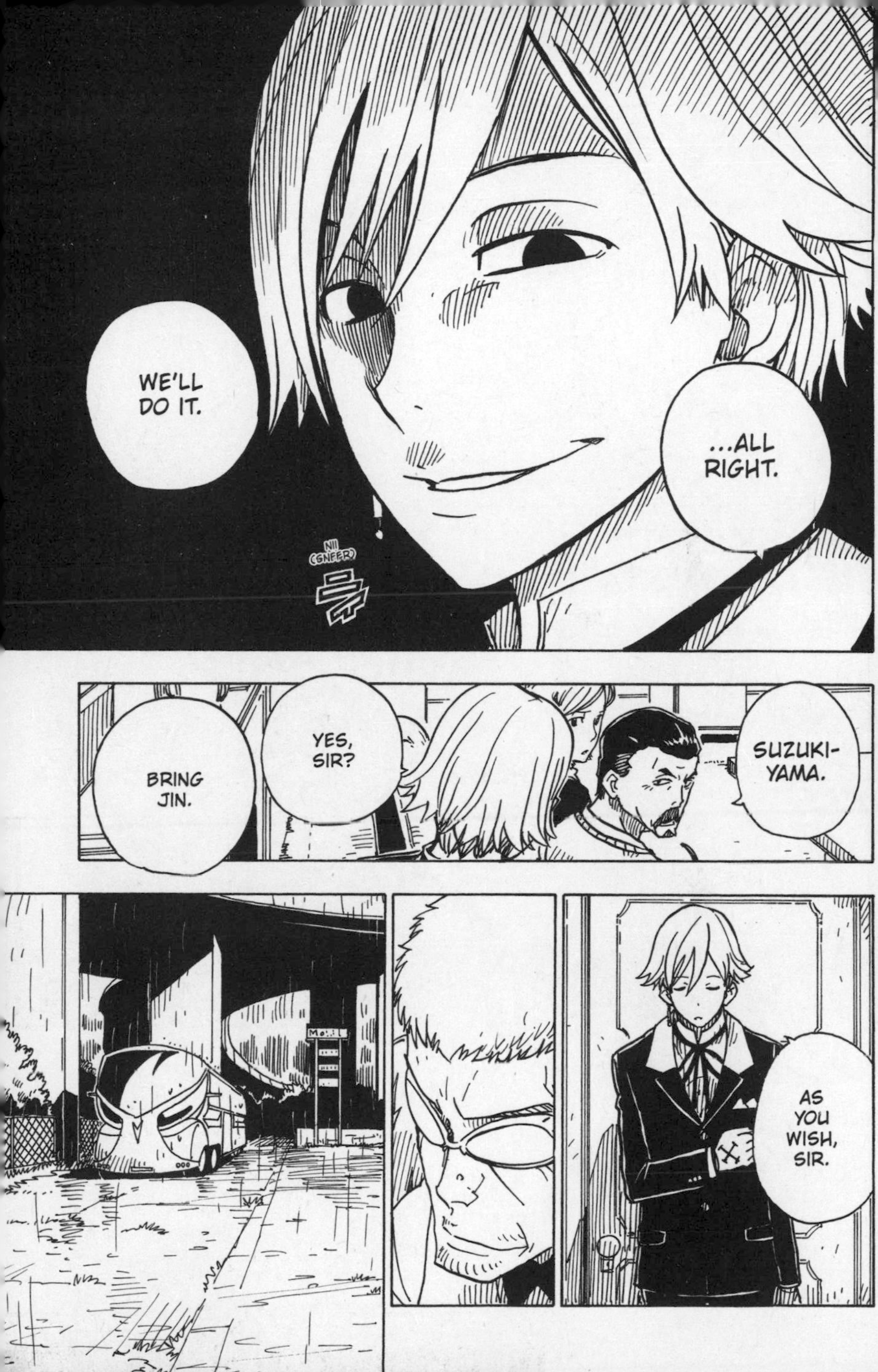
...ALL RIGHT.
WE'LL DO IT.
NII (SNEER)
SUZUKI-YAMA.
YES, SIR?
BRING JIN.
AS YOU WISH, SIR.

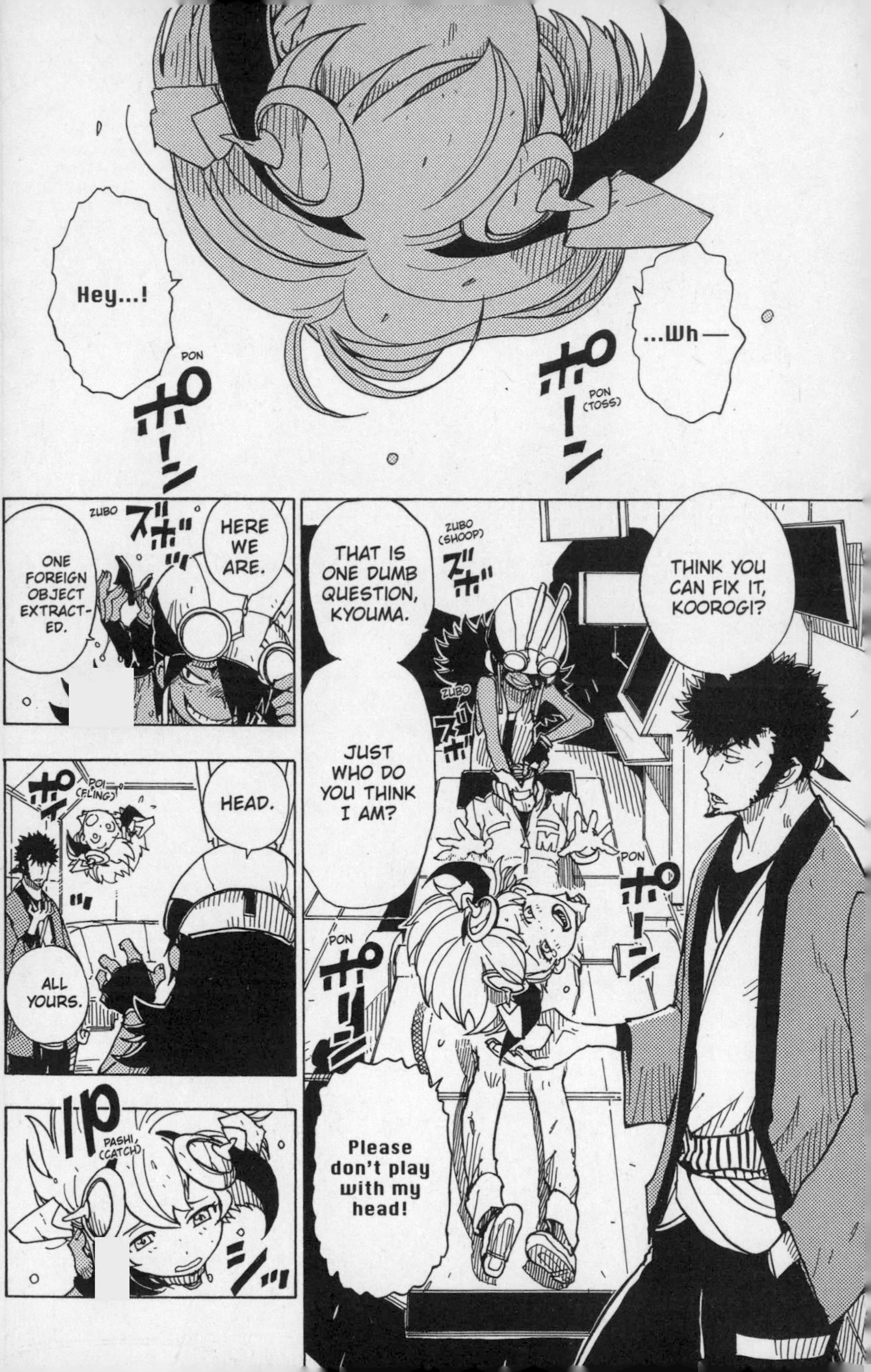
...Wh—
PON (TOSS)
PON
Hey...!
THINK YOU CAN FIX IT, KOOROGI?
ZUBO (SHOOP)
THAT IS ONE DUMB QUESTION, KYOUMA.
ZUBO
JUST WHO DO YOU THINK I AM?
PON
PON
Please don't play with my head!
HERE WE ARE.
ZUBO
ONE FOREIGN OBJECT EXTRACT-ED.
HEAD.
POI (FLING)
ALL YOURS.
PASHI, (CATCH)

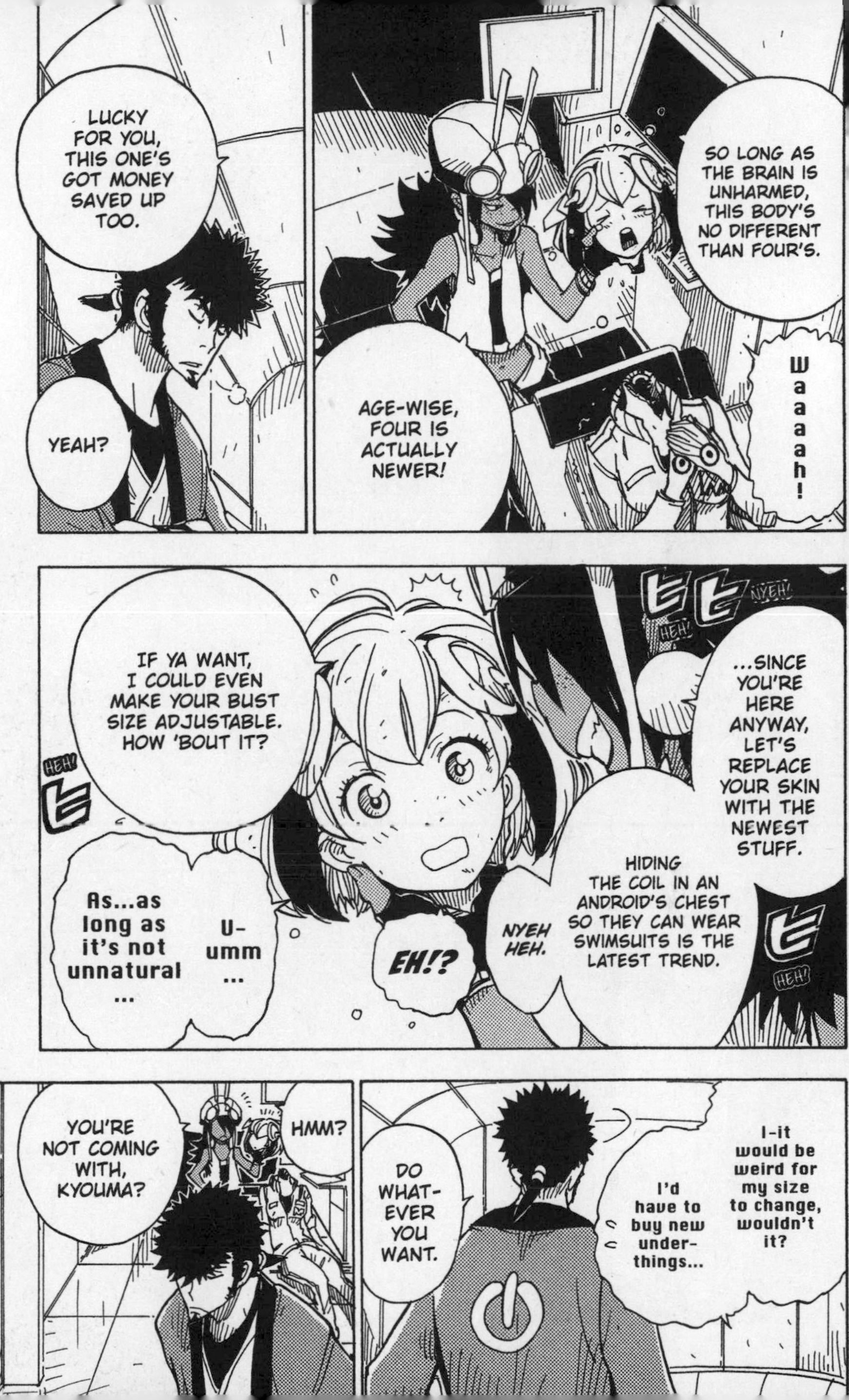
SO LONG AS THE BRAIN IS UNHARMED, THIS BODY'S NO DIFFERENT THAN FOUR'S.
Waaaah!
AGE-WISE, FOUR IS ACTUALLY NEWER!
LUCKY FOR YOU, THIS ONE'S GOT MONEY SAVED UP TOO.
YEAH?
NYEH!
HEH!
...SINCE YOU'RE HERE ANYWAY, LET'S REPLACE YOUR SKIN WITH THE NEWEST STUFF.
HEH!
HIDING THE COIL IN AN ANDROID'S CHEST SO THEY CAN WEAR SWIMSUITS IS THE LATEST TREND.
NYEH HEH.
EH!?
IF YA WANT, I COULD EVEN MAKE YOUR BUST SIZE ADJUSTABLE. HOW 'BOUT IT?
HEH!
U-umm...
As...as long as it's not unnatural...
I-it would be weird for my size to change, wouldn't it?
I'd have to buy new under-things...
DO WHAT-EVER YOU WANT.
HMM?
YOU'RE NOT COMING WITH, KYOUMA?

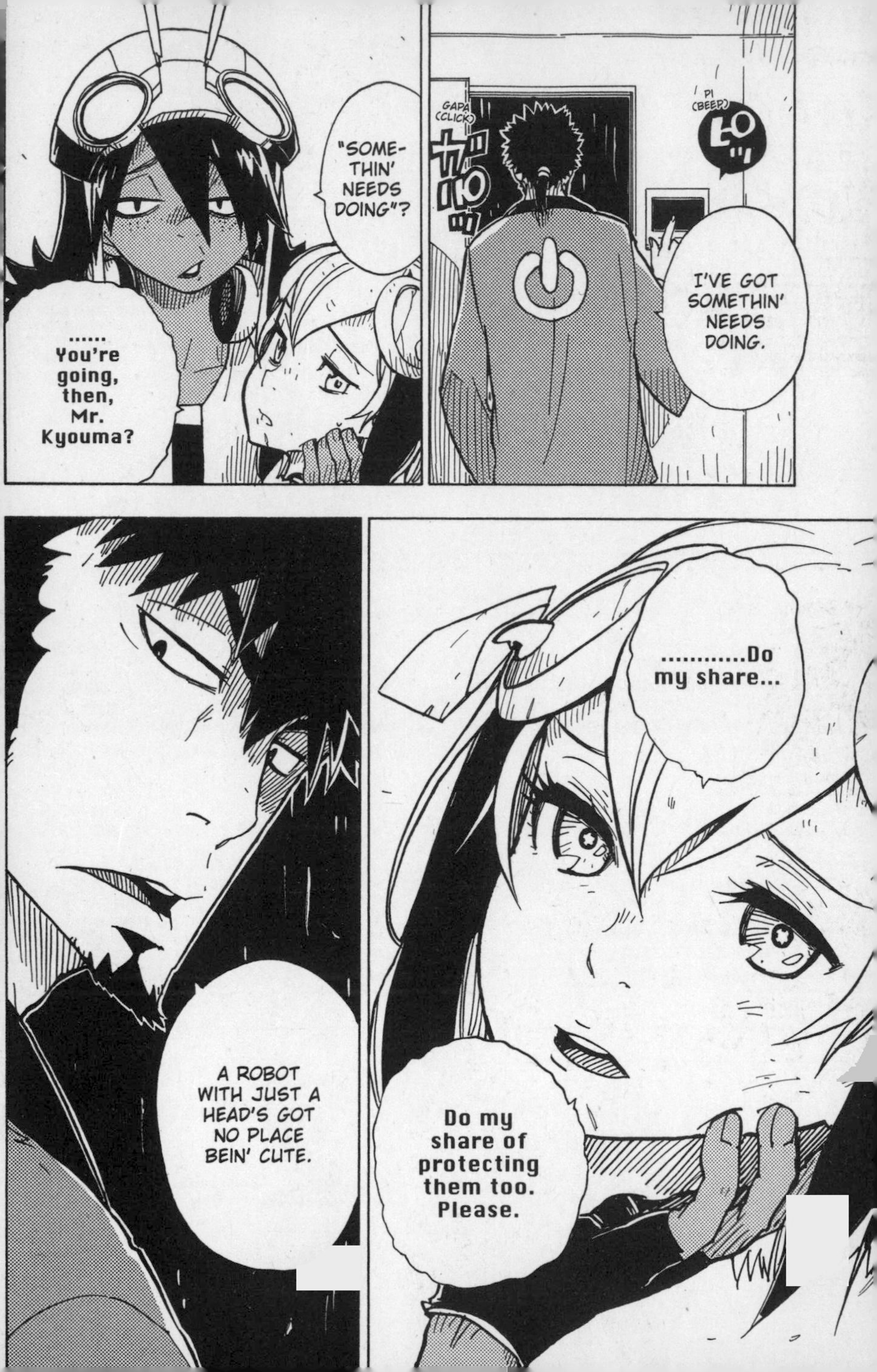
PI (BEEP)
GAPA (CLICK)
I'VE GOT SOMETHIN' NEEDS DOING.
"SOMETHIN' NEEDS DOING"?
...... You're going, then, Mr. Kyouma?
............Do my share...
Do my share of protecting them too. Please.
A ROBOT WITH JUST A HEAD'S GOT NO PLACE BEIN' CUTE.

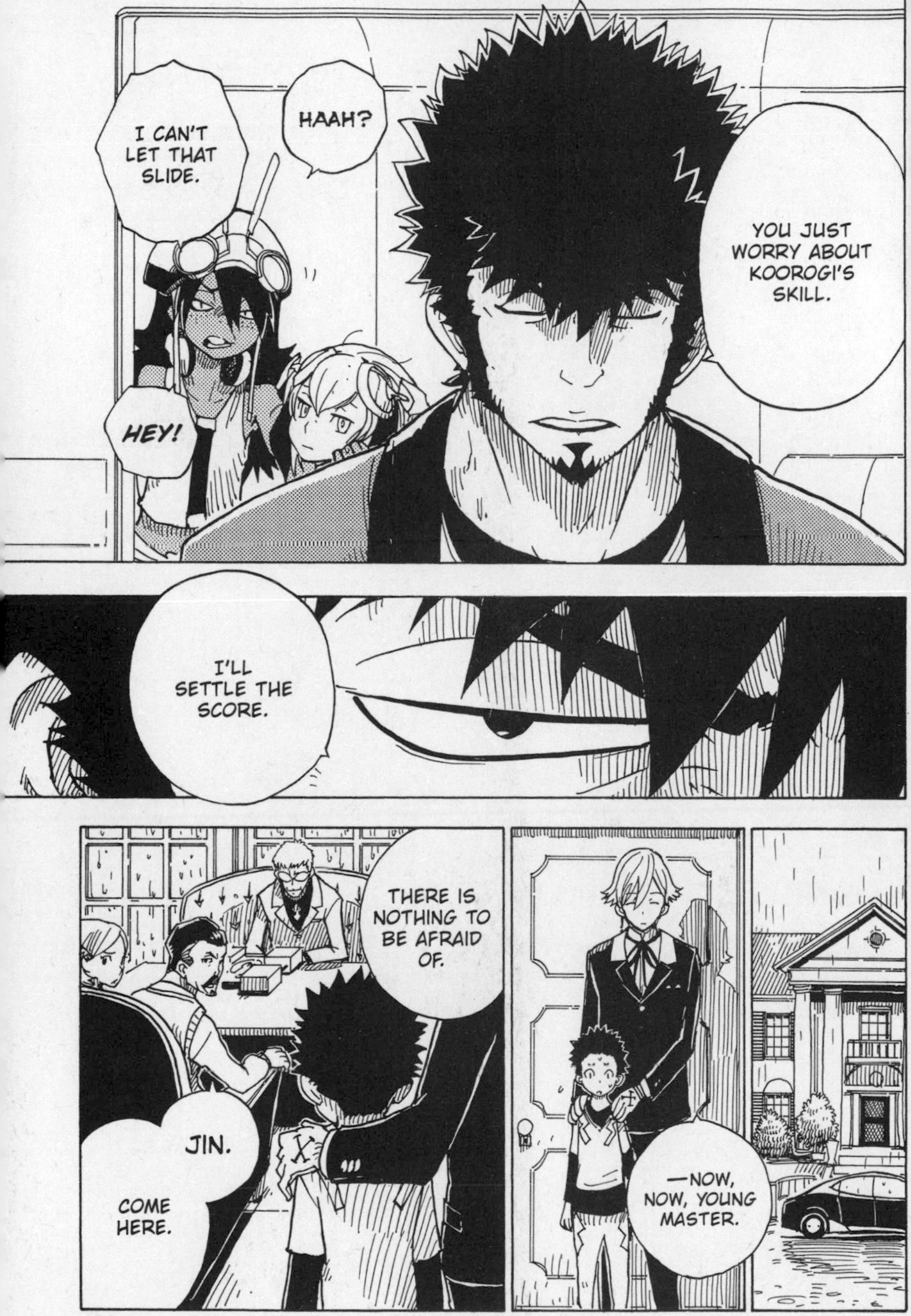
YOU JUST WORRY ABOUT KOOROGI'S SKILL.
HAAH?
I CAN'T LET THAT SLIDE.
HEY!
I'LL SETTLE THE SCORE.
—NOW, NOW, YOUNG MASTER.
THERE IS NOTHING TO BE AFRAID OF.
JIN.
COME HERE.

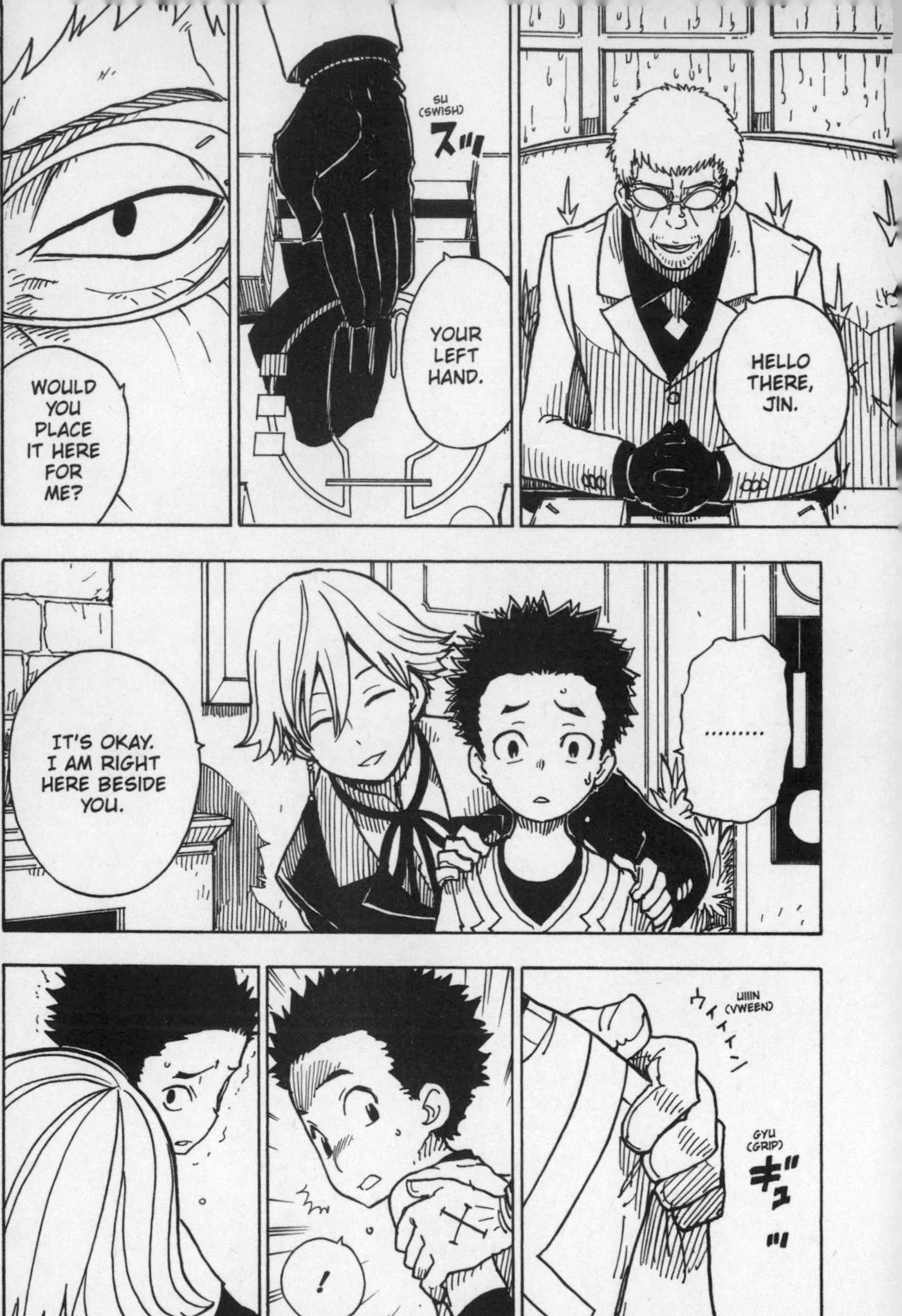
HELLO THERE, JIN.
SU (SWISH)
ズッ
YOUR LEFT HAND.
WOULD YOU PLACE IT HERE FOR ME?
....
IT'S OKAY. I AM RIGHT HERE BESIDE YOU.
UIIIN (VWEEN)
ウィィィン
GYU (GRIP)
ギュッ
!

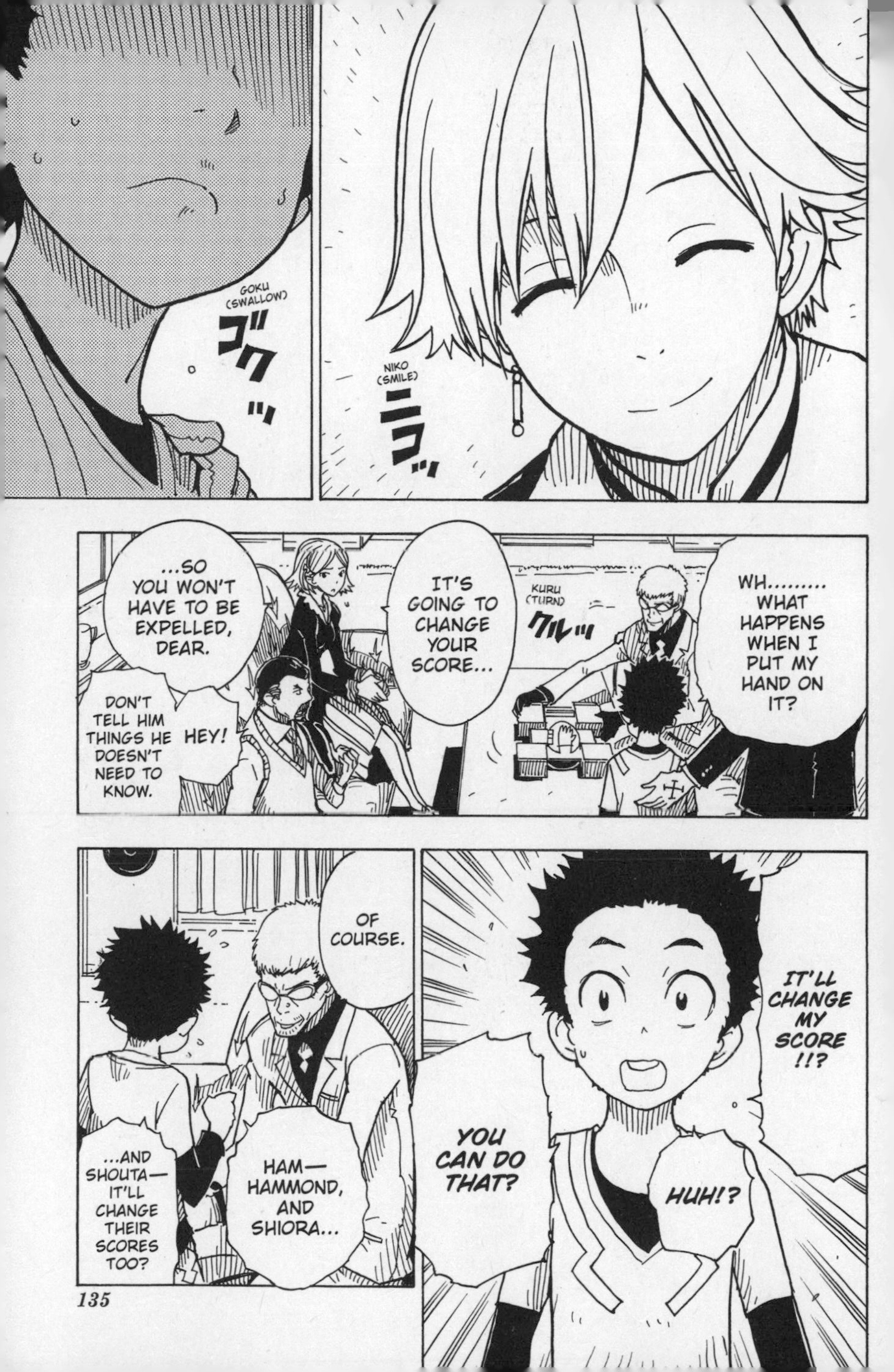
NIKO (SMILE)
ニコッ
GOKU (SWALLOW)
ゴクッ
WH......... WHAT HAPPENS WHEN I PUT MY HAND ON IT?
KURU (TURN)
クルッ
IT'S GOING TO CHANGE YOUR SCORE...
...SO YOU WON'T HAVE TO BE EXPELLED, DEAR.
HEY!
DON'T TELL HIM THINGS HE DOESN'T NEED TO KNOW.
IT'LL CHANGE MY SCORE!!?
HUH!?
YOU CAN DO THAT?
OF COURSE.
HAM—HAMMOND, AND SHIORA...
...AND SHOUTA—IT'LL CHANGE THEIR SCORES TOO?

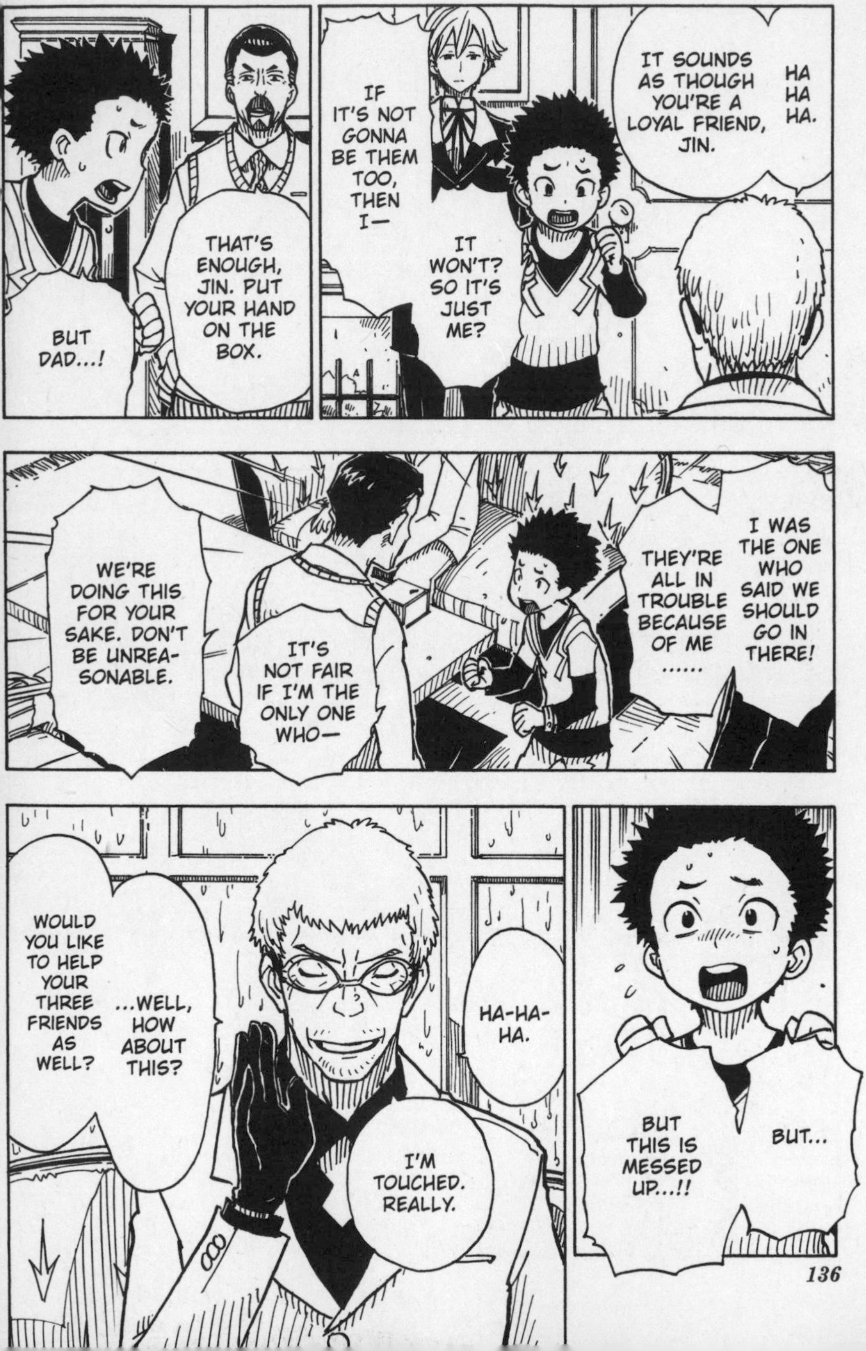
IT WON'T? SO IT'S JUST ME?
IF IT'S NOT GONNA BE THEM TOO, THEN I—
HA HA HA.
IT SOUNDS AS THOUGH YOU'RE A LOYAL FRIEND, JIN.
THAT'S ENOUGH, JIN. PUT YOUR HAND ON THE BOX.
BUT DAD...!
I WAS THE ONE WHO SAID WE SHOULD GO IN THERE!
THEY'RE ALL IN TROUBLE BECAUSE OF ME......
IT'S NOT FAIR IF I'M THE ONLY ONE WHO—
WE'RE DOING THIS FOR YOUR SAKE. DON'T BE UNREA-SONABLE.
BUT...
BUT THIS IS MESSED UP...!!
HA-HA-HA.
I'M TOUCHED. REALLY.
...WELL, HOW ABOUT THIS?
WOULD YOU LIKE TO HELP YOUR THREE FRIENDS AS WELL?

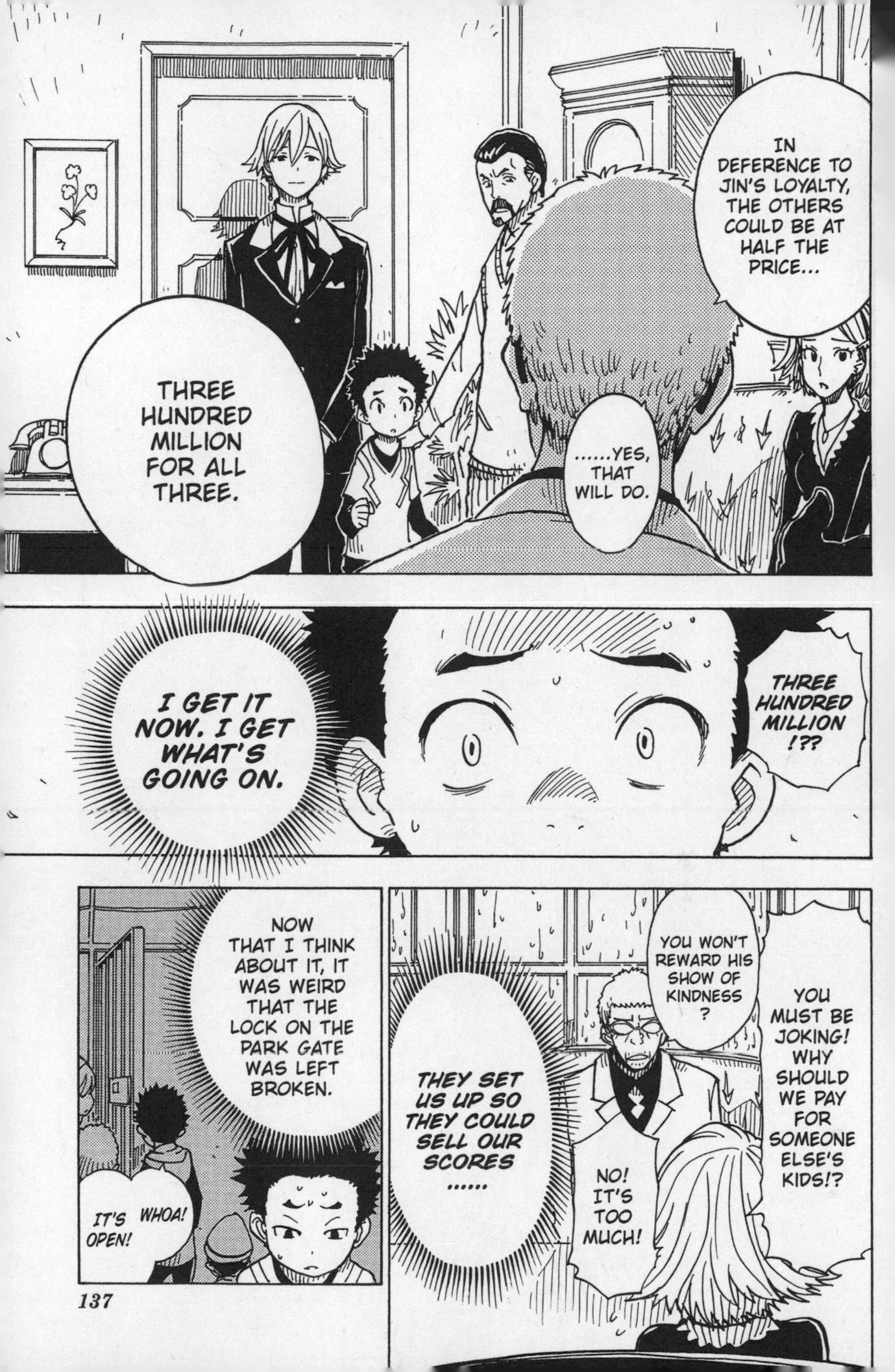
IN DEFERENCE TO JIN'S LOYALTY, THE OTHERS COULD BE AT HALF THE PRICE...
THREE HUNDRED MILLION FOR ALL THREE.
......YES, THAT WILL DO.
THREE HUNDRED MILLION !??
I GET IT NOW. I GET WHAT'S GOING ON.
YOU WON'T REWARD HIS SHOW OF KINDNESS ?
YOU MUST BE JOKING! WHY SHOULD WE PAY FOR SOMEONE ELSE'S KIDS!?
NO! IT'S TOO MUCH!
THEY SET US UP SO THEY COULD SELL OUR SCORES ......
NOW THAT I THINK ABOUT IT, IT WAS WEIRD THAT THE LOCK ON THE PARK GATE WAS LEFT BROKEN.
WHOA!
IT'S OPEN!

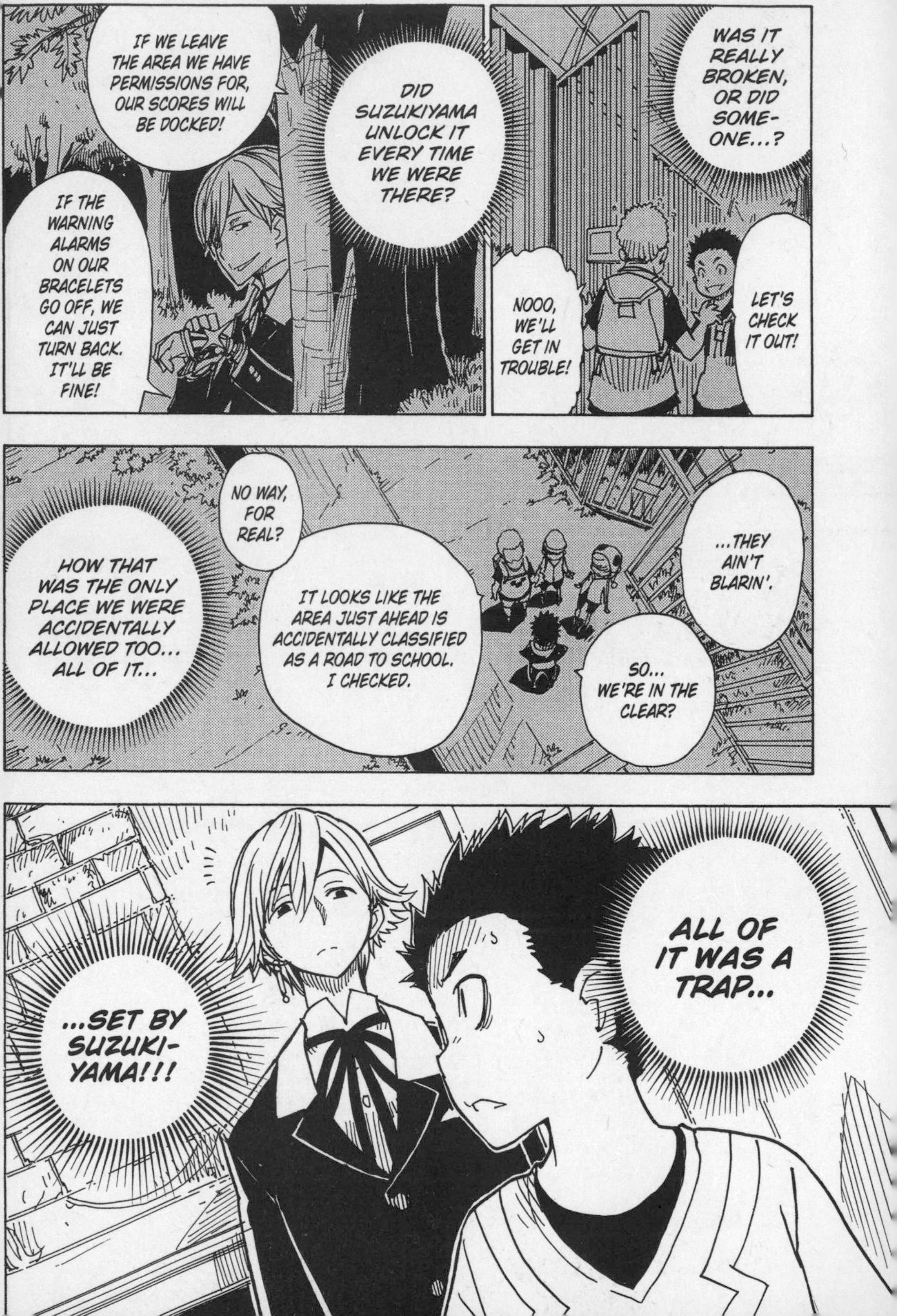
WAS IT REALLY BROKEN, OR DID SOME-ONE...?
LET'S CHECK IT OUT!
NOOO, WE'LL GET IN TROUBLE!
DID SUZUKIYAMA UNLOCK IT EVERY TIME WE WERE THERE?
IF WE LEAVE THE AREA WE HAVE PERMISSIONS FOR, OUR SCORES WILL BE DOCKED!
IF THE WARNING ALARMS ON OUR BRACELETS GO OFF, WE CAN JUST TURN BACK. IT'LL BE FINE!
...THEY AIN'T BLARIN'.
SO... WE'RE IN THE CLEAR?
IT LOOKS LIKE THE AREA JUST AHEAD IS ACCIDENTALLY CLASSIFIED AS A ROAD TO SCHOOL. I CHECKED.
NO WAY, FOR REAL?
HOW THAT WAS THE ONLY PLACE WE WERE ACCIDENTALLY ALLOWED TOO... ALL OF IT...
ALL OF IT WAS A TRAP...
...SET BY SUZUKI-YAMA!!!

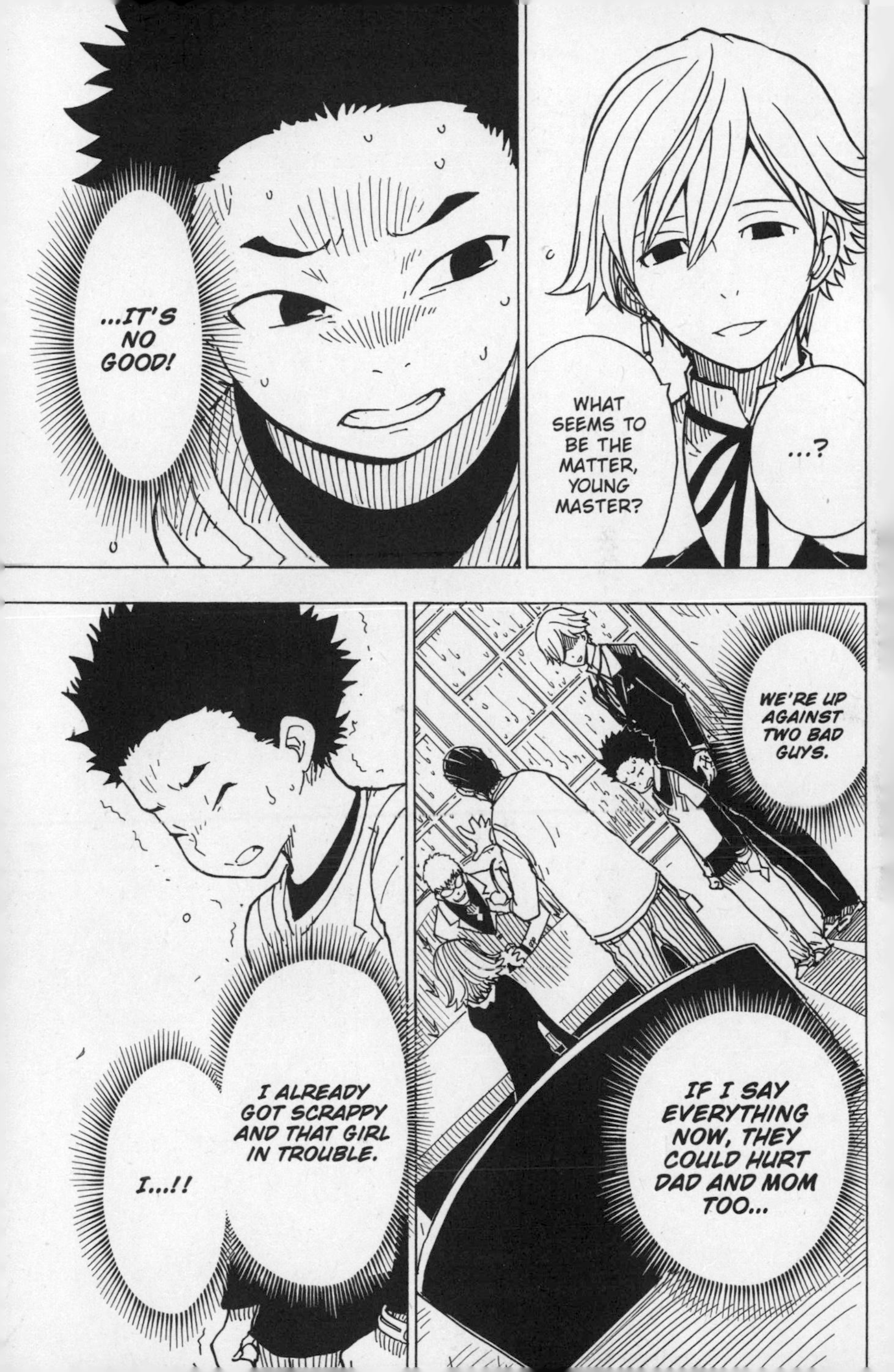
...?
WHAT SEEMS TO BE THE MATTER, YOUNG MASTER?
...IT'S NO GOOD!
WE'RE UP AGAINST TWO BAD GUYS.
IF I SAY EVERYTHING NOW, THEY COULD HURT DAD AND MOM TOO...
I ALREADY GOT SCRAPPY AND THAT GIRL IN TROUBLE.
I...!!

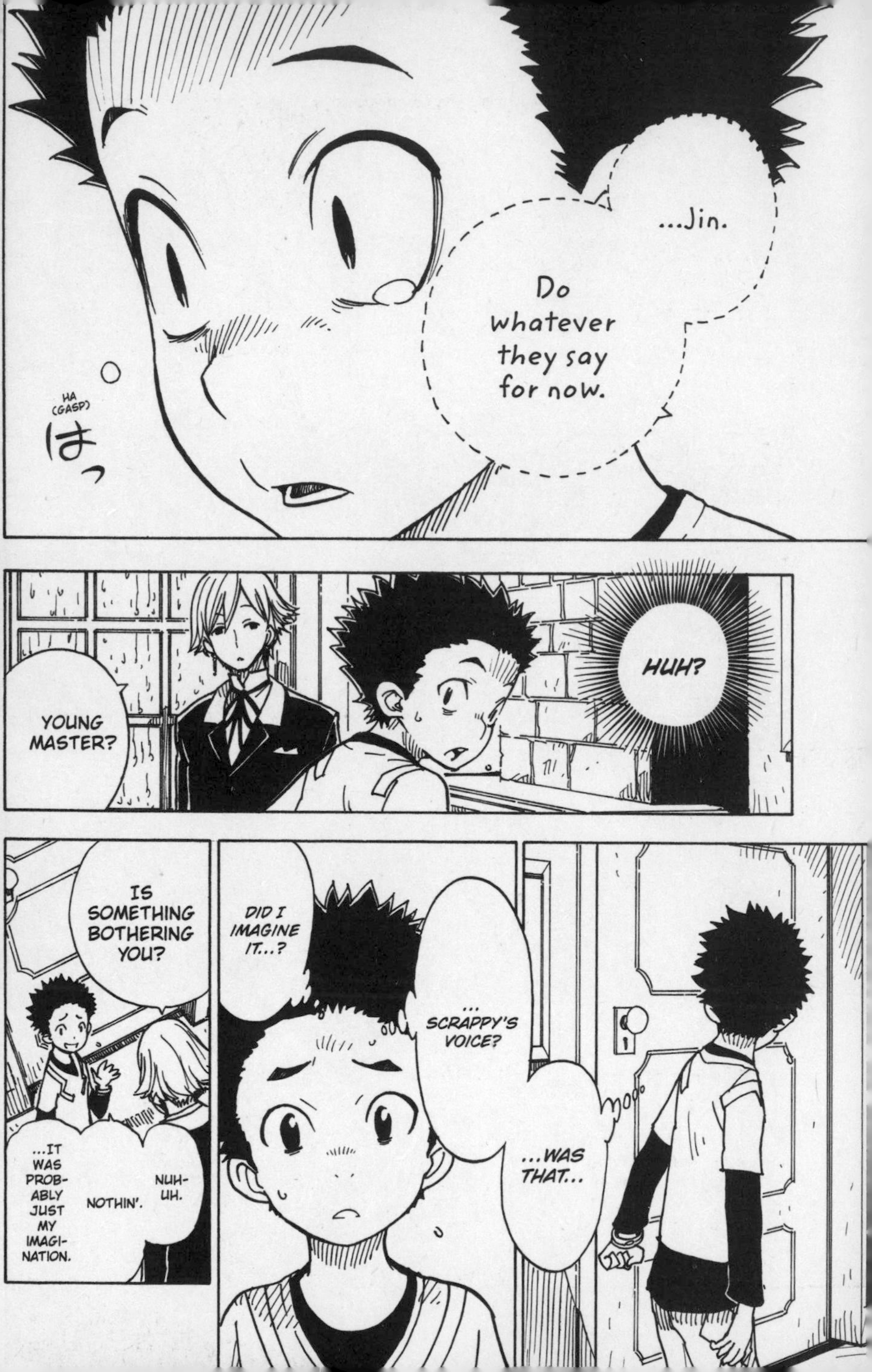
...Jin.
Do whatever they say for now.
HA (GASP)
はっ
HUH?
YOUNG MASTER?
...WAS THAT...
...SCRAPPY'S VOICE?
DID I IMAGINE IT...?
IS SOMETHING BOTHERING YOU?
NUH-UH.
NOTHIN'.
...IT WAS PROBABLY JUST MY IMAGINATION.

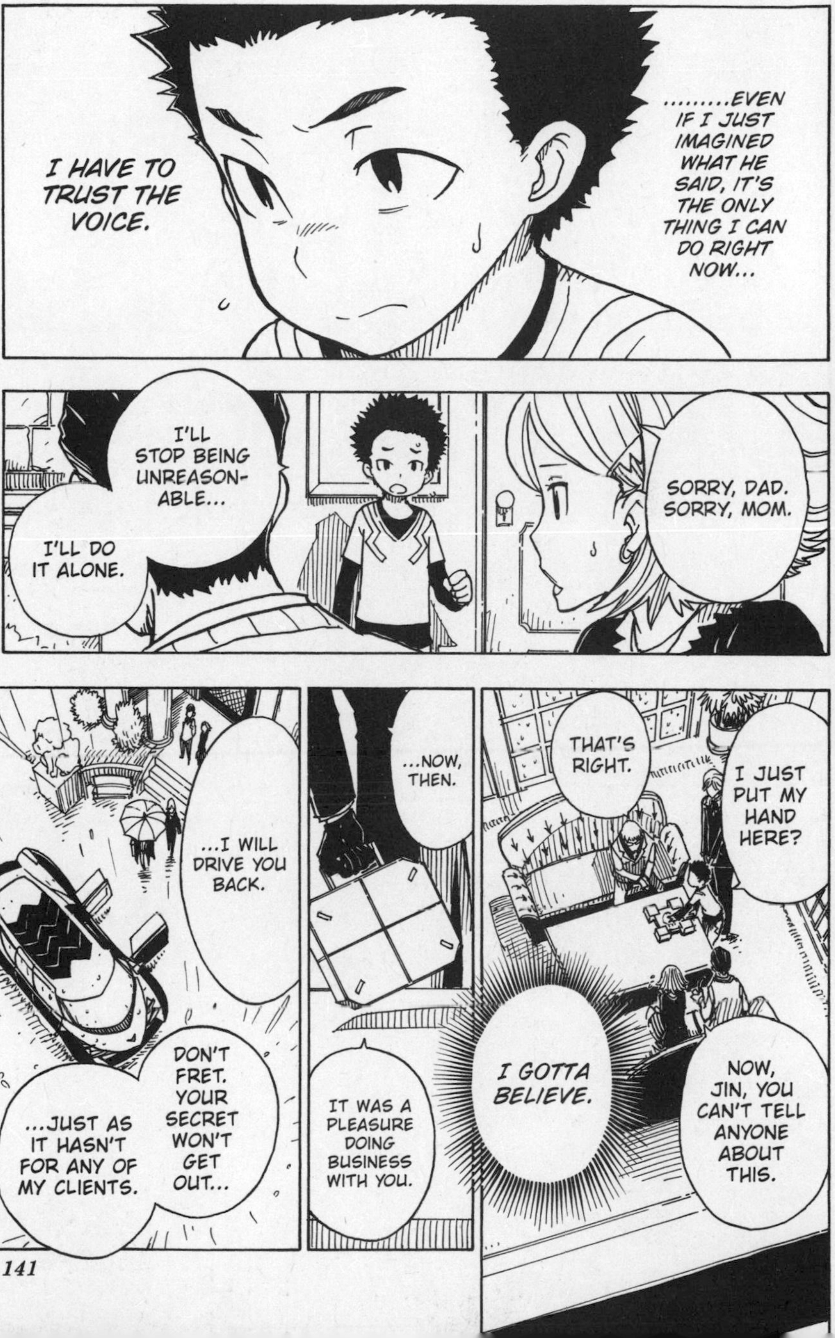

........EVEN IF I JUST IMAGINED WHAT HE SAID, IT'S THE ONLY THING I CAN DO RIGHT NOW...
I HAVE TO TRUST THE VOICE.
SORRY, DAD. SORRY, MOM.
I'LL STOP BEING UNREASON-ABLE...
I'LL DO IT ALONE.
I JUST PUT MY HAND HERE?
THAT'S RIGHT.
NOW, JIN, YOU CAN'T TELL ANYONE ABOUT THIS.
I GOTTA BELIEVE.
...NOW, THEN.
IT WAS A PLEASURE DOING BUSINESS WITH YOU.
...I WILL DRIVE YOU BACK.
DON'T FRET. YOUR SECRET WON'T GET OUT...
...JUST AS IT HASN'T FOR ANY OF MY CLIENTS.

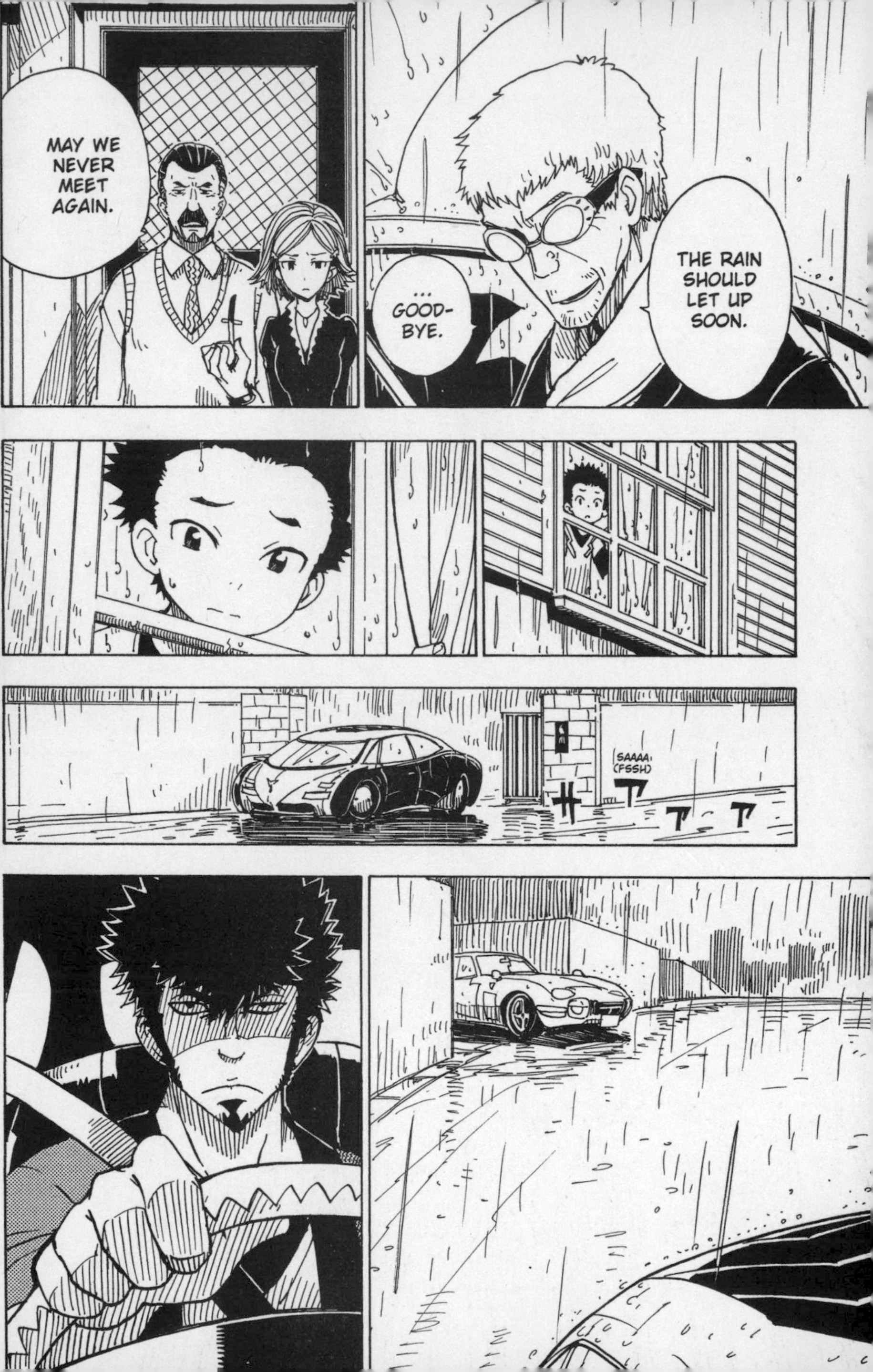
THE RAIN SHOULD LET UP SOON.
...GOOD-BYE.
MAY WE NEVER MEET AGAIN.
SAAAA (FSSH)
サァァァ

FILE.14
CHASE

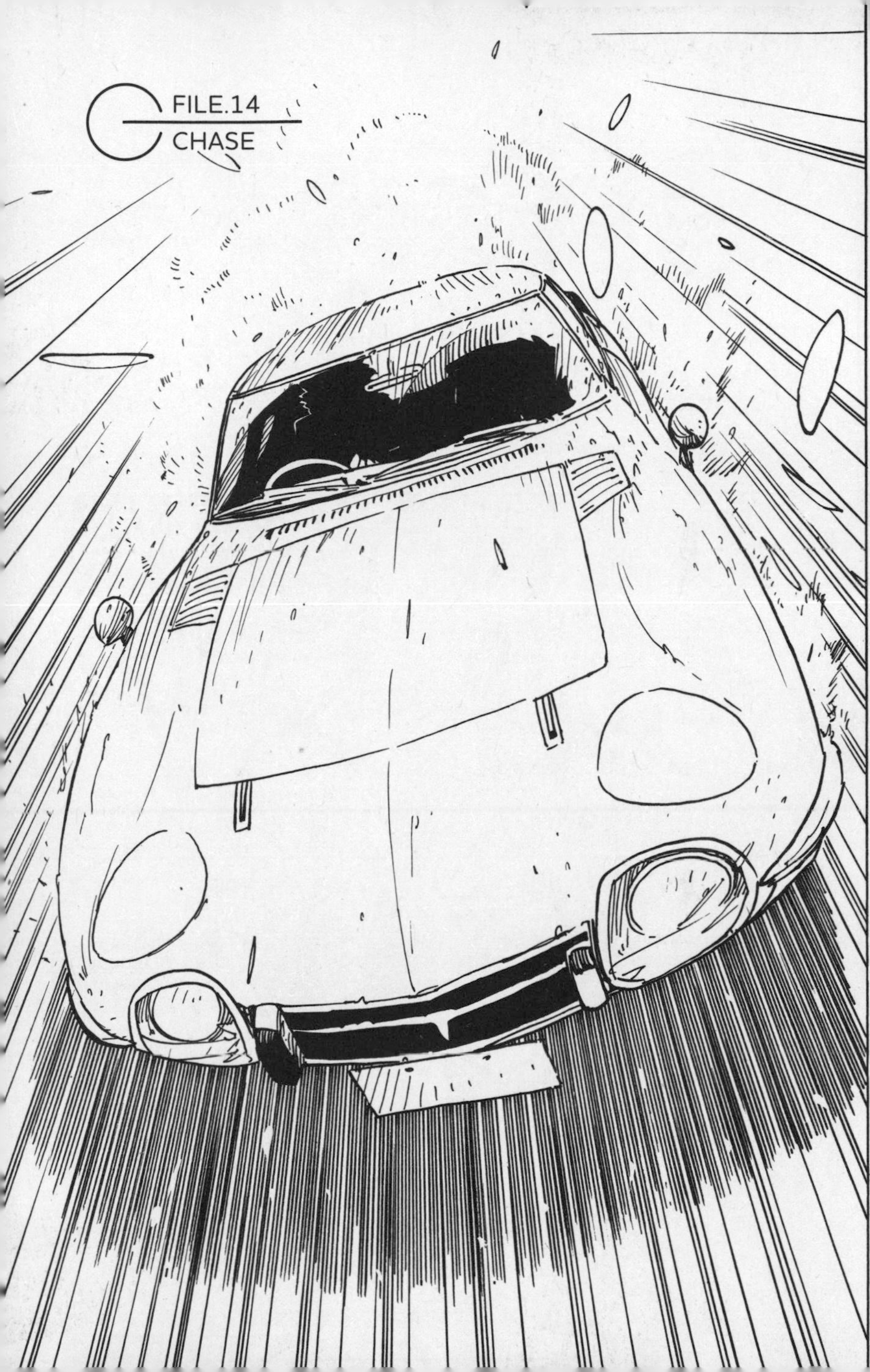

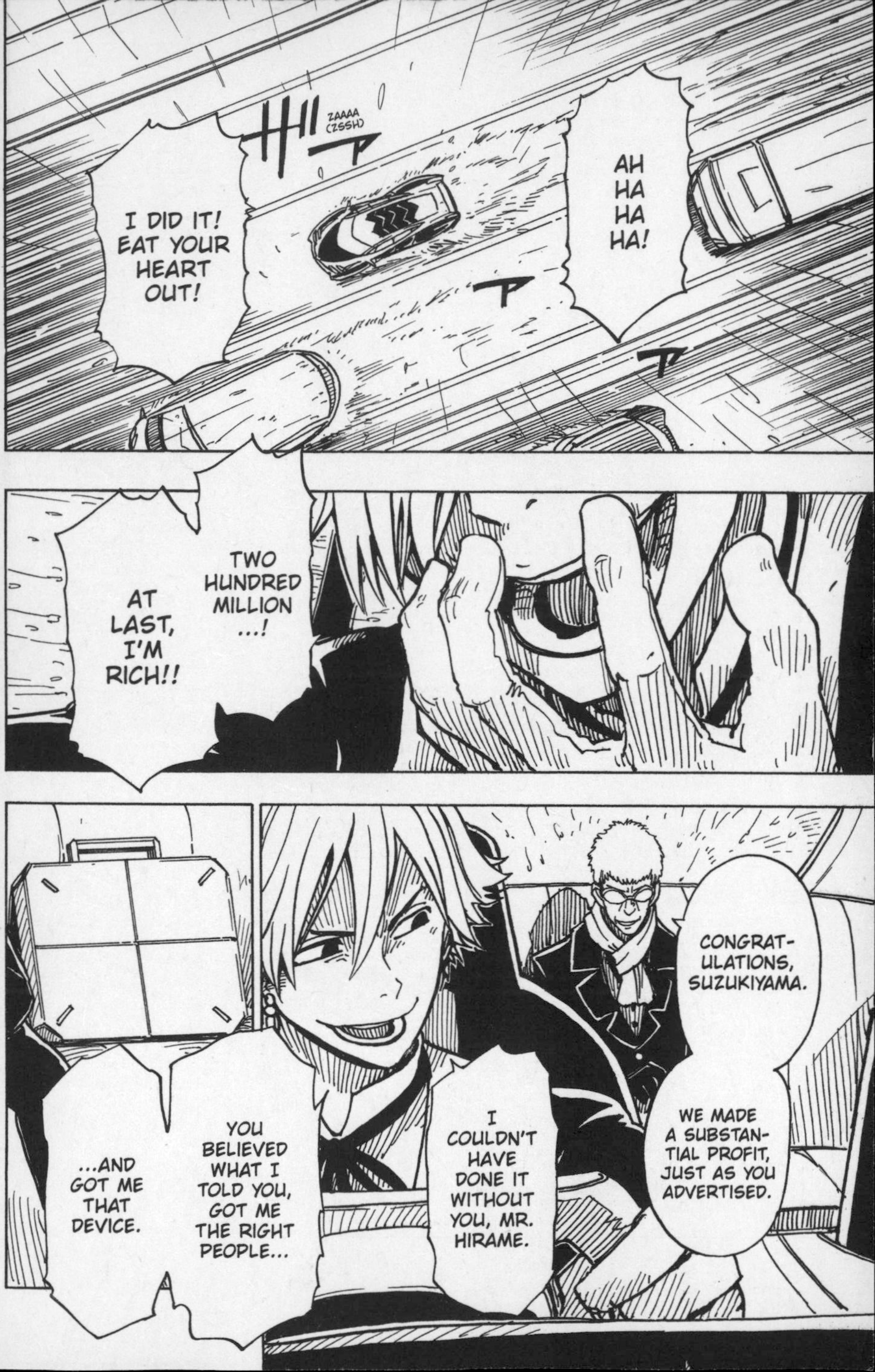
AH HA HA HA!
ZAAAA (ZSSH)
I DID IT! EAT YOUR HEART OUT!
TWO HUNDRED MILLION ...!
AT LAST, I'M RICH!!
CONGRAT-ULATIONS, SUZUKIYAMA.
WE MADE A SUBSTAN-TIAL PROFIT, JUST AS YOU ADVERTISED.
I COULDN'T HAVE DONE IT WITHOUT YOU, MR. HIRAME.
YOU BELIEVED WHAT I TOLD YOU, GOT ME THE RIGHT PEOPLE...
...AND GOT ME THAT DEVICE.

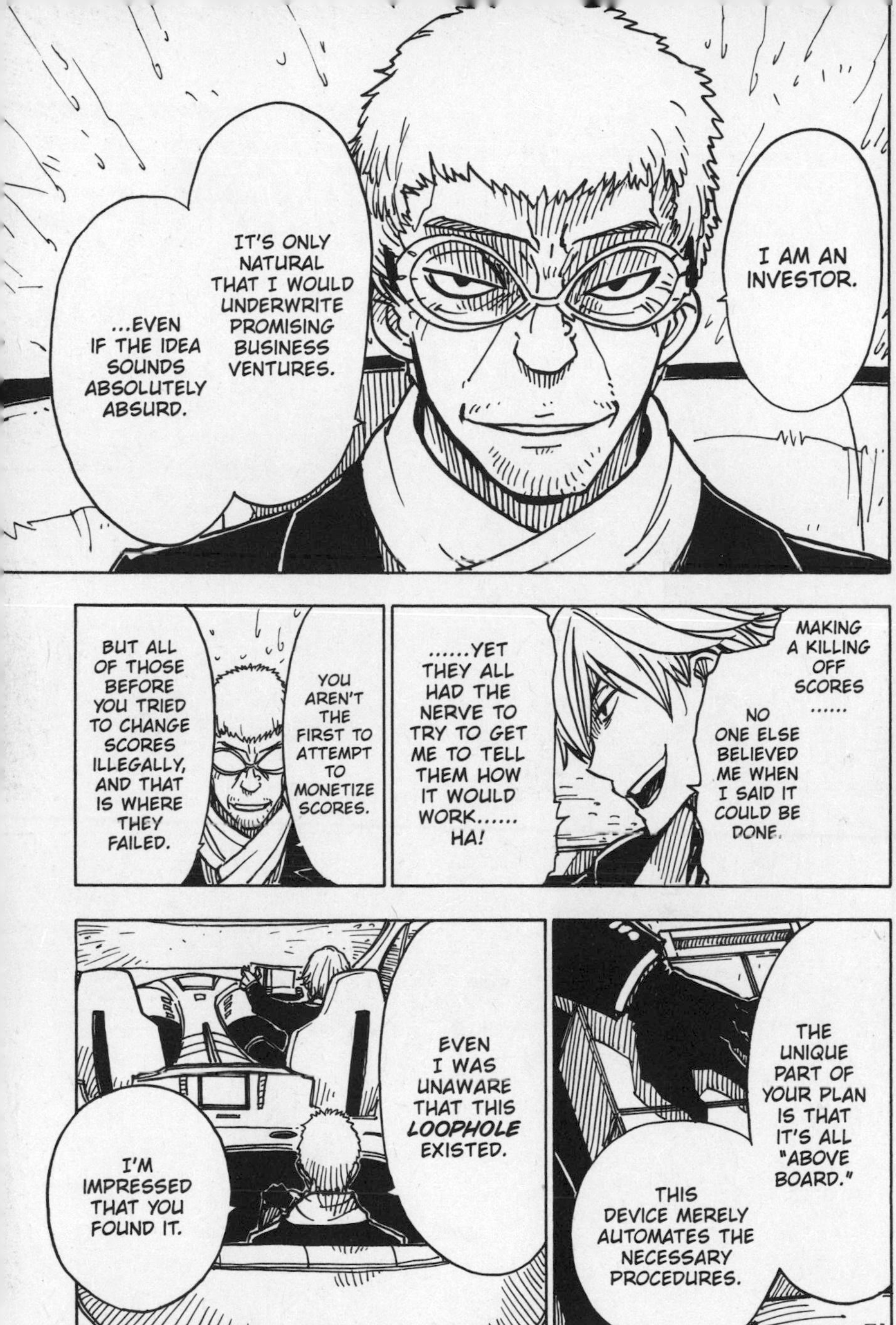
I AM AN INVESTOR.
IT'S ONLY NATURAL THAT I WOULD UNDERWRITE PROMISING BUSINESS VENTURES.
...EVEN IF THE IDEA SOUNDS ABSOLUTELY ABSURD.
MAKING A KILLING OFF SCORES......
NO ONE ELSE BELIEVED ME WHEN I SAID IT COULD BE DONE.
......YET THEY ALL HAD THE NERVE TO TRY TO GET ME TO TELL THEM HOW IT WOULD WORK...... HA!
YOU AREN'T THE FIRST TO ATTEMPT TO MONETIZE SCORES.
BUT ALL OF THOSE BEFORE YOU TRIED TO CHANGE SCORES ILLEGALLY, AND THAT IS WHERE THEY FAILED.
THE UNIQUE PART OF YOUR PLAN IS THAT IT'S ALL "ABOVE BOARD."
THIS DEVICE MERELY AUTOMATES THE NECESSARY PROCEDURES.
EVEN I WAS UNAWARE THAT THIS *LOOPHOLE* EXISTED.
I'M IMPRESSED THAT YOU FOUND IT.

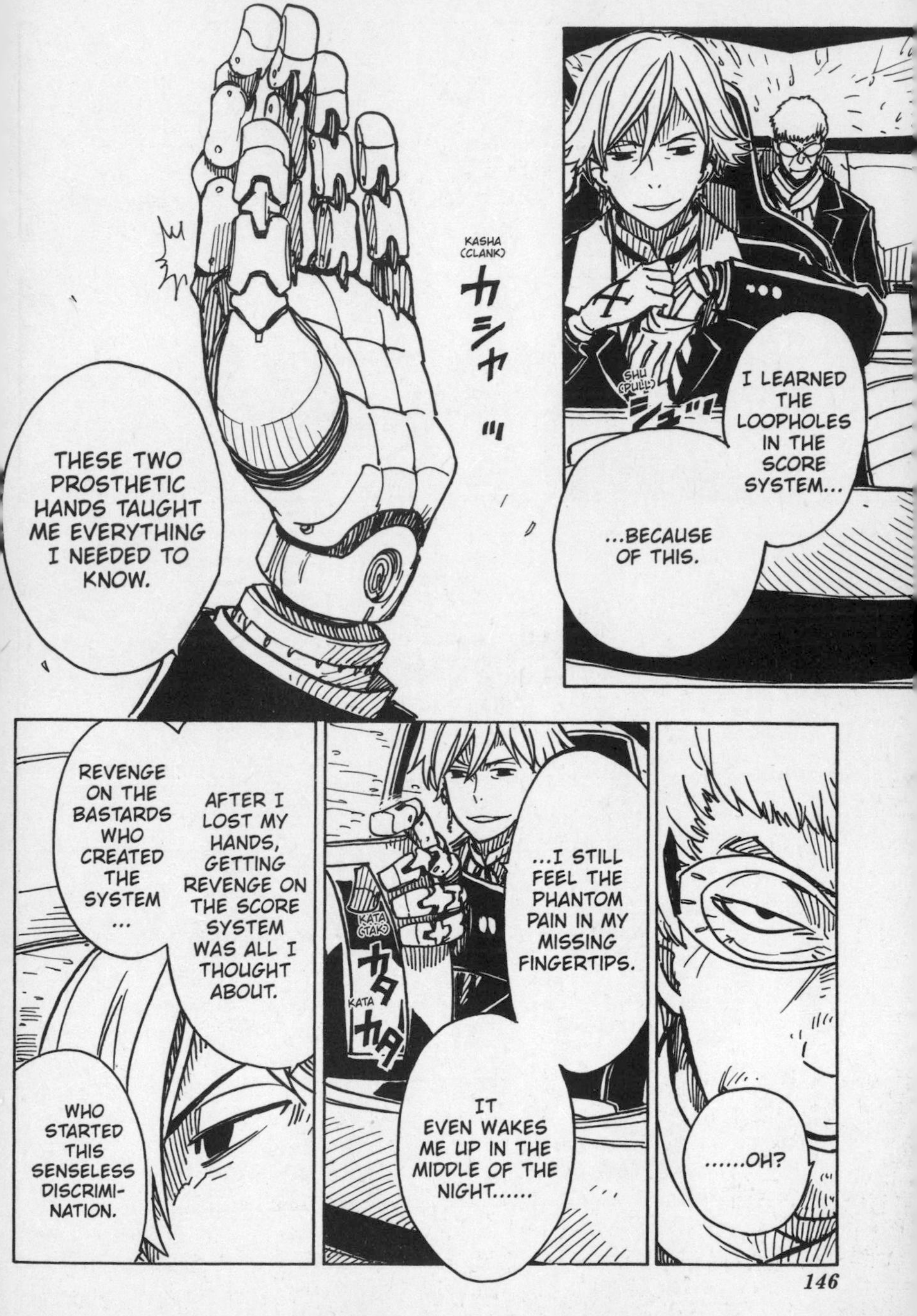
SHU (PULL)
ジュッ
I LEARNED THE LOOPHOLES IN THE SCORE SYSTEM...
...BECAUSE OF THIS.
KASHA (CLANK)
カシャッ
THESE TWO PROSTHETIC HANDS TAUGHT ME EVERYTHING I NEEDED TO KNOW.
......OH?
...I STILL FEEL THE PHANTOM PAIN IN MY MISSING FINGERTIPS.
KATA (TAK)
カタ
KATA
カタ
IT EVEN WAKES ME UP IN THE MIDDLE OF THE NIGHT......
AFTER I LOST MY HANDS, GETTING REVENGE ON THE SCORE SYSTEM WAS ALL I THOUGHT ABOUT.
REVENGE ON THE BASTARDS WHO CREATED THE SYSTEM...
WHO STARTED THIS SENSELESS DISCRIMI-NATION.

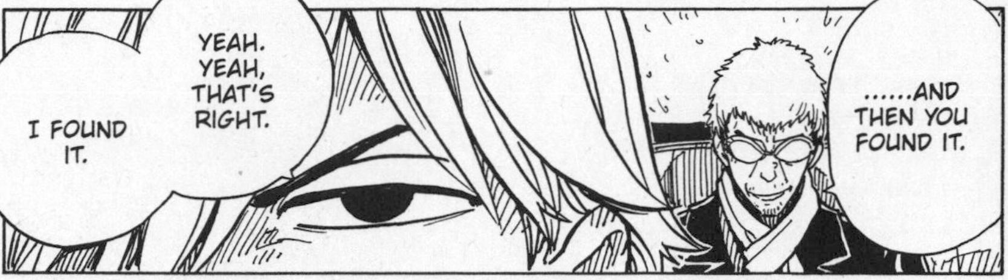
......AND THEN YOU FOUND IT.
YEAH. YEAH, THAT'S RIGHT.
I FOUND IT.

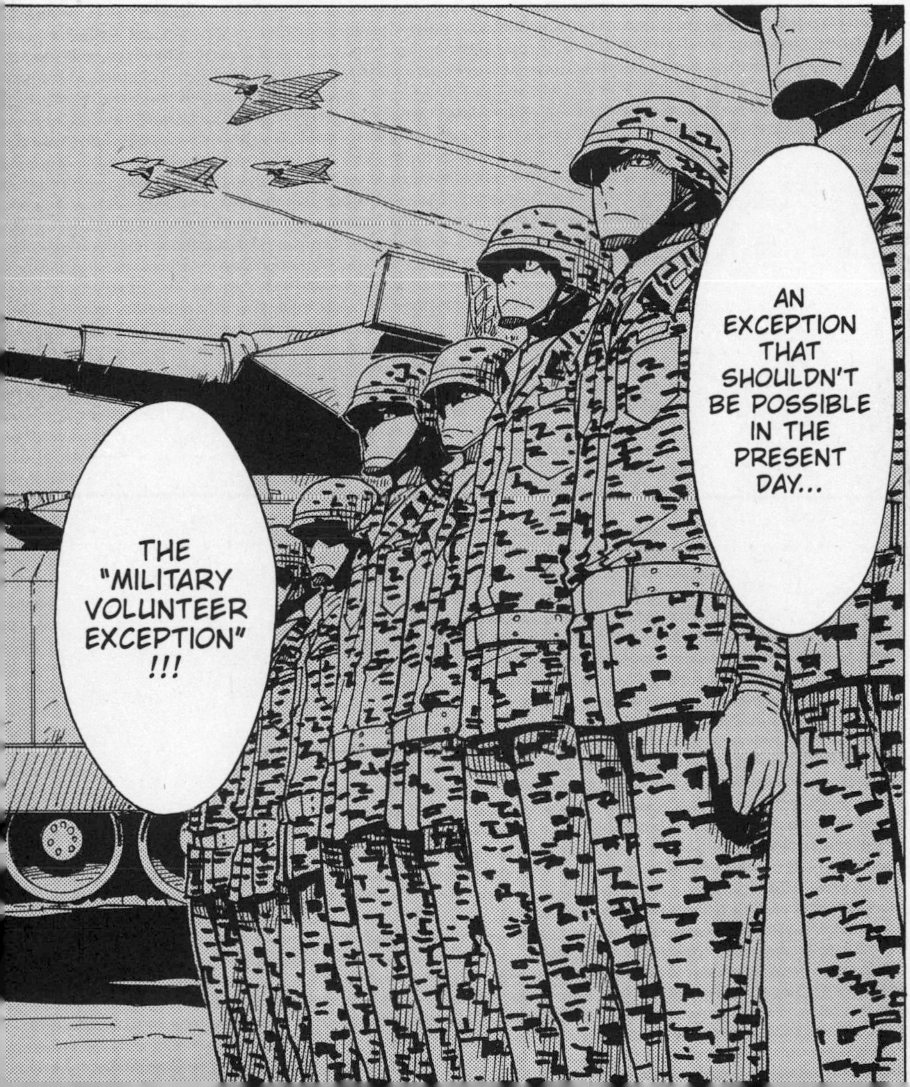
AN EXCEPTION THAT SHOULDN'T BE POSSIBLE IN THE PRESENT DAY...
THE "MILITARY VOLUNTEER EXCEPTION"!!!

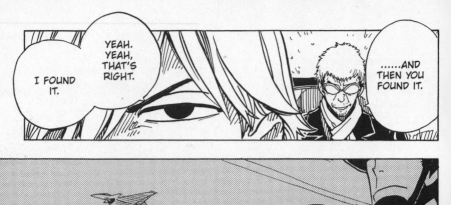

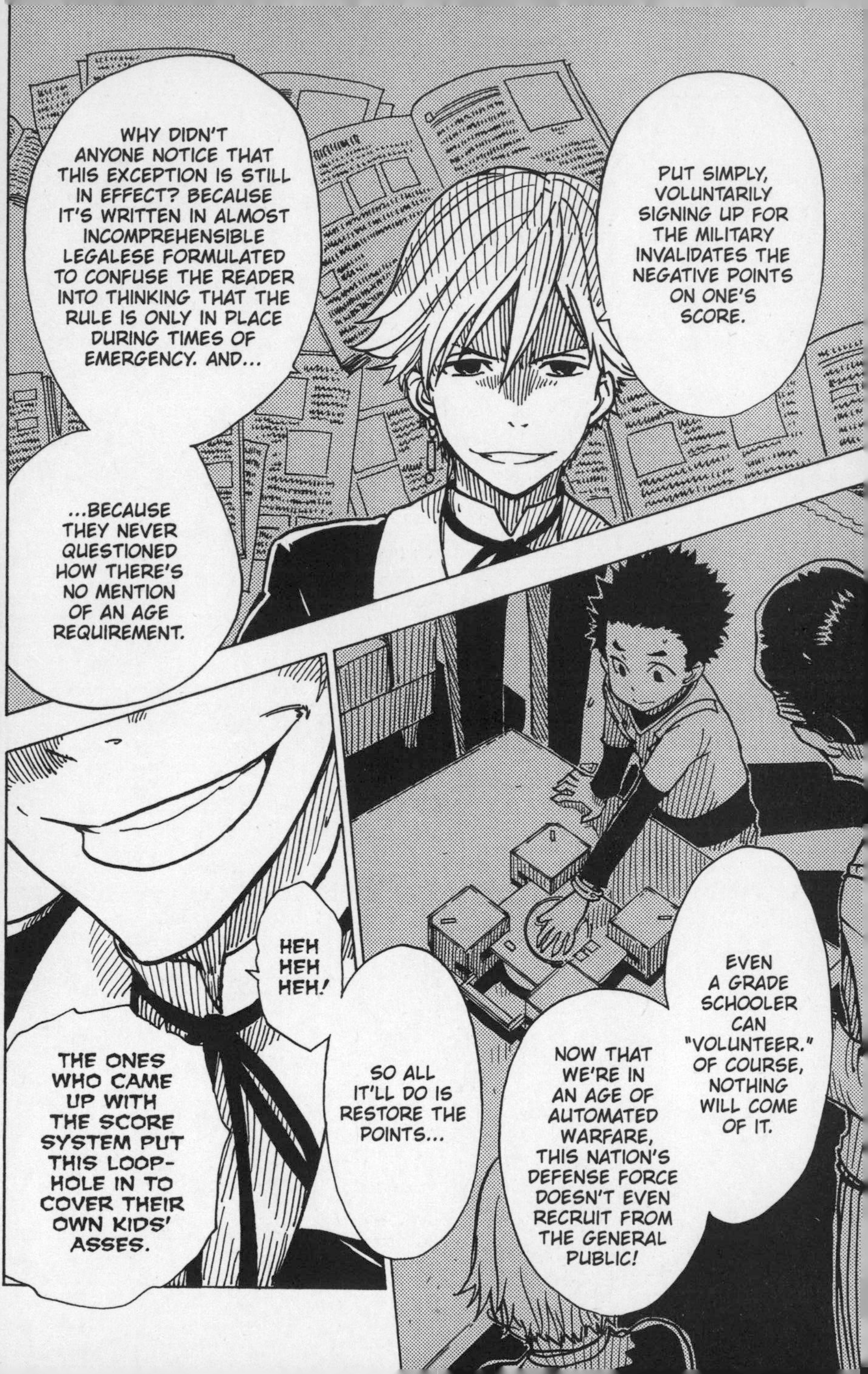
PUT SIMPLY, VOLUNTARILY SIGNING UP FOR THE MILITARY INVALIDATES THE NEGATIVE POINTS ON ONE'S SCORE.
WHY DIDN'T ANYONE NOTICE THAT THIS EXCEPTION IS STILL IN EFFECT? BECAUSE IT'S WRITTEN IN ALMOST INCOMPREHENSIBLE LEGALESE FORMULATED TO CONFUSE THE READER INTO THINKING THAT THE RULE IS ONLY IN PLACE DURING TIMES OF EMERGENCY. AND...
...BECAUSE THEY NEVER QUESTIONED HOW THERE'S NO MENTION OF AN AGE REQUIREMENT.
EVEN A GRADE SCHOOLER CAN "VOLUNTEER." OF COURSE, NOTHING WILL COME OF IT.
NOW THAT WE'RE IN AN AGE OF AUTOMATED WARFARE, THIS NATION'S DEFENSE FORCE DOESN'T EVEN RECRUIT FROM THE GENERAL PUBLIC!
SO ALL IT'LL DO IS RESTORE THE POINTS...
HEH HEH HEH!
THE ONES WHO CAME UP WITH THE SCORE SYSTEM PUT THIS LOOP-HOLE IN TO COVER THEIR OWN KIDS' ASSES.

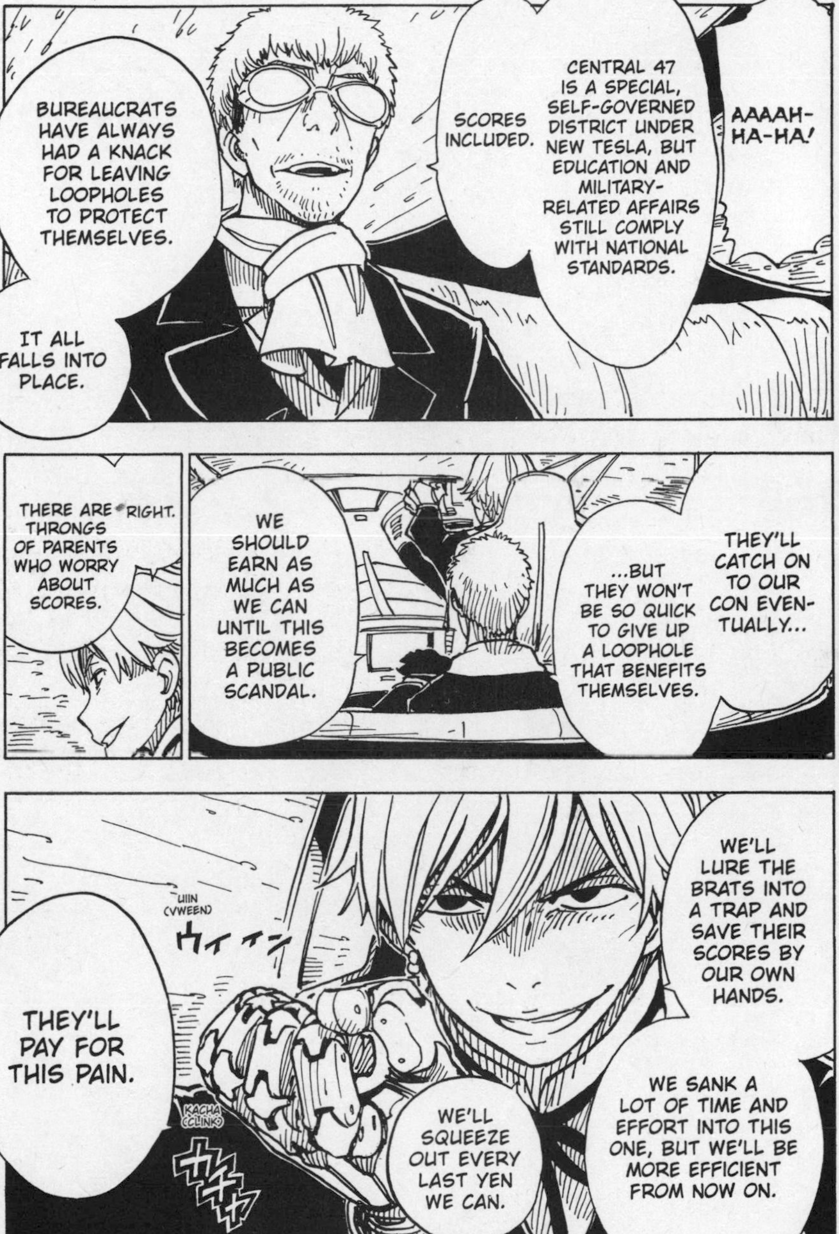
AAAAH-HA-HA!
CENTRAL 47 IS A SPECIAL, SELF-GOVERNED DISTRICT UNDER NEW TESLA, BUT EDUCATION AND MILITARY-RELATED AFFAIRS STILL COMPLY WITH NATIONAL STANDARDS.
SCORES INCLUDED.
BUREAUCRATS HAVE ALWAYS HAD A KNACK FOR LEAVING LOOPHOLES TO PROTECT THEMSELVES.
IT ALL FALLS INTO PLACE.
THEY'LL CATCH ON TO OUR CON EVEN-TUALLY...
...BUT THEY WON'T BE SO QUICK TO GIVE UP A LOOPHOLE THAT BENEFITS THEMSELVES.
WE SHOULD EARN AS MUCH AS WE CAN UNTIL THIS BECOMES A PUBLIC SCANDAL.
RIGHT.
THERE ARE THRONGS OF PARENTS WHO WORRY ABOUT SCORES.
WE'LL LURE THE BRATS INTO A TRAP AND SAVE THEIR SCORES BY OUR OWN HANDS.
WE SANK A LOT OF TIME AND EFFORT INTO THIS ONE, BUT WE'LL BE MORE EFFICIENT FROM NOW ON.
UIIN (VWEEN)
ウィィ―ン
WE'LL SQUEEZE OUT EVERY LAST YEN WE CAN.
KACHA (CLINK)
カチャ
THEY'LL PAY FOR THIS PAIN.

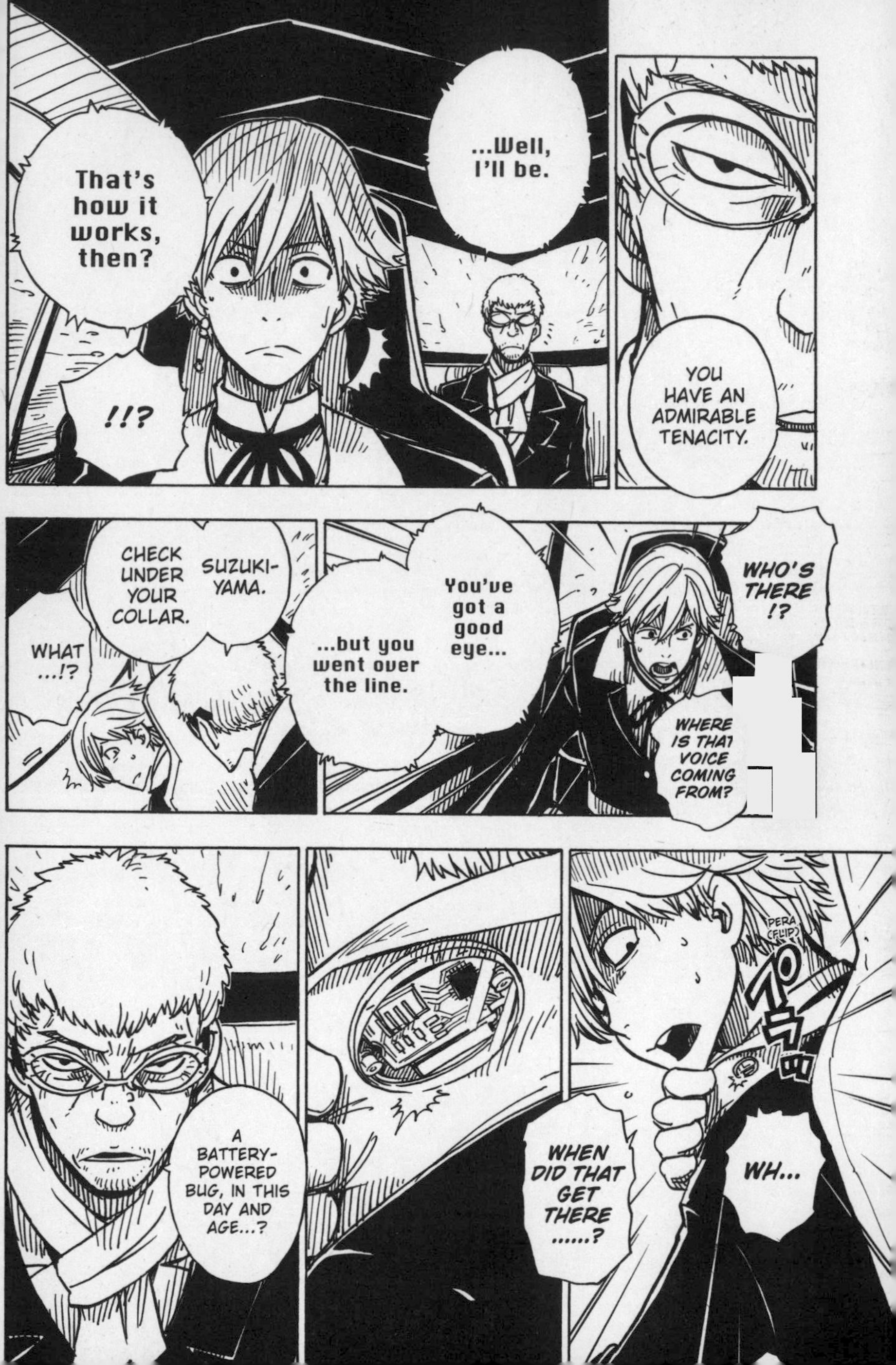
YOU HAVE AN ADMIRABLE TENACITY.
...Well, I'll be.
That's how it works, then?
!!?
WHO'S THERE !?
WHERE IS THAT VOICE COMING FROM?
You've got a good eye...
...but you went over the line.
SUZUKI-YAMA.
CHECK UNDER YOUR COLLAR.
WHAT ...!?
PERA (FLIP)
WH...
WHEN DID THAT GET THERE ......?
A BATTERY-POWERED BUG, IN THIS DAY AND AGE...?

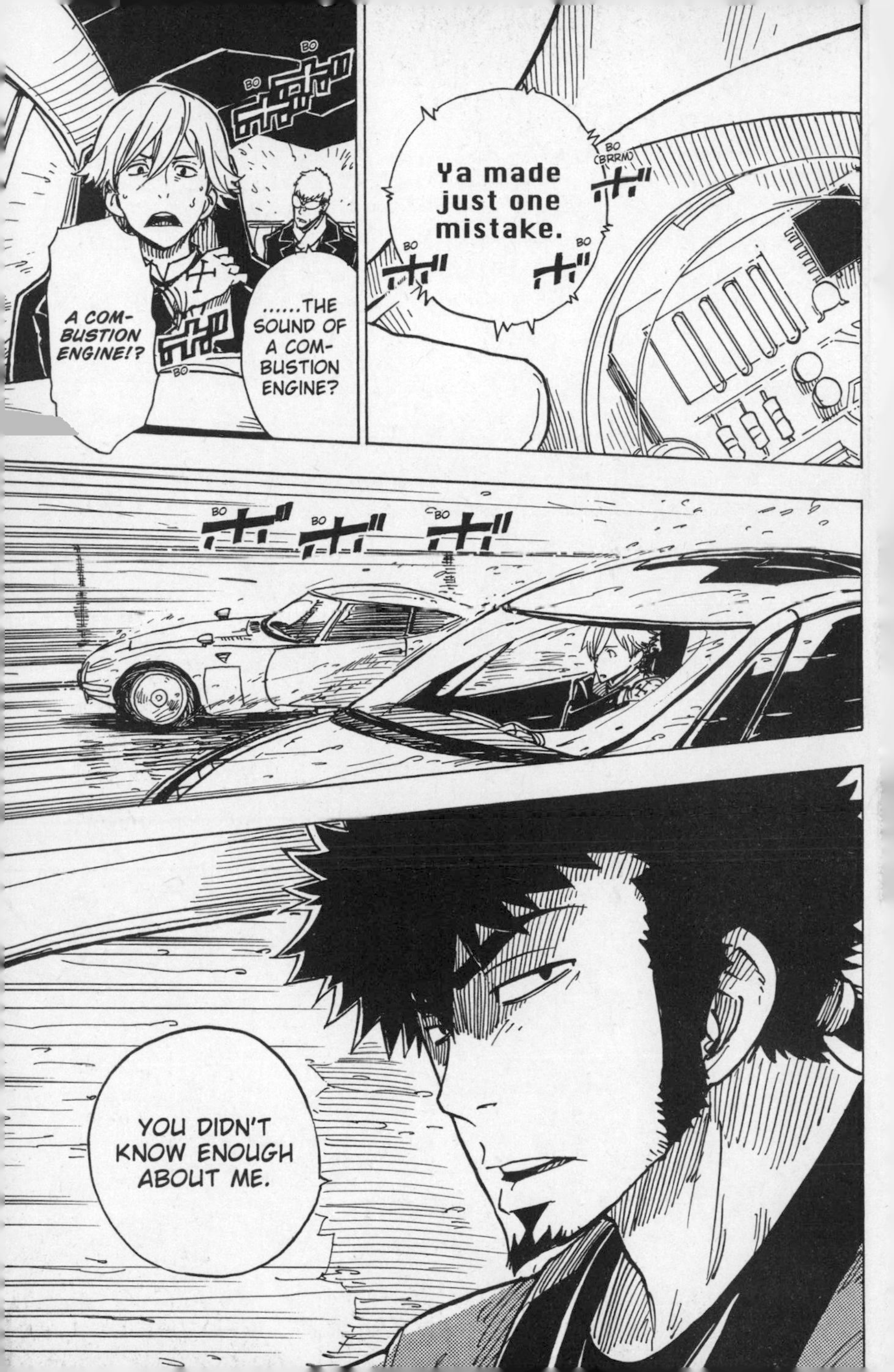
BO (BRRM)
Ya made just one mistake.
BO
BO
BO
BO
......THE SOUND OF A COM-BUSTION ENGINE?
A COM-BUSTION ENGINE!?
BO
BO
BO
BO
YOU DIDN'T KNOW ENOUGH ABOUT ME.

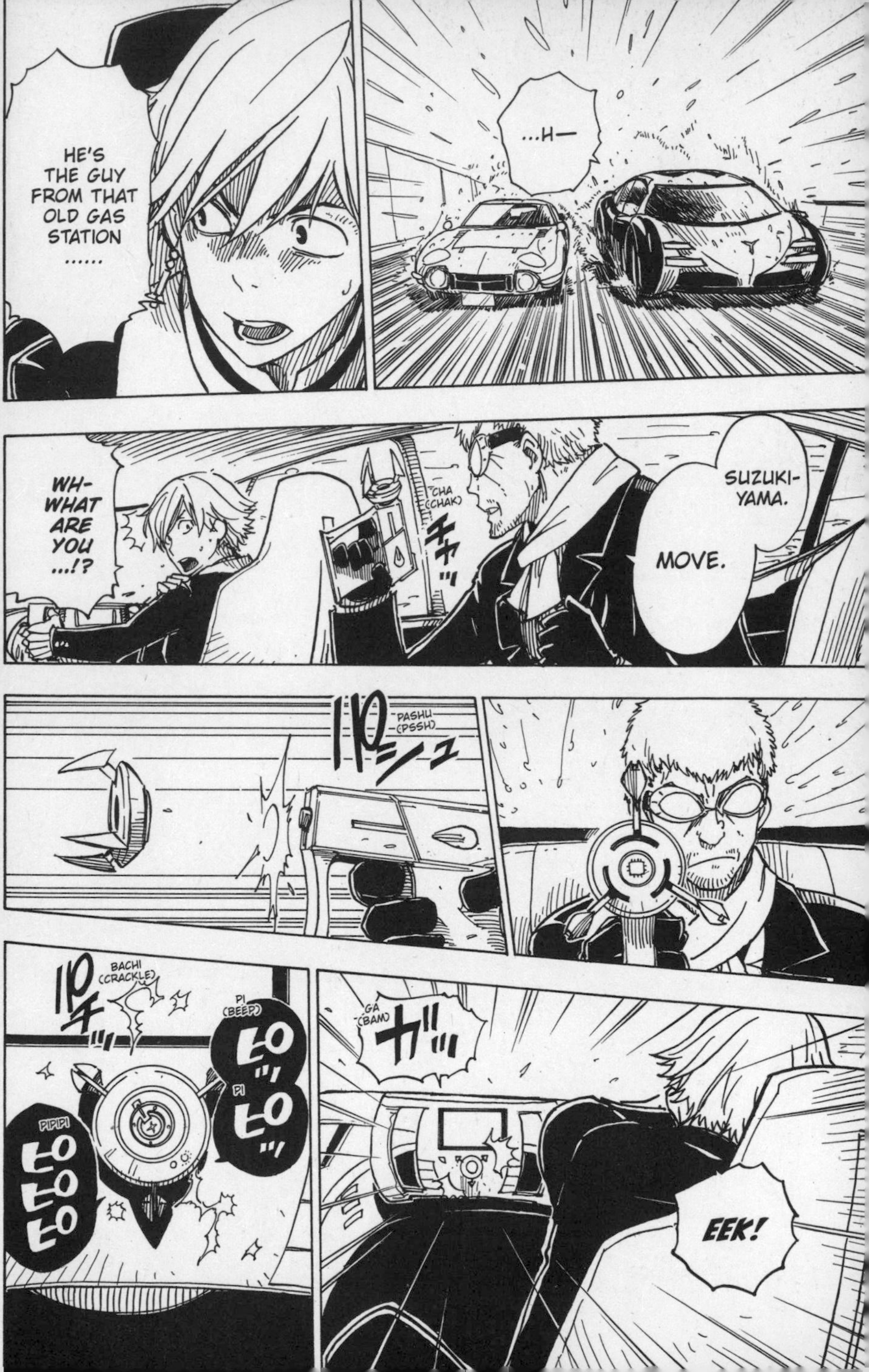
...H—
HE'S THE GUY FROM THAT OLD GAS STATION ......
SUZUKI-YAMA.
MOVE.
CHA (CHAK)
WH-WHAT ARE YOU ...!?
PASHU (PSSH)
GA (BAM)
EEK!
PI (BEEP)
PI
PIPIPI
BACHI (CRACKLE)

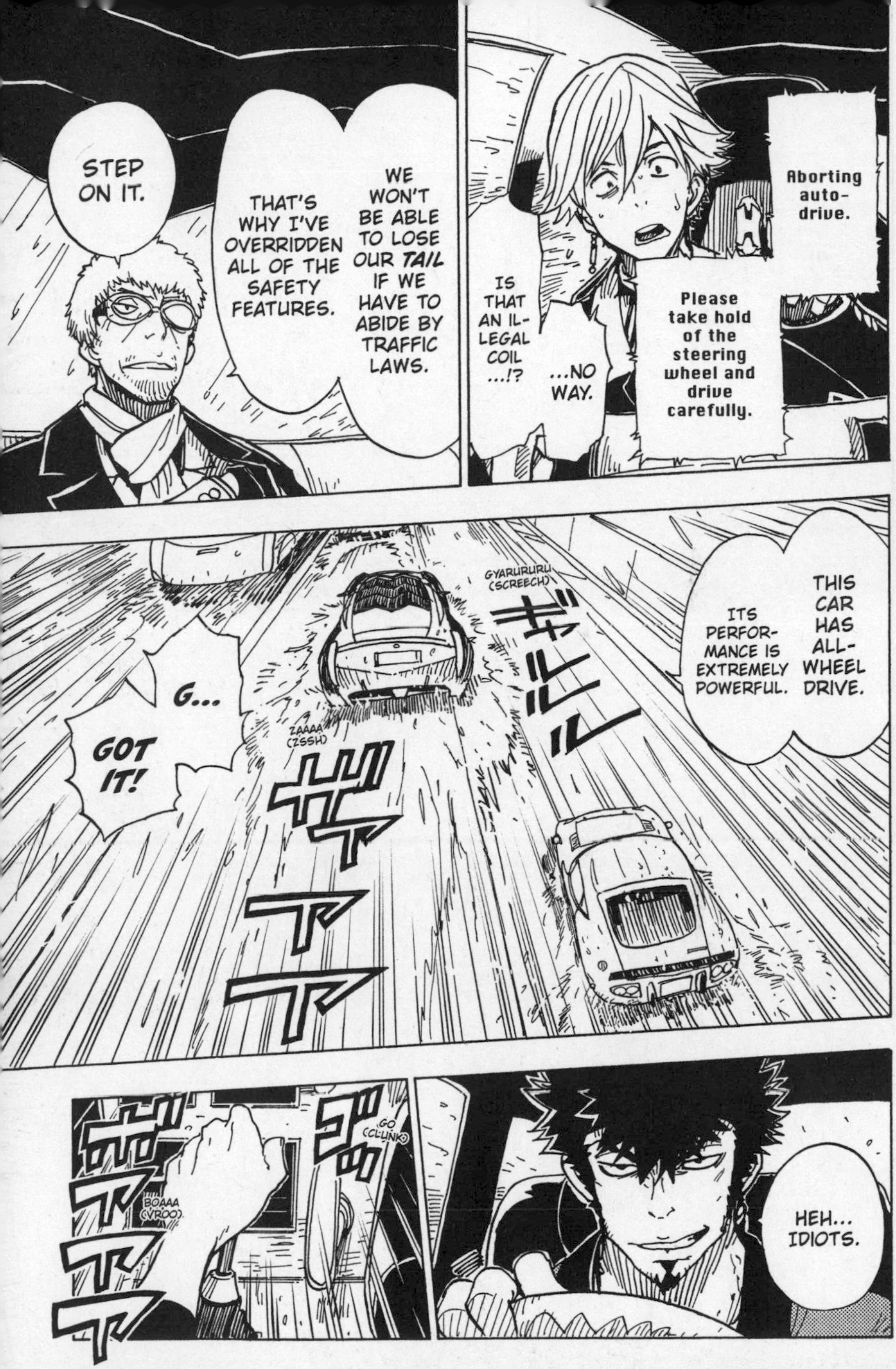
Aborting auto-drive.
Please take hold of the steering wheel and drive carefully.
...NO WAY.
IS THAT AN ILLEGAL COIL ...!?
WE WON'T BE ABLE TO LOSE OUR *TAIL* IF WE HAVE TO ABIDE BY TRAFFIC LAWS.
THAT'S WHY I'VE OVERRIDDEN ALL OF THE SAFETY FEATURES.
STEP ON IT.
THIS CAR HAS ALL-WHEEL DRIVE.
ITS PERFORMANCE IS EXTREMELY POWERFUL.
GYARURURU (SCREECH)
ZAAAA (ZSSH)
G... GOT IT!
HEH... IDIOTS.
GO (CLUNK)
BOAAA (VROO)

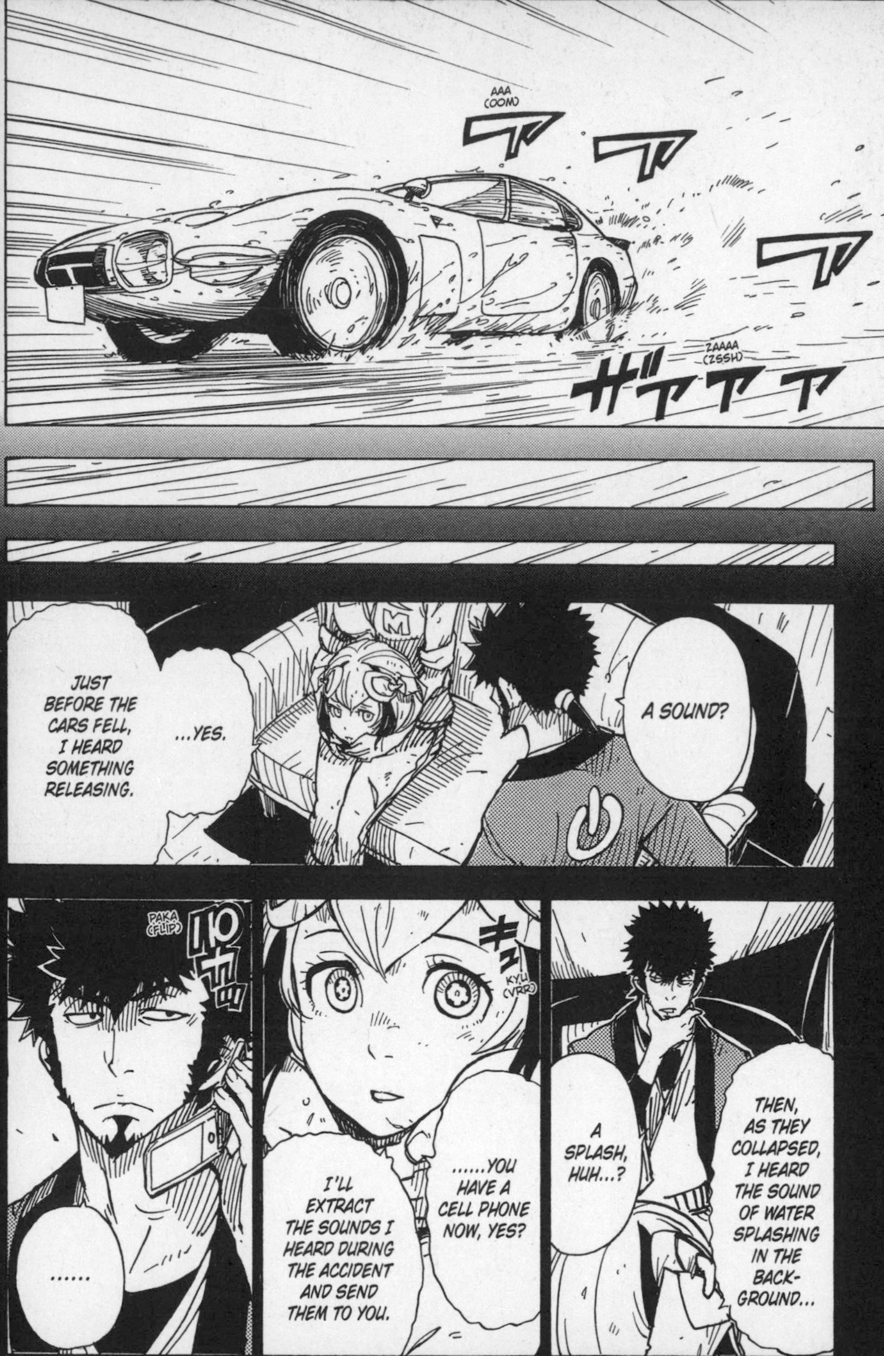
AAA (OOM)
ァァァ
ZAAAA (ZSSH)
ザァァァ
A SOUND?
...YES.
JUST BEFORE THE CARS FELL, I HEARD SOMETHING RELEASING.
THEN, AS THEY COLLAPSED, I HEARD THE SOUND OF WATER SPLASHING IN THE BACK-GROUND...
A SPLASH, HUH...?
KYU (VRR)
キュ
......YOU HAVE A CELL PHONE NOW, YES?
I'LL EXTRACT THE SOUNDS I HEARD DURING THE ACCIDENT AND SEND THEM TO YOU.
PAKA (FLIP)
パカ
......

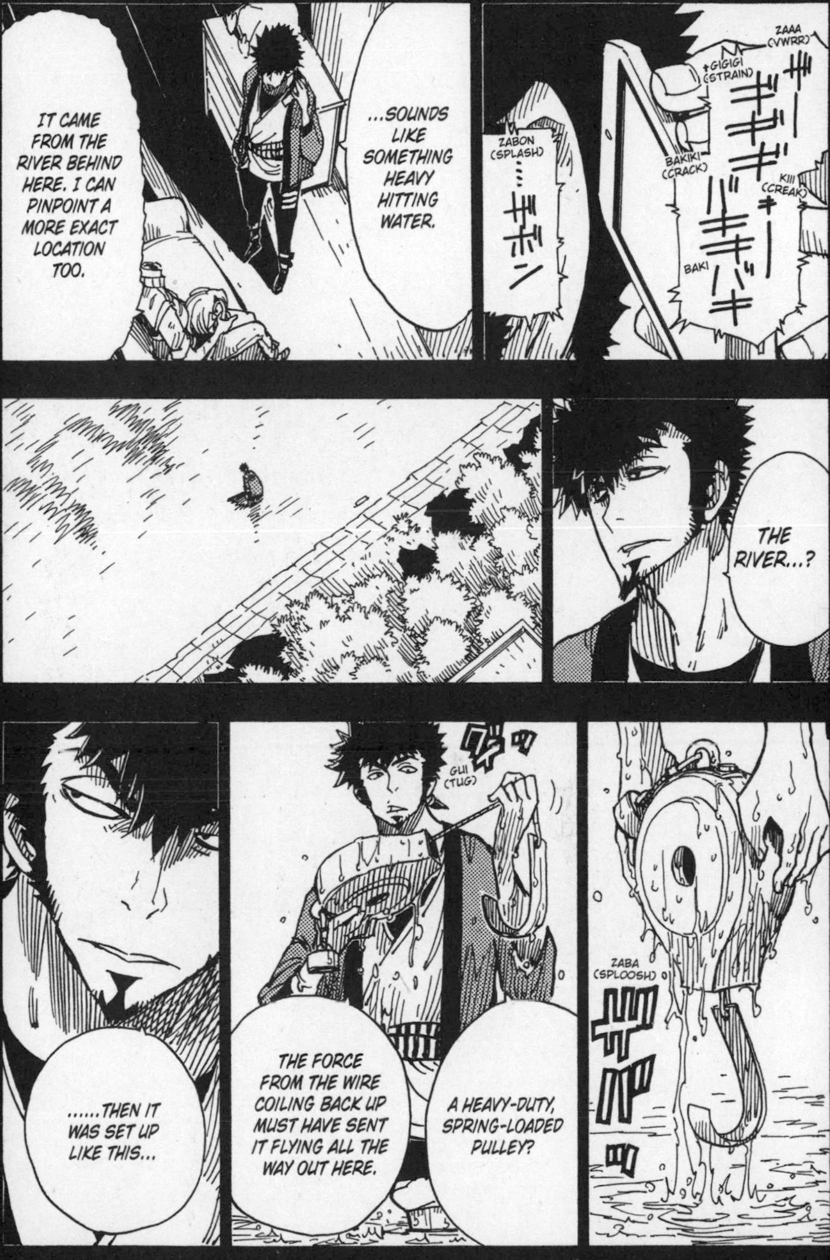
ZAAA (VWRR)
GIGIGI (STRAIN)
BAKIKI (CRACK)
KIII (CREAK)
BAKI
ZABON (SPLASH)
...SOUNDS LIKE SOMETHING HEAVY HITTING WATER.
IT CAME FROM THE RIVER BEHIND HERE. I CAN PINPOINT A MORE EXACT LOCATION TOO.
THE RIVER...?
ZABA (SPLOOSH)
GUI (TUG)
A HEAVY-DUTY, SPRING-LOADED PULLEY?
THE FORCE FROM THE WIRE COILING BACK UP MUST HAVE SENT IT FLYING ALL THE WAY OUT HERE.
......THEN IT WAS SET UP LIKE THIS...

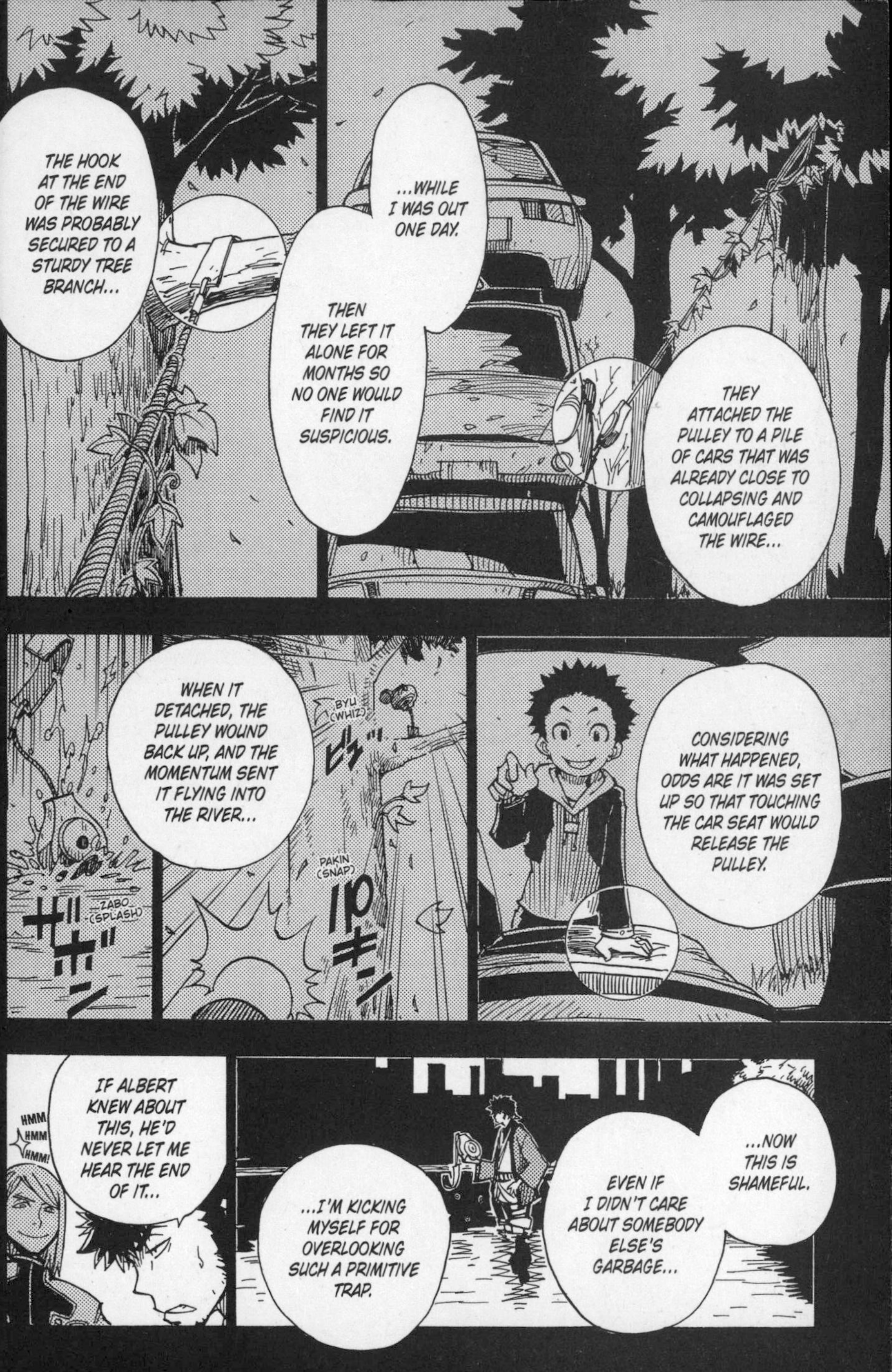
THEY ATTACHED THE PULLEY TO A PILE OF CARS THAT WAS ALREADY CLOSE TO COLLAPSING AND CAMOUFLAGED THE WIRE...
...WHILE I WAS OUT ONE DAY.
THEN THEY LEFT IT ALONE FOR MONTHS SO NO ONE WOULD FIND IT SUSPICIOUS.
THE HOOK AT THE END OF THE WIRE WAS PROBABLY SECURED TO A STURDY TREE BRANCH...
CONSIDERING WHAT HAPPENED, ODDS ARE IT WAS SET UP SO THAT TOUCHING THE CAR SEAT WOULD RELEASE THE PULLEY.
BYU (WHIZ)
PAKIN (SNAP)
WHEN IT DETACHED, THE PULLEY WOUND BACK UP, AND THE MOMENTUM SENT IT FLYING INTO THE RIVER...
ZABO (SPLASH)
...NOW THIS IS SHAMEFUL.
EVEN IF I DIDN'T CARE ABOUT SOMEBODY ELSE'S GARBAGE...
...I'M KICKING MYSELF FOR OVERLOOKING SUCH A PRIMITIVE TRAP.
IF ALBERT KNEW ABOUT THIS, HE'D NEVER LET ME HEAR THE END OF IT...
HMM HMM HMM!

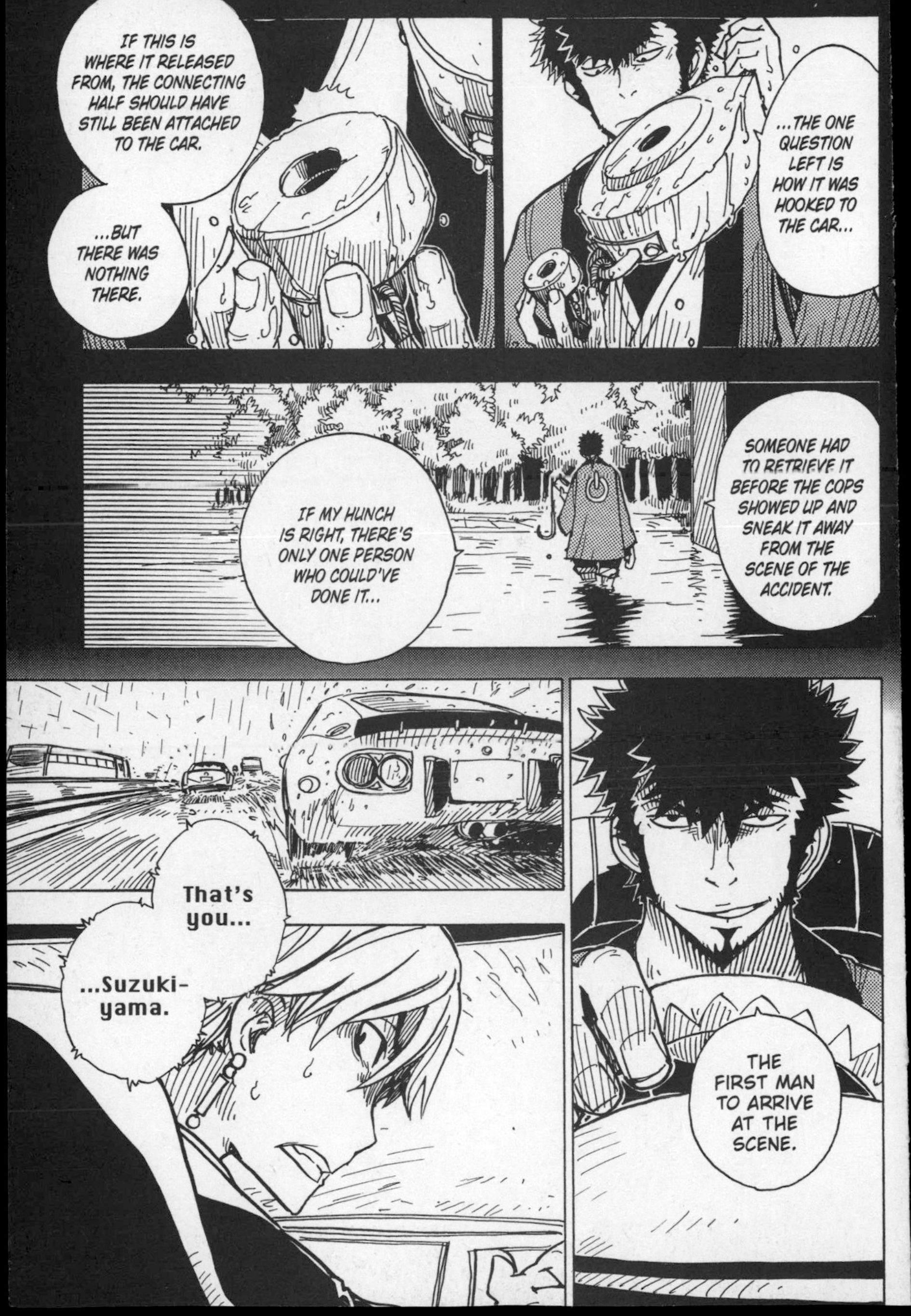
...THE ONE QUESTION LEFT IS HOW IT WAS HOOKED TO THE CAR...
IF THIS IS WHERE IT RELEASED FROM, THE CONNECTING HALF SHOULD HAVE STILL BEEN ATTACHED TO THE CAR.
...BUT THERE WAS NOTHING THERE.
SOMEONE HAD TO RETRIEVE IT BEFORE THE COPS SHOWED UP AND SNEAK IT AWAY FROM THE SCENE OF THE ACCIDENT.
IF MY HUNCH IS RIGHT, THERE'S ONLY ONE PERSON WHO COULD'VE DONE IT...
THE FIRST MAN TO ARRIVE AT THE SCENE.
That's you...
...Suzuki-yama.

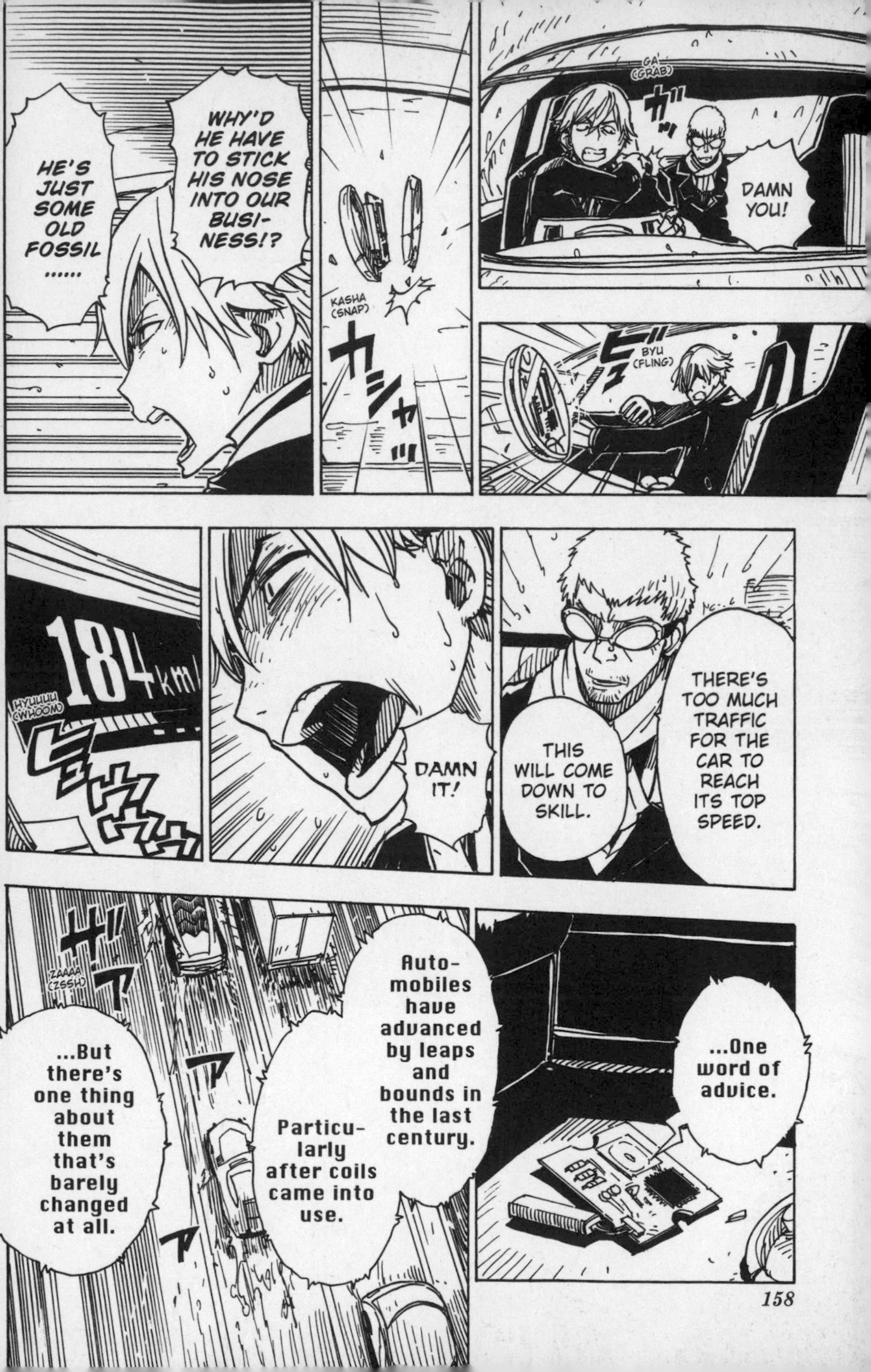
GA (GRAB)
DAMN YOU!
BYU (FLING)
KASHA (SNAP)
WHY'D HE HAVE TO STICK HIS NOSE INTO OUR BUSI-NESS!?
HE'S JUST SOME OLD FOSSIL ......
THERE'S TOO MUCH TRAFFIC FOR THE CAR TO REACH ITS TOP SPEED.
THIS WILL COME DOWN TO SKILL.
DAMN IT!
184km
HYUUUU (WHOOM)
...One word of advice.
Auto-mobiles have advanced by leaps and bounds in the last century.
Particu-larly after coils came into use.
...But there's one thing about them that's barely changed at all.
ZAAAA (ZSSH)

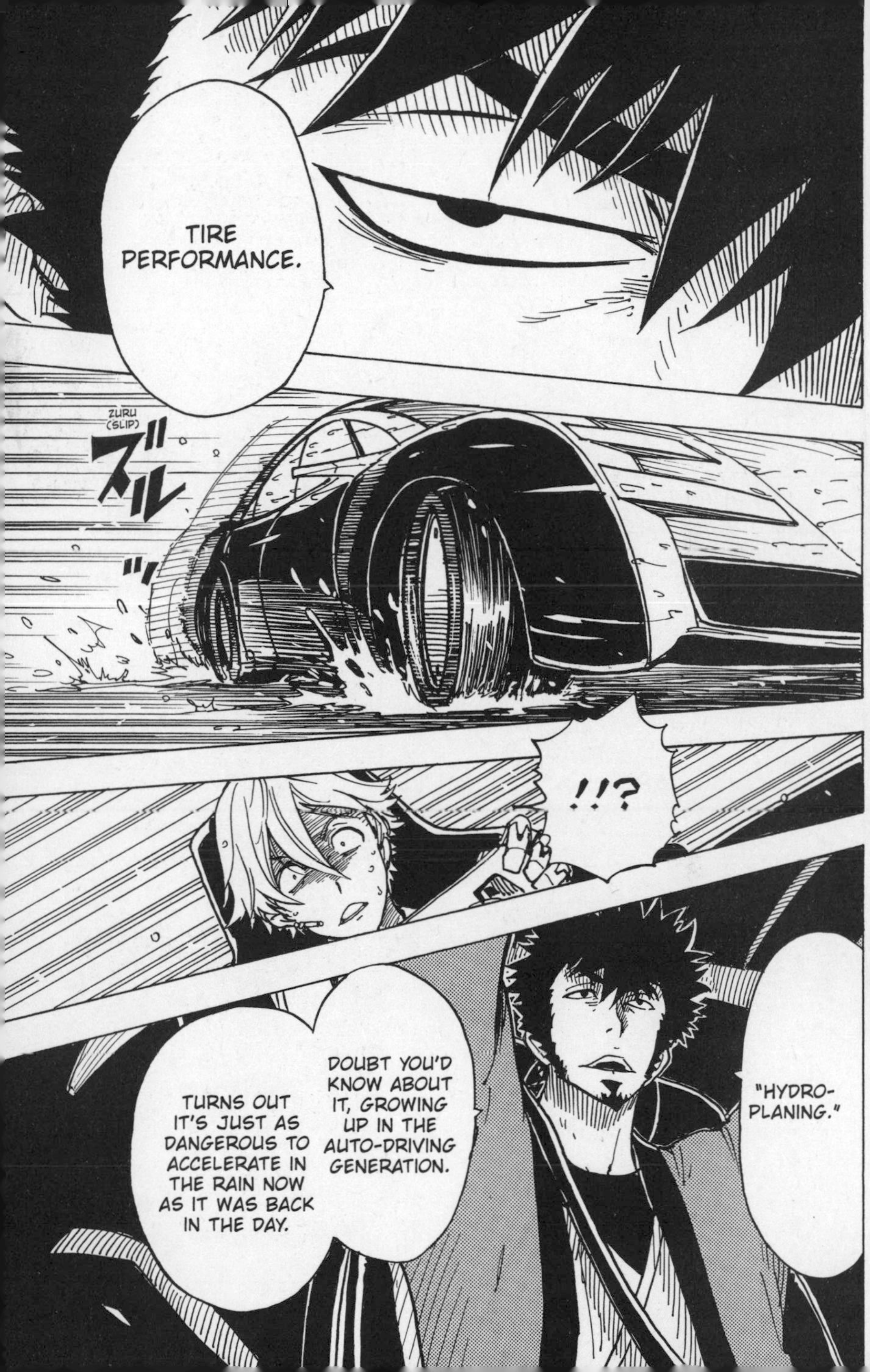
TIRE PERFORMANCE.
ZURU (SLIP)
ズル
!!?
"HYDRO-PLANING."
DOUBT YOU'D KNOW ABOUT IT, GROWING UP IN THE AUTO-DRIVING GENERATION.
TURNS OUT IT'S JUST AS DANGEROUS TO ACCELERATE IN THE RAIN NOW AS IT WAS BACK IN THE DAY.

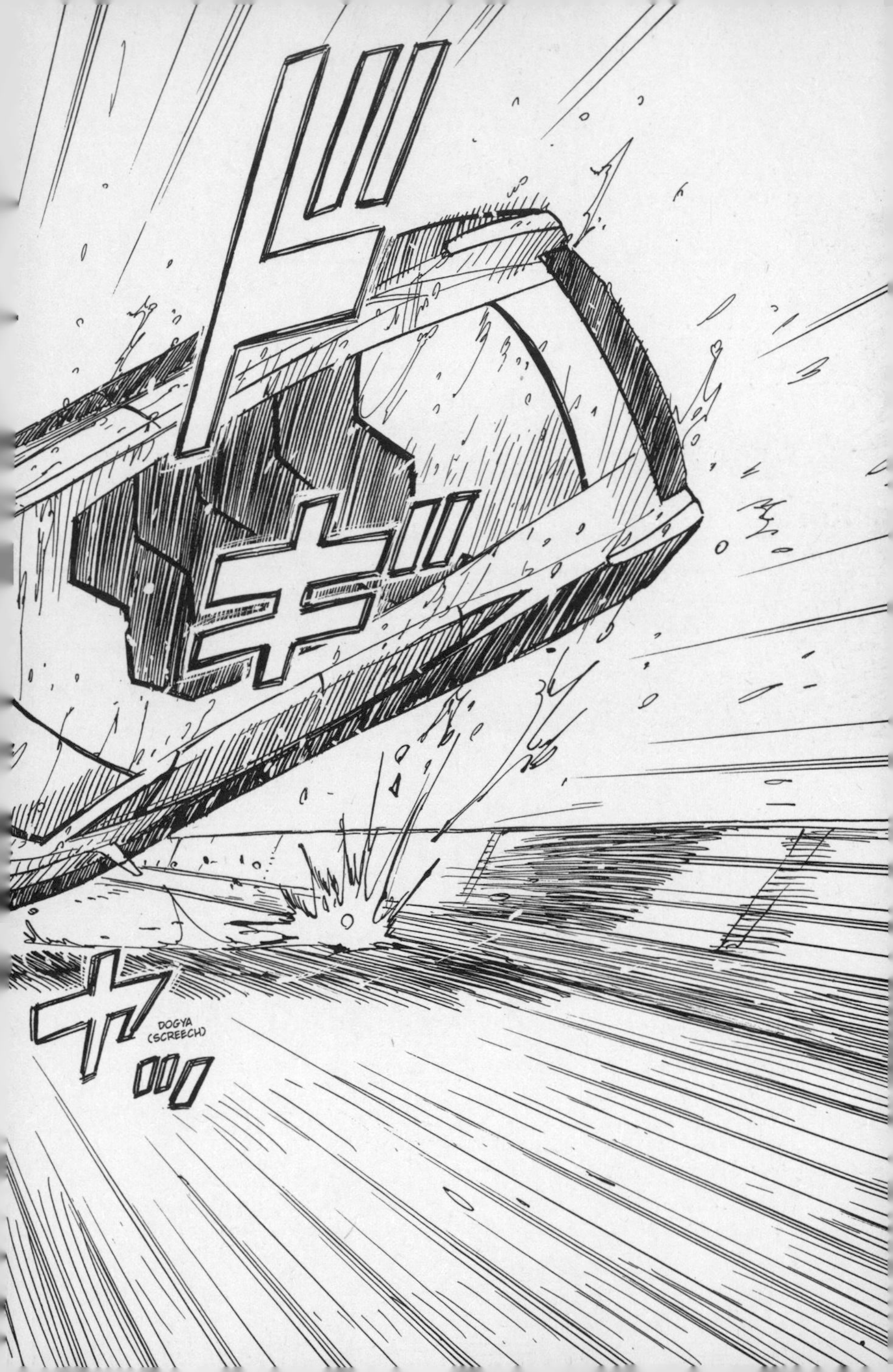
DOGYA
(SCREECH)

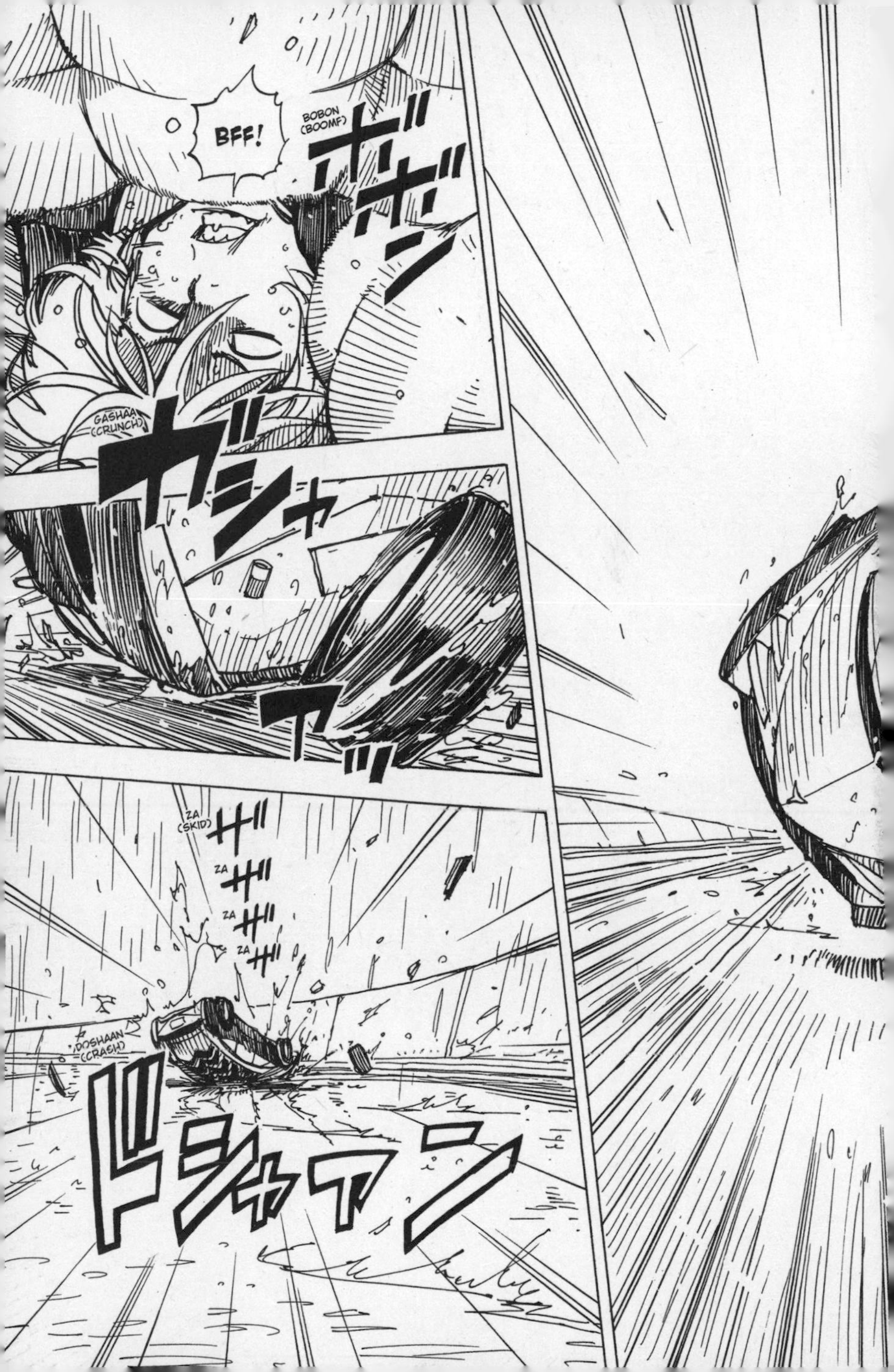
BFF!
BOBON (BOOMF)
GASHAA (CRUNCH)
ZA (SKID)
ZA
ZA
ZA
DOSHAAN (CRASH)

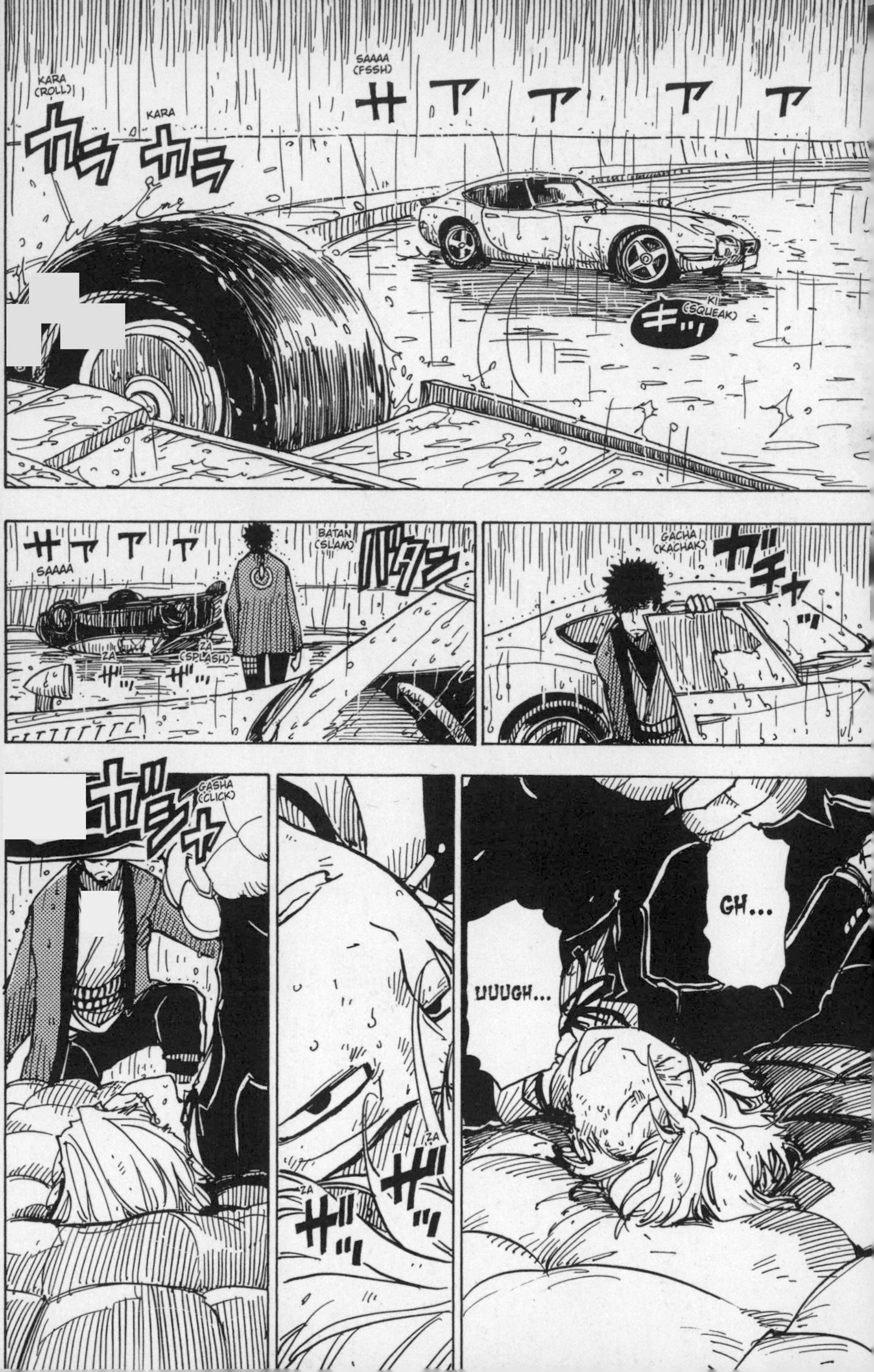
SAAAA (FSSH)
KARA (ROLL)
KARA
KI (SQUEAK)
GACHA (KACHAK)
BATAN (SLAM)
SAAAA
ZA
ZA (SPLASH)
GH...
UUUGH...
ZA
ZA
GASHA (CLICK)

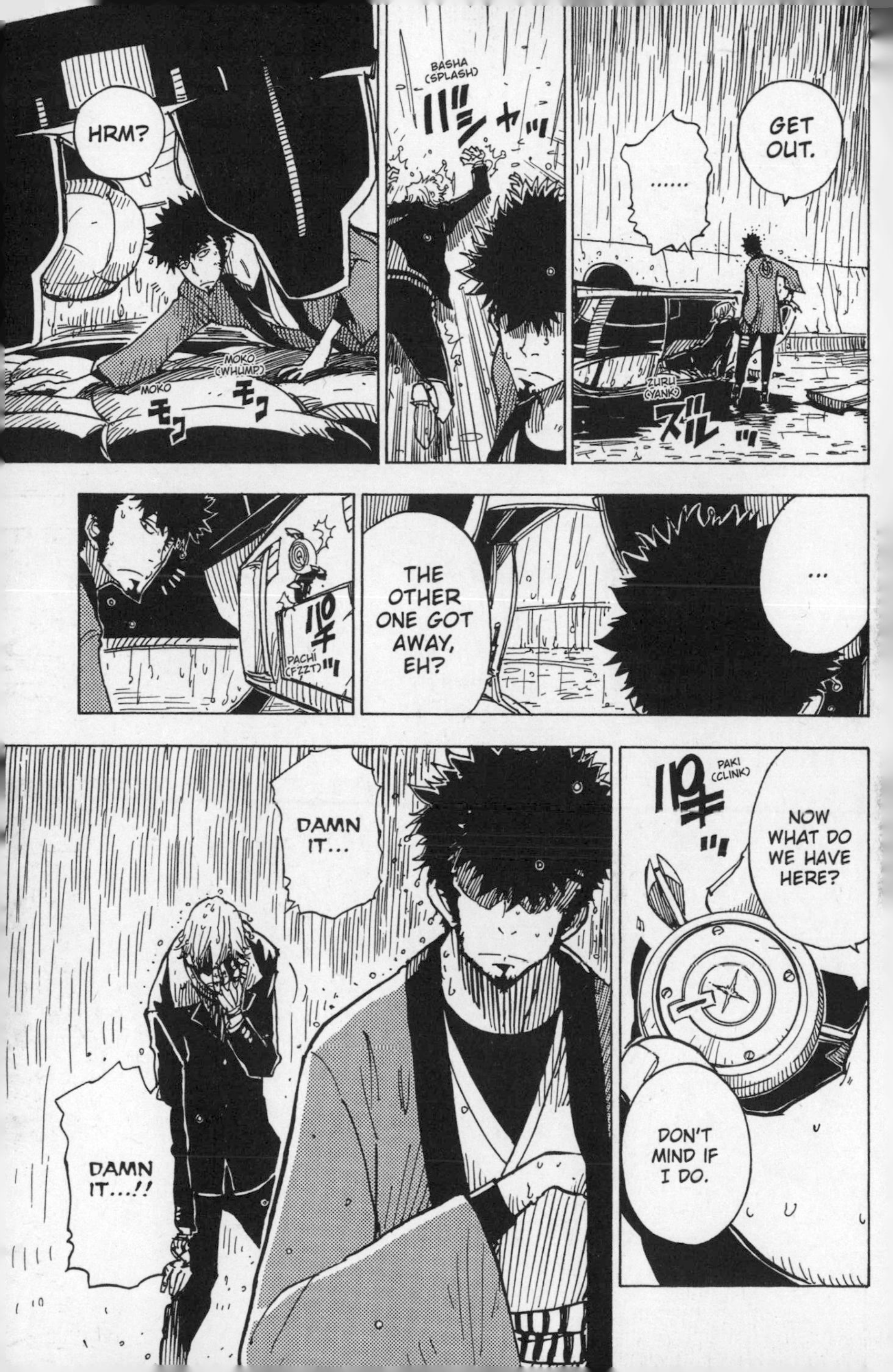
GET OUT.
......
ZURU (YANK)
BASHA (SPLASH)
HRM?
MOKO (WHUMP)
MOKO
...
THE OTHER ONE GOT AWAY, EH?
PACHI (FZZT)
PAKI (CLINK)
NOW WHAT DO WE HAVE HERE?
DON'T MIND IF I DO.
DAMN IT...
DAMN IT...!!

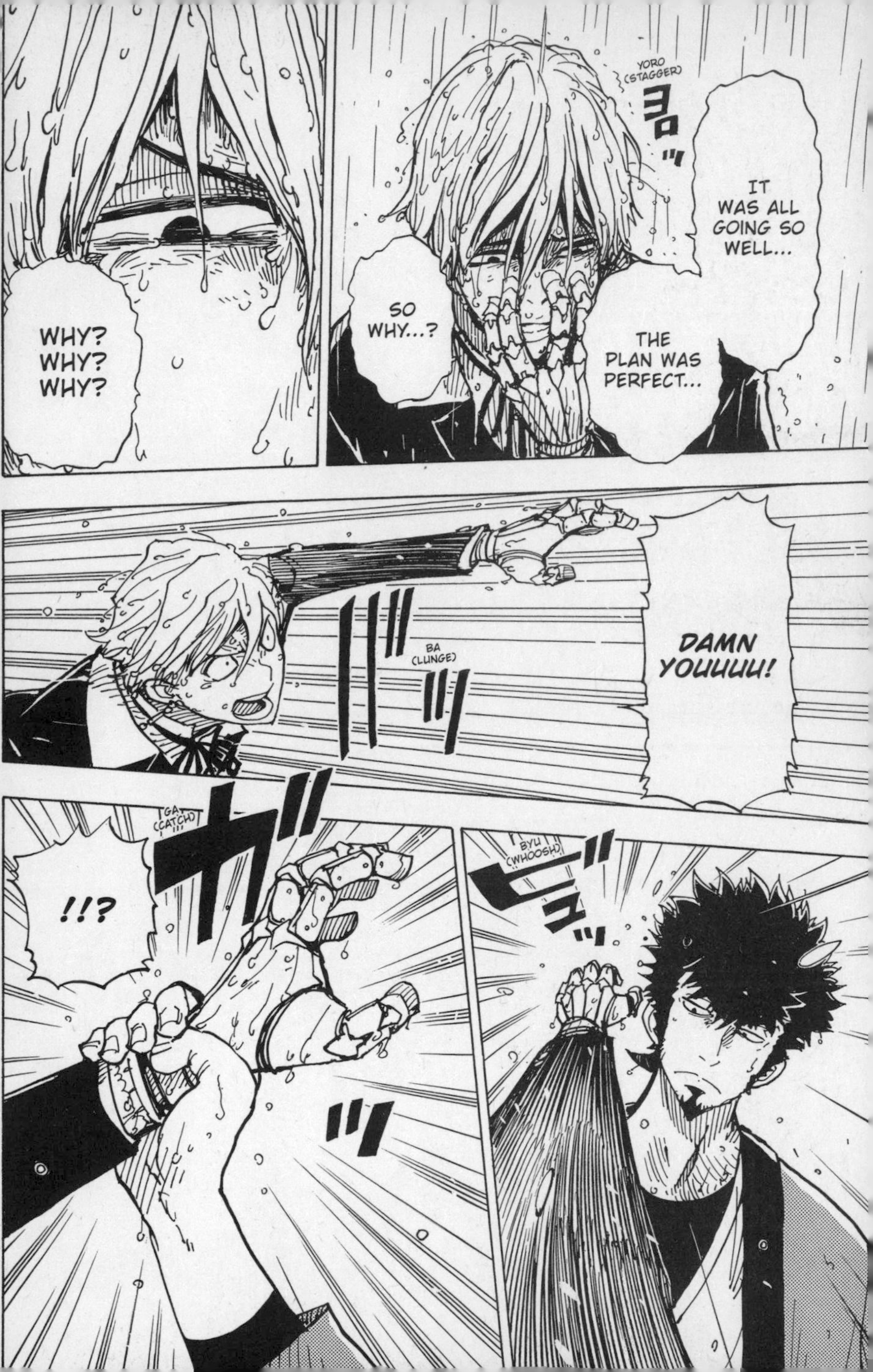
YORO (STAGGER)
IT WAS ALL GOING SO WELL...
THE PLAN WAS PERFECT...
SO WHY...?
WHY? WHY? WHY?
DAMN YOUUUU!
BA (LUNGE)
BYU (WHOOSH)
GA (CATCH)
!!?

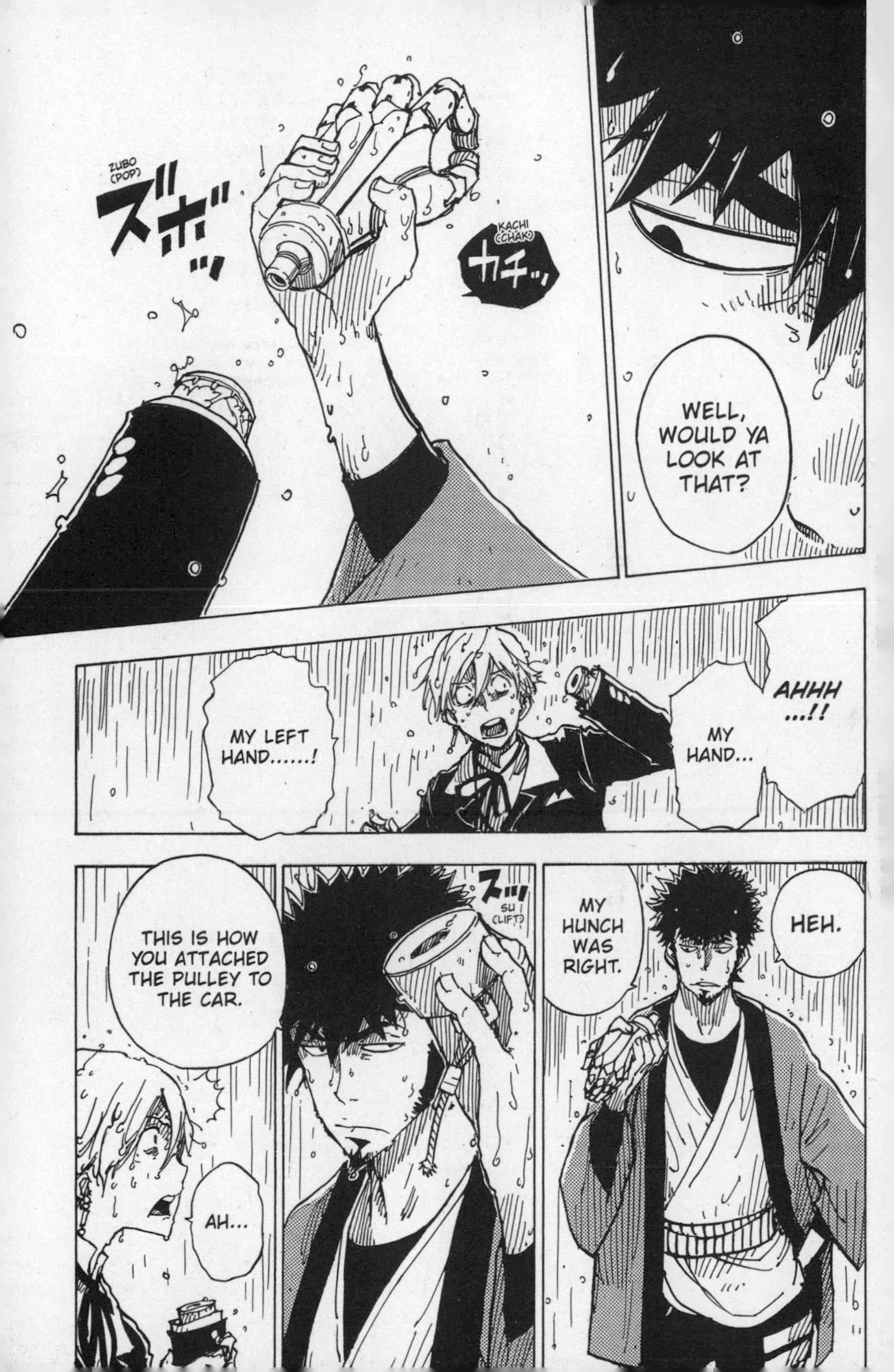
WELL, WOULD YA LOOK AT THAT?
KACHI (CHAK)
カチッ
ZUBO (POP)
ズボッ
AHHH...!!
MY HAND...
MY LEFT HAND......!
HEH.
MY HUNCH WAS RIGHT.
スッ
SU (LIFT)
THIS IS HOW YOU ATTACHED THE PULLEY TO THE CAR.
AH...

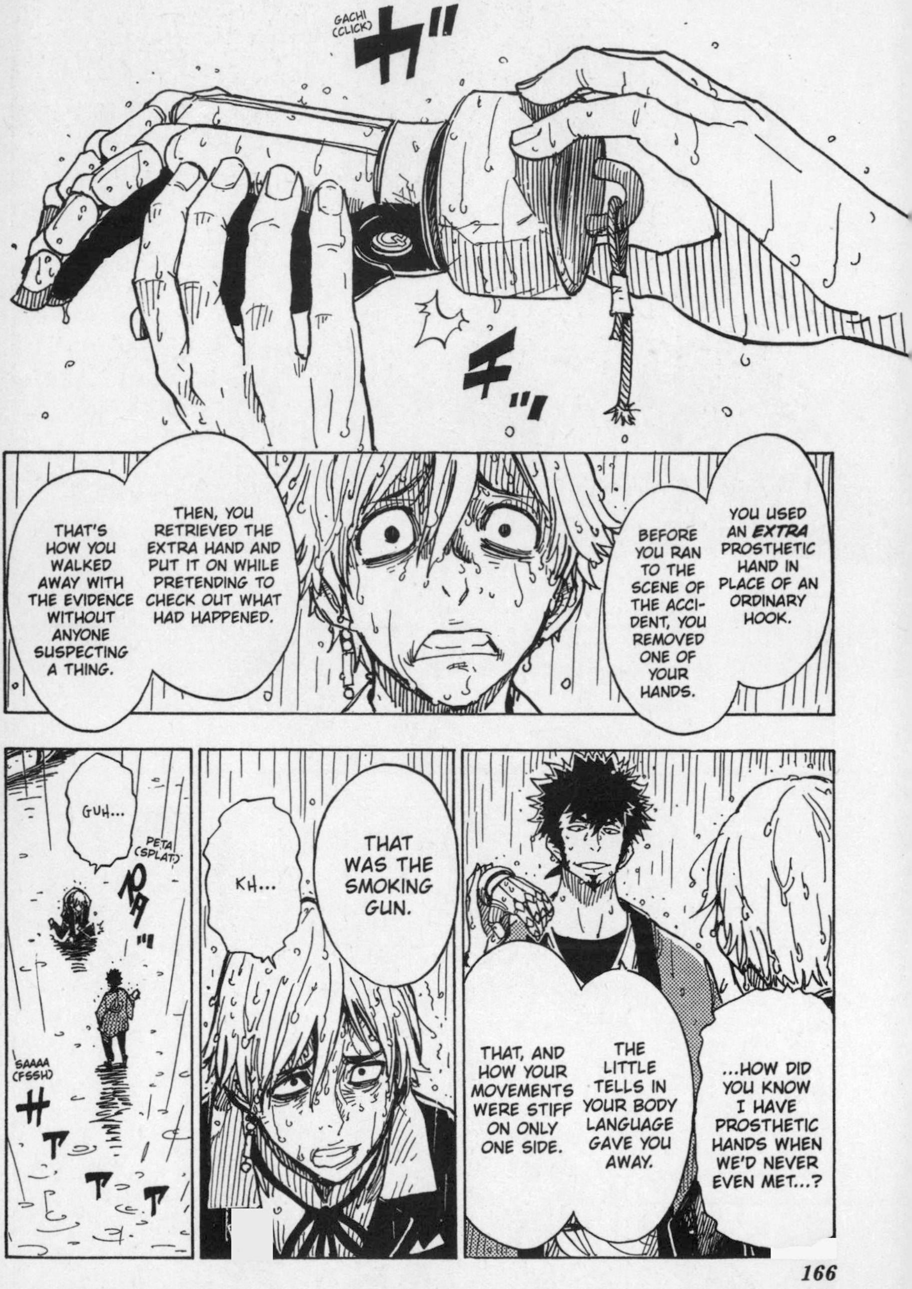
GACHI (CLICK)
YOU USED AN *EXTRA* PROSTHETIC HAND IN PLACE OF AN ORDINARY HOOK.
BEFORE YOU RAN TO THE SCENE OF THE ACCIDENT, YOU REMOVED ONE OF YOUR HANDS.
THEN, YOU RETRIEVED THE EXTRA HAND AND PUT IT ON WHILE PRETENDING TO CHECK OUT WHAT HAD HAPPENED.
THAT'S HOW YOU WALKED AWAY WITH THE EVIDENCE WITHOUT ANYONE SUSPECTING A THING.
...HOW DID YOU KNOW I HAVE PROSTHETIC HANDS WHEN WE'D NEVER EVEN MET...?
THE LITTLE TELLS IN YOUR BODY LANGUAGE GAVE YOU AWAY.
THAT, AND HOW YOUR MOVEMENTS WERE STIFF ON ONLY ONE SIDE.
THAT WAS THE SMOKING GUN.
KH...
GUH...
PETA (SPLAT)
SAAAA (FSSH)

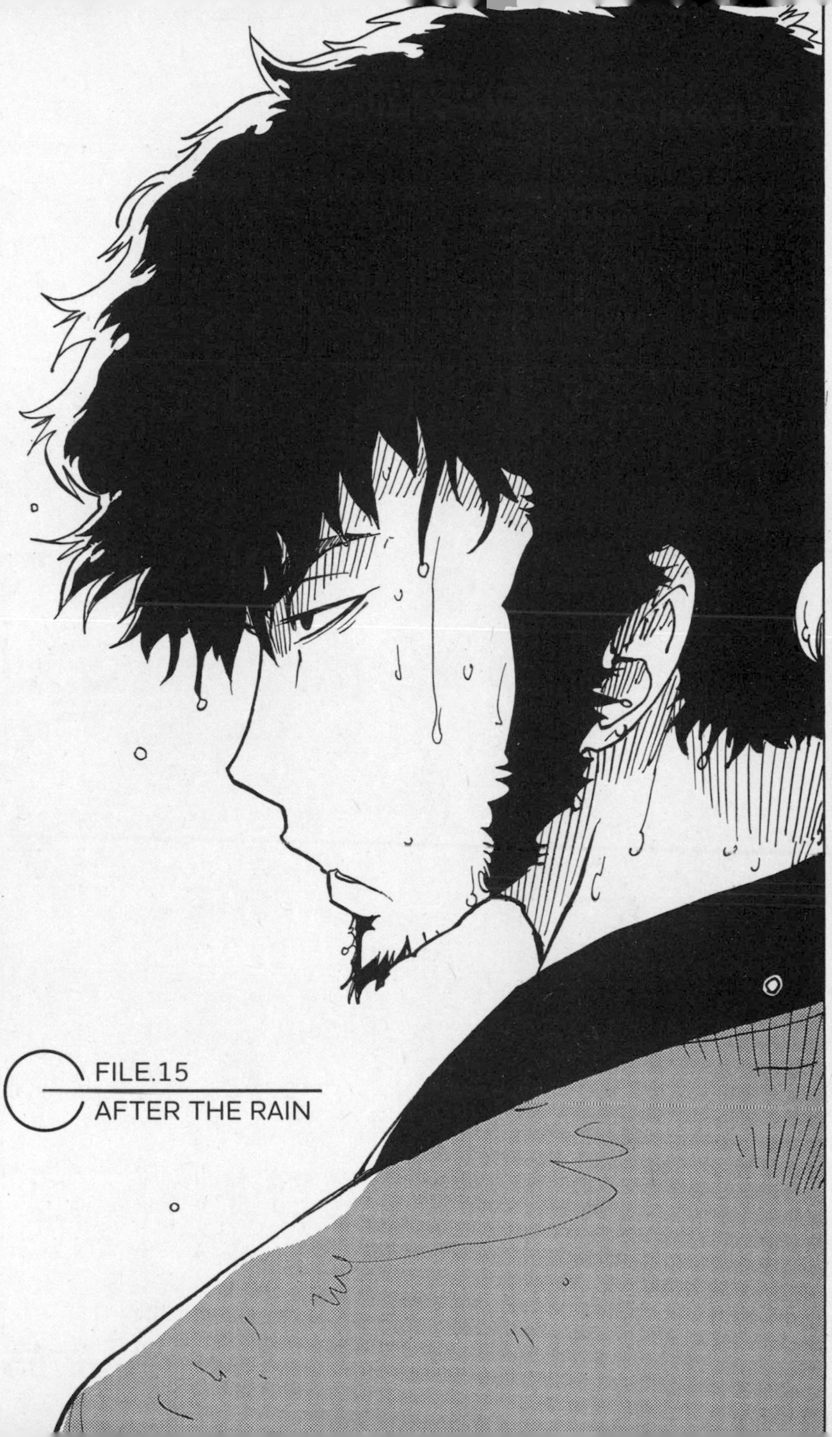
FILE.15
AFTER THE RAIN

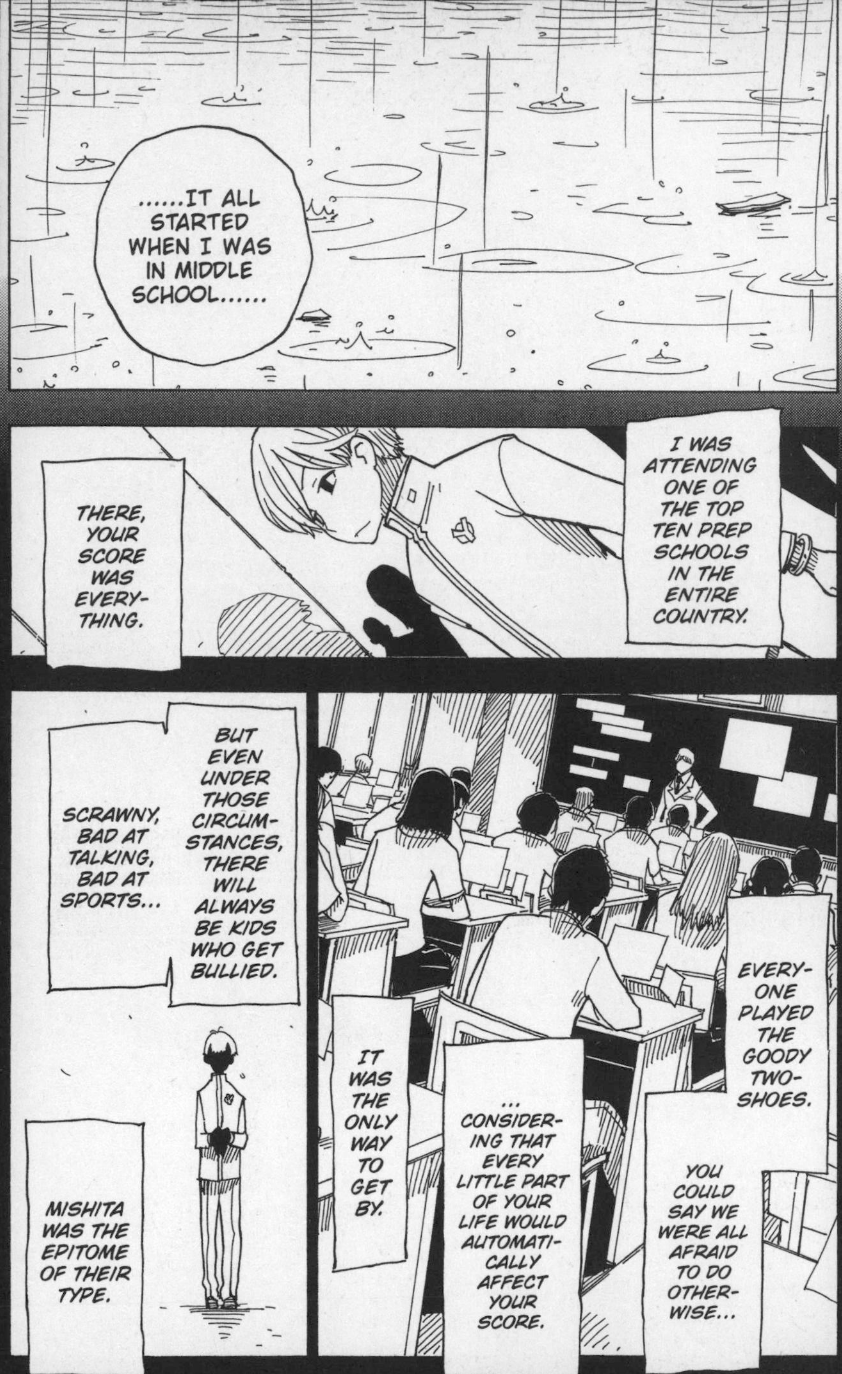
......IT ALL STARTED WHEN I WAS IN MIDDLE SCHOOL......
I WAS ATTENDING ONE OF THE TOP TEN PREP SCHOOLS IN THE ENTIRE COUNTRY.
THERE, YOUR SCORE WAS EVERYTHING.
EVERYONE PLAYED THE GOODY TWO-SHOES.
YOU COULD SAY WE WERE ALL AFRAID TO DO OTHERWISE...
...CONSIDERING THAT EVERY LITTLE PART OF YOUR LIFE WOULD AUTOMATICALLY AFFECT YOUR SCORE.
IT WAS THE ONLY WAY TO GET BY.
BUT EVEN UNDER THOSE CIRCUMSTANCES, THERE WILL ALWAYS BE KIDS WHO GET BULLIED.
SCRAWNY, BAD AT TALKING, BAD AT SPORTS...
MISHITA WAS THE EPITOME OF THEIR TYPE.

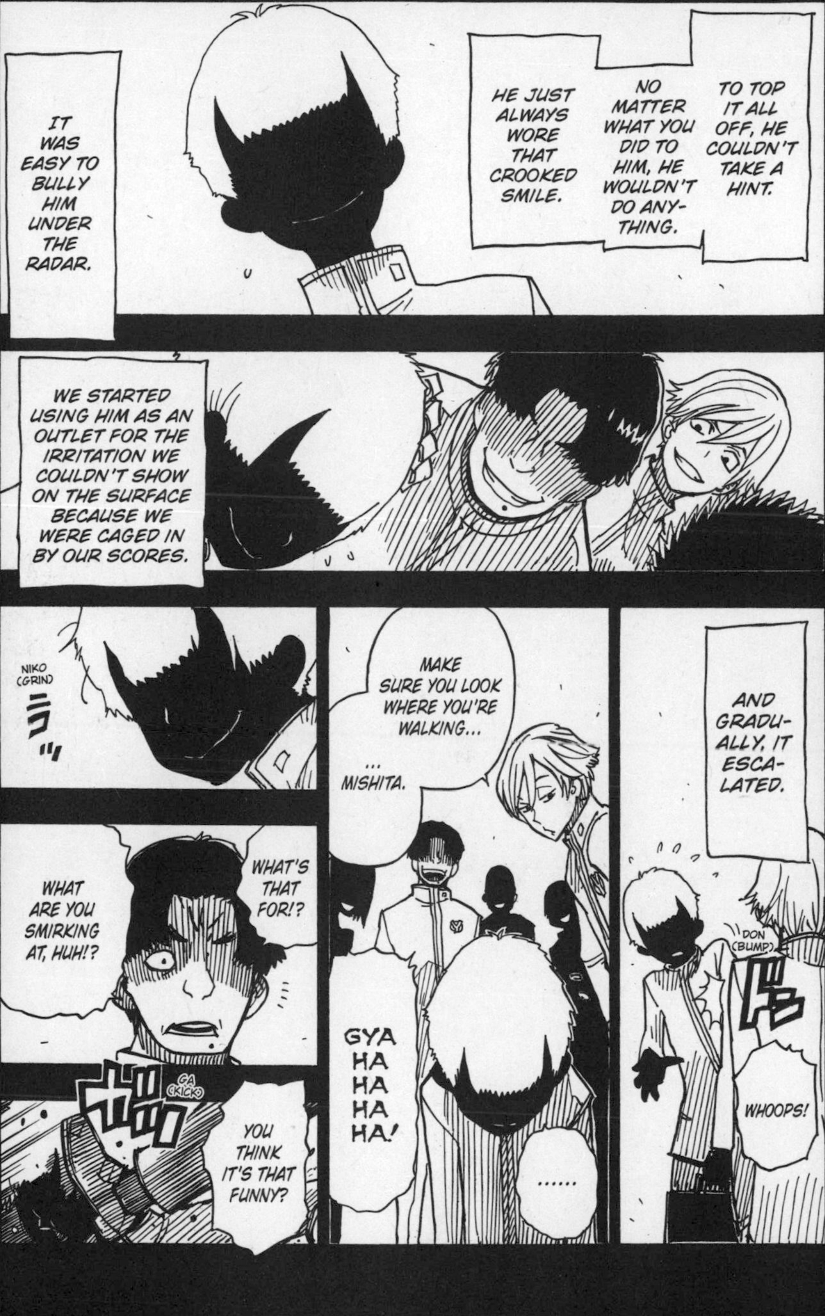
HE JUST ALWAYS WORE THAT CROOKED SMILE.
NO MATTER WHAT YOU DID TO HIM, HE WOULDN'T DO ANYTHING.
TO TOP IT ALL OFF, HE COULDN'T TAKE A HINT.
IT WAS EASY TO BULLY HIM UNDER THE RADAR.
WE STARTED USING HIM AS AN OUTLET FOR THE IRRITATION WE COULDN'T SHOW ON THE SURFACE BECAUSE WE WERE CAGED IN BY OUR SCORES.
AND GRADUALLY, IT ESCALATED.
DON (BUMP)
WHOOPS!
MAKE SURE YOU LOOK WHERE YOU'RE WALKING...
...MISHITA.
GYA HA HA HA HA!
......
NIKO (GRIN)
WHAT'S THAT FOR!?
WHAT ARE YOU SMIRKING AT, HUH!?
GA (KICK)
YOU THINK IT'S THAT FUNNY?

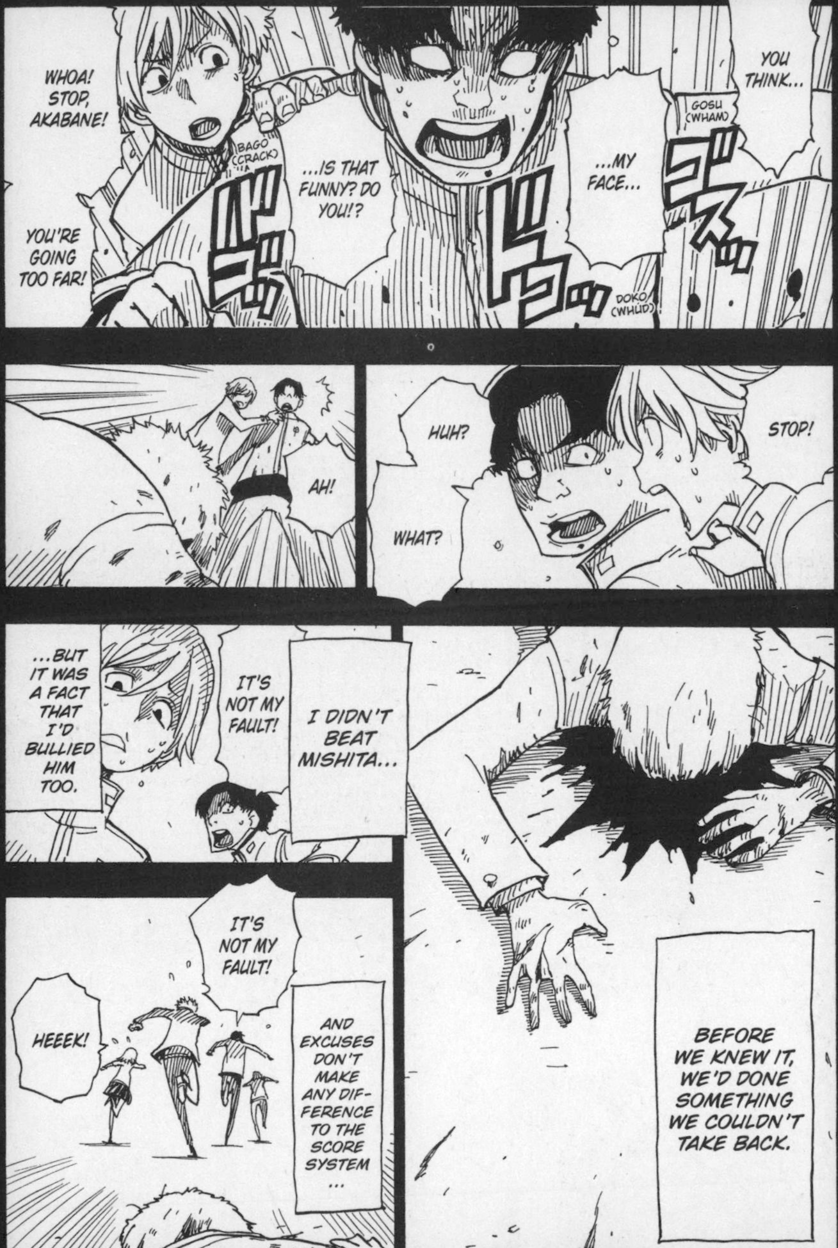
YOU THINK...
GOSU (WHAM)
...MY FACE...
DOKO (WHUD)
...IS THAT FUNNY? DO YOU!?
BAGO (CRACK)
WHOA! STOP, AKABANE!
YOU'RE GOING TOO FAR!
STOP!
HUH?
WHAT?
AH!
BEFORE WE KNEW IT, WE'D DONE SOMETHING WE COULDN'T TAKE BACK.
I DIDN'T BEAT MISHITA...
IT'S NOT MY FAULT!
...BUT IT WAS A FACT THAT I'D BULLIED HIM TOO.
AND EXCUSES DON'T MAKE ANY DIFFERENCE TO THE SCORE SYSTEM...
IT'S NOT MY FAULT!
HEEEK!

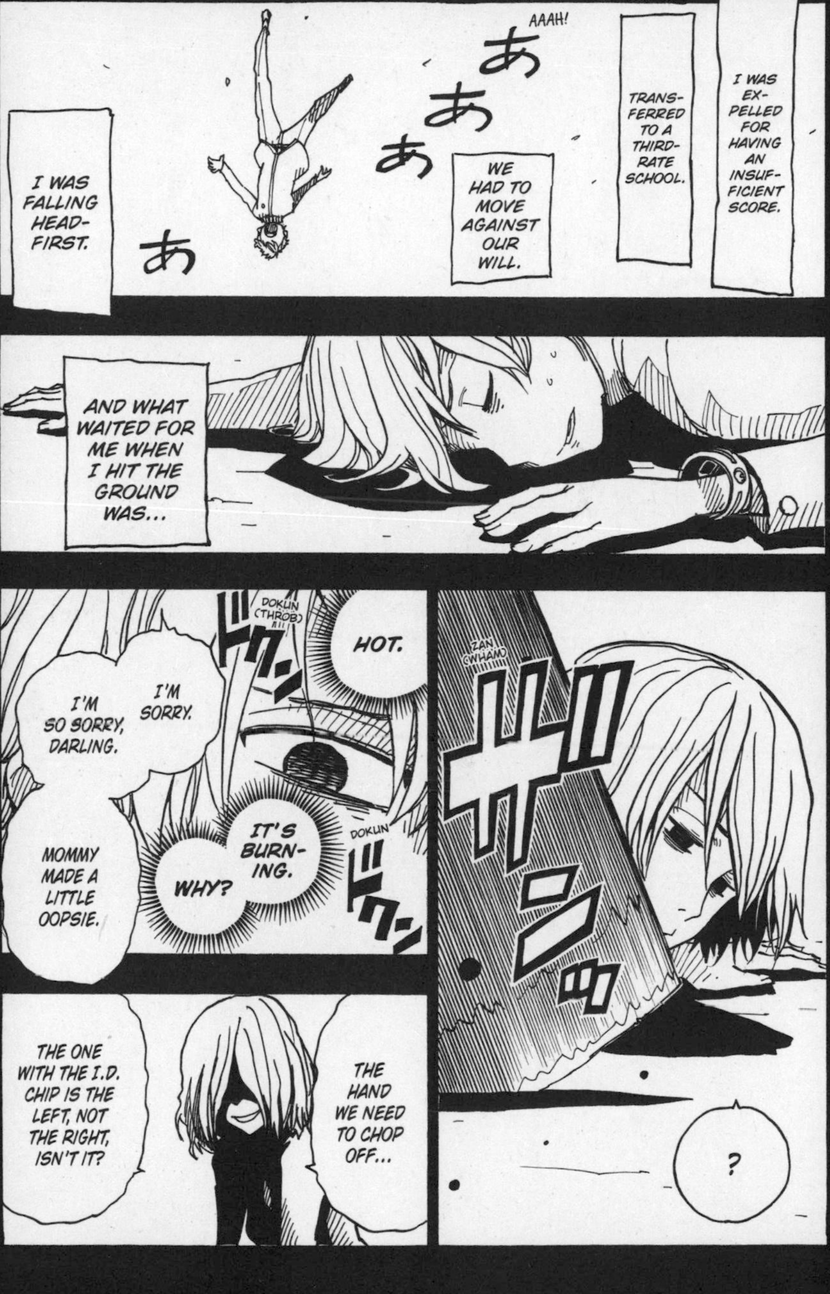
I WAS EXPELLED FOR HAVING AN INSUFFICIENT SCORE.
TRANSFERRED TO A THIRD-RATE SCHOOL.
AAAH!
あ あ あ あ
WE HAD TO MOVE AGAINST OUR WILL.
I WAS FALLING HEAD-FIRST.
AND WHAT WAITED FOR ME WHEN I HIT THE GROUND WAS...
ZAN (WHAM)
?
DOKUN (THROB)
HOT.
DOKUN
IT'S BURNING.
WHY?
I'M SORRY.
I'M SO SORRY, DARLING.
MOMMY MADE A LITTLE OOPSIE.
THE HAND WE NEED TO CHOP OFF...
THE ONE WITH THE I.D. CHIP IS THE LEFT, NOT THE RIGHT, ISN'T IT?

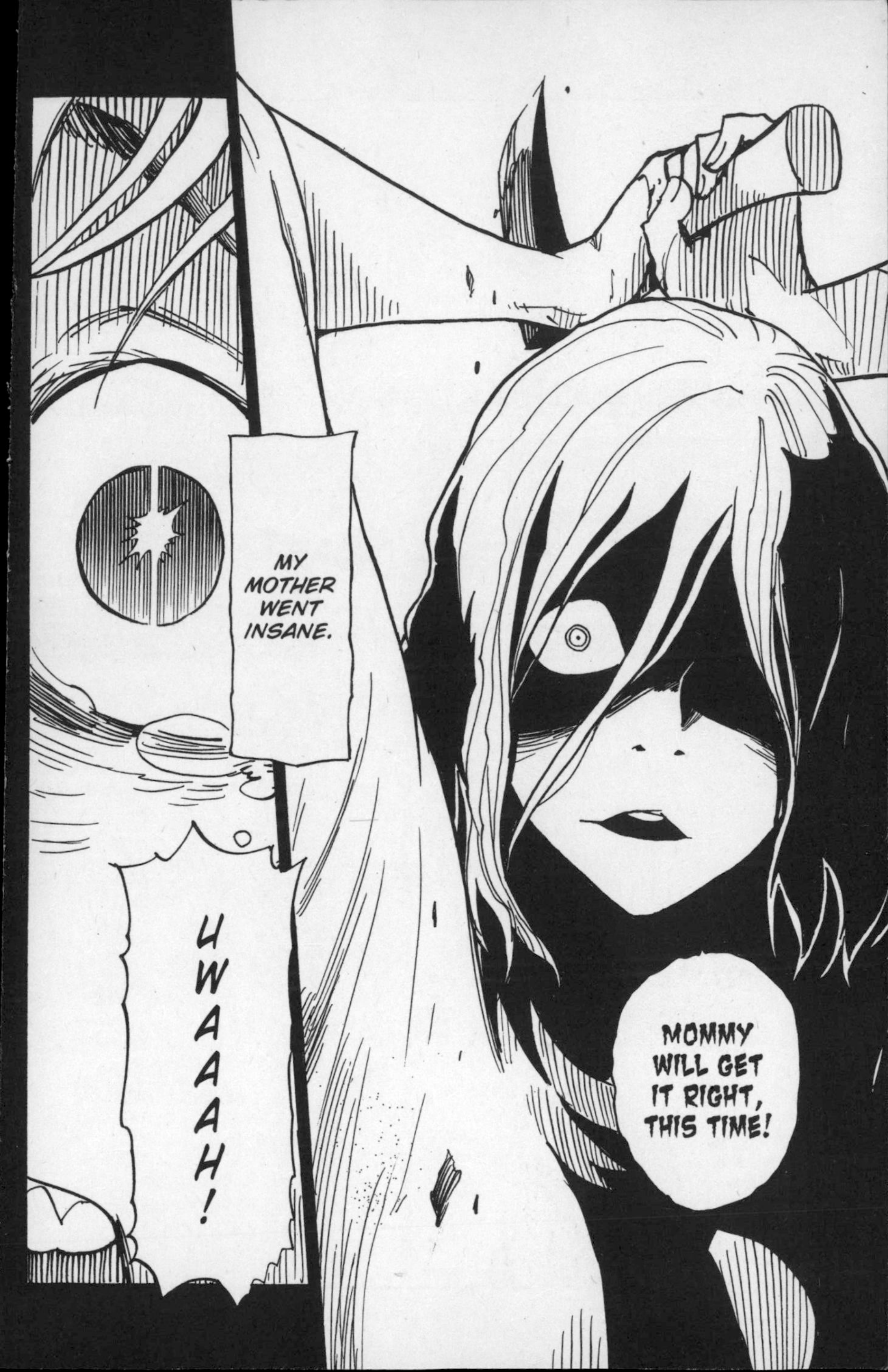
MY MOTHER WENT INSANE.
MOMMY WILL GET IT RIGHT, THIS TIME!
UWAAAAAH!

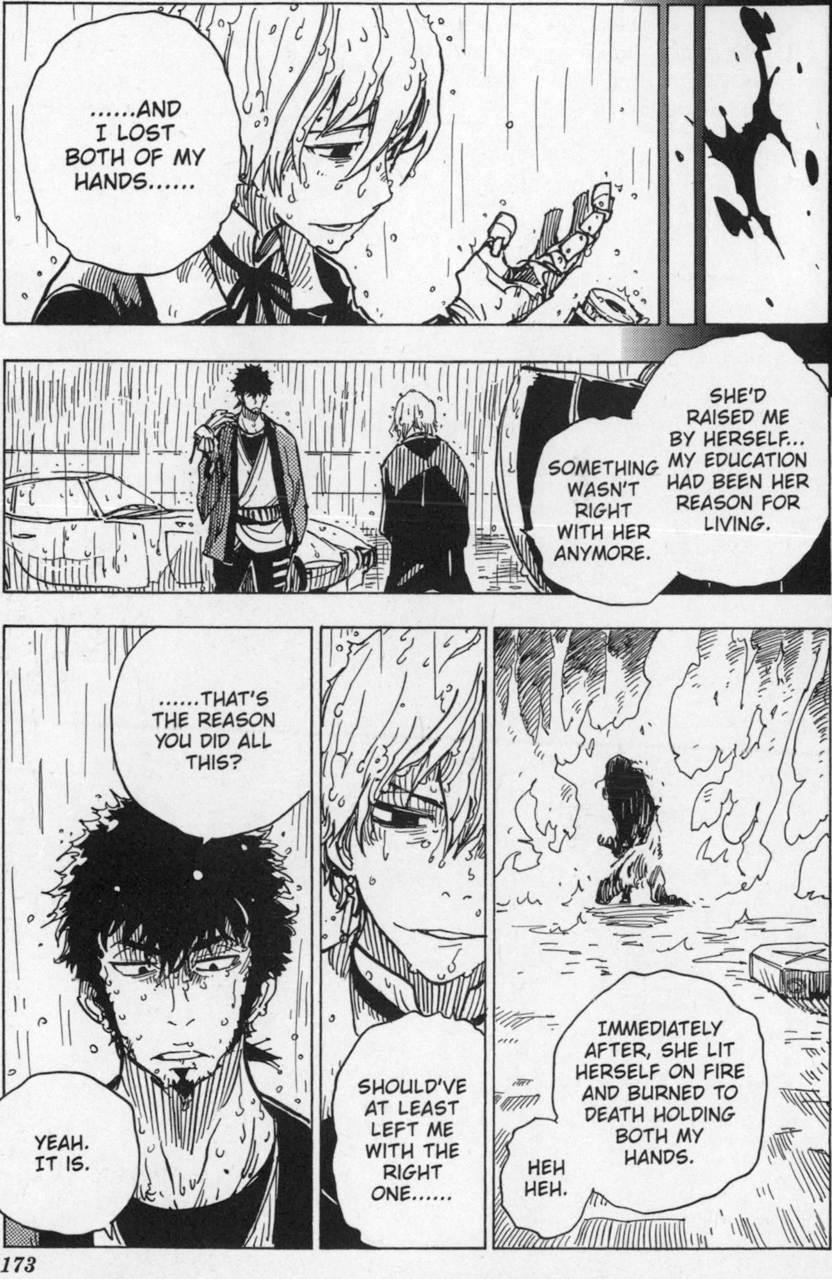
......AND I LOST BOTH OF MY HANDS......
SHE'D RAISED ME BY HERSELF... MY EDUCATION HAD BEEN HER REASON FOR LIVING.
SOMETHING WASN'T RIGHT WITH HER ANYMORE.
IMMEDIATELY AFTER, SHE LIT HERSELF ON FIRE AND BURNED TO DEATH HOLDING BOTH MY HANDS.
HEH HEH.
SHOULD'VE AT LEAST LEFT ME WITH THE RIGHT ONE......
......THAT'S THE REASON YOU DID ALL THIS?
YEAH. IT IS.

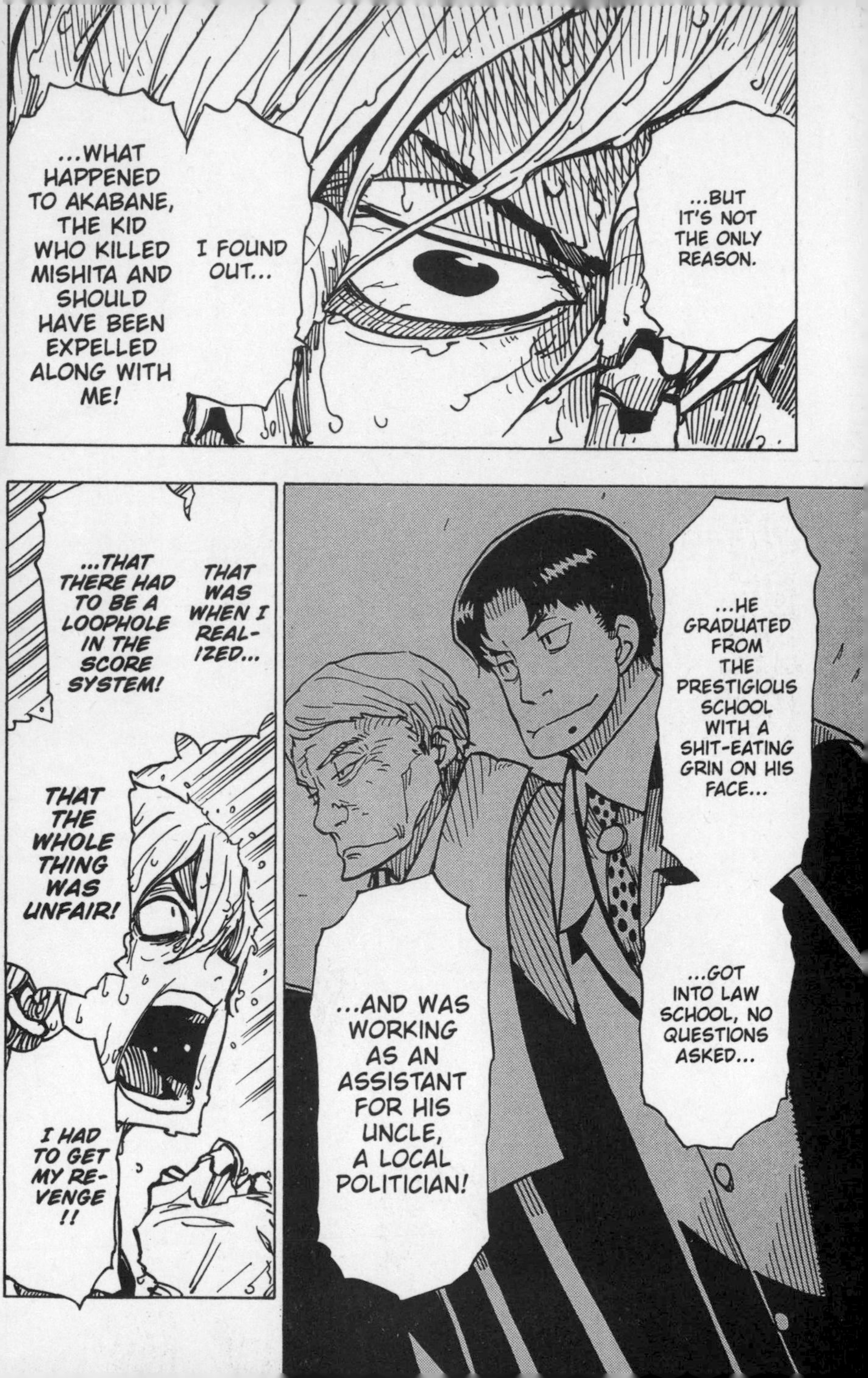
...BUT IT'S NOT THE ONLY REASON.
I FOUND OUT...
...WHAT HAPPENED TO AKABANE, THE KID WHO KILLED MISHITA AND SHOULD HAVE BEEN EXPELLED ALONG WITH ME!
...HE GRADUATED FROM THE PRESTIGIOUS SCHOOL WITH A SHIT-EATING GRIN ON HIS FACE...
...GOT INTO LAW SCHOOL, NO QUESTIONS ASKED...
...AND WAS WORKING AS AN ASSISTANT FOR HIS UNCLE, A LOCAL POLITICIAN!
THAT WAS WHEN I REAL-IZED...
...THAT THERE HAD TO BE A LOOPHOLE IN THE SCORE SYSTEM!
THAT THE WHOLE THING WAS UNFAIR!
I HAD TO GET MY RE-VENGE!!

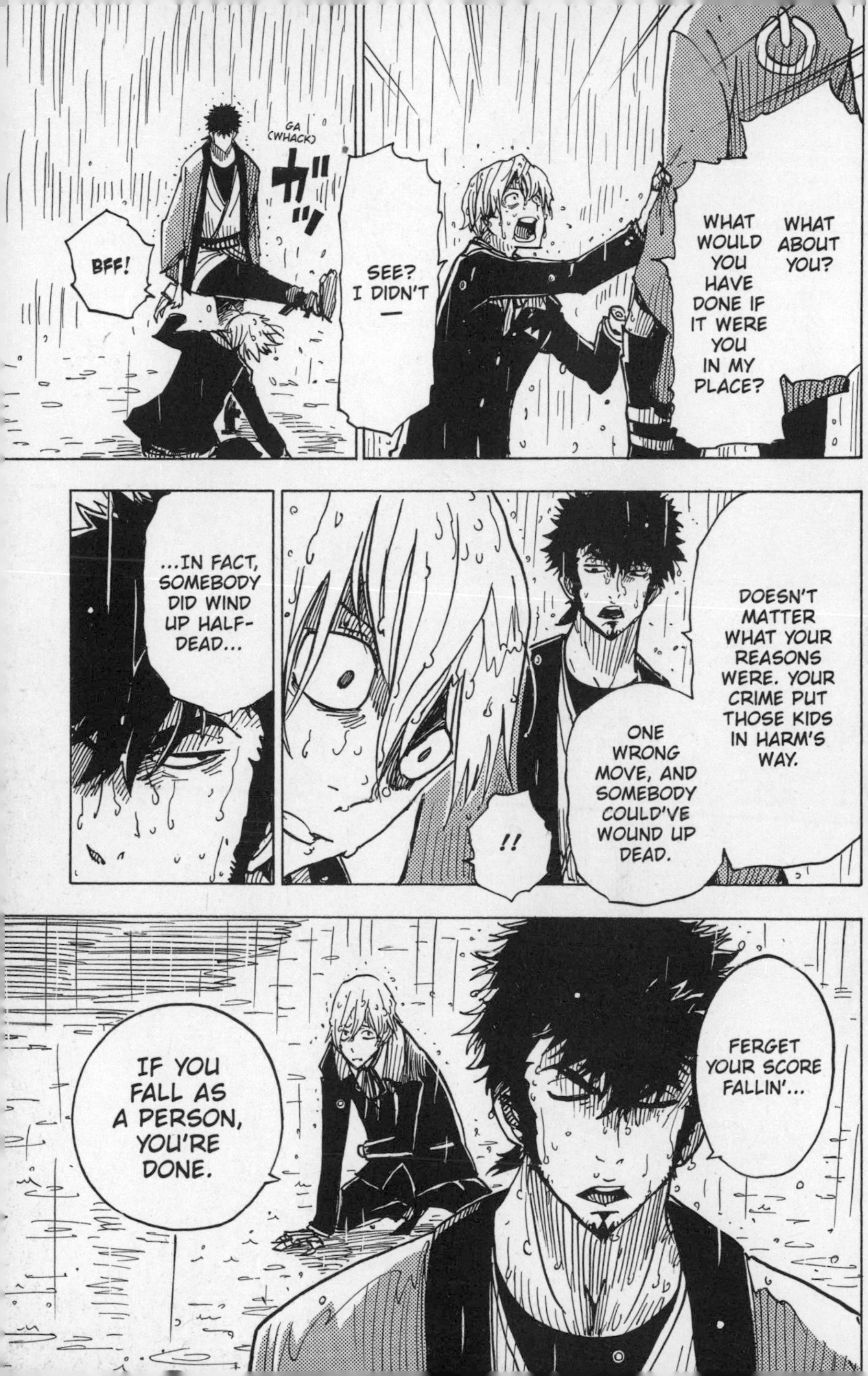
WHAT ABOUT YOU?
WHAT WOULD YOU HAVE DONE IF IT WERE YOU IN MY PLACE?
SEE? I DIDN'T —
ガッ
GA (WHACK)
BFF!
DOESN'T MATTER WHAT YOUR REASONS WERE. YOUR CRIME PUT THOSE KIDS IN HARM'S WAY.
ONE WRONG MOVE, AND SOMEBODY COULD'VE WOUND UP DEAD.
!!
...IN FACT, SOMEBODY DID WIND UP HALF-DEAD...
FERGET YOUR SCORE FALLIN'...
IF YOU FALL AS A PERSON, YOU'RE DONE.

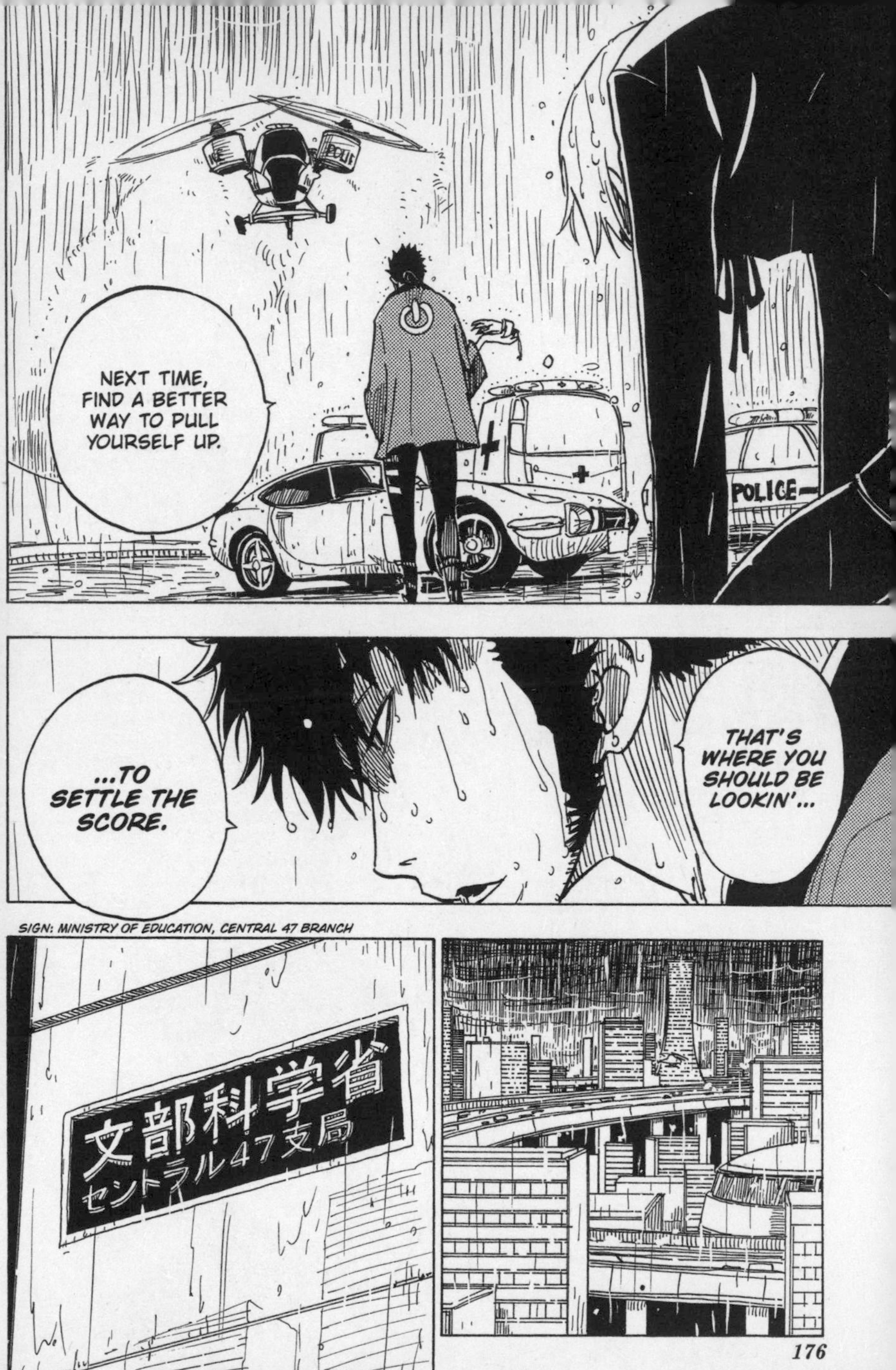
NEXT TIME, FIND A BETTER WAY TO PULL YOURSELF UP.
THAT'S WHERE YOU SHOULD BE LOOKIN'...
...TO SETTLE THE SCORE.
SIGN: MINISTRY OF EDUCATION, CENTRAL 47 BRANCH
文部科学省
セントラル47支局

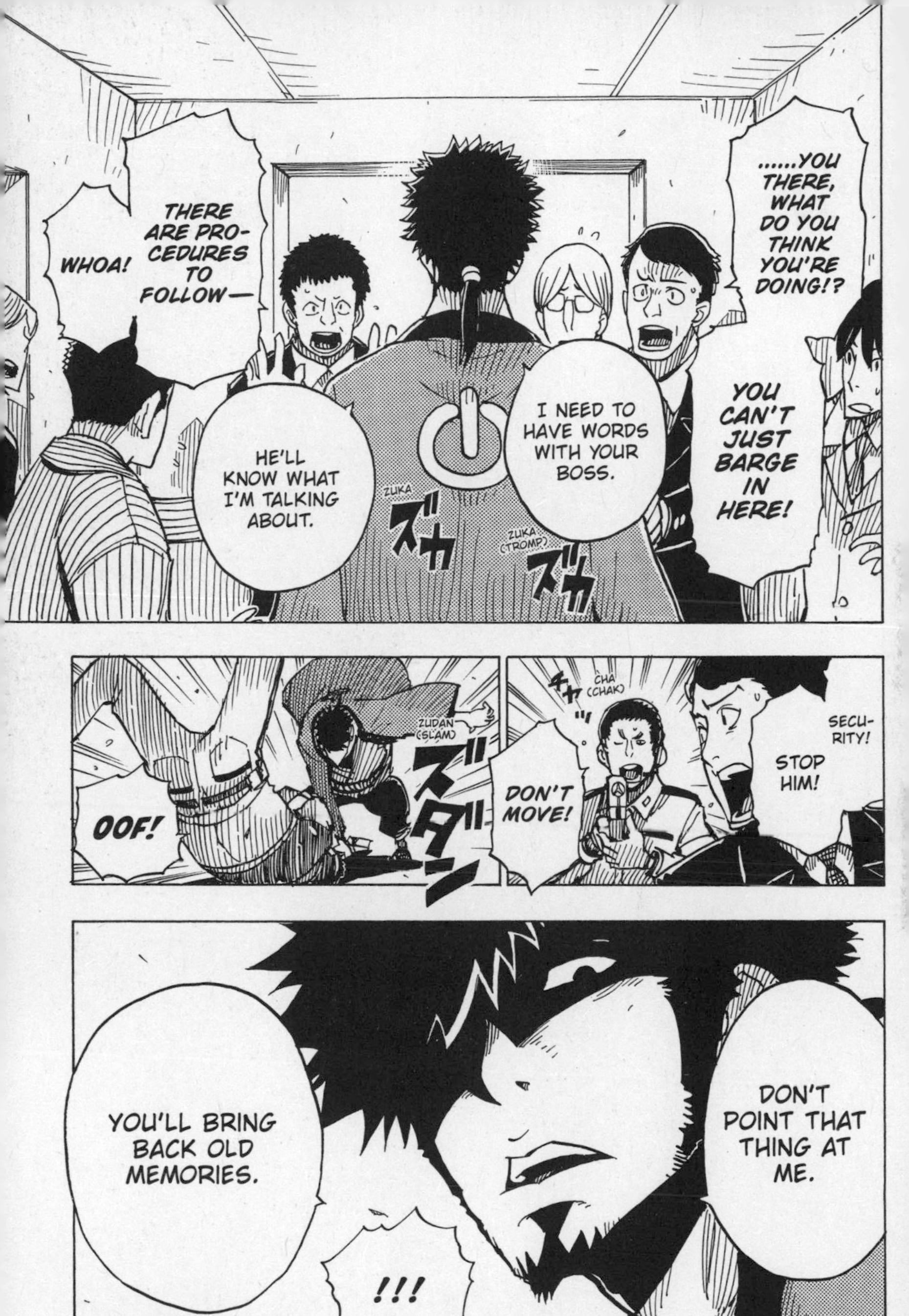
......YOU THERE, WHAT DO YOU THINK YOU'RE DOING!?
YOU CAN'T JUST BARGE IN HERE!
I NEED TO HAVE WORDS WITH YOUR BOSS.
ZUKA (TROMP)
ZUKA
HE'LL KNOW WHAT I'M TALKING ABOUT.
THERE ARE PROCEDURES TO FOLLOW—
WHOA!
SECURITY!
STOP HIM!
CHA (CHAK)
DON'T MOVE!
ZUDAN (SLAM)
OOF!
DON'T POINT THAT THING AT ME.
!!!
YOU'LL BRING BACK OLD MEMORIES.

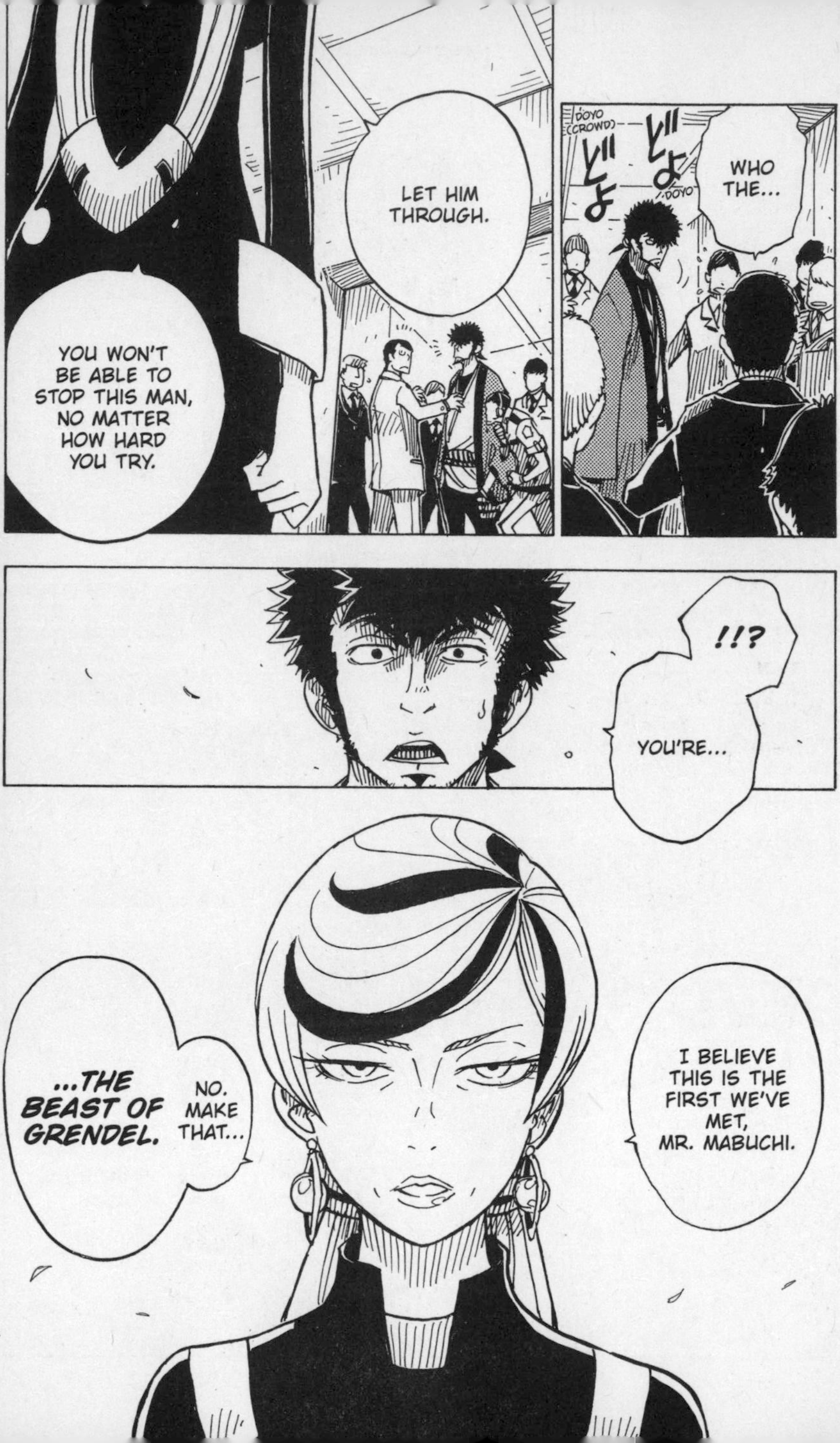
DOYO (CROWD)
どよ どよ
DOYO
WHO THE...
LET HIM THROUGH.
YOU WON'T BE ABLE TO STOP THIS MAN, NO MATTER HOW HARD YOU TRY.
!!?
YOU'RE...
I BELIEVE THIS IS THE FIRST WE'VE MET, MR. MABUCHI.
NO. MAKE THAT...
...THE BEAST OF GRENDEL.

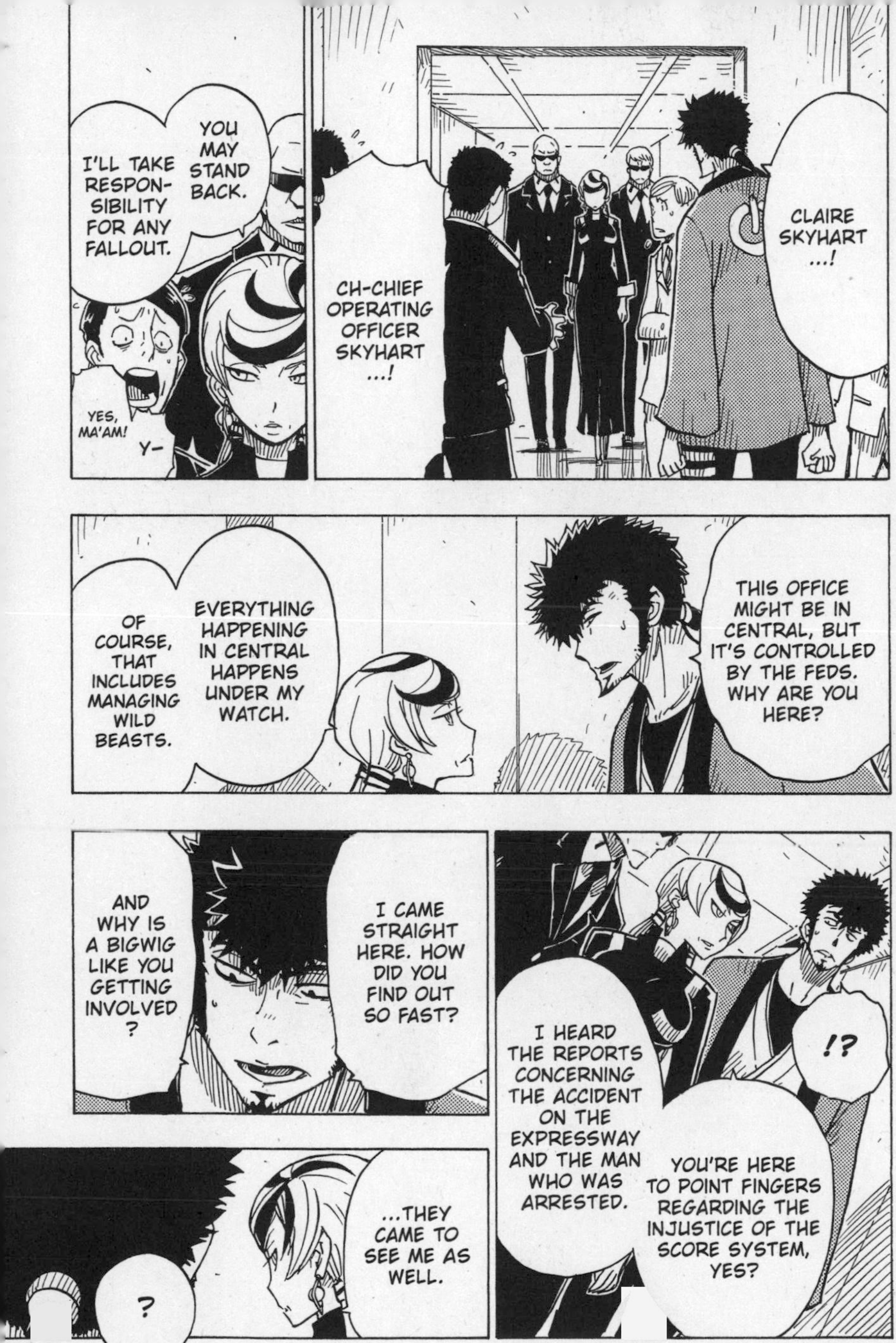
CLAIRE SKYHART ...!
CH-CHIEF OPERATING OFFICER SKYHART ...!
YOU MAY STAND BACK.
I'LL TAKE RESPON-SIBILITY FOR ANY FALLOUT.
Y-
YES, MA'AM!
THIS OFFICE MIGHT BE IN CENTRAL, BUT IT'S CONTROLLED BY THE FEDS. WHY ARE YOU HERE?
EVERYTHING HAPPENING IN CENTRAL HAPPENS UNDER MY WATCH.
OF COURSE, THAT INCLUDES MANAGING WILD BEASTS.
I HEARD THE REPORTS CONCERNING THE ACCIDENT ON THE EXPRESSWAY AND THE MAN WHO WAS ARRESTED.
!?
YOU'RE HERE TO POINT FINGERS REGARDING THE INJUSTICE OF THE SCORE SYSTEM, YES?
I CAME STRAIGHT HERE. HOW DID YOU FIND OUT SO FAST?
AND WHY IS A BIGWIG LIKE YOU GETTING INVOLVED ?
...THEY CAME TO SEE ME AS WELL.
?

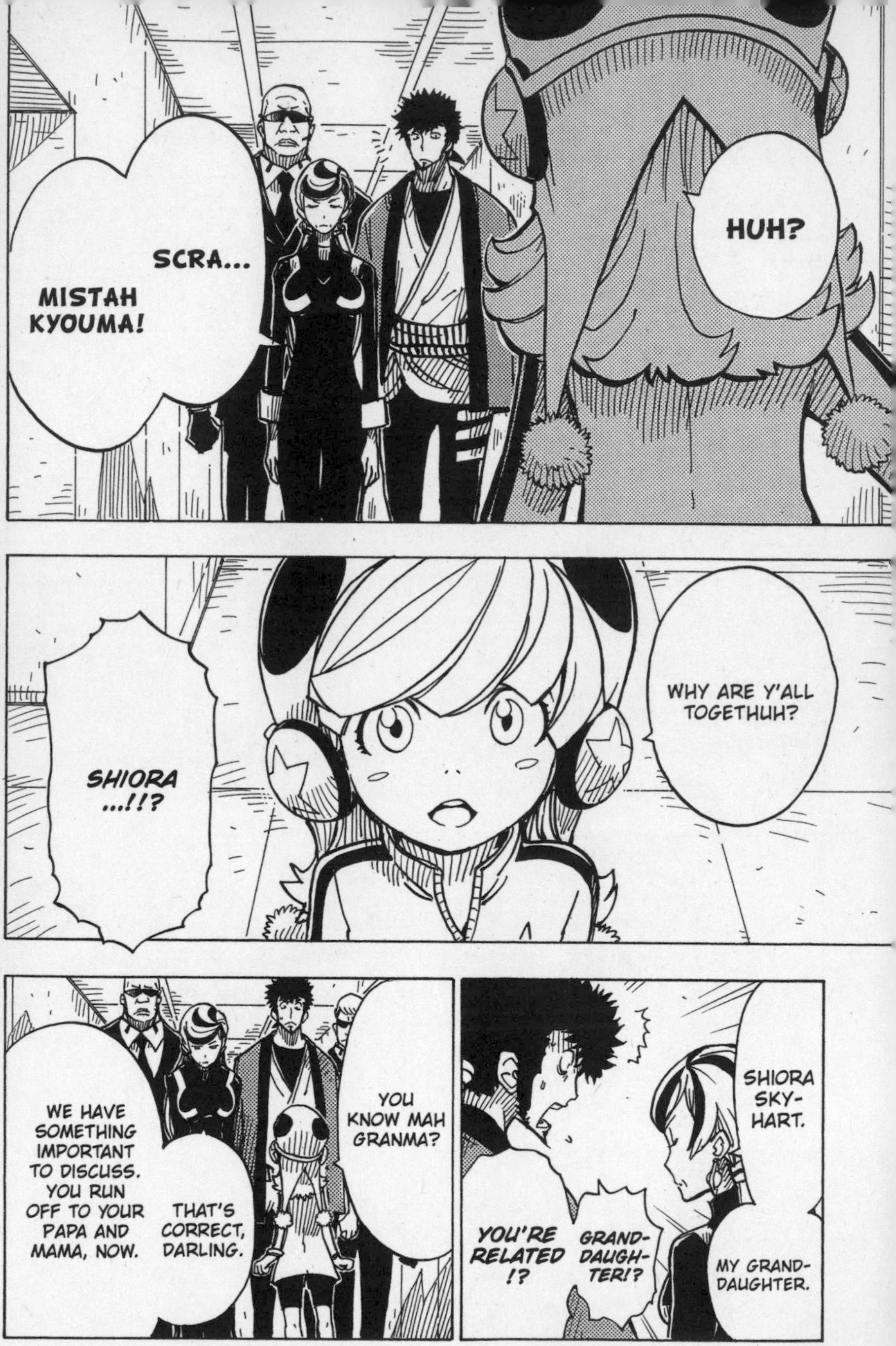
HUH?
SCRA...
MISTAH KYOUMA!
WHY ARE Y'ALL TOGETHUH?
SHIORA ...!!?
SHIORA SKY-HART.
MY GRAND-DAUGHTER.
GRAND-DAUGHTER!?
YOU'RE RELATED !?
YOU KNOW MAH GRANMA?
THAT'S CORRECT, DARLING.
WE HAVE SOMETHING IMPORTANT TO DISCUSS. YOU RUN OFF TO YOUR PAPA AND MAMA, NOW.

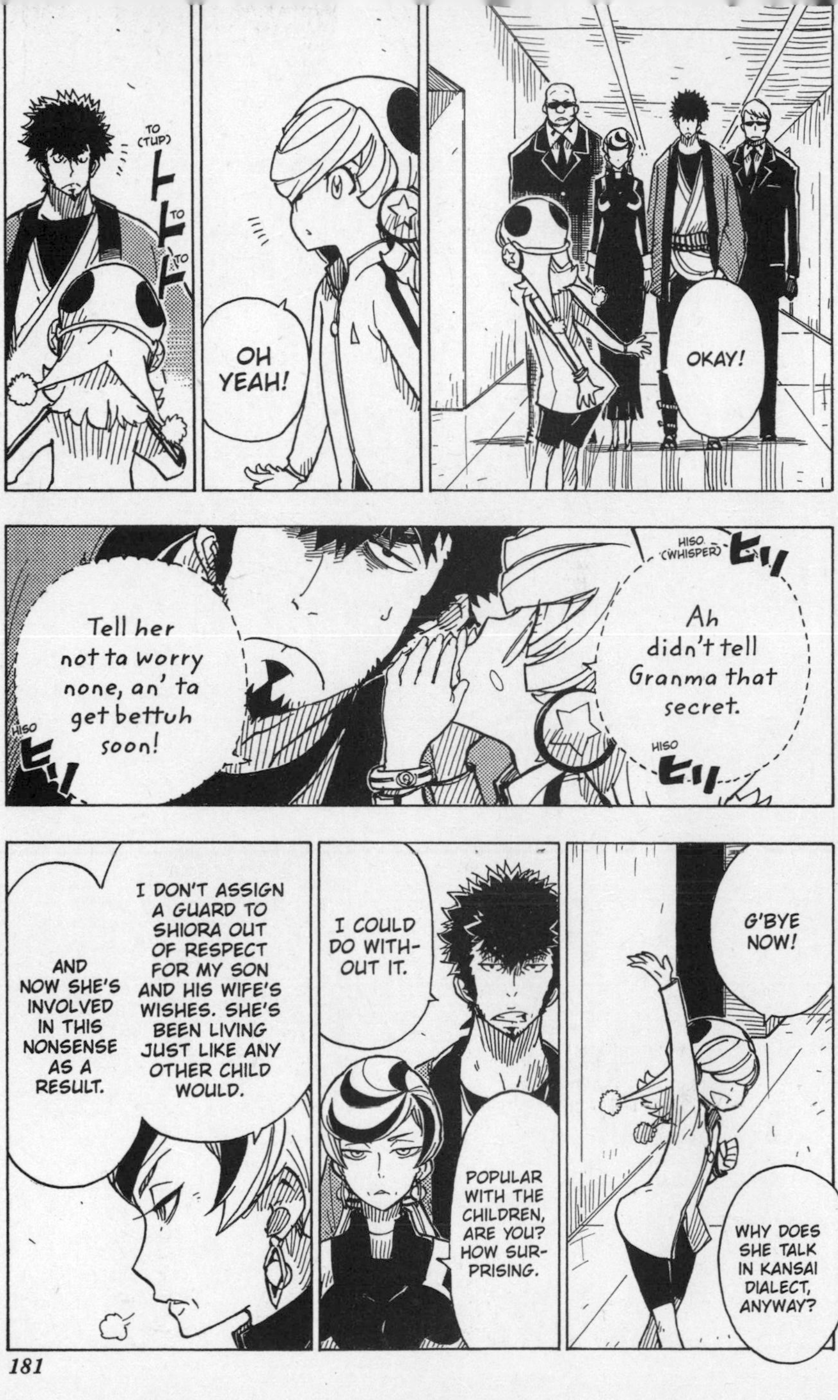
OKAY!
OH YEAH!
TO (TUP)
TO
TO
HISO. (WHISPER)
Ah didn't tell Granma that secret.
HISO
Tell her not ta worry none, an' ta get bettuh soon!
HISO
G'BYE NOW!
WHY DOES SHE TALK IN KANSAI DIALECT, ANYWAY?
I COULD DO WITH-OUT IT.
POPULAR WITH THE CHILDREN, ARE YOU? HOW SUR-PRISING.
I DON'T ASSIGN A GUARD TO SHIORA OUT OF RESPECT FOR MY SON AND HIS WIFE'S WISHES. SHE'S BEEN LIVING JUST LIKE ANY OTHER CHILD WOULD.
AND NOW SHE'S INVOLVED IN THIS NONSENSE AS A RESULT.

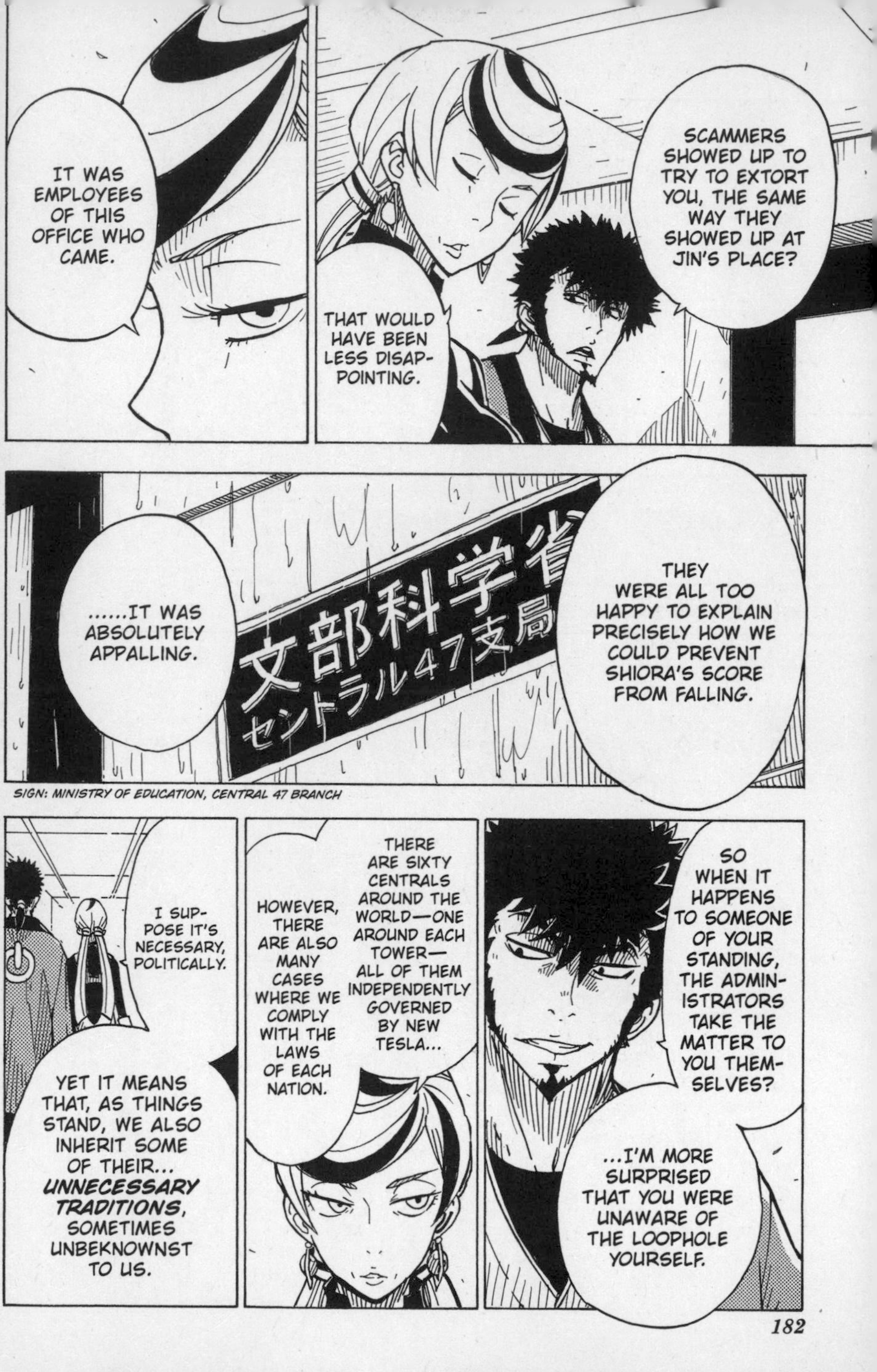
SCAMMERS SHOWED UP TO TRY TO EXTORT YOU, THE SAME WAY THEY SHOWED UP AT JIN'S PLACE?
THAT WOULD HAVE BEEN LESS DISAP-POINTING.
IT WAS EMPLOYEES OF THIS OFFICE WHO CAME.
文部科学省
セントラル47支局
THEY WERE ALL TOO HAPPY TO EXPLAIN PRECISELY HOW WE COULD PREVENT SHIORA'S SCORE FROM FALLING.
......IT WAS ABSOLUTELY APPALLING.
SO WHEN IT HAPPENS TO SOMEONE OF YOUR STANDING, THE ADMIN-ISTRATORS TAKE THE MATTER TO YOU THEM-SELVES?
...I'M MORE SURPRISED THAT YOU WERE UNAWARE OF THE LOOPHOLE YOURSELF.
THERE ARE SIXTY CENTRALS AROUND THE WORLD—ONE AROUND EACH TOWER—ALL OF THEM INDEPENDENTLY GOVERNED BY NEW TESLA...
HOWEVER, THERE ARE ALSO MANY CASES WHERE WE COMPLY WITH THE LAWS OF EACH NATION.
I SUP-POSE IT'S NECESSARY, POLITICALLY.
YET IT MEANS THAT, AS THINGS STAND, WE ALSO INHERIT SOME OF THEIR... ***UNNECESSARY TRADITIONS***, SOMETIMES UNBEKNOWNST TO US.

SIGN: MINISTRY OF EDUCATION, CENTRAL 47 BRANCH

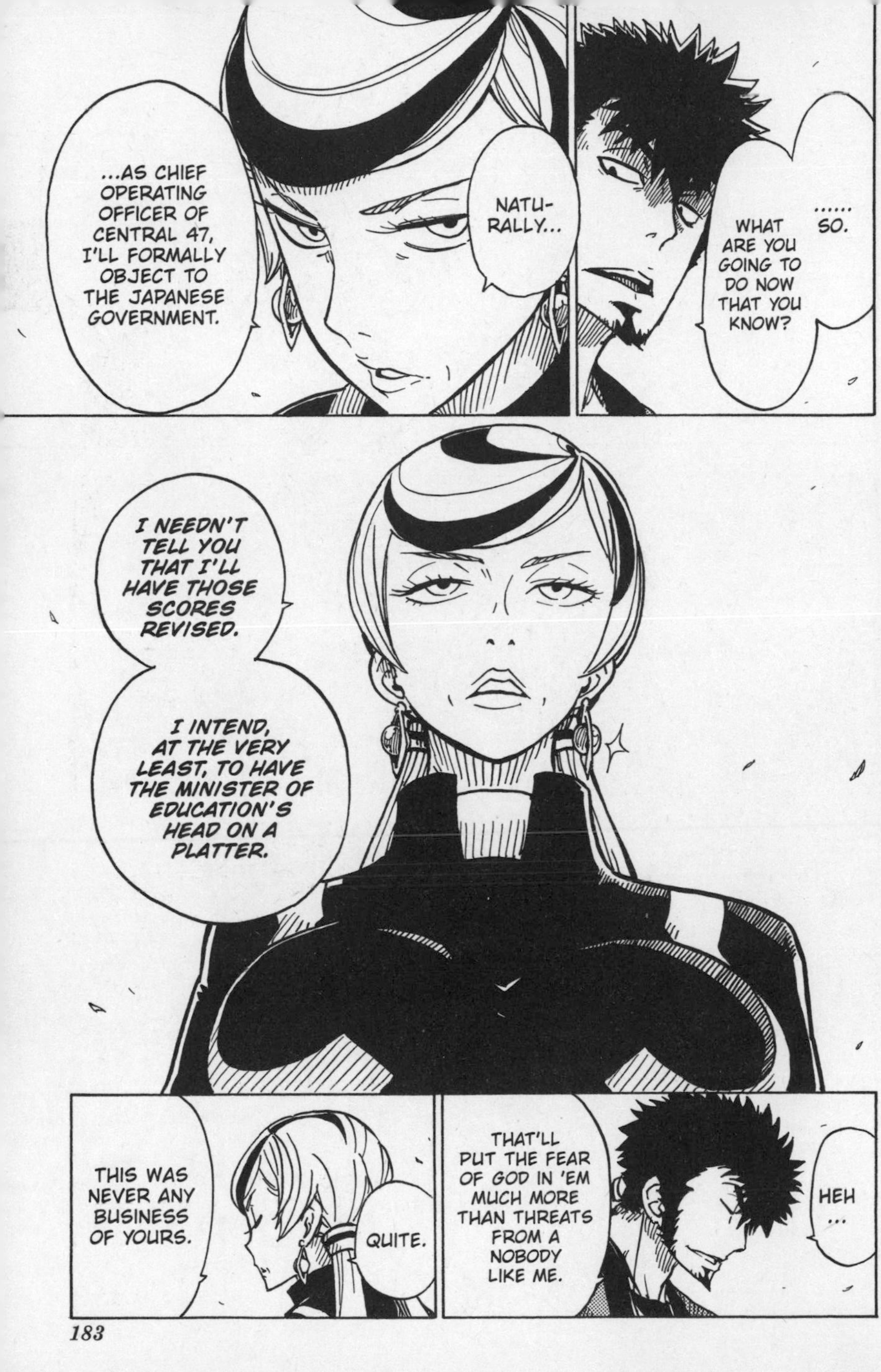
......SO.
WHAT ARE YOU GOING TO DO NOW THAT YOU KNOW?
NATU-RALLY...
...AS CHIEF OPERATING OFFICER OF CENTRAL 47, I'LL FORMALLY OBJECT TO THE JAPANESE GOVERNMENT.
I NEEDN'T TELL YOU THAT I'LL HAVE THOSE SCORES REVISED.
I INTEND, AT THE VERY LEAST, TO HAVE THE MINISTER OF EDUCATION'S HEAD ON A PLATTER.
HEH ...
THAT'LL PUT THE FEAR OF GOD IN 'EM MUCH MORE THAN THREATS FROM A NOBODY LIKE ME.
QUITE.
THIS WAS NEVER ANY BUSINESS OF YOURS.

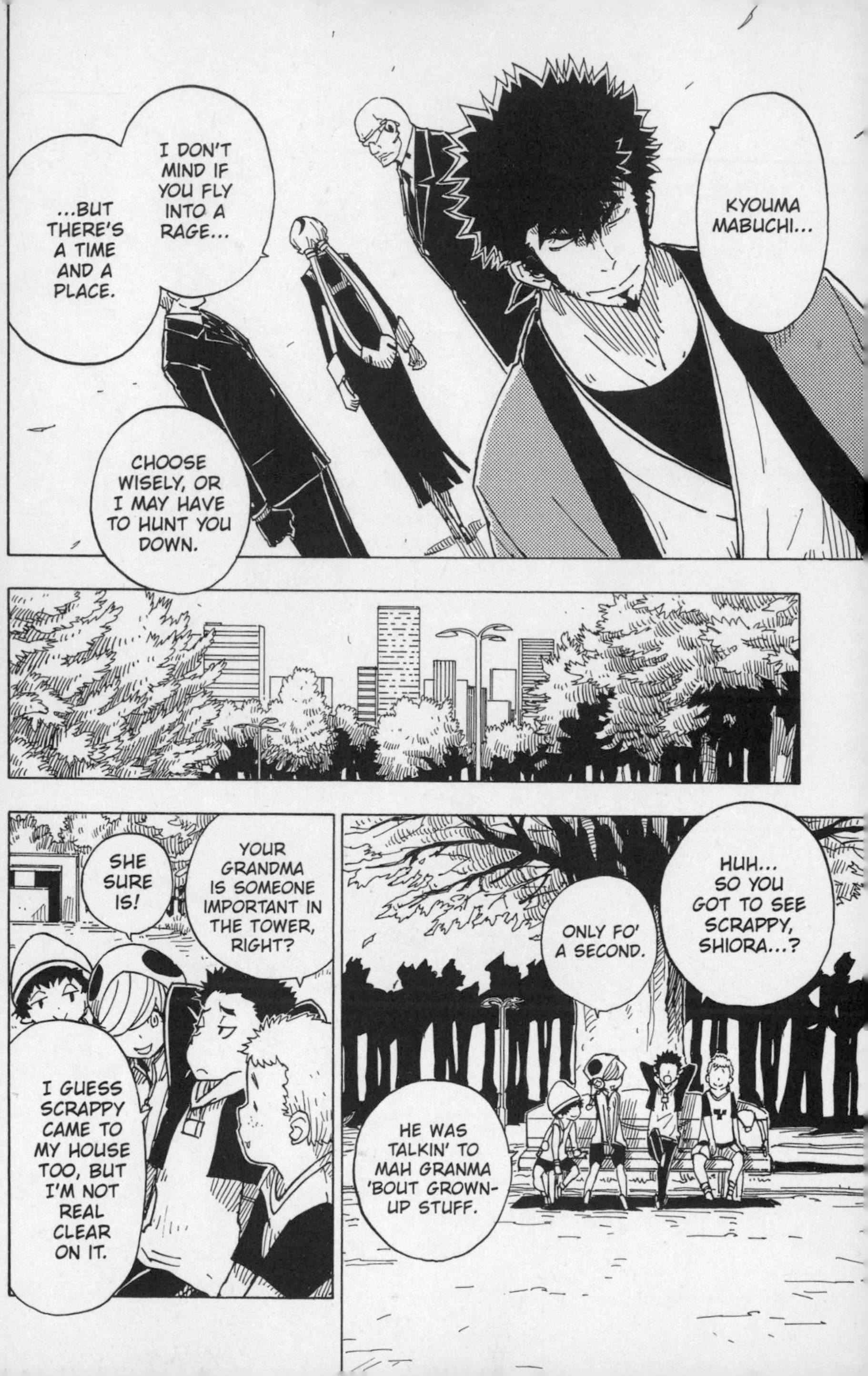
KYOUMA MABUCHI...
I DON'T MIND IF YOU FLY INTO A RAGE...
...BUT THERE'S A TIME AND A PLACE.
CHOOSE WISELY, OR I MAY HAVE TO HUNT YOU DOWN.
HUH... SO YOU GOT TO SEE SCRAPPY, SHIORA...?
ONLY FO' A SECOND.
HE WAS TALKIN' TO MAH GRANMA 'BOUT GROWN-UP STUFF.
YOUR GRANDMA IS SOMEONE IMPORTANT IN THE TOWER, RIGHT?
SHE SURE IS!
I GUESS SCRAPPY CAME TO MY HOUSE TOO, BUT I'M NOT REAL CLEAR ON IT.

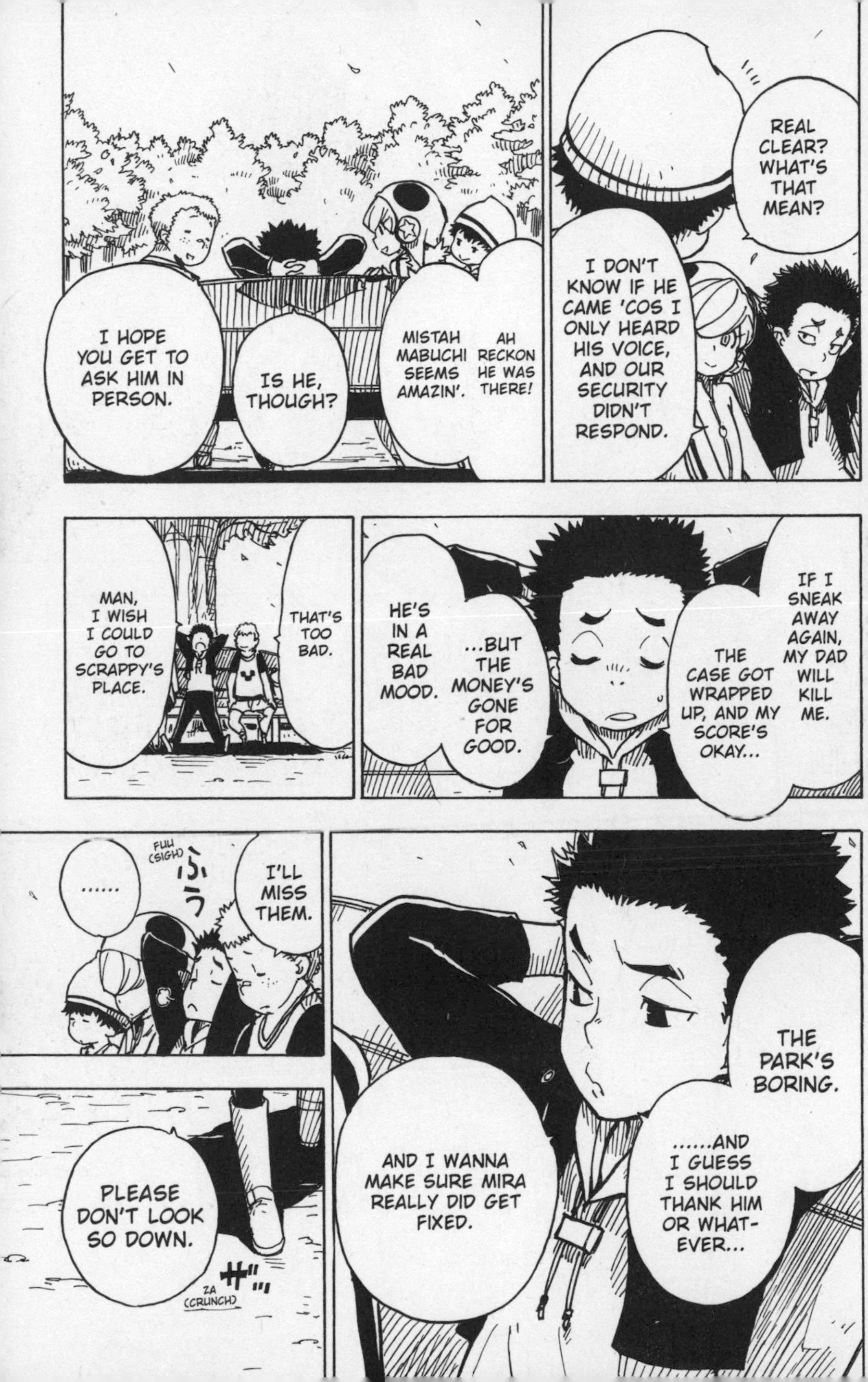
REAL CLEAR? WHAT'S THAT MEAN?
I DON'T KNOW IF HE CAME 'COS I ONLY HEARD HIS VOICE, AND OUR SECURITY DIDN'T RESPOND.
AH RECKON HE WAS THERE!
MISTAH MABUCHI SEEMS AMAZIN'.
IS HE, THOUGH?
I HOPE YOU GET TO ASK HIM IN PERSON.
IF I SNEAK AWAY AGAIN, MY DAD WILL KILL ME.
THE CASE GOT WRAPPED UP, AND MY SCORE'S OKAY...
...BUT THE MONEY'S GONE FOR GOOD.
HE'S IN A REAL BAD MOOD.
THAT'S TOO BAD.
MAN, I WISH I COULD GO TO SCRAPPY'S PLACE.
THE PARK'S BORING.
......AND I GUESS I SHOULD THANK HIM OR WHATEVER...
AND I WANNA MAKE SURE MIRA REALLY DID GET FIXED.
I'LL MISS THEM.
ふう
FUU (SIGH)
......
ザッ
ZA (CRUNCH)
PLEASE DON'T LOOK SO DOWN.

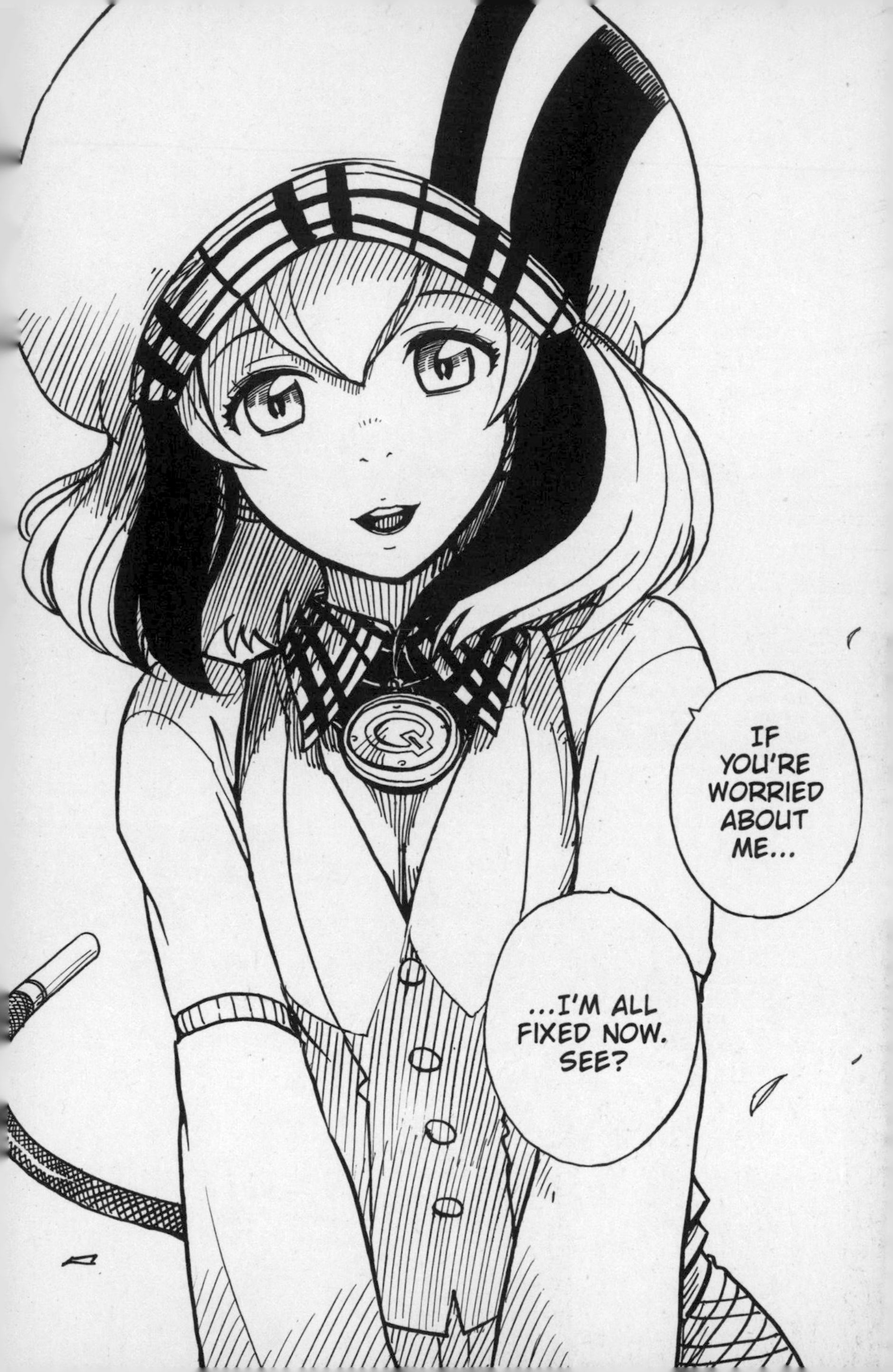
IF YOU'RE WORRIED ABOUT ME...
...I'M ALL FIXED NOW. SEE?

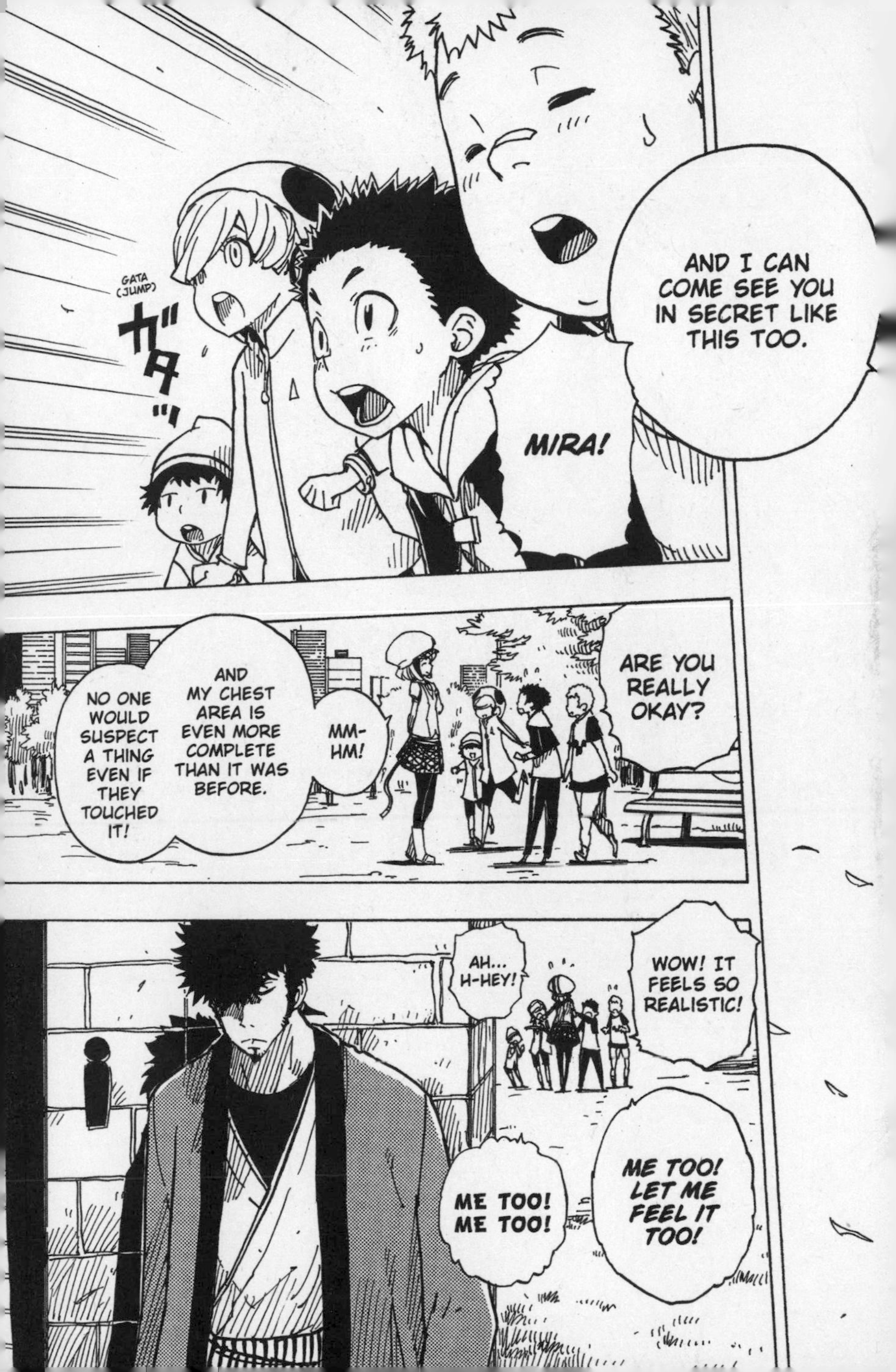
AND I CAN COME SEE YOU IN SECRET LIKE THIS TOO.
MIRA!
GATA (JUMP)
ガタッ
ARE YOU REALLY OKAY?
MM-HM!
AND MY CHEST AREA IS EVEN MORE COMPLETE THAN IT WAS BEFORE.
NO ONE WOULD SUSPECT A THING EVEN IF THEY TOUCHED IT!
WOW! IT FEELS SO REALISTIC!
AH... H-HEY!
ME TOO! LET ME FEEL IT TOO!
ME TOO! ME TOO!

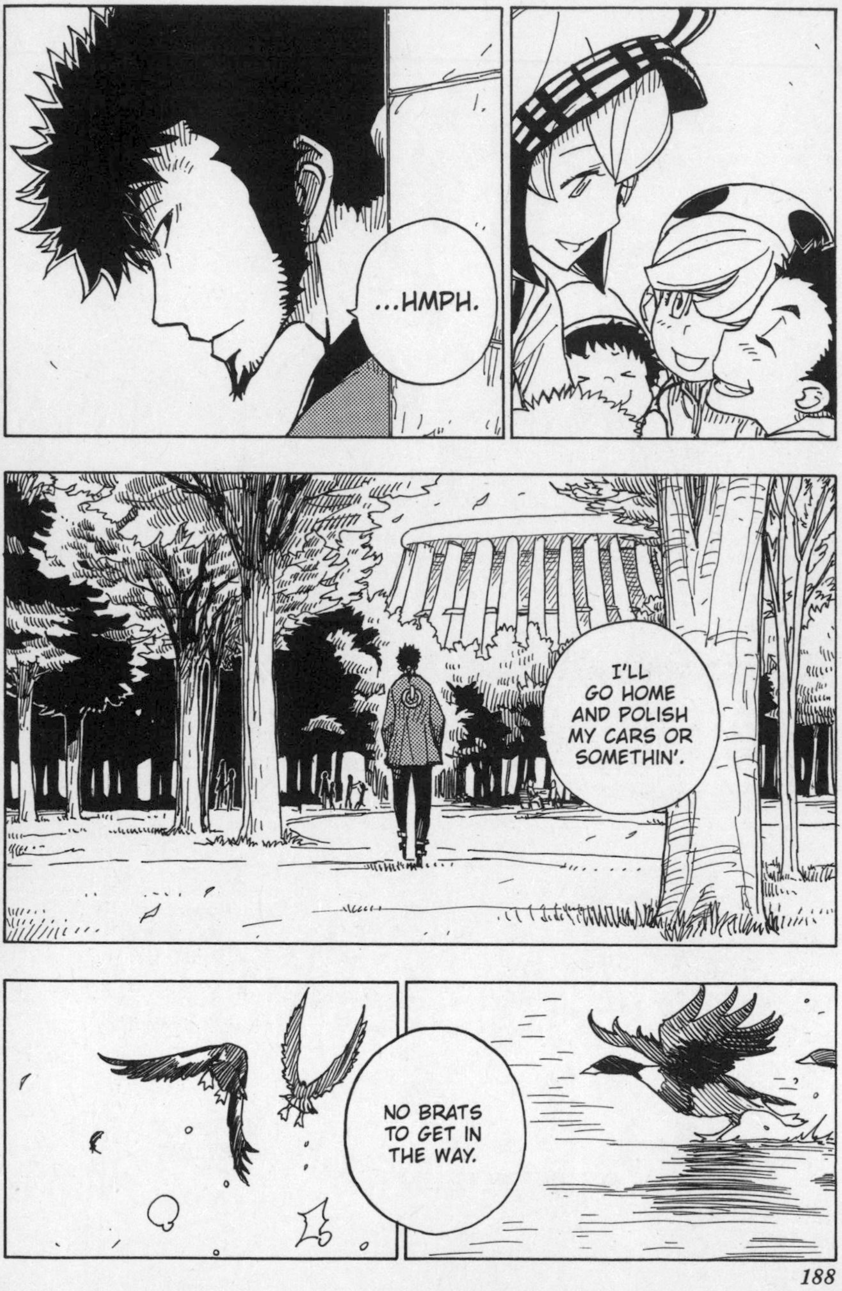
...HMPH.
I'LL GO HOME AND POLISH MY CARS OR SOMETHIN'.
NO BRATS TO GET IN THE WAY.

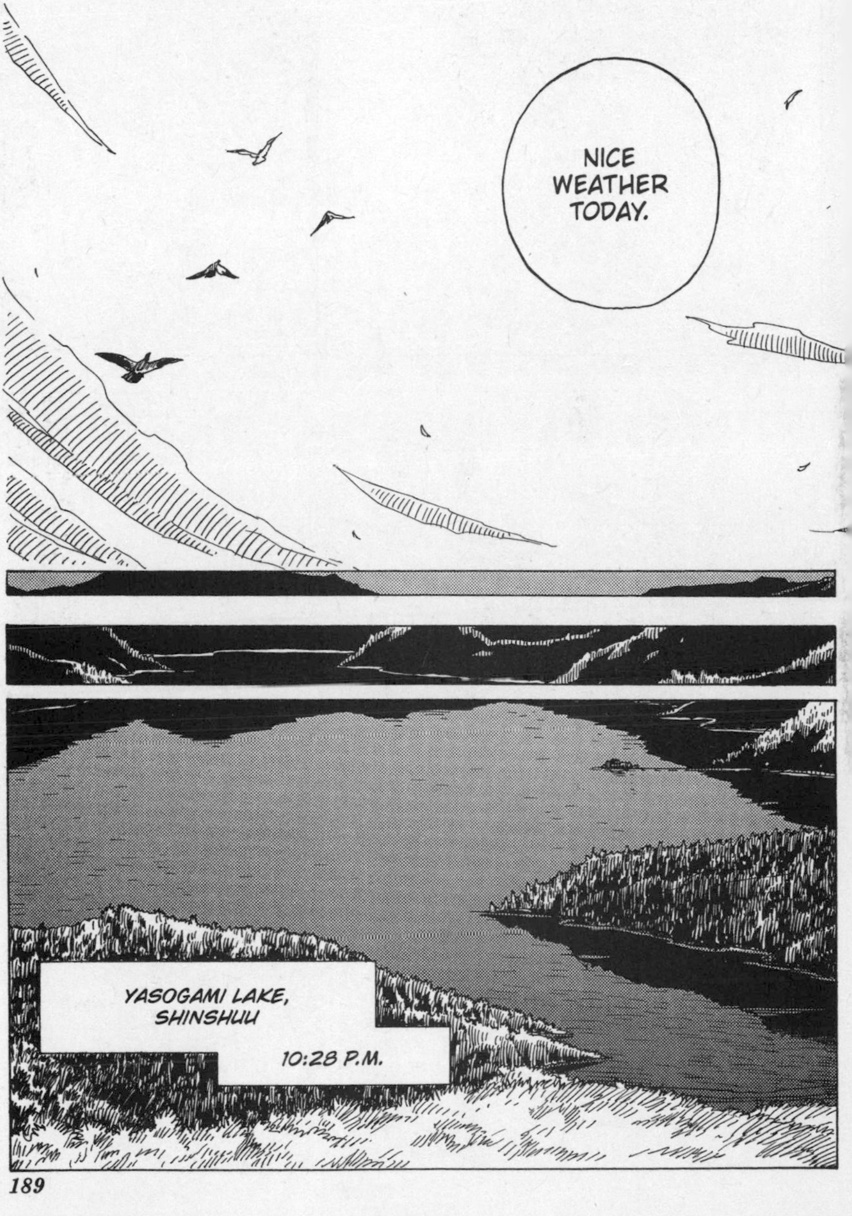
NICE WEATHER TODAY.
YASOGAMI LAKE, SHINSHUU
10:28 P.M.

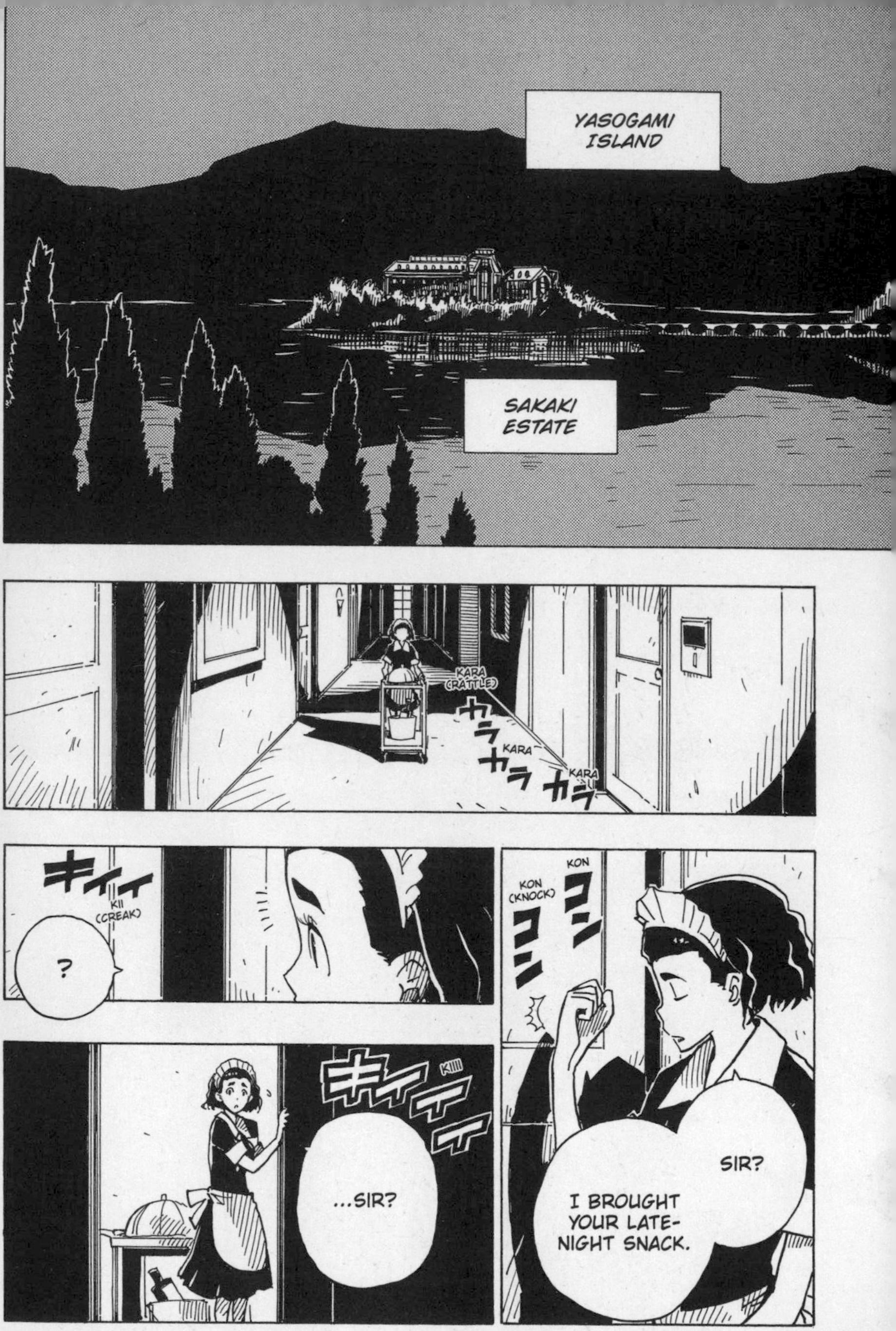

YASOGAMI ISLAND
SAKAKI ESTATE
KARA (RATTLE)
KARA
KARA
KON
KON (KNOCK)
SIR?
I BROUGHT YOUR LATE-NIGHT SNACK.
KII (CREAK)
?
KIIII
...SIR?

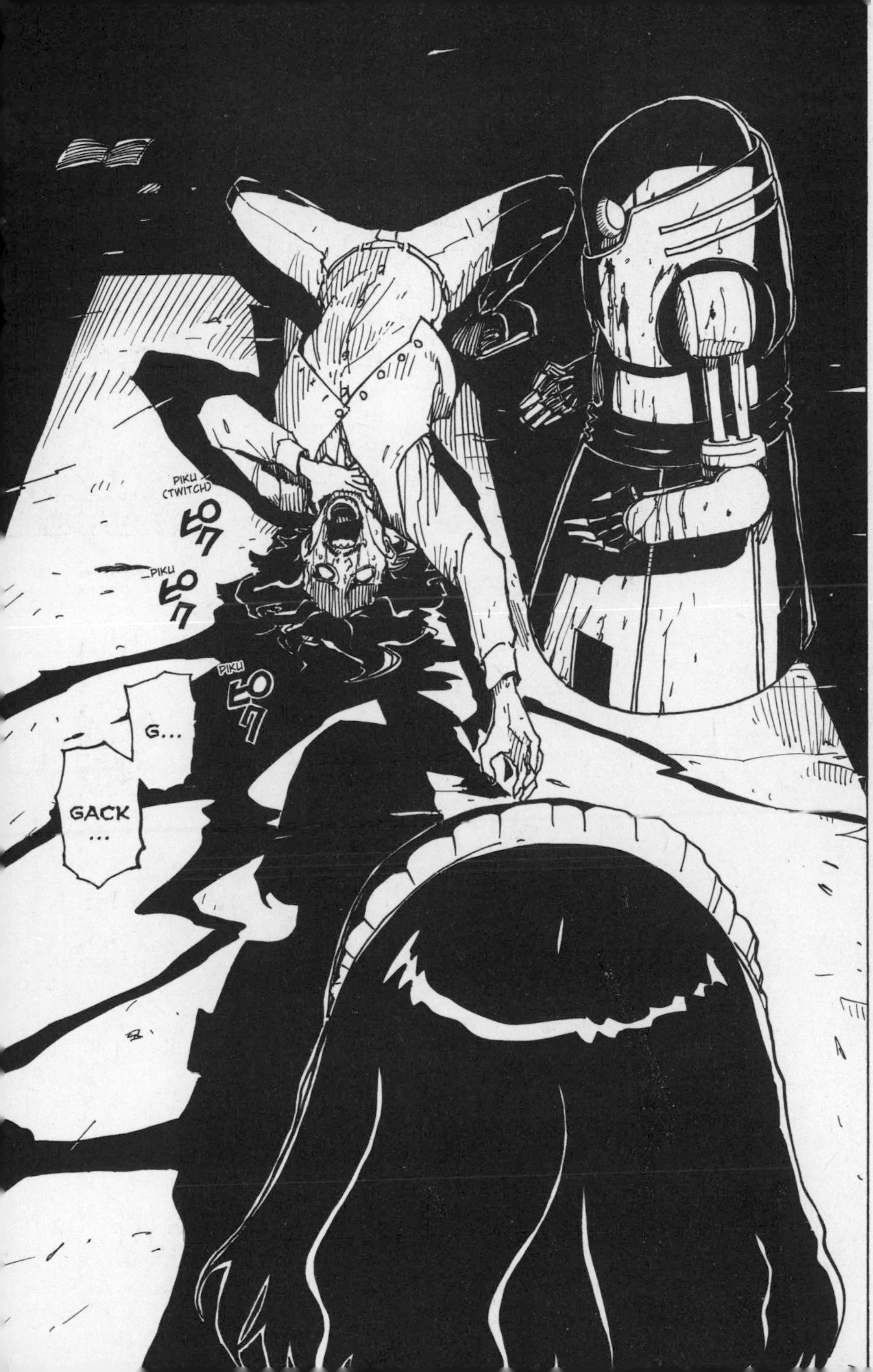
PIKU (TWITCH)
ピク
PIKU
ピク
PIKU
ピク
G...
GACK ...

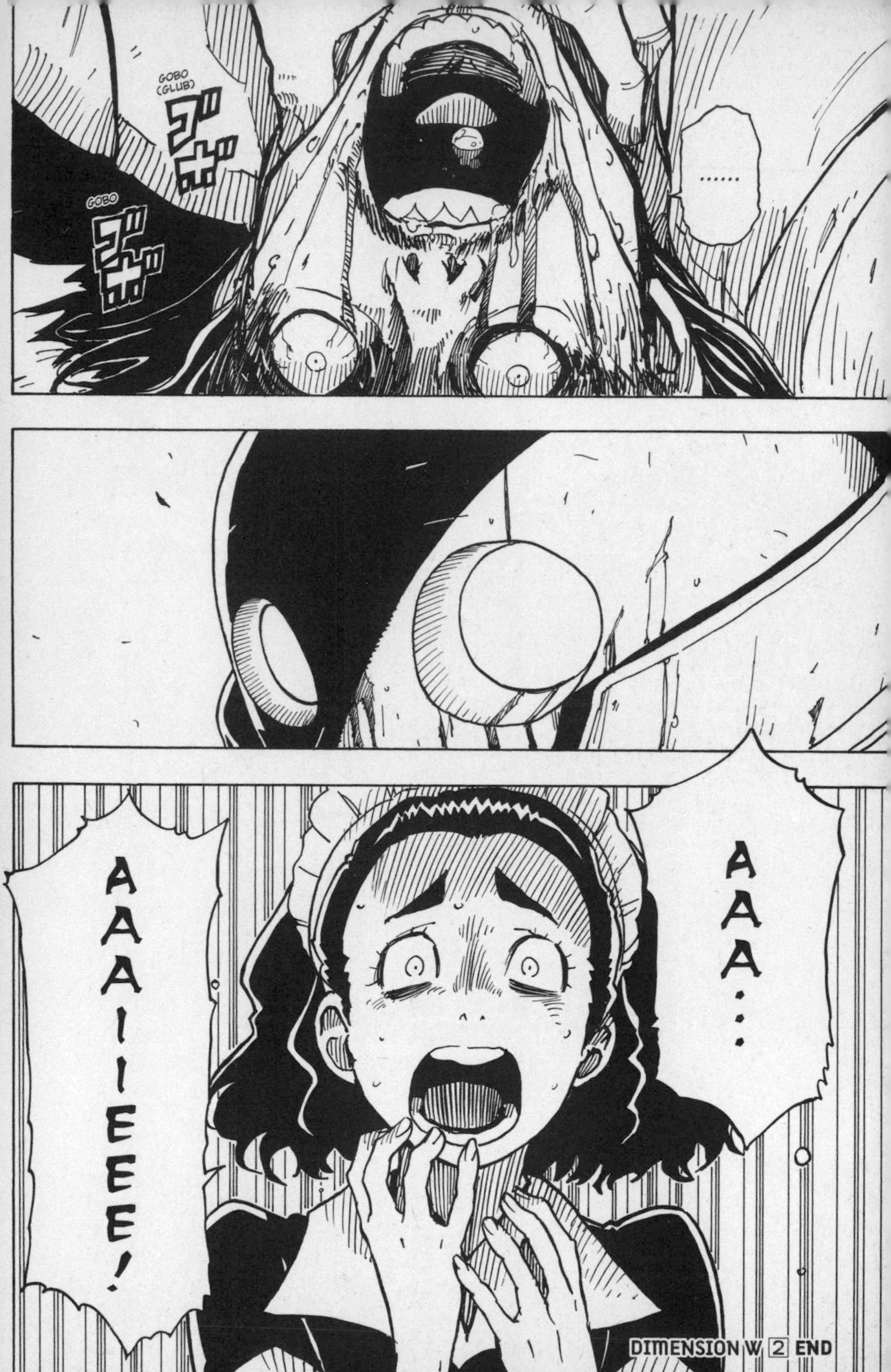

......
GOBO (GLUB)
ゴボ
GOBO
ゴボ
AAA...
AAAIIEEE!
DIMENSION W 2 END

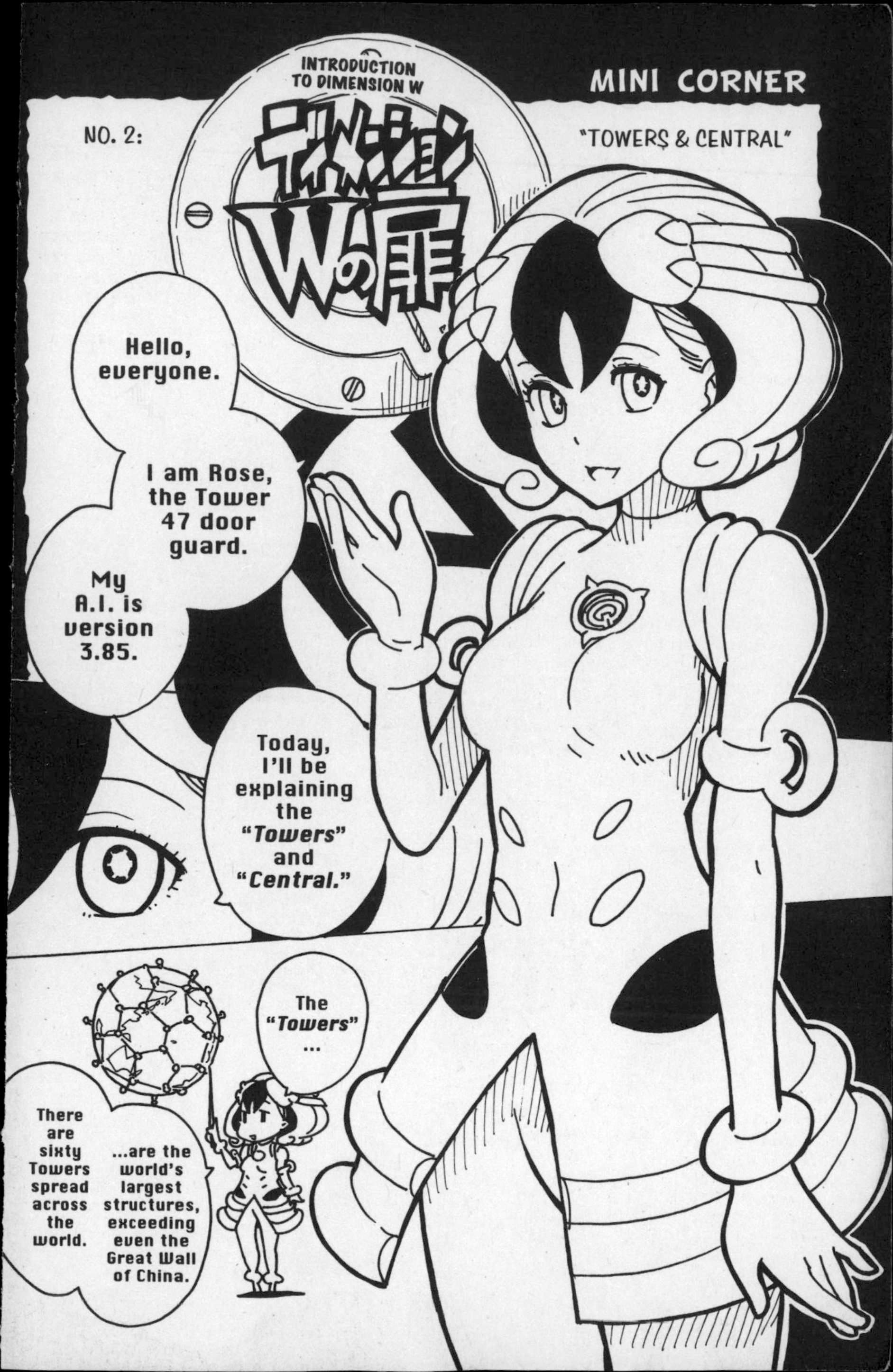
MINI CORNER
INTRODUCTION TO DIMENSION W
ディメンションWの扉
NO. 2:
"TOWERS & CENTRAL"
Hello, everyone.
I am Rose, the Tower 47 door guard.
My A.I. is version 3.85.
Today, I'll be explaining the "*Towers*" and "*Central.*"
The "*Towers*" ...
...are the world's largest structures, exceeding even the Great Wall of China.
There are sixty Towers spread across the world.

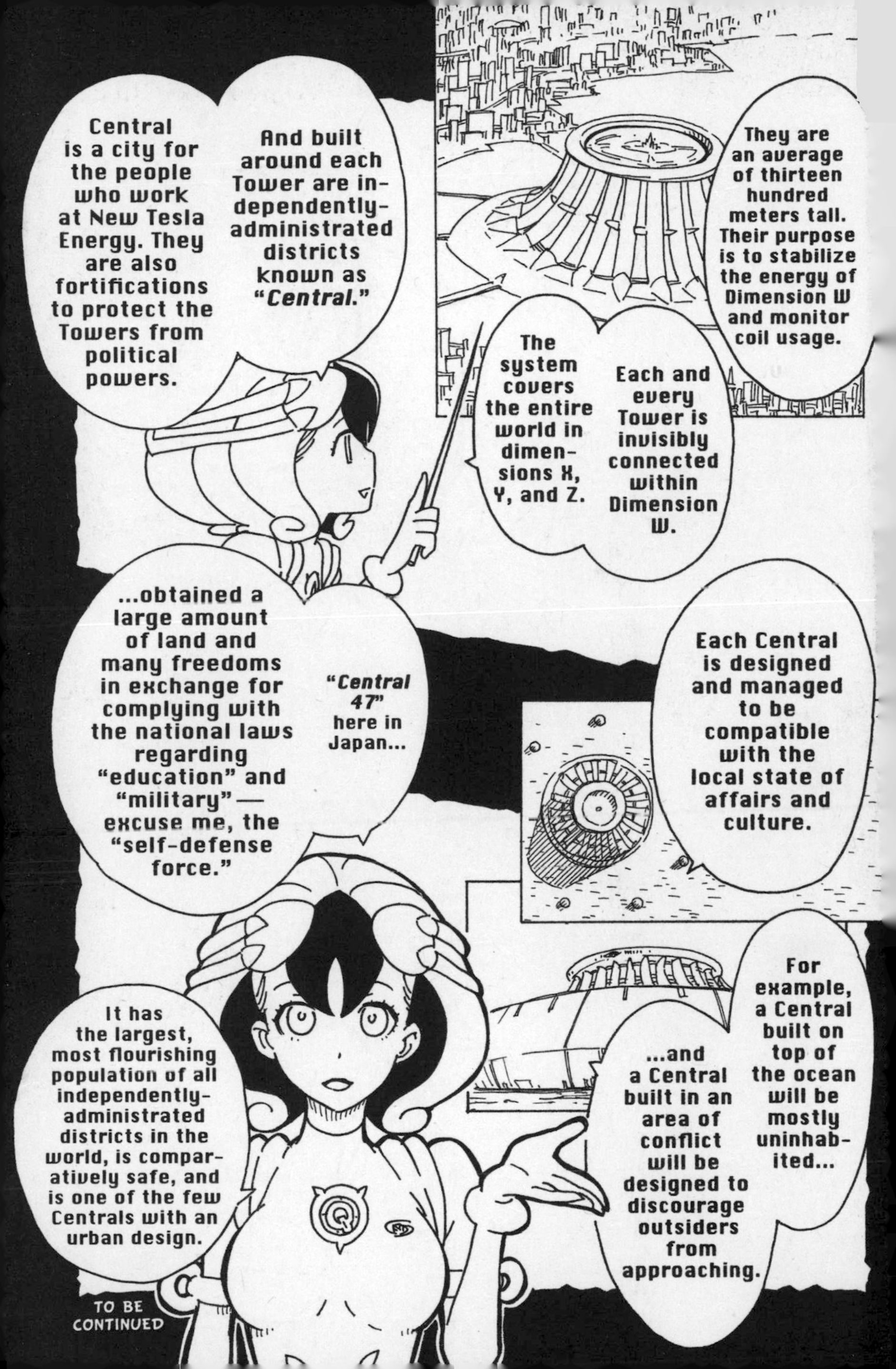
They are an average of thirteen hundred meters tall. Their purpose is to stabilize the energy of Dimension W and monitor coil usage.
Each and every Tower is invisibly connected within Dimension W.
The system covers the entire world in dimensions X, Y, and Z.
And built around each Tower are independently-administrated districts known as "*Central.*"
Central is a city for the people who work at New Tesla Energy. They are also fortifications to protect the Towers from political powers.
Each Central is designed and managed to be compatible with the local state of affairs and culture.
"*Central 47*" here in Japan...
...obtained a large amount of land and many freedoms in exchange for complying with the national laws regarding "education" and "military"—excuse me, the "self-defense force."
For example, a Central built on top of the ocean will be mostly uninhabited...
...and a Central built in an area of conflict will be designed to discourage outsiders from approaching.
It has the largest, most flourishing population of all independently-administrated districts in the world, is comparatively safe, and is one of the few Centrals with an urban design.
TO BE CONTINUED

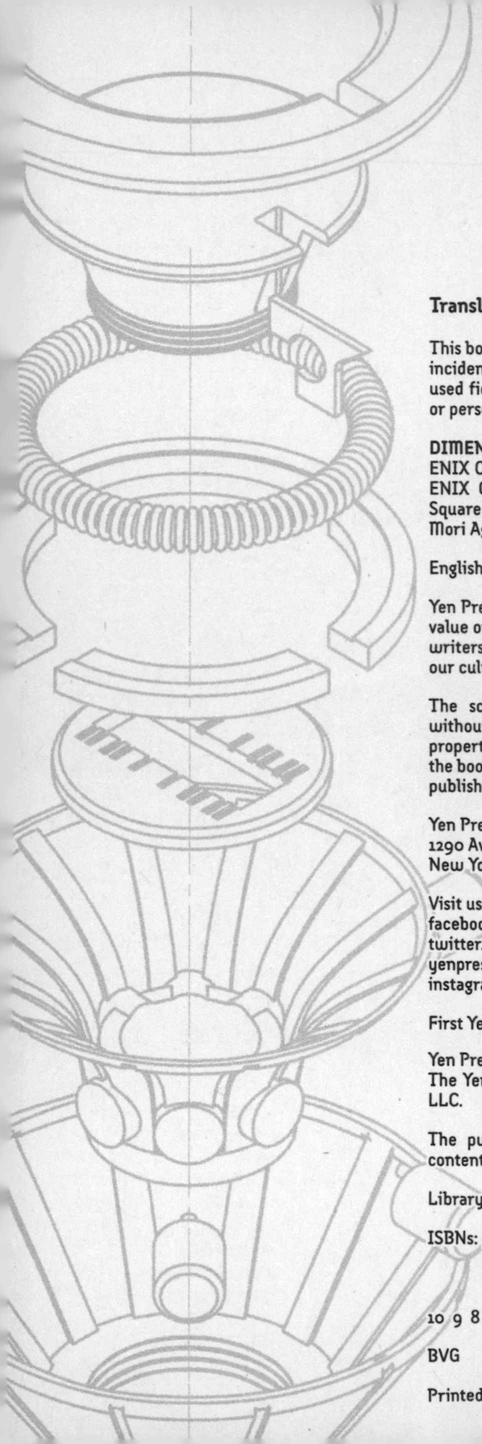

Dimension W

by Yuji Iwahara

Translation: Amanda Haley • Lettering: Phil Christie

DIMENSION W Volume 2 ©2012 Yuji Iwahara/SQUARE ENIX CO., LTD. First published in Japan in 2012 by SQUARE ENIX CO., LTD. English translation rights arranged with Square Enix Co., Ltd. and Yen Press, LLC through Tuttle-Mori Agency, Inc.

English translation © 2016 SQUARE ENIX CO., LTD.

Yen Press
1290 Avenue of the Americas
New York, NY 10104

Visit us at yenpress.com
facebook.com/yenpress
twitter.com/yenpress
yenpress.tumblr.com
instagram.com/yenpress

First Yen Press Edition: May 2016

Yen Press is an imprint of Yen Press, LLC.
The Yen Press name and logo are trademarks of Yen Press, LLC.

Library of Congress Control Number: 2015956889

ISBNs: 978-0-316-27221-6 (paperback)
978-0-316-27675-7 (ebook)
978-0-316-27676-4 (app)

10 9 8 7 6 5 4 3 2

BVG

Printed in the United States of America